OUT-STANDING LIVES

Profiles of Lesbians and Gay Men

Michael Bronski, Consulting Editor
Foreword by Jewelle L. Gomez
Christa Brelin and Michael J. Tyrkus, Editors

VISIBLE INK PRESS

Detroit New York Toronto London

Outstanding Lives: Profiles of Lesbians and Gay Men

Published by Visible Ink Press™
a division of Gale Research
835 Penobscot Building
Detroit, MI 48226-4094

Visible Ink Press is a trademark of Gale Research

Cover photo of Charles Busch © David Morgan.

Back cover photo of Nancy K. Bereano © Jill Posener.

Art Director: Michelle DiMercurio

Most Visible Ink Press™ books are available at special quantity discounts when purchased in bulk by corporations, organizations, or groups. Customized printings, special imprints, messages, and excerpts can be produced to meet your needs. For more information, contact Special Markets Manager, Visible Ink Press, 835 Penobscot Bldg., Detroit, MI 48226. Or call 1-800-776-6265.

ISBN 1-57859-008-6

Library of Congress Cataloguing-in-Publication Data

Outstanding lives : profiles of lesbians and gay men / Christa Brelin
    and Michael J. Tyrkus, editors ; Michael Bronski, consulting editor.
        p.   cm.
    Includes bibliographical references and index.
    ISBN 1-57859-008-6
    1. Lesbians—Biography.   2. Gay men—Biography.   3. Gays—
Biography.   I. Brelin, Christa.   II. Tyrkus, Michael J., 1970–   .
III. Bronski, Michael.
HQ75.3.O97   1997
305.9'0664—dc21   97-11522
                                                                                      CIP

ADVISORY BOARD

CONTENTS

FOREWORD

As you open this volume of Outstanding Lives: Profiles of Lesbians and

Gay Men a first question might be: Why a book such as this one? That

A Place •

to Begin

question, sure to be on the lips of some, is better approached by framing

another query: What is a lesbian or gay man? This has been debated by

psychiatrists, politicians, doctors, parents, theologians, and talk show

hosts for so long the question has ceased to have meaning. We might as

well ask: Who is a person in a crowd? The answer will be as different as

each individual, different from decade to decade, different from one

culture to another. Social, literary, and media images of who lesbians

and gay men are have been of little or no assistance in answering the inquiry. Each new representation of lesbians and gay men is embraced or rejected as representing (or not representing) the whole group, leaving in its wake a cacophony of images: the shy, sensitive student, flamboyant drag queen, flannel-shirted "woodsbian," ice-pick wielding siren, universal earth mother, bikeless leatherman, effete opera buff, repressed librarian, golfer, skater, waiter. . . . Lesbians and gay men are, of course, all of these things and more.

It wasn't until relatively recently that the question could even be formed. Social historian Dennis Altman pointed out in his 1982 book *The Homosexualization of America:* "The existence of large numbers of women and men whose self-definition is homosexual, and who regard homosexual relationships as the primary ones in their lives, is largely confined to modern Western societies, and it seems to be possible only under the particular social formations of urbanization and industrialization." First the Industrial Revolution, then World War II helped to increase the mobility of the population, irrevocably altering the idea of the norm in society. The subsequent development of more extensive systems of national communications, the burgeoning economic independence of women, and the growth of more urban areas continued to change the face of life throughout the world. Among other opportunities, these developments offered individuals a chance to pursue same-sex relationships not as simply stolen moments, but as defining elements of a social life. Lesbians and gay men could begin to establish the symbols and signals that would make them known to each other, and begin to create social circles. Although it was still safer to maintain a discreet silence within a "special friendship," lesbians and gay men began to see the first crack in the wall of isolation and invisibility.

Even with this societal shift, the time still had not (and has not) arrived when lesbian/gay life is looked upon without comment or judgment by some segments of the population. But from the very first stirrings for lesbian/gay rights during the mid–twentieth century, the movement toward an open life as a homosexual has been steady and consistent. But why is it important to know who is a lesbian or gay man?

When we enter a room and see an apple on a table, what do we see? Some would just say "an apple." Others would say a "rome" or "gravenstein" or "baking apple." But it is often the context which gives depth of meaning to a concept. If the apple sits on a table that has seen very little food, an apple might mean saving someone's life. If it is on a table in a palatial estate it might mean a snack for the maid or for a dieting patriarch. It could be one person's entire dinner, or just the beginning of a pie. For those with a Christian heritage that apple might suggest something much more significant than it does to those who adhere to

Native American spiritual beliefs, or to a Buddhist. Looking at the context tells us so much more than just "an apple."

The same is true of people. If there were no hunger in the world, maybe just "an apple" would have all the resonance it needs. If there were no fear of, or discrimination against, lesbians and gays, maybe just "a person" would do. But our social instinct is to name, to define, even when those appellations become confining or negative. And the designee, in turn, often learns to cling to the name, in order to create space to exist in the world.

In making that safe place, the naming has often created a box many individuals fight to escape. So there will always be those who would never consider calling themselves lesbian or gay even though their lives fit such a description. So it may be time to shed the traditional view that "labeling" a person as lesbian or gay diminishes them as individuals or taints their accomplishments. One can just as easily suggest that adding the information about an individual's homosexuality opens a door, taking us further into that person's experience. As we learn each new facet of a personality we see the individual as more whole, complete. What do we know when we know that Edward Albee is gay? Or that James Baldwin, Leonard Bernstein, Martina Navratilova, Bayard Rustin, or Tennessee Williams are lesbians or gay men? By acknowledging the homosexual orientation of individuals we, by implication, refute the ironclad assumption of the heterosexual nature of society and history. That refutation makes the individual and our world not smaller, but bigger.

Whether their accomplishments are directly related to or obviously reflect their lives as lesbians or gay men is not the core issue. To enjoy the music of Aaron Copland or to read the poetry of Adrienne Rich, acknowledging their gayness, gives an added context for their lives and their work that can deepen the appreciation for their accomplishments. If we are able to consider the diverse talents of so many individuals in light of their mutual gayness we can expunge some of the empty stereotypes that limit our thinking, and postulate the infinite variety of ways that gayness is manifest in culture and society.

Singer Alberta Hunter, for example, entertained audiences for over sixty years with her ladylike delivery of suggestive lyrics. Recording her first song in 1921, Hunter's mellow blues voice delighted listeners from Harlem's Apollo Theatre to Chez Florence in Paris and back to the Cookery in New York City's Greenwich Village, where she performed until her death in the 1984. She recorded the sound track for Robert Altman's 1977 film, *Remember My Name,* which included much of her own original music and brought her talents to the attention of a new generation of fans.

Despite her impish performance persona Hunter was also known to be a tough business woman. This ease with contrasts is also evidenced in Hunter's projection of a demure (and always heterosexual) playfulness in counterpoint to the sometimes racy implications of the lyrics of her songs. Her carefully constructed ladylike image and the layers of sexual innuendo take on a deeper resonance in light of her long-term lesbian relationships.

The complexities of individual identity are labyrinthine. Whether an individual has been in the position (historical, financial, or political) to be openly lesbian or gay is not an issue in this compilation. As always, what must be held most significant is how a person lives and contributes to the society. And in many cases it has been difficult or impossible for individuals to either allow sexual orientation to be openly acknowledged or to make it an overt element in his or her accomplishments. The opportunity for such openness is directly influenced by class, ethnicity, history, profession, acculturation, etc.—all the variables that help make us who we are. This volume places within a valuable social/historical context many well-known citizens of the world for whom such a book would have been beyond their imagination. This contextualization allows us to see more than just an apple.

But to create such a book means that some people will, of practical necessity, be left out. The committee of advisors pored over lists of names for almost a year with the resulting conclusion (the same as the chant at every Lesbian/Gay Pride March): "We Are Everywhere." Consequently, many people—well-known pioneers, significant historical figures, local leaders—do not appear here. What *is* here is a glimpse at the spectrum that lesbian/gay life and accomplishment encompasses. The book stands as a reference point, a place to begin, a door to open.

Other readers might wonder about some individuals they would define as bisexual, or question how transsexuals or transvestites fit in. Again, this volume is meant to illuminate the discussion of lesbian/gay life, not set the definitive parameters for that discussion. The term "bisexual" has changed in implication over time and the bisexual movement, which has taken shape through the 1990s, will continue to help refine how we identify ourselves, as will transgender activists. Because the discussion of identity is still being framed, included in this book are some individuals who will also be grouped, under other circumstances, with bisexual or transgendered people. These inclusions do not dismiss the unique position of bisexuals or ignore the complex discussions raised by transgender identity; they, again, suggest a place to begin.

In this way *Outstanding Lives* offers the fullest possible spectrum of what has been lesbian and gay life during this century.

**By Jewelle L. Gomez,
San Francisco State
University, 1996**

PREFACE

Biography has traditionally been viewed as a sort of map of history. The

lives of the great and the near great were seen as the locations in which

history happened. Presidents, generals, statesmen, and writers were the

fixed points—the geographic sites—where the overwhelming march

and morass of "history" could be defined, delineated. Biographies were

composed of facts and details that dovetailed with the historical record,

the way a map corresponds to terrain and roadway. The problem with

this was twofold: the proper subject of biography was assumed to be (for

the most part) white men, and the proper method of writing biography

was simply to relate the facts of public life. This all changed with Lytton

Strachey who, in his studies of Florence Nightingale, Cardinal Newman, and Queen Victoria, among others, invented the radical ideas that the private life was as important as—perhaps even more important than—the public, and that men were not the only people who could change the world. If biography was a map to history Strachey insisted that much of the map was—up until then—an invisible one.

The notion that the lives of non-white men might be important was a tremendous shift in how biography, and history, was conceptualized; we now realize that such a limitation is wrongheaded and inaccurate. The notion that the personal life was as vital as the public, however, was downright revolutionary. The privatization of emotions and sexuality has been a primary form of social regulation. What happened in the public sphere was history, what happened in private was, well, private. When Strachey claimed the "private" as within the reach of biography he seriously disrupted how the world was ordered. The "private" realm of feelings, emotions, and sexuality were now seen as relevant not only to the individual subjects of biography, but to how they lived in the world. In a poem about German artist Kathe Kollwitz, Muriel Rukeyser has written: "What would happen if one woman told the truth about her life?/The world would split open." By simply discussing, openly and honestly, the sexuality of noted women and men, *Outstanding Lives: Profiles of Lesbians and Gay Men* presents us, quite frankly, with a world split open.

The seventy biographies here are a map to recent history. Reading them locates us in time and place, pinpointing moments of historical conflict and surveying movements of change and upheaval. But because they deal openly with the sexuality of their subjects, they present us with an increasingly visible map: what has been, in many cases, hidden, is now manifest. It is possible to divide the subjects in *Outstanding Lives* into two groups. The first are women and men who are acknowledged, historical figures, such as Alvin Ailey, Aaron Copland, Alberta Hunter, and Bayard Rustin, among many others. By discussing the often complex sexual identities of these subjects, *Outstanding Lives* is attempting to shed new light on how we examine and understand the past. The second group of subjects are contemporary people who are living now, or have recently lived, as openly lesbian or gay, some of whom are active members in a broad range of political and cultural activities that constitute the gay liberation movement: Paula Gunn Allen, Margarethe Cammermeyer, Harry Hay, Essex Hemphill, Audre Lorde, Barbara Smith, to name only a few. These women and men have already made themselves visible, their lives and accomplishments established on the visible map of history.

It would be a mistake to read *Outstanding Lives* as a standard volume of historical, political, and cultural biographies that happens to mention its subjects' sexual orientation. That new information—while interesting—would simply be another, more or less consequential, fact. The reality is that sexual orientation is integral to identity and activity. What is interesting is not that Tennessee Williams had homosexual desires (and acted upon them) but how this affected his thinking and work. The importance of sexual desire on the private and public life is enormous. Before his death in 1995, gay African American Essex Hemphill wrote: "I speak for thousands, perhaps hundreds of thousands of men who live and die in the shadows of secrets, unable to speak of the love that helps them endure and contribute to the race." The profundity of sexuality and desire shapes how we all view the work, how we work, what we create. What would James Baldwin's work have been like if he were not a homosexual? What does her lesbianism have to do with how Roberta Achtenberg sees her role in the world and politics? Who would the women and men who create contemporary lesbian and gay culture be today if they were heterosexual? The experience of being lesbian or gay is not simply a sexual one that exists in the realm of the private, but one that affects how lesbians and gay men view and change the world in which they live. *Outstanding Lives* not only attempts to give new and more honest "facts" about its subjects, but allows its readers a new way to interpret these lives and the culture in which they live. It provides us with a new map—now visible—of the world split open.

**By Michael Bronski,
Consulting Editor**

INTRODUCTION

Outstanding Lives: Profiles of Lesbians and Gay Men celebrates the lives and accomplishments of seventy remarkable individuals. From American politician Roberta Achtenberg to Italian filmmaker Franco Zeffirelli, these contemporary lesbians and gay men have shared their gifts, broken new ground, and influenced those around them with their talent and courage.

Those profiled in *Outstanding Lives* were selected by a seven-member advisory board, in conjunction with the consulting editor and the editors. We created an initial list of more than 600 influential gays and lesbians, then whittled it down to 275 profiles, which are included in the comprehensive *Gay & Lesbian Biography,* published by St. James Press. From those names, we selected the seventy that appear within these pages. Certainly, these individuals are not the only nor even the "best" figures of note. But their accomplishments are indeed exceptional, and we believe they represent well the larger community.

The outstanding lives profiled in this book come from virtually every industry and all walks of life. Politicians like Roberta Achtenberg and Barney Frank are here, as well as entertainers like Charles Busch, Marga Gomez, Holly Hughes, and RuPaul. Pat Califia and Joan Nestle, who have greatly influenced current theory on sexual dynamics, and Metropolitan Community Church founder Troy Perry coexist here. Alongside athletes like Greg Louganis and Martina Navratilova are virtuoso dancers Alvin Ailey and Rudolf Nureyev. A variety of musicians are represented here, from Leonard Bernstein, Aaron Copland, and Stephen Sondheim to Melissa Etheridge, Alberta Hunter, and k.d. lang. Along with filmmakers like Pedro Almodovar, Debra Chasnoff, Pratibha Parmar, Marlon Riggs, and Franco Zeffirelli are editors and publishers like Nancy K. Bereano, Michael Denneny, Barbara Grier, and Cherrie Moraga, as well as writers and scholars such as Paula Gunn Allen,

Dorothy Allison, James Baldwin, Martin Duberman, Allen Ginsberg, Essex Hemphill, Audre Lorde, Adrienne Rich, Kitty Tsui, Gore Vidal, Tennessee Williams, and many more. Naturally, multicultural and political activists take their place within these pages: Harry Hay, Cleve Jones, Phyllis Lyon, Del Martin, Simon Nkoli, Bayard Rustin, Barbara Smith, Urvashi Vaid, Merle Woo, and others.

You'll find the resources from which we've drawn these profiles in the section called A Closer Look, which follows the biographies, and the Index will guide you to the many individuals and organizations mentioned throughout the book.

Writer/activist Jewelle Gomez sets the stage for this volume in her Foreword, pondering such questions as: *Why a book such as this one? What is a lesbian or gay man? How do individuals who might be better defined as bisexual, transsexual, or transvestite fit in here?* And in his Preface, consulting editor Michael Bronski describes these profiles as a map to recent history. "Because they deal openly with the sexuality of their subjects," he writes, "they present us with an increasingly visible map: what has been, in many cases, hidden, is now manifest."

We present these profiles as your map to recent history: an honest assessment of some outstanding lives of our time.

CONTRIBUTORS

Lee Arnold
Sandra Brandenburg
Ira N. Brodsky
Joann Cerrito
Mary C. Churchill
Elizabeth Hutchinson
   Crocker
Renee R. Curry
Susie Day
Joseph E. DeMatio
Danielle M. DeMuth
Joseph M. Eagan
Carolyn Eckstein-Soule
Jean Edmunds

Marian Gracias
R. Ellen Greenblatt
Loie B. Hayes
Karen Helfrich
Debora Hill
Robert F. Jones
Judith C. Kohl
David Levine
Michael A. Lutes
Jacquelyn Marie
James P. McNab
D. Quentin Miller
Tom Musbach
Michael E. O'Connor

Teresa Ortega
Andrea L.T. Peterson
Annmarie Pinarski
Joanna Price
Shawn Stewart Ruff
Marvin S. Shaw
Charles Shively
Jerome Szymczak
Nicolas Tredell
Michael J. Tyrkus
Jonathan Wald
Gary Westfahl
Catherine A. Wiley
Les K. Wright

Heartfelt •

thanks to these

chroniclers

of history

PHOTO CREDITS

Photo of **Roberta Achtenberg,** p. 2, courtesy Reuters/Bettmann; Photo of **Alvin Ailey,** p. 8, courtesy AP/Wide World Photos; Photo of **Edward Albee,** p. 16, courtesy AP/Wide World Photos; Photo of **Paula Gunn Allen,** p. 22, courtesy AP/Wide World Photos; Photo of **Dorothy Allison,** p. 26, courtesy AP/Worldwide Photos; Photo of **Pedro Almodovar,** p. 34, courtesy AP/Wide World Photos; Photo of **James Baldwin,** p. 38, by Carl Van Vechten, courtesy Library of Congress; Photo of **Arthur Bell,** p. 46, courtesy AP/Wide World Photos; Photo of **Nancy Bereano,** back cover and p. 50, by Jill Posener, courtesy Jill Posener; Photo of **Leonard Bernstein,** p. 54, by Carl Van Vechten, courtesy Library of Congress; Photo of **Ron Buckmire,** p. 62, courtesy Ron Buckmire; Photo of **Charles Busch,** front cover and p. 66, by David Morgan, courtesy David Morgan; Photo of **Paul Cadmus,** p. 70, courtesy Corbis-Bettmann; Photo of **Pat Califia,** p. 78, by Marc Geller, courtesy Marc Geller; Photo of **Michael Callen,** p. 84, courtesy AP/Wide World Photos; Photo of **Margarethe Cammermeyer,** p. 88, courtesy AP/Wide World Photos; Photo of **Debra Chasnoff,** p. 92, by Irene Young, courtesy Debra Chasnoff; Photo of **Michael Denneny,** p. 104, courtesy Michael Leo Denneny; Photo of **Martin Duberman,** p. 108, by Gene Bagnato, courtesy Martin Duberman; Photo of **Melissa Etheridge,** p. 112, courtesy AP/Wide World Photos; Photo of **Lillian Faderman,** p. 118, courtesy Lillian Faderman; Photo of **Barney Frank,** p. 126, courtesy UPI/Corbis-Bettmann; Photo of **Allen Ginsberg,** p. 134, courtesy Archive Photo/Saga/Capri; Photo of **Jewelle Gomez,** p. 142, by D. Sabin, courtesy Jewelle Gomez; Photo of **Marga Gomez,** p. 146, by Linda Sue Scott, courtesy Irene Pinn; Photo of **Barbara Grier,** p. 152, courtesy Barbara Grier; Photo of **Marilyn Hacker,** p. 158, by Robert Giard, courtesy Robert Giard; Photo of **Barbara Hammer,** p. 166, by Glenn Halverson, courtesy Glenn Halverson; Photo of **Harry Hay,** p. 172, by Daniel Nicoletta, courtesy Daniel Nicoletta; Photo of **Essex Hemphill,** p. 180, courtesy Patented Photos; Photo of **David Hockney,** p. 184, courtesy UPI/Bettmann; Photo of **Holly Hughes,** p. 192, by John Lovett, courtesy John Lovett; Photo of **Alberta Hunter,** p. 198, courtesy The Bettmann Archive; Photo of **Karla Jay,** p. 206, by Jill Posener, courtesy Jill Posener; Photo of **Bill T. Jones,** p. 210, courtesy AP/Wide World Photos; Photo of **Cleve Jones,** p. 218, courtesy AP/Wide World Photos; Photo of **Jonathan Ned Katz,** p. 226, courtesy Jonathan Ned Katz; Photo of **Larry Kramer,** p. 234, courtesy AP/Wide World Photos; Photo of **k.d. lang,** p. 240, courtesy AP/Wide World Photos; Photo of **Audre Lorde,** p. 246, by Dagmar

Thanks to the •

following

individuals and

organizations

OUT-STANDING LIVES

Profiles of Lesbians and Gay Men

ROBERTA ACHTENBERG

Although the lesbian and gay community would likely hail Roberta   **1950–** •

Achtenberg for such achievements as being the first lesbian—in fact, the

first openly gay person—ever to be nominated by the president and   ***American*** •

confirmed by the U.S. Senate (she was appointed to the position of   ***politician***

Assistant Secretary for Fair Housing and Equal Opportunity by Presi-

dent Bill Clinton in 1993) or for being a member of the San Francisco

Board of Supervisors, Achtenberg sees her own accomplishments in a

much different light.

Although Achtenberg readily acknowledges that her appointment by President Clinton—and the Senate's confirmation—was "a milestone for the [gay and lesbian] movement," she does not feel that the appointment itself was the most significant thing. This reasoning comes about because she measures her own successes by a different standard: "The most important thing about being the Assistant Secretary for Fair Housing," she says, "is being the best Assistant Secretary that ever was—

not for the sake of being the best," but for affecting change and for being effective in the position.

"Doing the job right," she reiterates, "is more important than being the first" to hold the position. It is this outlook that she brings to life's challenges, driving her to accomplish and enabling her to see success where others might not.

On 20 July 1950, Roberta Achtenberg was born to Beatrice and Louis Achtenberg. The Achtenbergs, a family of six, lived in Inglewood, near Los Angeles, California. The daughter of immigrant parents who owned a small store, Achtenberg learned at home what would serve as the foundation for a lifetime of accomplishment: respect "for the values of family, hard work, and community."

Influenced by her brother's struggle to be independent in spite of his use of a wheelchair, she vowed early on to help those in need. Her career has been about precisely this ambition—helping those in need by challenging and changing the status quo, and by making legal and governmental protections available and accessible to those requiring them. To date, the measure of her own success has been based on how well she has effected change: how many people have had the circumstances of their lives changed, for the better, because of her work.

Achtenberg and her partner, former San Francisco Municipal Court Judge Mary C. Morgan—the first openly lesbian judge in the United States—have been together since 1983. Morgan, who is currently a Deputy Assistant Attorney General at the Department of Justice, has temporarily relocated to Washington, D.C., with Achtenberg and their son, Benji, where they will remain until both of them complete their tenure with the Clinton Administration.

- *Achievements*

and Career

Milestones

Prior to the 1992 presidential election, Achtenberg was one of the first elected officials in California to endorse Clinton. In fact, she campaigned extensively for the candidate, serving as National Co-Chair of Clinton-Gore '92 and later as Clinton's appointee to the prestigious Platform Drafting Committee. She was also selected to address the Democratic National Convention in defense of that platform. Shortly after Clinton took office, Achtenberg was appointed Assistant Secretary for Fair Housing and Equal Opportunity, and one of the most grueling Senate confirmation hearings followed.

As Assistant Secretary of Fair Housing and Equal Opportunity Achtenberg was the chief enforcement officer of the federal Fair Housing Act and of civil rights laws governing Department of Housing and Urban Development (HUD) programs. Among the many things she has accomplished, she ranks her work with housing at the top of the list: "integrating housing, restructuring the bureaucracy, housing people." Among other things, she took on the Ku Klux Klan to successfully integrate the public housing in one Texas community; she helped more than 13,000 low-income families find new homes after the 1994 earthquake in Northridge, Los Angeles; and she even developed the first ever national Best Practices Fair Lending Agreement with the Mortgage Bankers of America and a Best Practices Agreement with the National Association of Home Builders. According to HUD Secretary Henry G. Cisneros, under whom Achtenberg worked, she "made a substantial difference in the lives of many Americans who might otherwise have faced housing discrimination."

Also high up on her own list is her work as legal director for the Lesbian Rights Project of Equal Rights Advocates (1984–1988)—fighting for "family rights of gay and lesbian people"; and the publication of her book, *Sexual Orientation and the Law,* which she calls a resource "very much needed . . . for lawyers representing lesbian or gay clients." Of providing this essential volume, Achtenberg says, "I was glad to have done it."

As County Supervisor in San Francisco, Achtenberg was an advocate for "basic things": families, children, a cleaner environment, crossing guards, etc. "Someone needs to do that stuff," she says. "I got to do it." She also penned the city's original "Sunshine" ordinance that allowed full public scrutiny of virtually every aspect of city government. She later drafted legislation to improve water recycling, promote ground water reclamation, and to require city agencies to protect the environment by reducing the use of wasteful paper products.

Chief among her concerns as supervisor was childcare for low income families. During her time on the San Francisco Board of Supervisors she worked for legislation to require developers either to build childcare facilities or to contribute to a childcare fund for low income families. Her efforts resulted in legislation providing monthly childcare subsidies to graduates of job training programs as well as a guaranteed $10 million annual allocation to establish and administer a children's budget. But one of her proudest accomplishments while on the Board is her legislation establishing the San Francisco Commission on National Service, which has made substantial progress in promoting and directing the work of young people in San Francisco's neighborhoods.

Before her tenure on the San Francisco Board of Supervisors, Achtenberg had already distinguished herself as one of the country's leading civil rights attorneys. She has taught at the Stanford Law School, served as dean at the New College of California School of Law, and as a member of the Board of Directors of the San Francisco Neighborhood Legal Assistance Foundation.

In 1989 Achtenberg was selected by the United Way of the Bay Area as Management Volunteer of the Year, and in 1993 she was the California Senate's Woman of the Year for the Third Senate District. She has also received much recognition and many honors for her efforts on behalf of women's and gay and lesbian rights. Among them is the Lifetime Achievement Award, which the Lambda Legal Defense and Education Fund presented to her in 1990.

She also received, during her time as Assistant Secretary for Fair Housing and Equal Opportunity, the National Performance Review's Golden Hammer Award from Vice President Al Gore for "streamlining her office's grant-making program, for saving the federal government millions of dollars, and for improving the quality of service to the public."

• *Losing or*

Winning?

Although the greatest challenge of her career might appear to have ended in failure, Achtenberg says of her attempt to win the 1995 San Francisco mayoral race: "I thought I did extremely well. I was wildly successful. The only thing I didn't do was win."

In a campaign where she was severely out-financed by her opponents, Achtenberg did do extremely well. So, will she run again? "We'll see," she says. More important than whether she won or lost, or whether she'll run again, she says, is what she took away from the campaign—the realization that "there is life after loss"—something that she says "many [political hopefuls] don't realize."

The belief in a "life after loss" is clearly evidenced by her return in February 1996, after the San Francisco mayoral race, to HUD, where she continues to chip away at the endless layers of bureaucracy, seeking to eliminate redundancy within the agency, and working for a more efficient, effective system.

Upon returning to HUD, Achtenberg assumed the position of Senior Advisor to HUD Secretary Cisneros. In that capacity she works to develop and implement Clinton Administration and Departmental policy on housing, home ownership, and community-based economic development. When emergencies arise, it is her job to quickly formulate and implement effective solutions.

Achtenberg maintains that she has no ultimate career goals. "That's not how I do my [life]. I don't do something [in order] to do something else," she maintains. In 1996 she returned to California to live so that her son could "start middle school back in San Francisco" in the fall. "It is important," she adds, "for him to spend his adolescence and high school years at home." Despite living in San Francisco, Achtenburg maintains her office in Washington, D.C.

It is safe to say that whatever lies ahead will be a continuation of her commitment to eradicate discrimination, to make the basics readily available to the average person, and to continue to fight for change in government—whether through legislation or within the bureaucracy.

Clearly her greatest contributions to the gay and lesbian movement would have to be the publication of her book, *Sexual Orientation and the Law* and her appointment as Assistant Secretary for Fair Housing and Equal Opportunity—controversial, she says, only because the radical right made it so.

"You don't know what it's going to be like," Achtenberg says of the ordeal of going through the historic, grueling Senate confirmation of her appointment where she endured not only the routine questioning of the Senate committee, but also withstood the attacks on her character by Jesse Helms and other Senate bigots. "You [draw from] other burdens you have borne" when you face something this difficult, and you get through it. Achtenberg maintains the process wasn't nearly the big deal for her, however, that it was for the public.

"Doing a good job," she stresses, "is exceedingly important . . . wanting to lead your city . . . [tapping into] people's best instincts, not their worst fears." These are the things that Achtenberg considers more important than all of the firsts she has accomplished.

A Giant Step or •

Two for the

Movement

**Profile by
Andrea L. T. Peterson**

ALVIN AILEY

A lvin Ailey was perhaps the greatest black modern dancer-choreog-

rapher in the United States. He was the founder of the primarily black

Alvin Ailey Dance Theater and was influential in dance circles, espe-

cially to young black—but also white and Asian—dancers and

choreographers. He grew up in the black south of Texas in the 1930s and

1940s, moved to Los Angeles at age 12, and started taking modern

dance with Lester Horton when he was 18. He studied off and on at

various California colleges, majoring in languages, from 1949 to 1953

but finally quit to devote his full attention to dance. He formed his dance

company in New York and toured internationally starting in the 1960s.

Ailey and his troupe were extremely well received, particularly in

1931–1989 ·

African American ·

dancer and

choreographer

9 •

Europe, Africa, and Asia. He choreographed many dances, from black spiritual to jazz to classical themes. Many were tributes to important people in his life: Lester Horton, his first teacher; Duke Ellington; or most especially, his mother, to whom he dedicated *Cry*. His company had its financial troubles; it often foundered but continued after his death in 1989, under the tutelage of his premier dancer, Judith Jamison.

Born in Rogers, Texas on 5 January 1931, Ailey grew up in poverty-stricken, rural, segregated Texas towns, picking cotton with his mother, Lula Elizabeth (Cliff) Cooper. His father, Alvin Ailey Sr., a laborer, gave him a name but nothing else; he left when young Ailey was six months old. These childhood experiences, as well as attending the Baptist church, made Ailey aware of his black roots. His dances came directly from these roots; his famous *Revelations* draws from the church's baptism by total immersion in water, and *Blues Suite* from the rough honky-tonk bars and dance halls such as the Dew Drop Inn in Navasota, Texas. As Ailey put it in his autobiography *Revelations,* "Many of the same people who went to the Dew Drop Inn on Saturday night went to church on Sunday morning. In dance I deal with these two very different worlds."

As a young boy, he moved to Los Angeles with his mother who found work in an aircraft company. He was athletically built but preferred gymnastics to football. In high school he had a love for languages and literature and was soon reading Spanish classics.

The Los Angeles schools gave him a much better education than the segregated schools of the South. He was taken on a school trip to the Ballet Russe de Monte Carlo and soon roamed the theatre district himself. There he saw dance films, popular singers and bands like Billie Holiday and Duke Ellington, and his first black dance troupe, that of the influential Katherine Dunham. He later brought some of Dunham's dances out of retirement and restaged them with his dance company.

When Ailey saw Carmen de Lavallade, a black student, dance a Mozart piece in high school, he was enchanted and convinced to try dancing classes with her at the Lester Horton studio. Horton was a white, gay male, an innovator in dance, who was a pivotal force in Ailey's life. Horton's dance was eclectic, outside traditional dance forms, using influences from Japanese theatre to American Indian dances in his school. This style attracted the shy young Ailey and started him dancing and visualizing his own dance forms. He later became an eclectic choreographer and teacher himself. Brenda Dixon, in *Black American Literature Forum,* called Ailey's choreography "a fusion of Black forms, modern dance, and ballet." Clive Barnes, the dance critic in *Ballet News,* explained that "Ailey has attempted to run his company along the lines of a classic dance troupe rather than a modern dance original. He has always seen his company as essentially a repertory dance company with himself as the principal choreographer . . . finding its repertory from the full range of American modern dance."

When Lester Horton died in 1953, Ailey took over the company, whose principal dancers were Carmen de Lavallade and James Truitte, both important people in Ailey's life. He started dancing duets with Carmen and went on with her to work with Jack Cole in Hollywood. He had, however, started choreographing his own material and needed to create his own style.

In 1954, Ailey went to New York as a featured dancer in the Broadway show *House of Flowers* and stayed on to dance in Harry Belafonte's *Sing Man Sing* and with Lena Horne in *Jamaica* in 1957. He acted in plays such as *Carefree Tree* and had the starring role in the short-lived Broadway play *Tiger, Tiger, Burning Bright* in 1962. Meanwhile, he studied dance with a series of teachers, including Martha Graham, Hanya Holm, and Karel Shook, but was never completely happy with their styles.

Ailey Finds His •

Niche on

Broadway

Ailey choreographed his first pieces in 1954: *According to St. Francis* for James Truitte was an homage to Horton, and *Mourning, Mourning* for Carmen de Lavallade derived from Tennessee Williams' writings. Both were performed at the Jacob's Pillow Dance Festival.

Ailey painstakingly put together a troupe, rehearsing in out-of-the-way places, and gave his inaugural concert on 30 March 1958. His guest artist was a black dancer and later a well-known choreographer, Talley Beatty, from Katherine Dunham's troupe. The dances were all choreographed by Ailey: *Ode and Homage* to his teacher, Lester Horton, *Redonda* with Latin music and themes, and the durable *Blues Suite* from his experience of Southern honky-tonk bars. The audience was enthusiastic.

The second concert, 21 December 1958, premiered *Arriette Oubliee* to Debussy music. It was danced by Ailey and de Lavallade and showed Ailey's versatility as a dancer and choreographer. January 1960 saw the third concert, in which *Revelations,* Ailey's masterpiece based on the Southern Baptist traditions and using black spirituals and gospel songs, was premiered. Since then, *Revelations* has been the dance most asked for and expected in concerts. The finale—"Rocka My Soul in the Bosom of Abraham"—moves and uplifts audiences of all colors and languages.

Ailey continued to choreograph pieces for other companies: *Ariadne* for the Harkness Ballet with Maria Tallchief in the title role, *Carmen* for the Metropolitan Opera in 1973, and *Precipice* for the Paris Opera in 1983. His *Knoxville: Summer of 1915* was called his most autobiographical work. Its theme from James Agee's *Death in the Family* concerned a child who is loved but not understood. This theme of aloneness is also echoed in his *Hermit Songs,* sung in 1961 by Leontyne Price with music by Samuel Barber and danced by Ailey himself. His dancing was called exceptional. As Doris Hering wrote in *Dance Magazine,* "he reminds one of a caged lion full of lashing power that he can contain or release at will."

The dance company found a home at the Clark Center for Performing Arts in the YWCA in New York. From 1958 to 1965 Ailey danced with the company as well as choreographing and generally holding the company together. His company was primarily black as he felt it important that black dancers were given a chance to dance; they were not accepted in most dance and ballet companies. As he stated in an interview on the video *An Evening with the Alvin Ailey American Dance Theatre,* he had "grown up in a country which is intensely racist" and was making a "social and political statement" with a primarily black company. He wanted to continue the "black tradition which started with his black forefathers"; he wanted a "popular" company that his family and people in Texas could relate to. Later in the more militant 1960s, he was chastised for allowing white and Asian dancers into his black troupe.

Early in the life of his dance company, he took his dancers on international tours, and they often found a more receptive audience than in the United States; one audience in Germany applauded for an hour. His company was often asked to represent the United States at foreign festivals, such as the Paris Festival of Nations and the Premiere Festival Mondial des Arts in Dakar, Senegal, in 1966. In 1963 for their first international tour, they traveled first to Rio for a festival and then on to London and Paris. In 1965, they toured nine European countries for three months. In 1970 they were the first American dance troupe to tour the Soviet Union, to overwhelming success.

Finances were always difficult and Ailey often felt that he would have to disband the company, sometimes actually disbanding them but always pulling them together again. Dancers came and left, looking for more secure jobs, often disgruntled with Ailey. As one of his colleagues recalls in the book *Judith Jamison: Aspects of a Dancer,* "Alvin came to New York with a Southern Baptist conscience, a prim idea of right and wrong. He was idealistic and committed, and that made him hard to work with, and for. Alvin did not spare himself. He saw no reason to spare other people."

1965 was a pivotal year. Ailey stopped dancing and turned the running of the business—the dance theater, with its training company, the Alvin Ailey Repertory Ensemble, and the Alvin Ailey American Dance Center for young, talented, and often poor youngsters—over to other people, such as Ivy Clark, his general manager, and a board of directors.

Also in 1965, Judith Jamison, who was to become an important figure in Ailey and the company's life, made her debut. As Jamison said later in her biography, *Judith Jamison: Aspects of a Dancer,* the company, even after Ailey stopped dancing, was "still very patriarchal. The concentration was on the men." In a *Dance Magazine* article by Sylviane Gold, however, Jamison recognized Ailey's greatness as a teacher who "made sure that your influence was eclectic but that you realized what your roots were."

He designed the beautiful and mesmerizing *Cry,* dedicated to his mother and all black women everywhere, especially for Jamison; it became her signature piece.

In the late 1970s, Ailey lost close friends and associates to illness and death and became depressed, turning to drugs. The deaths of Duke Ellington (with whom he had collaborated on *The River,* which Ellington did not have a chance to see before his death) and Joyce Trisler, an old friend and dancer from the Horton days, affected him greatly. He thought he might end up like Trisler, dying a lonely death at an early age; her body lay for several days in her apartment before being found. He felt he might die immediately so he decided to, as he tells it in *Revelations,* "live quickly and get all that I could from what time I had left."

He connected with Abdullah, an Arab boy he had met earlier in Paris. "We found the best hashish and the best cognac in town and began to smoke and drink like two wild people—and to enjoy each other." Then he started on cocaine, spending four hundred dollars a week on the drug. In a drug-induced state, he still choreographed, particularly *Memoria* for Trisler to the music of Keith Jarrett.

Finally things became too much for his young lover, and Abdullah left him to live at the International House. Ailey describes his manic state as he raised a ruckus at the residence looking for the young man he thought he would have a "perfect relationship" with. He was apprehended and taken to Bellevue Hospital. In 1980 he ran through an apartment house yelling "fire" and broke into a woman's apartment; again he was hospitalized. After weeks of care, he went on lithium, stopped taking drugs and drinking, lost weight, and most importantly, started choreographing again.

His first post-hospital piece was *Phases* to music by Max Roach for dancer Masazumi Chaya. The piece made him "happy" and whole again, and his autobiography, *Revelations,* ends on this upbeat note.

Ailey went on to choreograph other pieces and keep his dance troupe going into the 1980s. In 1984, he and his troupe enjoyed a tremendous success at their twenty-five-year anniversary at the New York City Center, where 80 Ailey dancers gathered together. Ailey called this event, in an article in *Ebony,* "a wonderful family gathering. It was one of my most memorable experiences."

In twenty-five years, the Alvin Ailey Dance Theater had been seen by fifteen million people in forty-eight states and forty-four countries on six continents. They had been first in many areas, including the first black modern dance company at the Metropolitan Opera, the first American modern dance company in the Soviet Union and China, and the first American dance company to be awarded a National Endowment of the Arts long-term residency. Ailey was also awarded the 1975 *Dance Magazine* award, the 1979 Capezio award, and the 1976 NAACP Spingarn medal. In 1976 Ailey organized an Ellington festival for the bicentenary of the American Revolution, and specially composed the light-hearted *Pas de Duke* for the interesting duet of Judith Jamison and Mikhail Barishnikov.

Throughout his life, Ailey was a private person, often not even inviting friends or associates to his apartment. His relationships were part of this private life but seemed to come second to his overpowering creativity as a choreographer and his devotion to his dance theater. Ailey stated in *Revelations* that, at an early age, he knew all the gay youth in school and had "a lot of homosexual fantasies before I ever got into doing anything actually physical." Once when he was fifteen he found himself dressing in his mother's clothes to go to a party in drag. His friends at the time were having sex with an older man but he did not participate. Later in his autobiography he was somewhat open about his affair with young Abdullah, but only as it related to his breakdown. He did state that he seemed to get involved with younger men throughout his life, often ones who robbed him. Few, if any, articles, obituaries, or biographies ever mentioned his sexual preference. In an *Advocate* review of *Revelations,* however, John Weir opines that "the book is coy about Ailey's homosexuality and indeed about the whole course of his romantic and sexual life." The 1996 biography *Alvin Ailey: A Life in Dance* uses new material, especially Ailey's poems and short prose pieces from the Black Archive of Mid-America in Kansas City, Missouri, to discuss his sexuality more completely. A piece from his younger years begins, "He had always clung to the thought that the thin boy would someday return to him, and that they together would find something more beautiful and real." A poem from the 1960s has these lines: "several hard-hipped hustlers and more I am I will always be queers gazing at the crotches of small thick-thighed magazines—sighing—'oh'." Again, these were private pieces not known to his friends until after his death.

In the end, Ailey was primarily a lover of dance and insisted that dance should come from the people and be delivered back to the people. The credo that best sums up Ailey and his philosophy of dance was written for the Alvin Ailey Dance Theater program in London in 1964:

> The cultural heritage of the American Negro is one of America's richest treasures. From his roots as a slave, the American Negro—sometimes sorrowing, sometimes jubilant, but always hopeful—has created a legacy of music and dance which has touched, illuminated, and influenced the most remote preserves of world civilization.
>
> I and my dance theatre celebrate, in our programme, this trembling beauty. We bring to you the exuberance of his jazz, the ecstasy of his spirituals, and the dark rapture of his blues.

Though Alvin Ailey died 1 December 1989 of HIV complications, this "exuberance, ecstasy, and rapture" lives on in his dances and in the Alvin Ailey Dance Theater, now under the capable leadership of Judith Jamison and Masazumi Chaya.

Profile by
Jacquelyn Marie

EDWARD ALBEE

1928– •

*W*ith his first play, Edward Albee caught the attention of the

theatrical world. He soon followed this success with the wildly popular

Who's Afraid of Virginia Woolf? *as well as several other award-winning*

American •

plays. On the whole, Albee's work is substantial and includes eight full-

playwright

length plays, nine one-act plays, and five theatrical adaptations of

novels. But critical backlash against Albee has also been considerable,

most notably a homophobic attack that has been leveled against him

throughout his career. Regardless, as Michael Bronski writes, Albee "has

maintained his position as one of the most important playwrights of the

contemporary theater."

Edward Franklin Albee was born probably somewhere in Virginia, although his official place of birth is listed as Washington, D.C., on 12 March 1928. Within just a few weeks he was adopted by Reed and Frances Albee. Though he wasn't born "in a theater," he was clearly born to it, as his later career would prove. Albee's father was, at the time, part owner of the Keith-Albee vaudeville circuit, which had been started by his father, Edward Franklin Albee II, whom the young Albee was named after. Albee's childhood, spent primarily among the well-to-do in Larchmont, New York, was filled with horses, toys, pets, and rolling landscapes, but his education was frequently interrupted by winter vacations to warmer climates, and his emotional well-being was routinely challenged by his mother's constant reminders that he was adopted. It was fortunate for Albee that his maternal grandmother lived with the family. She was the ally who, in later years, encouraged him and set up a trust fund that enabled Albee to leave home at an early age. He left home in 1950. Albee's grandmother died in 1959, and the following year he dedicated his play *The Sandbox* to her.

• *Schooling*

School and Albee were not the best of friends. Not only were his early studies at Rye Country Day School in Westchester interrupted by vacations, but he would also frequently cut classes. By the age of eleven he was enrolled in the first of several boarding schools—The Lawrenceville School in New Jersey, from which he was eventually expelled for failing to attend classes. He also attended the Valley Forge Military Academy in Pennsylvania and Choate School in Connecticut. While he did not do well academically at any of them, he enjoyed his time at Choate, where his teachers encouraged his writing (primarily poetry at this time). By the age of twelve Albee had written his first play, *Aliqueen,* a three-act sex farce. But it was his poetry that got Albee the most attention. In 1947, one of his poems was published in *Kaleidoscope,* a Texas-based literary magazine.

Albee attended Trinity College in 1946, but lack of interest and commitment led him to drop out after only a year and a half. He returned home and took a writing job at the local radio station. In the early 1950s Albee spent some time in Italy, where he wrote a novel. During this time he met W. H. Auden, received advice from Thornton Wilder, and was greatly influenced by the work of Tennessee Williams. The composer William Flanagan was Albee's closest friend and roommate during these years. Returning to New York, he settled in Greenwich Village and spent the next ten years living in a series of places and working at a variety of jobs. Among these vocations, the job Albee liked most was as a messenger for Western Union from 1955–58.

Living on the cusp of his third decade was apparently motivational for Albee, and he quit his job with Western Union just before his birthday. In just three weeks, he wrote *The Zoo,* the play that would gain him entry into the world of drama. The play, however, was rejected across the board by several New York producers until it eventually found its first audience at the Schiller Theater Werkstatt in Berlin on 28 September 1959.

But *The Zoo,* Albee's first social commentary attacking individual and social apathy, failed to firmly establish him as a playwright. He soon followed up his first play with *The Sandbox, The American Dream,* and *The Death of Bessie Smith.* Within his new plays, Albee came down hard on "the substitution of artificial for real values" in American society, and tried to illustrate how relationships in society are valued primarily in commercial terms. Following the promise of his first offering, these three plays helped to solidify Albee's reputation as a promising new play-wright. Albee once observed, "Fearful personalities utilize power to destroy and not to heal." He hoped to demonstrate these things on stage. Albee had been applauded in Europe, Turkey, South America, and several places in the United States, but it wasn't until *Who's Afraid of Virginia Woolf?,* in 1962, that he became recognized as a major New York playwright. The play was an unparalleled success and it catapulted Albee to a level of fame he had not previously known. The following year, *Who's Afraid of Virginia Woolf?* won a Tony award.

Albee, who maintains that he intended to entertain as well as offend, could not have been surprised to find that the play that brought him due recognition as a playwright and a handful of awards also garnered harsh criticism. Although gay themes are conspicuously absent from Albee's work, he makes no secret of his own homosexuality. Some critics have maintained that his sexuality has influenced his understanding of heterosexuality as portrayed in his plays. Still others have argued that the characters in *Who's Afraid of Virginia Woolf?* closely resemble squabbling gay male couples. In fact, in 1961 Howard Taubman attacked what he saw as an overpowering homosexual influence on American theater. According to Bronski, this article was primarily concerned with "three unnamed playwrights who attacked marriage and women but were really writing about dysfunctional gay relationships." The playwrights were of course William Ing, Tennessee Williams, and Albee. This type of criticism is the kind usually levelled against Albee. In terms of his sexuality, however, Albee had been aloof in the past but has been more open in recent years. But, as Bronski points out, criticism of Albee has always been hostile toward his homosexuality in two extremes: "As a somewhat closeted writer, Albee was attacked for artistic inauthenticity; as an openly gay writer he was attacked for his sexuality."

Nearly a dozen plays followed *Who's Afraid of Virginia Woolf?*, but none was such a sweeping success—nor were any quite so controversial. Among them have been *Tiny Alice* (1964), *A Delicate Balance* (1966), *Everything in the Garden* (1967), *Seascape* (1975), and *The Man Who Had Three Arms* (1983); Albee won a Pulitzer Prize for both *A Delicate Balance* and *Seascape*.

• *The Theatre of*

the Absurd

Albee has long been identified with the "Theatre of the Absurd," an identification Albee himself might consider absurd. In a 1962 *New York Times Magazine* article he posed the question, "Which Theatre Is the Absurd One?" With this question, he doesn't just wonder if it is, he actually posits the sentiment that the so-called real theater which panders to the public's illusory self-images might, in fact, be the truly absurd one. This is very much in keeping with Albee's contempt for misguided American values and misplaced priorities.

Albee is living proof that—as there was life well before Broadway—there is, for him, also life after Broadway. Since his Broadway production *The Man Who Had Three Arms* in 1983, Albee has directed numerous productions in countless cities and he has taught a playwriting course in search of new writers who can "contribute something to the theater as an art form." His recent play *Three Tall Women* won a Pulitzer as well as numerous other awards. Throughout his career, the importance of Albee's body of work has been soiled by homophobic critics. As Bronski puts it, it has become "fashionable to dismiss much of Albee's work for a variety of reasons." Albee's work must eventually be reevaluated without the hurtful and ignorant approach that has been used in the past.

Profile by
Andrea L. T. Peterson

PAULA GUNN ALLEN

*P*aula Gunn Allen is one of the most important Native American

1939– •

writers and intellectuals of the twentieth century. She is perhaps most

highly regarded for her poetry, though her acclaim as a novelist and

Native American •

literary scholar cannot be denied. Her scholarship on American Indian

writer and

understandings of gays and lesbians ("two-spirits") represents some of

scholar

the most significant work on the subject, and it has laid the groundwork

for more accurate and culturally relevant research in this area.

Allen was born Paula Marie Francis on 24 October 1939 in Cubero, New Mexico, a Spanish land grant town near Laguna Pueblo. Laguna, Lakota, and Scottish on her mother's side and Lebanese on her father's, Allen is one of five children born to Ethel Gottlieb Francis and E. Lee Francis, a former Lieutenant Governor of New Mexico. Growing up in a rural environment, she attended mission school locally then continued her Roman Catholic education in Albuquerque, where she attended convent boarding school.

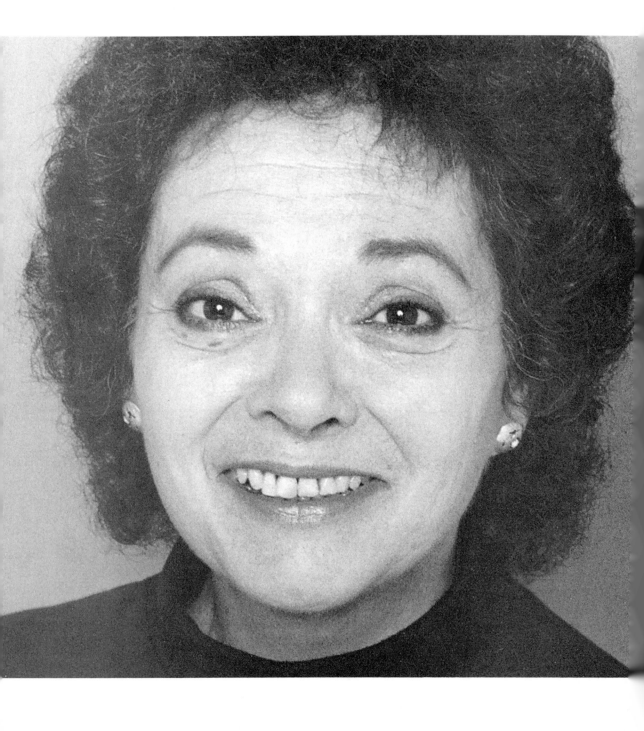

As an undergraduate at the University of Oregon, Allen earned her bachelor of arts degree in literature in 1966. Two years later, she completed a master of fine arts degree in creative writing at the same institution. She went on to attain a Ph.D. in American studies from the University of New Mexico, Albuquerque in 1975.

While Allen never planned on becoming a Native American scholar, she has nonetheless made her mark on academia. She has taught at several universities, most notably the University of California, Berkeley. She presently is a professor of English at the University of California, Los Angeles. Her curricula span a variety of fields, including Native American studies, women's studies, literature, and philosophy.

As a scholar, Allen is probably most well known for two groundbreaking books: *Studies in American Indian Literature: Critical Essays and Course Designs,* which she edited, and *The Sacred Hoop: Recovering the Feminine in American Indian Traditions.* The former is a foundational work in the area of teaching and interpreting Native literature. In the latter, a collection of essays, Allen argues for and engages in a gynocentric, or woman-centered, understanding of American Indian traditions and cultures.

While her scholarship has always been accessible and intelligible to non-academics, she has initiated a series of books that appear directed to a broader audience. These works include *Spider Woman's Granddaughters: Traditional Tales and Contemporary Writing by Native American Women, Grandmothers of the Light: A Medicine Woman's Sourcebook,* and *Voice of the Turtle: American Indian Literature 1900–1970.* The edited anthologies demonstrate the existence of a rich and enduring body of literature written by Native American writers whose works have been excluded from the American canon. The sourcebook, relying on a traditional method of teaching—storytelling—attempts to educate a non-Indian audience deluded by romantic portrayals of Native American spirituality.

Reaching a •

Wider Audience

As an artist, Allen has written one novel, *The Woman Who Owned the Shadows,* and seven collections of poetry. Only beginning to receive the critical attention it deserves, the novel powerfully depicts the cycle of spiritual death and recovery of Ephanie Atencio, a Native woman of mixed heritage. Allen skillfully situates Ephanie and her struggle not only in modern urban American Indian life but also in the time of the grandmothers, the mythic matrix that fundamentally structures her consciousness. Allen's poetry, however, reveals most deeply the multitudinous reality that is the heart of her creative thought. Her words are soundings of the complex and beauteous universe that Allen both points to and evokes in her writing. She draws on and articulates in contemporary life the power of thought and language, understood by Lagunas since long ago. She has been recognized for her writing with grants from the Ford Foundation and the National Endowment for the Arts.

In various genres, Allen has addressed Native American lesbian and gay ways of life. Her essay "*Hwame, Koshkalaka,* and the Rest: Lesbians in American Indian Cultures," published in *The Sacred Hoop,* remains an important contribution to the field. She also has written several poems with lesbian and gay themes, including "Koshkalaka, Ceremonial Dyke" and "Never Cry Uncle" (both in *Wyrds*) and "Some Like Indians Endure" *(Living the Spirit). Raven's Road,* a novel in progress, also features a Native American lesbian character. Chapters of this novel have appeared as "Deep Purple" *(Spider Woman's Granddaughters),* "Selections from *Raven's Road" (Living the Spirit),* and "The Medicine Song of Allie Hawker" *(Intricate Passions).*

That Allen has been married during the course of her life with persons of the opposite sex and same sex is not surprising in light of the cultural understandings of many Native communities. As she herself has written, "I am not especially defined by my sex life, nor complete without it" *(Intricate Passions).* She has three grown children. Allen is important not only because of her writing on two-spirits, but also because of her participation in gay and lesbian communities on the West Coast, where she has lived on and off for many years.

Profile by
Mary C. Churchill

DOROTHY ALLISON

*S*ince the 1970s Dorothy Allison has written for feminist, lesbian,

and gay newspapers and periodicals, but it was the publication of her

first novel in 1992 that pushed her into the national spotlight. Bastard

Out of Carolina, *which Allison describes to Alexis Jetter as "a heroic story*

about a young girl who faces down a monster," was a finalist for a

National Book Award and won both the Ferro Grumley and Bay Area

Book Reviewers Awards for fiction. While not wholly autobiographical

nor explicitly lesbian, the novel explores the dramatic effects of emotion-

al, physical, sexual, and psychic violence on personal identity from a

lesbian-feminist point of view. These themes shape Allison's entire body

of writing and have engendered both critical acclaim and controversy.

1949– •

American •

writer

Dorothy Allison was born in 1949 in Greenville, South Carolina, to Ruth Gibson Allison, a poor fifteen year old who dropped out of school in the seventh grade to work as a waitress. Allison fondly remembers the women of her family—her aunts and grandmothers—as dazzling and outrageous storytellers. Yet, her childhood and adolescence are marked most painfully by the physical and sexual abuse she endured at the hands of her stepfather from the time she was five years old. While Allison told Jetter that she "has made peace" with her stepfather, her mother's complicity in the abuse has been much more difficult to reconcile. Despite the pained ambivalence that characterizes her feelings, Allison credits her mother with instilling in her a defiant pride and strong sense of self. Although she died of cancer in 1990 at the age of fifty-six, just three months before the completion of Bastard, Ruth Allison remains a strong presence in her daughter's life and writing.

Much of Allison's writing directly addresses her abusive upbringing as well as her class background. Her parents worked in a series of blue-collar jobs—her mother as a cook, fruit packer, and clothes launderer, her stepfather as a route salesman. In her essay "A Question of Class," Allison explains that, for a time, she was able to "run away from [her] own life" and the myths she had internalized about growing up poor. In the late 1960s, she literally escaped her family life by attending Florida Presbyterian College in St. Petersburg on a National Merit Scholarship. There, she embraced feminism and the women's movement, lived in lesbian-feminist collectives, and attended consciousness raising sessions. She credits feminism with saving her life. In the essay "Believing in Literature," she writes that feminism offered her "a vision of the world totally different from everything [she] had ever assumed or hoped."

After earning a bachelor's degree in 1971, Allison worked in a series of jobs as a salad girl, substitute teacher, and maid, finding steady employment but long hours at the Social Security Administration. In addition, she helped publish a feminist magazine, volunteered in a child-care center, and answered the phones at a rape crisis center. Allison managed to stay away from her family for almost a decade and eventually moved north in 1979 to New York City. There, she attended the New School for Social Research and earned a master's degree in anthropology. At the same time, she worked at *Conditions,* a small feminist magazine, where she wrote grant applications, raised funds, edited other people's writing, and finally published some of her own work. Although writing was an act of resistance and a means to understand her past, Allison admits that until 1974, when she published her first poem, she built a ritual fire each year and burned every word she produced—journals as well as short stories and poetry.

In 1983, Long Haul Press published Allison's first book, *The Women Who Hate Me,* a collection of poetry that was expanded and reprinted in a 1990 edition by Firebrand Books. With razor-sharp precision and exactitude, these poems explore love, sexual desire, betrayal, and bitterness. The first poem, "Dumpling Girl," establishes Allison's method for the entire volume, weaving memory and metaphor together with specific experience. Here, food is the catalyst for memory. The speaker of the poem celebrates her Southern heritage by identifying herself simultaneously as a "southern dumpling child, biscuit eater, tea sipper, okra slicer, [and] gravy dipper." Quickly, this catalogue is transformed into a meditation on lovemaking, a testament to the "butterfat shine" of her lover's thighs and the sweet rock salt taste of her belly. While similar themes of hunger, appetite, and desire run through the volume, the playful eroticism of "Dumpling Girl" is replaced in other poems by anger, regret, or sadness. In the book's title poem, for instance, Allison emphasizes the stinging ambivalence of desire, writing that

> The women who hate me cut me
> as men can't. Men don't count.
> I can handle men. Never expected better
> of any man anyway.

The poems as a collection are driven by Allison's pursuit of the truth about the vicissitudes of her sexual desires. Her poem "She Plays It Tight," for example, describes the object of her desire with provocative language suggesting sadomasochism:

> A woman I love
> really thinks she can make of herself
> a boy
> a lean-hipped
> hard-eyed
> cold-hearted
> piece of
> rough trade.

A self-proclaimed "transgressive lesbian," Allison has always written and spoken candidly about sexuality, exploring taboo topics such as promiscuity and butch/femme role playing. Indeed, in an interview with *The Kenyon Review,* Allison affirms that she belongs to a "perverse" literary tradition of "iconoclasts" and "queers." This unwavering point of view, however, has placed her at odds with certain segments of the feminist and lesbian communities and in the spotlight of the corrosive sex wars of the 1980s.

As Lillian Faderman explains in *Odd Girls and Twilight Lovers,* the sex wars saw cultural feminists and sex radicals divided over the issue of what constituted responsible, feminist expressions of lesbian sexuality. On the one hand, cultural feminists maintained that images of violence, domination, and control are not only harmful but anathema to lesbian ethics. On the other hand, sexual radicals encouraged lesbians to enjoy "freewheeling sexuality" and to reappropriate lust as a positive virtue. Allison's commitment to sexual freedom linked her to the sex radicals and provoked some feminists to label her work "pornographic."

In 1982, as the sex wars were developing, Allison was picketed by anti-pornography feminists at a symposium on sexuality at Barnard College where she was scheduled to speak. At the time, Allison was an outspoken founding member of The Lesbian Sex Mafia, "an old-fashioned consciousness raising group whose whole concern would be the subject of sex." The group championed free sexual expression and, as Allison explains in the essay "Public Silence, Private Terror," "concentrated on attracting members whose primary sexual orientation was s/m, butch/femme, fetish specific, or otherwise politically incorrect." In this same essay, Allison recounts how her affiliation with the Lesbian Sex Mafia and the Barnard incident disrupted her life. Mainstream feminists and colleagues alike labeled her an antifeminist writer and a pawn of the patriarchy; anonymous phone callers urged her boss to fire her; and she was expelled from the Sex Mafia. In an interview with the *Advocate,* she claims that the worse accusation "was that I was guilty of child sexual abuse because of the writing I was doing."

Despite the Barnard controversy, Allison remained convinced that sexuality was a vital issue both in political organizing and in her literary vision. "Public Silence, Private Terror" clarifies that for Allison "the struggle came down to an inner demand that [she] again look at sexual fear from [her] own perspective, without giving in to the impulse to hide, deny, or wall off desire itself." The 1988 collection *Trash,* published by Firebrand, testifies to this commitment. The preface succinctly explains that Allison's motives for writing are "to put on the page a third look at what I've seen in life—the condensed and reinvented experience of a cross-eyed working class lesbian, addicted to violence, language, and hope, who has made the decision to live." The voice of the first-person fictional narrator in *Trash* clearly expresses this motivation and unifies the volume.

Allison's Fiction •

Wins Acclaim

The stories in *Trash* are variously focused on childhood experiences, physical violence, poverty, class politics, and lesbian sexuality. The themes of personal, sexual, and physical violence emerge in myriad settings. In "Mama," the narrator recounts her stepfather's beatings, disclosing the survival tactics she learned to master. She writes: "When my stepfather beat me I pulled so deeply into myself I lived only in my eyes, my eyes that watched the shower sweat on the bathroom walls, the pipes under the sink, my blood on the porcelain toilet seat, and the buckle of his belt as it moved through the air." In other stories, violent imagery merges with graphic depictions of sexual desire. In "Her Thighs," for example, the narrator explores her dangerous attraction to Bobby, "a wild-eyed woman, proud of her fame for running women ragged," candidly revealing that "Bobby loved to beat my ass, but it bothered her that we both enjoyed it so much."

While *Trash* won two Lambda Book Awards for lesbian fiction and lesbian small press book, *Bastard Out of Carolina* gained national recognition for Allison. Like *Trash,* the novel relies on the perspicacity of its first person narrator to drive the story. The voice in the novel belongs to Ruth Anne Boatwright, nicknamed Bone, who tells the story of her life and her world until she is thirteen years old. Beside Bone, a host of characters populate a deftly drawn setting recalling rural South Carolina in the 1950s. The novel's focus on Southern family life has evoked literary comparisons to Flannery O'Connor and William Faulkner. Bone's poor, white working-class Southern family is stubborn, violent, and, at the same time, fiercely loving. Bone worships her cadre of uncles—hard-drinking, wide-shouldered men who terrorize the county yet are protective and affectionate toward Bone and her cousins; her Aunt Raylene is also of special importance, an independent woman who once worked the carnivals and who had a female lover. However, Bone's most unforgettable and pernicious relationship is with "Daddy Glen," her stepfather, who abuses her in every conceivable way. Her mother knows about the abuse but fails to stop it.

The novel thus chronicles the treachery, intimacies, and hateful paradoxes of family love and Bone's attempts to understand the cruelty she endures. One of the hard-learned lessons that looms over the novel and into Bone's consciousness is "that we do terrible things to the ones we love sometimes." Randall Kenan, a gay novelist and book reviewer for *The Nation,* addresses the potential problems with the material of family drama that the novel presents. However, he argues that when *Bastard* succeeds, it does so by eluding the trap of Southern stereotypes and rendering Bone's milieu with devastating realism. To *The Kenyon Review* Allison speculates about the reasons for the novel's success with wide and varied audiences. She suspects that "an enormous range of people [can] relate emotionally to Bone's experience. . . . The level of emotional brutality that a lot of us have survived is appalling. The book is useful for in some ways it's a mirror you can look into." *New York Times* book reviewer George Garrett concurs that the novel's emotional authenticity coupled with its "living language" and "cumulative lyricism" signal the arrival of "a wonderful work of fiction by a major new talent." In 1996, a film version of *Bastard Out of Carolina* directed by Anjelica Houston aired on television, and Allison went to work on her second novel, entitled *Cavedweller.*

Allison revisits many of the themes of *Trash* and *Bastard Out of Carolina* in her first published collection of nonfiction essays, performance pieces, and autobiographical narratives entitled *Skin.* Some of the pieces are updated versions of earlier material while other essays were written especially for this volume. The subject matter ranges from details of Allison's lifelong commitment to feminist activism, to personal recollections of her experiences with pornography, to memories of her friend and mentor, the novelist Bertha Harris. Probably the most poignant essay echoes the title of the volume. "Skin, Where She Touches Me" remembers the two most important women in Allison's life—her mother and her first lover. Both have died, but Allison maintains she "cannot stop talking about them, retelling their stories, turning their jokes to parables and their stubborn endurance to legend." Allison admires and desperately loves both women, crediting them for shaping who she has become.

Allison continues to pay tribute to the women in her life with the publication in 1995 of *Two or Three Things I Know For Sure,* which originally was written for performance in the months following the completion of *Bastard Out of Carolina.* This multi-media piece was first performed in 1991 in San Francisco and has been substantially revised for written publication. While it is dedicated to her sisters, Allison claims that the characters are composites, "creations based on friends, family, and acquaintances." Moreover, family snapshots intermittently illustrate the written text. The title is Allison's touchstone throughout, a credo adapted from the words of an aunt whose declaration, "There's only two or three things I know for sure," offered the women of the family comfort in times of hardship.

Two or Three Things I Know For Sure details the molestation by her stepfather and its effects on her life. The "sweaty power of violence" and "the sweet taste of desire" merge for Allison in the image she conjures of her stepfather during rifle target practice. The rendition of this memory, among others, captures Allison's power as a storyteller who uses fiction not as therapeutic indulgence but as a method to save lives. The lives she elucidates here, including her own, are resilient and determined; the stories here, like the ones that distinguish her previous fictional efforts, are passionate and desperate. Yet, they "all have to be told in order not to tell the one the world wants." Indeed, Dorothy Allison's works

Skin *Talks* •

About Sex,

Class, and

Literature

Profile by
Annmarie Pinarski

attempt to come to terms with a host of experiences that the world would rather keep silent.

PEDRO ALMODOVAR

*P*edro Almodovar is a Spanish film director who takes full advan-

tage of the artistic freedom in his country since the death of Francisco

Franco. Under Franco's dictatorship, thirty-six years of cultural repres-

sion and censorship stifled progress in the arts. Almodovar began his

career as a filmmaker in 1980 when he produced his first feature film.

His work marks the beginning of a new era for Spain. Throwing caution

to the wind, he is garish and outlandish in style, openly homosexual,

and flaunts bizarre sex in his films. A favorite theme is relationships

among women, whom he finds more interesting than men. Explicit sex,

disregard for conventional morality, and twisted personalities mix with

satire and bathroom humor in controversial productions.

1951– •

Spanish •

filmmaker

Almodovar was born in 1951 and spent his earliest childhood in the small, poor village of Calzada de Calatrava. His father was a bookkeeper and gas station attendant, who made wine on the side for some extra income. His mother, Francisca Caballero, ran the home. Pedro had two sisters and one brother. When he was eight, the family moved to a different small town, Caceras, in the province of La Mancha. It was an isolated, cold region, where he never felt he belonged. Even though he was close to his family, he couldn't wait to leave and explore the big cities. He began school at age ten, when he was given a scholarship by some priests who found him teaching villagers how to read.

When Almodovar was seventeen he left Caceras for Madrid, intending to become the most modern hippie in the city. He adopted hippie clothing and earned a living selling crafts on the street. He went to work for the national telephone company two years later. While he was employed, he pursued creative ventures on the side. He began filming a series of short, silent films with a Super-8 camera. He attracted quite a cult following, showing his creations in schools, bars, or parties, and providing his own commentary to make up for their lack of sound. Using a pseudonym (Patty Diphusa, a fictional porn star), he created a series of torrid "memoirs." During this time he also performed with a punk-rock band known as Almodovar and McNamara. He joined an avant-garde theatre group, Los Goliardos. One of the actresses in the group, Carmen Maura, would later star in several of his films.

A contract from an underground newspaper propelled him on the road to notoriety. Almodovar produced an outrageous, brazen film called *Pepi, Luci, Bom y otras chicas del monton (Pepi, Luci, Bom and Other Girls on the Heap)*. It took a year and a half to make, resulting in a technically disconnected product. For example, characters sometimes appeared with different hair lengths in the same scene. It is a raw, sexual production, violating good taste at every turn. Appearing at the San Sebastian Film Festival in 1980, it received an angry reaction from audiences. This film is the only one of Almodovar's never released in the United States.

Underground •

Contract

Almodovar's second film is a pop musical, *Laberinto de pasiones (Labyrinth of Passion)*. Its cast includes far-fetched characters from the fringes of society—punk rockers, transvestites, and the bisexual son of a deposed Iranian emperor. It takes a humorous look at a section of society that cares more about instant gratification than traditional mores. Released in 1982, it played through 1990 in Madrid's most popular art theatre.

Until 1982, Almodovar was popular mostly in his own region. His international reputation grew with the release of *Dark Habits* in 1983. It played at the Venice and Miami film festivals in 1984, creating a name for him as an outlandish, garish director. *Dark Habits* satires the work of an imaginary order of nuns called the Humble Redeemers. The subversive portrayal of the nuns as drug addicts, murderers, and delinquents is, nevertheless, presented with humor. The sisters come across as crazy but likable. Almodovar often depicts Catholicism in an unfavorable light, growing out of early unpleasant memories from his school years. In both this film and his previous, the special effects and lighting are especially notable. He uses neon color, grotesque close-ups, dramatic music, and a fast pace to enhance his defiance of convention in subject matter.

- *Controversial*

Career—

Conventional

Success

Almodovar featured Carmen Maura, a friend from his early acting days, in *What Have I Done to Deserve This?* It was his first commercial success in Spain. The film depicts the life of a frenzied housewife in Madrid, satirizing the unfortunate growing pains of modern Spain in 1985. While it carries undertones of Almodovar's idealism, still there is no attempt at using a different technique to make his statement. Almodovar returns to his same combination of ribald humor and dirty talk. His next film was less successful. His intent with *Matador* was a commentary on the glamourization of death in traditional Spanish culture. However, most people who viewed it missed that message amidst the story of a disreputable matador, whose student attempts to rape the matador's mistress. *Matador* was shown at the Rio International Film Festival in 1986 and released in the United States in 1988, but it never did well at the box office in Spain.

Frustrated by disagreements with the financial backers of *Matador,* Almodovar put together his own production company, El Deseo, with his brother. Together they produced *La ley del deseo (Law of Desire)* with financial assistance from Spain's Ministry of Culture. This homosexual love story was Spain's biggest moneymaker in 1986. It became a favorite of international cult film devotees, appealing to both gay and straight audiences with its romance and humor.

He proceeded from there to produce his most acclaimed film, *Women on the Verge of a Nervous Breakdown,* which received an Oscar nomination for best foreign film in 1988. The New York Film Critics Circle cited it as the best foreign film, and Almodovar received a screenwriter's award at the Venice Film Festival. Carmen Maura starred in the role of an unmarried, pregnant television actress recently abandoned by her lover. *Women on the Verge of a Nervous Breakdown* is modeled on American comedies of the 1950s, such as *How to Marry a Millionaire.* But it is a comedy with a message about female loneliness. The characters are beautiful women in plush surroundings, with funny situations happening all around them. But meanwhile, the women are alone, and it is evident that beautiful things cannot make up for sadness within.

The contrast between this film and his next one, *Tie Me Up! Tie Me Down!* (1990) deserves note. *Tie Me Up! Tie Me Down!* departs from all of his previous work by actually turning in the direction of convention, sentiment, and optimism. In addition, Carmen Maura does not play the starring role. It's the controversial story of a former mental patient who kidnaps a porn star, ties her to a bed, and waits for her to fall in love with him. Many feminists criticized the film for the use of ropes as subliminal violence against women. Almodovar insists that is not the case, that the ropes are symbolic only of the difficulty of two people getting to know each other. Critical reaction was much the same, with many critics feeling the film was uninspiring and devoid of substantial meaning while others praised it as Almodovar's best work yet.

Whatever the case may be, filmmaking is Pedro Almodovar's obsession. He lives for the intensity and excitement of bringing his dreams alive. He even enjoys the challenge of limited budgets, which he says stimulate his creativity. He's a demanding director, praised by his actors for the excellence he pushes them to achieve. His films are about today, what is happening now, and he records a viewpoint of society that challenges the mainstream.

Profile by Carolyn Eckstein-Soule

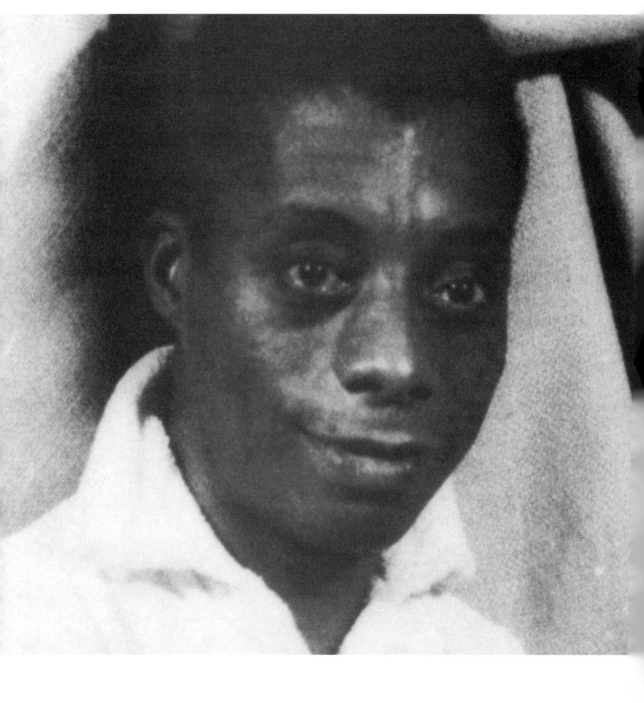

JAMES BALDWIN

I is nearly impossible to overestimate James Baldwin's importance as

a public figure, a visionary, and a storyteller. The author of some two

dozen books, Baldwin employed a wide range of voices and genres to tell

his personal story and the story of his nation over the course of his prolific

career. His six novels, seven collections of essays, and scattered short

stories, plays, and poetry all attest to the value of a struggle. For his

country, this struggle was the challenge to live up to its promise of liberty

for all of its citizens. For Baldwin, it was the challenge to forge an

identity as a gay, black man within this conflicted nation and to tell

other beleaguered Americans not to lose sight of their nation's promise.

1924–1987 •

African American •

writer

James Baldwin was born to Berdis Jones on 2 August 1924 in New York City's Harlem Hospital. His biological father left Berdis before James was born. His stepfather, David Baldwin, was a preacher and laborer who moved north from New Orleans in the early 1920s. One of nine children in the Baldwin household, James learned at an early age that the world was not always going to be fair to him. As a gay, black writer who grew up in Harlem during the Great Depression, he learned that, in fact, the world was going to be quite unfair to him. But his strong sense of spirituality, his renowned talents as a writer, and the support of his family and friends enabled him to forge ahead in his search for the elusive promise of social equality and acceptance.

Educated initially at New York's P.S. 24 and later at Frederick Douglass Junior High School, Baldwin was singled out at a young age for his talents: oration, singing, and writing. At the age of fourteen he discovered a talent for public speaking and gained notoriety as a young minister in several Harlem churches. Baldwin moved away from the impoverished community of his childhood when he was accepted to the mostly white, largely Jewish De Witt Clinton High School in the Bronx, where he became active on the school's literary magazine. He tried to work through his divided loyalty between church and school in the poems, plays, and stories that he contributed to the magazine. His budding awareness of his homosexuality and his growing love of the arts caused Baldwin to leave his church in 1940.

Guided by two notable mentors—the poet Countee Cullen and the painter Beauford Delaney—Baldwin began to discover that possibilities existed in the arts for a black man to locate his identity. After graduating from Clinton, he eventually gravitated to Greenwich Village where he was able to experiment with his writing and with his sexuality. Through the late 1940s he pursued sexual experiences with both men and women, but few of these encounters led to long-term relationships. He also experimented with his writing; he published a handful of essays and reviews and a short story, but he stopped short of "facing his 'demons' head-on," as David Leeming points out in his biography *James Baldwin*.

The Artist in

Exile

To face these *demons*, notably his sexuality and his troubled relationship with his stepfather, Baldwin did what many American writers had done a generation before: he went to Paris in 1948. There he wrote his first meditation on homosexuality in an essay entitled "The Preservation of Innocence," in which he writes of "the presence and passion of human beings, who cannot ever be labeled." It was also in Paris where he met Lucien Happersberger, a Swiss street boy of seventeen whom Baldwin later described as the love of his life. Over the next few years Baldwin came as close as he would ever come to fulfilling his dream of a domestic life and a monogamous relationship with a male lover. During this time, he was finally able to address his identity crisis in a prolific outburst of writing; he published a number of essays and completed his first novel, *Go Tell It on the Mountain*. The protagonist of this novel, John Grimes, strongly resembles the young Baldwin wrestling with his paternal and religious demons and emerging from the struggle as a strong, vital man ready to face more challenges. This powerful novel reflects Baldwin's claim in his 1955 essay "Autobiographical Notes" that: "One writes out of one thing only—one's own experience. Everything depends on how relentlessly one forces from this experience the last drop, sweet or bitter, it can possibly give."

Although it enabled him to resolve some personal conflicts through writing, his relationship with Lucien was far from perfect, as one can see from its fictional rendition in his second novel, *Giovanni's Room*. Virtually all of Baldwin's novels treat the topic of homosexuality to one degree or another, but *Giovanni's Room* is his most moving and extended meditation on the subject. Between his idyllic time with Lucien in Paris and Switzerland from 1949 to 1952 and the publication of *Giovanni's Room* in 1956, Baldwin traveled back and forth across the Atlantic, enjoying a reputation as a young writer of great renown from his first collection of essays, *Notes of a Native Son,* as well as from his first novel. His relationship with Lucien tapered off, and although some of his long-term attempts with subsequent lovers were somewhat successful, he never quite got over Lucien. Mirroring this difficulty in Baldwin's life, *Giovanni's Room* is a novel about the risks and vulnerabilities of love. Its protagonist, David, is an American living in Paris who leaves his fiancée for Giovanni. When he tells his fiancée of his plans to leave her, she tells him about love in a forceful manner reminiscent of Baldwin's days as a preacher:

> You never have loved anyone, I am sure you never will! You love purity, you love your mirror—you are just like a little virgin. . . . You will never let anyone *touch* it—man *or* woman. You want to be *clean*. You think you came here covered with soap and you think you will go out covered with soap—and you do not want to *stink*.

Unlike David, Giovanni is not afraid of "the stink of love," a quality that makes him a superior lover. Love requires risks, Baldwin believed, and it can only work if people aren't afraid of it. Baldwin's realization of the fact that love requires a willingness to open up had much to do with his own identity crises as a gay man in a straight world, as an unwanted stepson in a large family, and as an African American in a country dominated in every sense by its white majority population.

In 1957 Baldwin returned for an extended time to the United States in order to confront directly the racial problems that plagued his native country. He traveled through the American South, visiting such landmarks as the Tuskegee Institute and meeting such notable figures as Martin Luther King Jr. The Civil Rights Movement at this time was moving to the front burner, and Baldwin found his own anger coming to a slow boil. His struggle to determine his role in the movement is apparent from the title alone of his next collection of essays, *Nobody Knows My Name*. Race is a more prevalent topic than homosexuality in this book, but the two are related; as Baldwin himself writes in the introduction, "the question of color . . . operates to hide the graver questions of the self."

The theme of the struggle for identity is present throughout his work, but it is especially evident in his writings from the early 1960s, notably his widely acclaimed novel *Another Country*. On one level, this book seems to do what his essay "Many Thousands Gone" had done a dozen years earlier—it readdresses the way that Richard Wright had written about racial injustice in his influential 1940 novel *Native Son*. Baldwin writes in this essay, "*Native Son* finds itself at length so trapped by the American image of Negro life and by the American necessity to find the ray of hope that it cannot pursue its own implications." Baldwin's goal in *Another Country* was to pursue these implications, by employing his victim Rufus Scott not as a "social symbol" like Wright's victim Bigger Thomas, but as a real person whose death allows the novel's other characters to examine their own identities. The "other country" of the title exists within all of us; Americans must go there in order to address the problems that plague their nation.

Baldwin was justly famous by this point; his literary fame brought him in contact with writers like William Styron and Norman Mailer, actors like Sidney Poitier and Marlon Brando, and Civil Rights leaders like Malcolm X. Like Malcolm, Baldwin traveled to Africa in order to get a clearer sense of the movement, and when he returned he was prepared to throw himself into the thick of it as an activist both in the South and in New York. His new role as a spokesman landed him on the cover of *Time* on 17 May 1963; six days later he met with Attorney General Robert Kennedy to discuss the rising crisis of racial strife in America. His literature, notably his play "Blues for Mister Charlie" (produced on Broadway in 1963), also addressed the most controversial racial issues of the time. Race and homosexuality were part and parcel of his nation's identity crisis because, Baldwin felt, Americans were plagued by their tendency to label everything and everyone and to stigmatize an Other.

Ironically, some members of the Civil Rights Movement were uncomfortable with Baldwin's homosexuality; Eldridge Cleaver attacked Baldwin's sexual preference in his best-seller *Soul on Ice*. Such attacks did nothing to appease Baldwin's confusion about his place within his country and within the Civil Rights Movement. On one level he craved acceptance; on another level he had to remain true to his own sense of self. At times he allied himself with Cleaver, the Black Muslims, and the Black Panthers; at other times he associated with King's non-violent approach to the problem. Baldwin was a writer who rejected labels on every level, and his refusal to be tied to any group within the Civil Rights Movement is not unlike his restlessness in his relationships. He created a character named Black Christopher in his 1968 novel *Tell Me How Long the Train's Been Gone* who seems to embody both his political and sexual interests. Yet Baldwin is more like the flawed protagonist of the novel, Leo Proudhammer, than he is like the idealized Black Christopher. The distance between Baldwin and his characters such as Black Christopher are testimony to his capacity for self-evaluation.

In the late 1960s and early 1970s Baldwin gradually became disillusioned with both his role in the Civil Rights Movement and his personal relationships. His health was also in decline; hepatitis and years of drinking had damaged his liver considerably. He was worn down both mentally and physically. He shuttled continuously between Paris, Istanbul, and New York, and the title of his next collection of essays, *No Name in the Street,* indicates that he remained aware of his identity crisis and his displacement. Some negative reviews of it contributed to his depression, which was also fueled by the death or deterioration of a few close friends. His next novel, *If Beale Street Could Talk,* was his most involved fictional depiction of the tribulations of Black America. He gained some comfort through this period from his relationship with the artist Yoran Cazac, to whom he dedicated *Beale Street*. By the time of his fiftieth birthday party in 1974, he was proud of his accomplishments and ready to move forward.

The next few years saw him complete *The Devil Finds Work,* an extended essay on America focusing on film history, and his ambitious final novel *Just Above My Head*. This novel begins, like *Another Country,* with the decline and death of a character and continues with other characters' reactions to this death. But *Just Above My Head*'s Arthur Montana is a celebrity and a homosexual, more obviously like Baldwin than *Another Country*'s Rufus Scott. Despite his failing health and the demands of this novel, Baldwin remained energetic through this period.

Different •

Directions

He began and ended more personal relationships and embarked on a second career as an academic; he taught at Bowling Green University and at the five colleges in and around Amherst, Massachusetts well into the 1980s. His final work of non-fiction, *The Evidence of Things Not Seen,* focuses on the race problems that continued to haunt America in the 1980s. Although it was not as well received as earlier works, the intensity of *Evidence* proves how committed Baldwin was to social change even in his final years. When his health began to rapidly deteriorate in the mid-1980s he returned to the village of St.-Paul-de-Vence, where he died of liver cancer in 1987. A whole nation mourned his passing at his funeral at the Cathedral of Saint John the Divine in New York, but they also celebrated his life. Like a blues song, the funeral was at once a record of sadness and an expression of both joy and hope for the future.

Many have paid tribute to Baldwin's courage, his vision, and his art. In a collection of essays entitled *James Baldwin: The Legacy,* edited by Quincy Troupe, Toni Morrison writes to Baldwin: "You knew, didn't you, how I needed your language and the mind that formed it? How I relied on your fierce courage to tame wildernesses for me?" Chinua Achebe adds: "As long as injustice exists . . . the words of James Baldwin will be there to bear witness and to inspire and elevate the struggle for human freedom." Witness to a nation's errors, prophet of its future, and teller of its troubled stories, Baldwin remains one of the most inspirational authors of the twentieth century. In "Autobiographical Notes," Baldwin stated his simple goal: "I want to be an honest man and a good writer." He was all that and much, much more.

Profile by
D. Quentin Miller

ARTHUR BELL

A rthur Bell was one of New York City's most widely recognized gay

men in his time. As a journalist, author, and activist, he helped shape the

gay male cultural and political outlook that emanated from Greenwich

Village in the post-Stonewall era.

1939–1984 ·

American ·

journalist and

activist

Arthur Irving Bell was born on 6 November 1939, in Brooklyn, New York. His father, Samuel Bell, worked as a successful clothing manufacturer, while his mother, Claire (née Bodan) Bell, designed clothing. When he was in junior high school, Bell moved to Montreal with his family. Bell's early homosexual experiences began in a movie theater at the age of seventeen and quickly increased when he discovered some of the Manhattan bars and bathhouses where gay men congregated in the 1950s.

Returning to New York City permanently in 1960, Bell worked in publicity for Viking Press until 1968, when he became publicity director for children's books at Random House. In 1964 he began his long relationship with Arthur Evans, a film distributor who later pursued a Ph.D. in philosophy at Columbia University.

After the Stonewall riots of June 1969, Bell and Evans began attending meetings of the newly formed Gay Liberation Front (GLF), a radical group of homosexuals concerned with a variety of progressive issues. Dissatisfied with GLF's purpose, organization, and tactics, Bell joined GLF dissidents Jim Owles, Marty Robinson, and other activists at a 24 November 1969 meeting to begin a group solely dedicated to homosexual liberation. On 21 December 1969, a group that included Evans, Owles, and Robinson met in Bell's Greenwich Village apartment to formally adopt the Gay Activists Alliance (GAA) constitution and to elect its first officers. The new group's intention combined the activism of the GLF with the focus of the homophile groups founded prior to Stonewall.

Bell became a pivotal GAA member in the early 1970s. Because of his flexible schedule at Random House, he could participate in many of GAA's New York City "zaps"—confrontations with politicians such as Mayor Lindsay and media figures such as talk show host, Dick Cavett. He championed the rights of all homosexuals—including street transvestites such as Stonewall veteran Ray "Sylvia" Rivera—to participate in GAA. Most importantly, Bell served as GAA's first publicity chair, helping to build the organization's exposure and membership by using the skills and contacts he had developed in publishing. For several months he wrote a column—using the pseudonym "Arthur Irving"—publicizing GAA in *Gay Power,* a New York City biweekly newspaper. His media attention heightened when WOR-TV interviewed him as an openly gay man and homosexual rights activist for a three-segment profile that was aired in November of 1970. Although he gradually lessened his commitment to GAA, his influence on the organization was profound.

In late 1970 Bell's relationship with Evans ended, although the two would remain lifelong friends. Bell also resigned his position at Random House, intending to devote himself full time to writing and gay activism. He wrote film reviews for *Gay* and began writing feature articles for the *Village Voice,* beginning with a front-page article about gay politics on 13 August 1970. His account of his first year as a gay activist, *Dancing the Gay Lib Blues: A Year in the Homosexual Liberation Movement,* became one of the first books about gay liberation published by a mainstream publisher.

Touching another form of gay activism, Bell began covering the gay crime beat in early 1973, beginning with a *Village Voice* story about the murders of four gay men in New York City. When "Little John" Wojtowicz robbed a Brooklyn bank to finance a sex change operation for his lover (later portrayed in the film *Dog Day Afternoon*), Bell was called in to act as his mediator. He also reported about the sadistic serial killer Dean

Corll and Felix Melendez, who killed newspaper heir John Knight III. The latter slaying became the subject of Bell's second book, *Kings Don't Mean a Thing: The John Knight Murder Case,* which received mixed reviews after its publication. By this time, Bell was writing about crime, entertainment, politics, and gay liberation for several publications, including *Cosmopolitan, Esquire, Playboy,* and the *New York Times.* "Bell Tells," his weekly column that began in 1976 in the *Village Voice,* focused on the New York City entertainment and nightlife scene.

Bell died in New York City on 2 June 1984, of complications from diabetes. The *Village Voice,* in a 26 June 1984 article, provided an opportunity for his friends, including Arthur Evans, Harvey Fierstein, Arnie Kantrowitz, Merle Miller, Vito Russo, James M. Saslow, and Liz Smith, to share their memories of Arthur Bell.

Profile by
Joseph M. Eagan

NANCY K. BEREANO

*A*s an editor at Crossing Press, and later as publisher and editor of

Firebrand Books, Nancy K. Bereano has consistently produced quality

works by a broad spectrum of lesbian and feminist writers in a variety of

genres. Nancy Kirp Bereano was born 17 August 1942 in New York City

to Adele Relis Kirp and Herman "Hy" Kirp. Her mother was a homemak-

er, and her father owned a small wholesale food company that distribut-

ed canned fish. Of her parents, Bereano says: "My father is very

comfortable around language and words and so I think I got from my

dad a real sense of pleasure in language. Also an enormous drive, for

better or worse, to do something significant in life. From my mother, I got

a sense of aesthetics which is helpful when putting books into the world,

1942– ·

American ·

publisher

49 ·

and a sense of what it means to survive."

Growing up in New York, Bereano attended public school. Describing her childhood, Bereano says simply: "I read a lot and I was a *painfully* good girl." She auditioned successfully on the piano for entrance into the School of Music and Art, where she learned to play the cello. Bereano stayed in New York to attend Queens College, and shortly after graduating with a B.A. in English in 1963, married Philip L. Bereano. In 1968, after a two-year tour of duty in Washington, D.C., the couple moved to Ithaca, New York, where Philip attended Cornell University. The next year Bereano gave birth to her only child, Joshua. The couple divorced several years later.

In those days of the anti–Vietnam War movement, the university was a politically charged environment and it was not long until Bereano became active in grassroots organizing. Throughout the 1970s, she was engaged in various progressive movements, including anti-war activism, women's liberation, and welfare organizing. The skills and connections she acquired during these years provided a solid foundation for her upcoming career in publishing.

In 1980, Bereano took a part-time position at Crossing Press as editor of its Feminist Series. "At the time, I thought editing meant putting in commas," comments Bereano, and although she has since discovered differently, "it has turned out to be my right work." During her five years at Crossing Press, Bereano developed a penchant for acquiring manuscripts of such seminal feminist works as Audre Lorde's *Sister Outsider* and Marilyn Frye's *The Politics of Reality,* and attracting such noted authors as Charlotte Bunch, Michelle Cliff, Judy Grahn, Valerie Miner, Pat Parker, and Jane Rule.

It was shortly before starting work at Crossing Press that Bereano came out. "I didn't come out until I was 38. I was able to be a lesbian because of the feminist and lesbian movement," Bereano reflects. "Once I came out I felt like I had been given another opportunity in my life. I wouldn't have been able to come close to realizing whatever potential I have without living in a lesbian world."

While at Crossing Press, Bereano attended the second Women in Print Conference, an event that was to resonate strongly throughout her life, both professionally and personally. "It was mind boggling. I met everyone involved in lesbian and feminist publishing!" she recounts. She made valuable connections at the conference and became a key player in the Women in Print movement, drawing upon her political organizing and publishing skills. On a personal note, Bereano met Janis Kelly, one of the conference organizers and a member of the *off our backs* collective. The two quickly became lovers, forming a relationship that lasted ten years.

In October 1984, Bereano was fired from Crossing Press over creative differences. Drawing upon "a certain amount of anger and revenge" in addition to her considerable publishing skills and connections, Bereano started Firebrand Books the very next month. By April 1985, Firebrand had published its first three books. Over the years, Firebrand has gone on to publish over eighty books documenting the rich diversity of the lesbian and feminist experience and has won eleven Lambda Literary Awards and four American Library Association Gay, Lesbian, and Bisexual Book Awards. Among the prominent authors that Firebrand has published are Dorothy Allison, Alison Bechdel, Beth Brant, Cheryl Clarke, Leslie Feinberg, Jewelle Gomez, Judith Katz, Audre Lorde, Joan Nestle, Pat Parker, Cindy Patton, Minnie Bruce Pratt, Ruthann Robson, Barbara Smith, and Kitty Tsui. Bereano herself was awarded the 1996 Publisher's Service Award by the Lambda Literary Awards, which declared her "at the forefront of lesbian and small press publishing."

Bereano resides in Ithaca, New York with her lover since 1995, novelist Elisabeth Nonas. Reflecting on publishing, she says: "I really do believe that books have a power to help change the world and that has been true in my life. At the times in my life when there were momentous changes, books have been the way I've expanded my horizons. I feel like doing this is a kind of payback, helping to put back in the world lots of what I got out."

**Profile by
R. Ellen Greenblatt**

LEONARD BERNSTEIN

*M*usical Renaissance man Leonard Bernstein is the most protean

figure worldwide in twentieth-century music, with an unmatched flair

for showmanship and popular appeal. He had classic good looks with a

compact physique, deep-set hazel eyes, aquiline nose, and athletic

coordination. By nature he was good humored, personable, and gener-

ous. With his ebullient theatricality and his verve, erudition, and

magnetic allure, he seemed one of life's darlings. Not an innovator, he

was Shakespearean in his ability to assimilate what others had invented

and to set upon it the stamp of his own unique genius.

1919–1990 ·

American ·

composer and

conductor

Louis (later Leonard) Bernstein was born in Lawrence, Massachusetts, 25 August 1918, to first-generation American citizens Samuel Yosef and Jennie Resnick Bernstein, from the Jewish pale of the Ukraine. Samuel started life cleaning fish in the Fulton Street Market in New York,

then, thanks to a stint in a barbershop, became associated with a supplier of hair and beauty products. By 1930 he was the owner of the Samuel Bernstein Hair Company with a staff of fifty. This was the springboard to middle-class prosperity. It was thanks to this affluence that son Leonard would have access to good teachers and a superior education.

Leonard's tastes for music asserted themselves at the age of ten with the arrival of a mahogany upright piano, a gift from an aunt. His connection to the instrument was immediate and spontaneous. He soon asked for lessons, and within one year his teacher was assigning him Chopin nocturnes and preludes. He met his lifelong friend, Sid Ramin, at the age of twelve. Ramin later reported to biographer Humphrey Burton that he had no recollection of fourteen-year-old Bernstein having a regular girlfriend. "He held back from committing himself physically with either sex."

By age thirteen, Leonard had outgrown his local piano teacher, so his family chose a teacher at the New England Conservatory of Music. At about the same time, Leonard was admitted to the Boston Latin School. His classmates, who considered him a good first baseman, could not deter him from his 5:30 departure to practice his piano and do his homework even by cat calls of "fruit, fruit, sissy." There are no stories of his sexual leanings from this period of his life. His next piano teacher, Helen Coates, who started working with him when he was sixteen and eventually became his private secretary, was to enjoy with him a relationship that lasted fifty years.

Bernstein graduated with honors in 1931, first in English, and was admitted to Harvard. Two years later, he met the famous Greek conductor, Dimitri Mitropoulos, aged forty, who was honored at Harvard at a function during which Bernstein was invited to play. The conductor was so impressed by the young man's musical passion that he invited him to attend his rehearsals of the Boston Symphony Orchestra. Bernstein was profoundly affected by Mitropoulos' expressive style, which had recourse to flamboyant body language articulated by magnetism and physical power. It was he who persuaded Bernstein that he had the makings of a fine conductor. Along with Serge Koussevitzky, Mitropoulos discerned quite early Bernstein's prodigious potential and promoted him as a wunderkind.

Another early influence on Bernstein was Aaron Copland, whom he met while still at Harvard. Despite the twenty-year age gap, they enjoyed a close friendship over the next six years, and there is some evidence that they even became lovers, as Mitropoulos and Bernstein had also presumably done—though neither long-lasting. Copland gave his young friend invaluable advice as he took his first halting steps in composition and conducting. By the time of his senior year at Harvard, he began to confront his sexuality after discovering the New York gay colony, where guilt was apparently not a problem.

Even with a Harvard diploma now in his hand, Bernstein faced an uncertain future. He turned down his father's offer to join the family firm at $100 a week. Instead he joined a group of five unknown performers who sublet a New York apartment with a Steinway grand piano. Continued encouragement from Mitropoulos and Copland steered him toward conducting. It was perhaps through Copland's contact with Fritz Reiner that Leonard was admitted to the Philadelphia Curtis Institute of Music, which attracted both aspiring performers and composers. It was Mitropoulos—not Samuel Bernstein—who offered to pay the $75 a month that was not covered by the scholarship.

It was in the summer after his first year at Curtis that Bernstein had his introduction to the Berkshire Music Center at Tanglewood, a famous Massachusetts site of musical activities since 1937. Serge Koussevitzky, reigning director of the Boston Symphony, held court there. It began as a festival but soon included a vigorous training center for some three hundred students every summer. Along with four other students, Bernstein had been singled out to participate in Koussevitzky's conducting class and was selected to conduct the first concert of the season. In the audience were his parents along with sister Shirley, a student at Mount Holyoke, and brother Burtie, who was then eight. In a letter to Copland, who was also present at Tanglewood that summer, Leonard wrote, "Not seeing you is something of a shock, you understand. The summer was a revelation in that regard: neither of us (I hope) tired of the other (I had feared you might), and I came, in fact, to depend in many ways on you. I've never felt about anyone before as I do about you, completely at ease, and always comforted with you. This is not a love letter, but I'm quite mad about you."

H. Burton concludes that Bernstein had no great love affair during his student days other than his own love affair with music. More revealing, perhaps, is an observation of Bernstein's to Shirley Gabis, a Curtis student with whom he became close during his second year: "I have a canker in my soul."

Bernstein's first big break came at the age of twenty-five when he was asked by Artur Rodzinski to become his assistant conductor at the New York Philharmonic. His duties had him sitting in on all rehearsals and learning each score sufficiently well to substitute for the maestro at a moment's notice. He rented his first apartment in Carnegie Hall itself. Later that season, when he had to replace an ill Bruno Walter, he became the youngest person ever to direct a Philharmonic concert as well as the first American-born conductor to head a major orchestra. Though he had not even had time to rehearse with the orchestra, at the end of the nationally broadcast concert, the audience brought him back four times, and the critics covered him with bouquets in all the major New York newspapers.

Soon he was invited to appear with the Pittsburgh and Boston orchestras, and he was on his meteoric rise to international celebrityhood. Much of Bernstein's leap to fame is a study in timing. The following season three of his compositions had premieres in New York: his first musical, *On the Town;* his first symphony, *Jeremiah;* and his first ballet, *Fancy Free. Jeremiah* was selected by the New York Music Critics Circle as the outstanding classical work of the season. *Fancy Free,* a master-piece of American vernacular, claimed a new role for dance in musical comedy. Soon, he was besieged by numerous offers to conduct.

In 1945, Bernstein was guest conductor with fourteen different symphonies. From 1945 to 1948 he was conductor of the New York City Orchestra. In 1953 he became the first American to conduct at Milan's acclaimed La Scala with Maria Callas singing the starring role. Not one to concentrate only on work, he gives a glimpse of his personal life in a letter to Copland. "I miss you terribly and need your cynical ears for my latest tales of love and limb—from Montreal to San Francisco. Oh, what a divine one in San Francisco!"

Felicia Montealegre, born in Costa Rica in 1922 of a Chilean mother and American father, was twenty-four and in New York studying to be an actress when she met Leonard. She was slim, even delicate, educated by British Catholic nuns, and every inch a lady. According to some, it was love at first sight. They soon became engaged. But the engagement dragged on so long that Felicia finally called it off and plunged headlong into her own career, which soon had her in important television dramatic roles. By the end of 1949, she was elected as the female Most Promising Star of Tomorrow by members of the industry. Leonard and Felicia finally married within four years of their first meeting, Felicia aware of Leonard's attraction to men but confident that he would change. There were three children.

The 1950s, when Bernstein was in his thirties, were his most productive years. In 1956 *Candide* received the New York Theater Critic award. *The Serenade for Violin and String Orchestra with Percussion* won high critical praise in 1954. The previous year *Wonderful Town* was a long-run hit, but it was *West Side Story,* in 1957, that spoke most eloquently the language of contemporary music. Exploding with energy, animation, and feeling, it is a prodigious amalgamation of American musical strains—including jive and big-band jazz—and, with its highly lyrical love songs and Latino dance rhythms, a blend of opera, choreography, and musical comedy.

Bernstein's first season with the New York Philharmonic, where he was director from 1957 to 1969, ushered in a new age in the exploration of American music. Sometimes as pianist-soloist conducting from the keyboard, he commanded a vast repertory. He gave music lovers the opportunity to hear a new generation of composers: George Chadwick, Lukas Foss, Ned Rorem, and Gunther Schuller. He drew on his talents as an educator in TV appearances and phonograph recordings, the most notable of which were some fifty "Young People's Concerts" and his educational programs on the PBS cultural series "Omnibus."

With his children nearly grown, Bernstein became deeply involved with Tom Cothran, a relationship that threatened the equilibrium of his marriage. Tom even accompanied him as a "traveling secretary" in 1976 on a cross-country tour as part of the bicentennial celebrations.

Of Irish descent, Tom Cothran was twenty-four and music director of a San Francisco radio station. Bernstein was fifty-three, his hair now gray and the lines in his face quite conspicuous. During his twenty-year marriage Leonard had had his share of homosexual encounters. (No affairs with women are ever referred to by his biographer, though his sister Shirley declared him bisexual.) Tom's entry into his life marked the beginning of a strong emotional relationship with a man and the end of an intimate relationship with Felicia, who died two years later of inoperable lung cancer. Leonard believed himself responsible for his wife's death, a belief that cast its shadow over the twelve years that remained to him. He never forgot her whispered curse when he told her he was leaving her for Cothran: "You're going to die a bitter and lonely old man."

Bernstein's biographer, Humphrey Burton, speculates that when Cothran became stricken with AIDS in 1980, Leonard lost the "only person who might have filled the void left by Felicia." He now became noisy about the need to come out of the closet. Once, when he egged on Aaron Copland, in his eighties, to "come out," he got this curt reply: "I think I'll leave that to you, boy." During his final decade, he explored relationships with dozens of men, easily becoming enamored with the young conductors he worked with each year. At his daughter's wedding reception at the Waldorf-Astoria, with four hundred guests present, he ended his toast with a list of his new son-in-law's virtues, adding this boast in conclusion: "and he's *straight.*"

By now, whenever he went abroad, Bernstein was courted by monarchs and presidents and was often the guest of honor at public receptions and private parties, and he received prestigious awards. In France he was honored with the title of Commander in the Legion d'Honneur. The Germans gave him the coveted Hartmann medal. By 1985, with Karajan ailing, he had become the leading conductor in the German-speaking world. The $250,000 he received as part of the Siemens Prize he gave away to music colleges. Whenever he was invited to perform in Israel, he gave his fee back to the Israel Philharmonic. In London and Vienna, he was only paid half his international fee. He had become music's spokesman to the world and gave himself generously to a myriad of musical projects. In 1987 Bernstein, who apparently never tested HIV-positive, was part of the first "Music for Life" AIDS benefit at Carnegie Hall, which raised $1.7 million for patient care.

Even at age seventy, Leonard was falling in love with young protegees. Mark Stringer, a conducting student from Georgia who fell under his charm, wrote this tribute: "He was the most important man in my life, intellectually and emotionally. . . . He was an incredible intellectual stimulus. . . . No other human being had ever given me total trust, looking past all my emotional insecurities. . . . No one believed in me more. . . . So I poured every ounce of dedication into my work for him."

The violinist Isaac Stern predicted that Leonard Bernstein would be remembered as the man who taught America what classical music was. He is remembered too for his willingness to take risks in his excursions into avant-garde music and his preview talks to audiences. Bernstein used religious themes in his important non-theatrical works that treat a crisis in faith. Several vocal pieces follow biblical texts. Among his fourteen works for the theater, the most notable are the operetta *Candide* (1956), his Oscar-nominated film score for *On the Waterfront* (1954), and his musicals, *On the Town* (1944), *West Side Story* (1957), and *1600 Pennsylvania Avenue* (1967). Of his seventeen orchestral works for the concert hall, the most outstanding are his three symphonies *Jeremiah* (1944), *The Age of Anxiety* (1949), and *Kaddish* (1963). *Chichester Psalms* (1965) is a work for chorus and orchestra. *Mass* (1971), Bernstein's most original work, represents the synthesis that he sought between Broadway and the concert hall. A theater piece for singers and dancers, it was commissioned at the suggestion of Jacqueline Kennedy for the opening of the John F. Kennedy Center of the Performing Arts in Washington, D.C. He also authored five books, all of which are currently in print: *The Joy of Music* (1959), *Leonard Bernstein's Young People's Concerts* (1962), *The Infinite Variety of Music* (1966), *The Unanswered Question* (1976), drawn from his lectures at Harvard when he was the Charles Eliot Norton Professor of Poetry (1972–73), and *Findings* (1982). He also recorded over one hundred albums.

Joseph Machlis states: "He has a real flair for orchestration. The spice and balance of sonorities, the use of the brass in high register, the idiomatic writing that displays each instrument to its best advantage— all these show his deftness. His harmonic idiom is spicily dissonant, his jazz rhythms have vitality. The formal structure tends to be diffuse, as is natural with a temperament that is lyrical and prone to improvise."

Bernstein's attraction to the music of Copland and Stravinsky coupled with his reverence for Gustave Mahler and Richard Strauss gave his style a blend of neo-classic and post-Romantic elements, though, in the final analysis, he is a maverick who does not fit categories.

Leonard Bernstein died at his New York home in 1990 of a heart attack brought on by a pleural tumor, emphysema, fibrosis, and a series of pulmonary infections. He was buried next to his wife in the Greenwood Cemetery in Brooklyn.

Profile by
Robert F. Jones

RON BUCKMIRE

*G*ay computer activist and mathematician Ron Buckmire is the

founder of the Queer Resources Directory (QRD), the largest and oldest

repository of gay, lesbian, bisexual, transgender, and AIDS information

available on the Internet. Buckmire was born on 21 May 1968 in

Grenville, Grenada, to Rose Henry and Reginald Buckmire. The next

year his father brought the family to the United States while he attended

graduate school at the University of Massachusetts at Amherst, working

toward a Ph.D. in food science and nutrition. Ron's parents divorced in

1974, and in 1978 the family returned to the Caribbean, this time to

Barbados, where Dr. Buckmire worked for the Caribbean Development

Bank.

1968– ·

West Indian– ·

born mathemati-

cian and activist

While in Barbados, Buckmire developed into an avid chess player, becoming an international-level youth chess player from 1981 to 1986 and participating in championship competition in Finland, England, Scotland, and the United States. He was also Barbados Junior Champion for four consecutive years as well as a three-time Barbados National Champion. Buckmire's interest in chess continues today; currently he is a United States Chess Federation Senior Master ranked in the Top 250 in the United States.

In 1986, Buckmire returned to the United States to attend college. Just three years later, in 1989, he earned his bachelor's degree in mathematics magna cum laude at Rensselaer Polytechnic Institute in Troy, New York. He went on to get his master's in mathematics in 1992 and his Ph.D. in applied mathematics in 1994 at the same institution.

It was during his college days that Buckmire came out. In 1988 he began to question his sexuality and consulted what many at that time would have thought a surprising source of information—the Internet: "I came out pretty quickly, with the aid of computer-mediated communication." It didn't take long for Buckmire to turn into an activist. When asked what drew him to queer activism, Buckmire explains, "It just seemed like the obvious thing to do. I read a lot of books on gay history (*The Mayor of Castro Street,* etc.) and found out how few rights gays and lesbians had and was shocked. The arguments against equal rights for gays and lesbians are so illogical and internally inconsistent that it was completely natural to join the fight. Civil rights for all just makes sense." Asked what drew him to computer activism in particular, he simply states: "Because that was what I knew, and there wasn't much of it going on at the time."

During his years at Rensselaer Polytechnic Institute, Buckmire served as president of the Rensselaer Gay/Lesbian/Bisexual Association from 1991–93, and co-creator and executive producer of HomoRadio, the local queer radio show from 1992–94. He was also a member several campus advisory committees and even co-founded the Women Students Association in 1992.

But his most enduring contribution has been the creation of the Queer Resources Directory in the spring of 1991. Originally begun as an electronic archive for Queer Nation (QN), Buckmire realized that "a more extensive resource than just an archive for QN would be useful for the queer Internet community" and began the process of transforming the QRD into its current status as the premier queer site on the Internet whose "function is to provide as much information as possible on every facet and issue relating to sexual minorities." Comments Buckmire, who currently serves as executive director of the QRD: "Creating the QRD and seeing it used by people all over the world in numerous situations is extremely rewarding."

In January 1991, Buckmire met his partner, Dean Elzinga. The two met—where else—"Through the Internet! I came to LA to visit my sister (attending USC) and a number of soc.motss (USENET newsgroups for members of the same sex) gatherings were thrown together for me. At the third one it was just Dean and me and that was the beginning. . . ." Still together, the couple celebrates 13 January as their anniversary.

Currently, Buckmire has just completed a Minority Scholar-in-Residence Postdoctoral Fellowship and now serves as assistant professor in the Department of Mathematics at Occidental College in Los Angeles, California. His field of study centers around mathematical modelling and applied mathematics. Most of his work has been in theoretical aerodynamics and computational fluid dynamics.

Active in the queer immigration rights movement, Buckmire is a founding member of the Los Angeles Chapter of the Lesbian and Gay Immigration Rights Task Force. Buckmire comments: "I have spent 18 of my 28 years in the USA as a 'non-immigrant resident' but I hope to become a permanent resident soon."

Buckmire also works as contributing producer for *This Way Out,* an award-winning weekly international lesbian and gay radio magazine currently airing on almost 100 stations in seven countries. He remains active on the Internet. Remembering its importance in his coming out process, Buckmire assures safe space on the Internet for gays, lesbians, bisexuals, transgendered, and questioning people throughout the world by administering several queer electronic discussion lists, including: GGBB ("girl-girl-boy-boy") for gay and lesbian couples; GLBMATH for queer mathematicians; GLBPOC for queer people of color; HOMORADIO for those involved in radio programming for queers; MARRIAGE for activists working to gain the right of same-sex couples in the United States to marry; QI (Queer Immigration) to discuss the impact of immigration policies on queers; QUEERLAW for discussion of queer legal theory; and QUEERPLANET to enable queer activists and organizations the world over to network.

The Internet has become a vital tool in queer organizing, the "silicon solution" as Michelangelo Signorile terms it in his book *Queer in America,* due in large part to the efforts of Ron Buckmire. He has chiselled out "queer space" on the Internet by generously giving of his time and resources to ensure that lesbians, gays, bisexuals, and transgendered persons can access and disseminate all types of information on the Internet. Buckmire continues to protect the rights to this information by being a part of the lawsuit challenging the Communications Decency Act, which seeks to censor such information.

**Profile by
R. Ellen Greenblatt**

CHARLES BUSCH

*B*en Brantley has called actor-playwright Charles Busch "arguably

the most beloved drag performer in the New York theater." That classic of

high camp, Vampire Lesbians of Sodom, of which Busch was the author

and star—and a string of gleeful, wicked comedies have built his

reputation on a surefire show-biz formula of high heels, heart, and

happy endings.

1954– •

American actor •

and playwright

The young Busch was raised in a Jewish family in Hartsdale, a middle-class suburb outside of New York City. Busch grew up with two older sisters, Meg and Betsy (now, respectively, a producer of promotional spots for Showtime and a textile designer).

But when Busch was seven, his mother died, and for the next seven years he "sort of got lost in this world of old movies and trivia to block out the real world," he told Lisa Anderson in an interview for the *Chicago Tribune*. "I had this completely overblown sense of the romantic."

"He was saved by his Aunt Lillian—Lillian Blum—his mother's oldest sister and a former schoolteacher, who, with his father's permission, moved him to Manhattan and got him into the High School of Music and Art," reports Alex Witchel in the *New York Times*. "Chuck was always special," Blum, at the age of 85, related to Witchel. "But he was so shy it was almost pathological. . . . Before he moved in with me, I would pick him up in Hartsdale on a Friday afternoon, and he would be like a zombie. But the minute we crossed the river to New York he was absolutely a new boy."

His aunt's love and strong personality made all the difference. She insisted, for example, that he read the front page of the newspaper every day just to help him keep at least one foot in the real world. "I didn't do drugs," Busch explained to Witchel, "I did Warner Brothers movies." Thanks to Aunt Lillian, Busch graduated high school and went on to study drama at Northwestern University in Evanston, Illinois.

While in some ways a frustrating experience, college helped Busch define his own strengths as a performer. "I was dealt a strange hand," he told Witchel, "Too thin, too light, which is the euphemism for gay. I was never cast at Northwestern for basically these reasons, and finally, I thought maybe what's most disturbing about me is what is most unique: my theatrical sense, my androgyny, even identifying with old movie actresses." So Busch began writing his own material, including a play, *Sister Act,* in 1976 about Siamese twin showgirls. "It made a big sensation at Northwestern," Busch told Anderson. "They'd never seen anything like it."

After college, from 1978 to 1984, Busch toured the country in a one-person non-drag show he wrote called *Alone with a Cast of Thousands.* Between bookings he would come back to New York where he cleaned apartments, scooped ice cream, gave the odds on a betting line, or did whatever he could to make ends meet.

But by 1984, the bookings had all but dried up and Busch was ready to throw in the towel. His last hurrah was going to be a little skit—with Busch in drag—that he arranged to put on at the Limbo Lounge, a gay bar in Manhattan's East Village. The skit, which eventually became *Vampire Lesbians of Sodom,* turned out to be a great hit, and Busch and his collaborators, who called themselves the Theatre-in-Limbo, created a series of drag spectacles at the bar, including *Theodora, She-Bitch of Byzantium* and *Times Square Angel.*

With his usual indomitability of spirit, Busch decided to mount a commercial production of *Vampire Lesbians,* and after he went "to every friend, family member, and ex-lover to raise the money," the show opened at the Provincetown Playhouse in Greenwich Village (c. 1985), where it received nearly unanimous raves. "The audience laughs at the first line and goes right on laughing at every line to the end, and even at some of the silences," wrote D. J. R. Bruckner in a career-changing *New York Times* review.

Vampire Lesbians established the characteristics that typified Busch's comedies over the next nine years: manic energy, bigger-than-life female roles, fabulous and funny costumes, and sharp and knowing parodies of old film and fashion styles. In *Vampire Lesbians,* Busch spoofed the antics of 1920s silent pictures and their stars. *Psycho Beach Party* (1987) had its fun with 1960s beach-party movies while *The Lady in Question* (1989) targeted 1940s wartime dramas. *Red Scare on Sunset* (1991) used the conventions of film noire to tell a tale of Communist-baiting in Hollywood of the 1950s.

With his 1994 play *You Should Be So Lucky,* Busch gave himself his first non-drag role since hitting it big. The play is an updated Cinderella story in which Cinderella is a pathologically shy gay man, an electrologist who through the intervention of a fairy godmother—the enigmatic, elderly businessman Mr. Rosenberg—not only gets to go to the ball where he meets the man of his dreams, but is left Mr. Rosenberg's fortune, too.

Busch's recent projects include *Queen Amarantha,* with a juicy new over-the-top drag role for himself, for the 1996–97 New York season. He has also written the book for a musical, *The Green Heart,* in development at the Manhattan Theater Club.

Through the medium of his own plays, Busch both spoofs and lovingly inhabits an outsized and glamorous world that captivated and charmed him and many other gay men as children. "Drag is being more, more than you can be," he told Witchel. "When I first started drag I wasn't this shy young man but a powerful woman." In a *New York Times* interview with Patrick Pacheco, Busch said of appearing in drag: "It liberated within me a whole vocabulary of expression. It was less a political statement than an aesthetic one." He finishes the thought with, "I look kinda pretty in a dress," which may just be an attempt to dispel any air that there's something serious going on under all that Max Factor.

**Profile by
Ira N. Brodsky**

PAUL CADMUS

1904– ·

*"S*ailor Beware—Artist with Camera" blared the headline in a

Time *piece on artist Paul Cadmus after such paintings as "The Fleet's*

In," "Shore Leave," and "Sailors and Floosies," all of which depicted   **American** ·

sailors doing what comes most natural to them when they are off ship   **artist**

and at liberty—trying to pick up some willing girls they hope will be easy

sex—affronted the U.S. Navy. An admiral's influence got "Sailors and

Floosies" removed from the American Painting section of the Golden

Gate International Exposition in San Francisco in 1940. It was re-hung

soon afterward because the director of the Palace of Fine Arts at the

Exposition, Timothy Pflueger, stated, "If every picture to which some

may object was removed, none would remain."

It is a wry but appropriate footnote to the progress of acceptance of the subjects of art—and to Cadmus's status as a premier American artist especially—that "The Fleet's In" now hangs in the Naval Historical Center in Washington, D.C. Still, one wonders how much of the Navy's supposed wrath might really have been aroused by one striking detail: at the upper left, a sailor accepts a cigarette from a blonde civilian who is looking intently at him. Much the same kind of detail can be found in "Shore Leave," in which a sailor is being picked up by a similar civilian, who has markedly swishy characteristics.

It was such satiric depiction that earned Cadmus his reputation as an "enfant terrible" before he was out of his twenties. But actually, it is Cadmus's repeated drawing and painting of the vital, fresh young male in all his splendid proportions that demonstrates the artist's love of such a subject best and most idealistically. Though Cadmus has never stated directly in any public medium that he is gay, nor has such a careful biographer as his friend Lincoln Kirstein ever so indicated explicitly, the presumption that Paul Cadmus is gay is general and solidly believed. His close association with such obviously gay men as the poet W. H. Auden and the novelist E. M. Forster is further substantiation. Cadmus's long co-habitation with the singer and dancer Jon Anderson, many times his model as well, affirms his sexual orientation.

Some have made the erroneous assumption that the artist's name indicates a Greek origin, but there is no connection between the artist's lineage and the mythic Cadmus, founder of Thebes, grandfather of Labdacus, and great-grandfather of Oedipus. Actually, the family name is Dutch, and the artist's mother was from a Spanish family. Both parents were artists. Paul was born on 17 December 1904, when the family was living on 103rd Street in New York. He has one sister, Fidelma, who has posed for him.

Paul Cadmus entered the National Academy of Design when he was fifteen and rapidly acquired skills in drawing and printmaking. From 1928 to 1931, Cadmus worked as a commercial illustrator. Then, in 1931, he and close friend Jared French went to Europe, bought bicycles, and toured in France and Spain. After they had visited Madrid's Prado Museum, the two went to Mallorca, where they lived for two years. This period saw the genesis of Cadmus's style, with many drawings of Mallorcan seacoast scenes and bicyclists emerging. Ironically, some of his most famous works, such as "Shore Leave" and "Y.M.C.A. Locker Room," were produced there.

While some of Cadmus's creations from the 1930s, with their emphases on the male form and/or satiric interpretations, seemed entirely original with him, there were plenty of antecedents in both subjects. Thomas Eakens's "The Swimming Hole," with its depiction of nude adolescent boys freely disporting, and George Bellows's "Stag at Sharkey's," with the drama of a furious boxing match, both display a previously established enthusiasm for the robust male.

On the satiric side, William Gropper's "The Senate" makes fun of the windy politician, and Jack Levine's "The Feast of Pure Reason" skewers the cop, the ward heeler, and the plutocrat in solemn conference on the fate of humankind.

Satiric depiction continued to attract Cadmus, though such canvases contributed to his reputation as a troublesome rebel. One especially pungent example is "Coney Island," which aroused the resentment of the businessmen of that resort with its clustering of lumpy show-offs supposedly enjoying themselves at the shore.

Some subjects were part of a series. Particularly biting was "Aspects of Suburban Life," which was commissioned by the Treasury Relief Art Project in 1936, one of the public works projects of the Roosevelt era designed to employ artists. The Marina dock, regatta, commuter rush, polo, and golf all got treatments that mixed colorful liveliness with realizations of shallow play.

Cadmus also produced an urban series, of which "Subway Symphony" is a prime example. The cacophony of big city life, as Cadmus sees and hears it, is a phantasmagoria of near-freakish riders on the underground, some asleep, others listening to a boombox or blowing bubblegum, but all crammed together temporarily in all their idiosyncracies. It dates from the 1970s, indicating that Cadmus's interest in satirizing persisted long after his 1930s-era U.S. Navy depictions.

One example from his earlier period, "Greenwich Village Cafeteria," however, has a significant example of his daring on gay subject matter. At one side of this crowded, raffish bunch of diners is a man looking over his shoulder provocatively as he is about to enter a men's restroom.

Another example from the 1930s is "Venus and Adonis," a satire on a classical subject and a humorous depiction of a silly and sordid phenomenon of the time, the attempted seduction of the young male by a woman well past her age of attractiveness. In it, Adonis is shown as an athletic young man with tennis racket and balls trying to escape from a middle-aged woman with bleached blonde hair holding on to him desperately. Off to one side is a squalling Cupid. Obviously, the young man would much rather be with the other young men on the court in the background. The gay suggestion is a strong part of the satire.

Cadmus's deeper interest in the human dilemma is represented too, though, in a 1940 work called "Herrin Massacre," showing a brutal murder in the Illinois town of Herrin in 1925. A contract dispute had flared into a bloody riot, and twenty-six strike breakers hired by the coal company were killed by the union members. Though the massacre had actually occurred at the mine, Cadmus set his depiction in a cemetery, with the headstones as emphatic commentary. The painting was commissioned by *Life* magazine. Critical remarks in art periodicals called the work "just gory journalism," but Cadmus's love of the male body is evident in the partially stripped forms of the slain, and the circular, dramatic composition bespeaks the influence that the Italian masters of the Renaissance and following periods had on him.

Contrasting with such violence is the series Cadmus painted of ballet scenes in the late 1930s and early 1940s. The 1941 "Arabesque" captures the grace of both male and female dancers as they perfect their art in the rehearsal hall. Such studies emerged from daily observations Cadmus made at the School of American Ballet. He became even more involved with dance when he designed scenery and costumes for the ballet "Filling Station," which was set to the music of the gay composer Virgil Thomson. The interior Cadmus designed for the set used some of the same kinds of figures the artist had put into the "Aspects of Suburban Life" series, here transformed into comic silhouettes. Cadmus's costume for Lew Christensen in the *danseur noble* lead role as the mechanic was cut from transparent plastic, which showed off the dancer's splendid build.

It was during this period of working on the ballet drawings and paintings that Cadmus was introduced to the egg tempera technique of painting, a method first evolved in the Italian Renaissance by Cennino Andrea Cennini. More modern means of producing egg tempera were advanced by Daniel V. Thompson of Yale University, and Cadmus adapted those to his own use. The result was a light, creamy emulsion that facilitated fastidious handling of all subjects and resulted in a porcelain finish that gave completed works a lifelike glow.

Soon after his development of his own style of egg tempera, Cadmus applied it to what Lincoln Kirstein, in *Paul Cadmus,* called the "capstone of Cadmus's career." The work in question is the seven-panel "Seven Deadly Sins." While such a judgment could easily be thought premature, inasmuch as the artist is still living and working in his ninety-second year and has been doing so steadily in the intervening fifty years since "Seven Deadly Sins" was painted, the very nature of the work—subject and technique both—mark it as highly distinctive.

Painted in the years 1945–49, "Seven Deadly Sins" shocked the public probably even more than Cadmus's earlier notorious works. Of course, classification of sins has used various terms: "capital," "mortal," and "venial" being some of the most frequently used. Cadmus is most likely to be thought of as a lapsed Catholic, the devoutly practiced faith of his mother. His father was apparently staunchly atheistic. It would be too much of a stretch to presume a really religious intention to this work, however.

Nonetheless, the seven venial sins Cadmus found to be most ubiquitous among humans, though not necessarily the most condemnatory, are Lust, Pride, Sloth, Anger, Envy, Avarice, and Gluttony. The representation of each demonstrates a command of imagination and skill that so impresses the viewer that the series is a masterpiece.

For example, "Lust" is a bisexual (as are all the figures, really) encased totally in a condom, the hands clasped across a vacant crotch, the face a combination of satisfaction and desperation. The bisexuality is most obviously shown first, a chest of full, ripe breasts, and, beneath that, an abdomen of masculine abdominal muscles. The overall effect is an obsessed creature trapped in a transparent casing of its own creation.

"Anger" is a furiously red monster bristling with black spines and thorns and surrounded by splatters of blood. The total effect is a roar of uncontrolled rage. "Gluttony" is a human being incredibly bloated but still stuffing itself, even while its guts are bursting out of an enormously distended abdomen. The viewer's realization is that this sin knows no satiation.

While this seven does not include such sins as murder, idolatry, or adultery, which could be thought of as more definitely capital crimes, it is easy to see that those three, whose consequences are more deeply serious than the seven, are still linked. For instance, out of anger comes murder; out of lust comes adultery. So who is to say which "set" is the more important? W. H. Auden suggested to Cadmus that he produce a contrasting series on the Christian virtues, but the artist felt that the static, passive factors that are intrinsically present in the virtues did not lend themselves to any impressive representations.

During the same early 1940s period, Cadmus created many beach scenes, some of them from his sojourns at Fire Island, which was already a favorite as an artist's retreat but not yet the great gay magnet it later became. Possibly the most famous of these is "The Shower," with two nude male figures and, chastely draped nearby, a woman. The gay suggestion is there.

This period also includes another work in which satire re-appears: "Fantasia on a Theme by Dr. S." Its basis is a body typing theory of a constitutional psychologist named Dr. William Sheldon, among whose ideas were the classifications of ectomorph (thinner than average), mesomorph (average body weight and proportions), and endomorph (heavier and stockier than average). In the center of the painting are three figures representing the three body types: a skinny queen in a nelly pose, a plump slob, and between them a gloriously developed young blonde in an athletic pose. On the right side of the painting come two young women in dark glasses just turning their gaze at the sexy mesomorph. Cadmus has certainly not been above making fun of gay stereotypes.

But more natural to his idealistic conceptions of human beings and his admiration of attractive and promising young men are such pieces from the 1950s as "The Inventor," in which a young man has created a mobile of natural beach objects; "Aviator," in which a youth has made a kind of box kite that could be his dream of flight; and "Architect," a picture of an intent young man with the T-square and blueprint of his intended vocation.

However, the commenting creation was still showing up in Cadmus's later work. "Night in Bologna" (1958) shows a dramatic triangle of a pale (and probably gay) man alone at a cafe table in an arcade looking piercingly toward a virile soldier, who, in turn, is looking at the retreating, seductive form of a young woman.

But a work that more likely characterizes this later part of Cadmus's life is "Study of David and Goliath," in which Cadmus's companion—performer—model Jon Anderson is posed, while Cadmus himself is in front of a sketch pad looking over at the viewer with a smile.

With the collaboration of his early friend, fellow artist Jared French, Cadmus composed his credo as an artist in 1937. Among the more important statements is the following: "I believe that art is not only more true but also more living and vital if it derives its immediate inspiration and its outward form from contemporary life. The actual contact with human beings who are living and dying, working and playing, exercising all their functions and passions, demonstrating the heights and depths of man's nature, gives results of greater significance than those gained by isolation, introspection, or subjective contemplation of inanimate objects."

The accumulation of the creations of Paul Cadmus in the nearly sixty years since the statement of that credo bear it out powerfully.

Profile by Marvin S. Shaw

PAT CALIFIA

*P*at Califia is a writer, activist, and self-proclaimed troublemaker.

Since the early 1970s she has advocated for the rights of those individu-

als perceived by the mainstream as perverts and outcasts. She has

eloquently railed against sexual repression and repression in general.

Her twelve books and many articles and stories run the gamut from

cultural criticism to pornographic fiction to sexual how-to guides, and

she is widely regarded as an expert on sadomasochistic relationships.

Califia's work has provided both the impetus for and a chronicle of the

sex-radical movement in the United States.

1954– ·

American writer, ·

activist, and sex

researcher

Califia often writes about herself, and her writing provides the main source of information about her difficult growing up. Pat Califia was born in 1954, into a Mormon family. She came out in 1971, when she was seventeen, in her first year of college in Utah; the process was extremely difficult for her. The woman she desired, a fellow student, insisted on maintaining a purely platonic friendship. Califia's family disapproved of her sexuality, and school pressures mounted. Califia, distraught, wrote poetry and took drugs to cope, but ultimately a nervous breakdown forced her out of school.

She went on public assistance and quickly realized that, as she writes in the introduction to the third edition of *Sapphistry,* "There simply was not any room in the system for women, especially lesbians. I had to become involved in political activity or I would not survive." Moving into a women's center to heal, she became involved with a range of feminist causes. She participated in consciousness-raising for the Equal Rights Amendment and founded a women's center. She became active in movements addressing self-health, peace in Vietnam, and housing for poor people and minorities. Despite these activities, she felt unhappy in Utah; by the end of 1973, Califia had quit her $1.60-an-hour job at a bindery and moved to San Francisco.

Califia dove into feminist politics in San Francisco. She joined the Daughters of Bilitis, Del Martin and Phyllis Lyon's pioneer lesbian organization. She worked on the San Francisco Sex Information switchboard and became a sex educator. Discouraged that lesbians never called the switchboard, Califia began to lead groups on lesbian sexuality. *Sapphistry* (Naiad Press, 1980), her first book, came out of these workshops.

Sapphistry was a straightforward guide to lesbian sex and sexuality, revolutionary in its treatment of lesbian sexuality. The book became enormously successful and eclipsed the few previous sex manuals written by lesbians (such as the *Joy of Lesbian Sex*). Columbia University's Department of English and Comparative Literature recently listed *Sapphistry,* along with Sigmund Freud's *Theory of Sexuality* and Margaret Mead's *Coming of Age in Samoa,* as a book that shaped twentieth-century ideas about sexuality:

> Where many texts had assumed that women intuitively knew how to perform sexually with each other, Califia recognized that many women felt unsure of their erotic abilities or embarrassed by their desires, and emphasized communication and openness in sex. Completely unfazed by the variety of sexual fantasies and practices among women, Califia's attitude throughout the book is an explicitly feminist combination of unabashed celebration and cool reportage of lesbian desire. For the first time many lesbians—those with disabilities, women growing older, teenage lesbians,

- **Writes**

Ground-

breaking

Lesbian Sex

Manual

women whose sexual activities included sadomasochism, group sex or role-playing—saw their sexuality discussed in a nonjudgmental, common sense way.

Sapphistry quickly found a large audience, and has been reprinted three times and translated into German.

With the success of her first endeavor, Califia branched out, writing about women's culture and feminist politics; she also began writing erotica and about erotica. Her articles appeared in various venues, including *Vector, Sisters, Focus, Black Maria, The Lesbian Tide, Heresies,* and the *Advocate,* for which she wrote a regular column. In addition, Califia's research on lesbian sex was published in the *Journal of Homosexuality.*

Califia has become known as a powerful voice for the freedoms of social outsiders, sexual and otherwise. She supports anyone who addresses social and economic inequity in society, whatever their specific subject, and her definition of radical embraces a diverse range of people. As she writes in *Public Sex:*

> Being a sex radical means being defiant as well as deviant. It means being aware that there is something unsatisfying and dishonest about the way sex is talked about (or hidden) in daily life. It also means questioning the way our society assigns privilege based on adherence to moral codes. If you believe that inequities can only be addressed through extreme social change, then you qualify as a sex radical, even if you prefer to get off in the missionary position and still believe there are only two genders.

Expert on •

Working-Class

Lesbians and

Sadomasochism

She has often focused on communities previously underrepresented, and her stances have not always been popular with mainstream feminists and lesbians. She strongly supports pornography, sex clubs, deviant sex of all kinds—including NAMBLA, the National Man-Boy Love Association, despite its disavowal by every major lesbian and gay rights group in America.

Two of her most common topics are working-class lesbians and lesbians who have sadomasochistic sex, two outcast communities that she regards as anti-assimilationist. Califia is widely regarded as an expert on sadomasochism in general and on lesbian s/m relationships in particular. Her book *Sensuous Magic* is a how-to guide to sadomasochism for beginners, and she has served as editor on numerous collections of leather erotica and instructions. Her popular novel *Doc and Fluff*

(Alyson Publications, 1990) deals with these communities; an often violent and over-the-top science-fiction novel about a pair of outlaw women, it is filled with tough love and rough sex.

Califia's most recent book is *Public Sex* (Cleis Press, 1994), a collection of essays examining sex, feminism, censorship, and economics in the United States, Canada, and Great Britain. Califia's other books include a collection of her *Advocate* columns published as *The Advocate Adviser: America's Most Popular Gay Columnist Tackles the Questions That the Others Ignore* (Alyson Publications, 1991). She has written two collections of erotic fiction, *Macho Sluts* (Alyson Publications, 1988) and *Melting Point* (Alyson Publications, 1993), contributed to many other collections, and edited collections, including *Doing It for Daddy* (Alyson Publications, 1994) and *The Lesbian S/M Safety Manual* (Lace Publications, 1988).

Most recently Califia has become a speaker for lesbian safe sex, openly discussing the previously taboo subject of lesbian drug use. Her work against censorship is ongoing: she has campaigned actively against anti-pornography laws, from child pornography cases to the 1996 Communications Decency Act, which attempts to eliminate pornography from the World Wide Web. In 1995 she contributed to *Forbidden Passages: Writings Banned in Canada* (Cleis Press, 1995), published to raise funds for Canada's Little Sister's Book and Art Emporium in its lawsuit against a section of the Canadian Customs Acts that allowed customs officers to seize books, videos, and other materials as they entered the country.

In 1994 Califia said, on the publication of *Public Sex,* "Today, at the amazing age of forty, I am trying to cause as much trouble as I did when I was twenty-five." She is also solidifying her stance with professional training—she is currently completing her M.A. in counseling psychology at the University of San Francisco. Her continued dedication to sexual, political, and informational freedom has earned her the respect of activists and deviants around the world.

Profile by Jonathan Wald

MICHAEL CALLEN

1955–1993 ·

Performer, ·

songwriter, and

AIDS activist

"*I* was diagnosed with AIDS before the term AIDS even existed. . . .

According to the best estimate, of the 1,049 Americans diagnosed with

AIDS during 1982, twenty-five are still alive. . . . I am one of the lucky

ones." In 1990, Michael Callen began his highly autobiographical book,

Surviving AIDS, *with those words. A devout atheist, he did not believe in*

providence, only luck. But he had a lot more going for him than luck in

the relatively short period he was alive. He was a soloist and lead singer

with the Flirtations (a five-man a cappella *group), a legal secretary,*

writer, and composer; yet it was his role as an AIDS activist that many

will remember most.

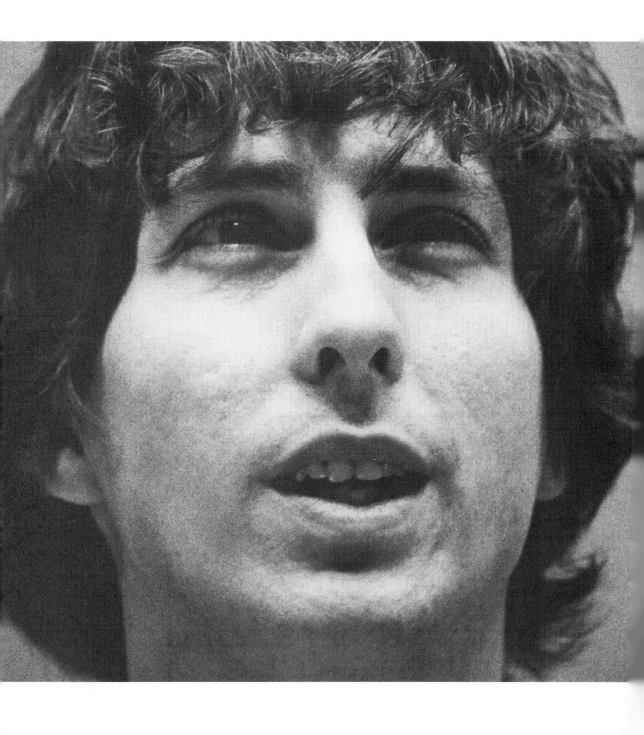

Of Native American and Pennsylvania Dutch stock, Callen was born in 1955 in Rising Sun, Indiana, and raised in Hamilton, Ohio. He attended Boston University on a musical scholarship and graduated in 1977. He moved to New York, working by day as a legal secretary and singing on the side. In *Surviving AIDS* he wrote, "At that time, I had been transformed from a silly, immature, lonely Midwesterner into a silly, immature, lonely urban gay man. . . . I only halfheartedly pursued singing. There were too many other distractions—mostly sex." He took up sex with militant zeal. He further explained: "Some of us believed that we could change the world through sexual liberation and that we were taking part in a noble experiment. . . . Unwittingly, and with the best of revolutionary intentions, a small subset of gay men managed to create disease settings equivalent to those of poor third-world nations in one of the richest nations on earth." He was diagnosed with GRID (Gay-Related Immune Deficiency) in 1982. Influenced by his physician Dr. Joe Sonnabend's multifactor theory (i.e., that repeated assaults on the immune system by many common sexually transmitted diseases and drug use result in a suppressed immune system), he became an AIDS activist.

In 1983 Michael Callen wrote, with Richard Berkowitz and Richard Dworkin, *How to Have Sex in an Epidemic: One Approach*. In that same year he, with other activists, created an AIDS self-empowerment movement and instituted the term "People with AIDS" (PWA) in lieu of "victim." He helped found the PWA Coalition and became the founding editor of its *Newsline*. He edited two volumes under the title *Surviving and Thriving with AIDS:* volume one was *Hints for the Newly Diagnosed* (1987), and volume two, *Collected Wisdom* (1988). He wrote and co-wrote several articles, testified before Congress, and appeared on national and local talk and interview shows. He was well known for his disdain for several AIDS drugs, especially AZT, which he routinely referred to as toxic. He devoted a whole chapter to AZT in *Surviving AIDS* and summed up: "I consider AZT to be Drano in pill form—pure, lethal poison. Anyone who takes AZT without examining all the evidence is a fool."

In 1991, *U.S. News & World Report* featured twelve personal narratives on HIV/AIDS; Michael Callen's was one of them:

> I'm still alive thanks to luck, Classic Coke and the love
> of a good man [Richard Dworkin]. . . . I want to devour
> every drop of life's preciousness. I'm determined to
> compress my life into a few years, and that impatience
> has made me take greater risks, say what's really on my
> mind, write more songs than ever. I'm happier now

than I've ever been. I don't mean to reduce AIDS to an Est seminar and recommend everyone should get it, but when humans are faced with catastrophe, they can either give in or fight. I've chosen to maintain an exhausting schedule as a singer and activist. I challenge the image that all people with AIDS are incapacitated. For me, it's more like having the flu for the rest of my life.

Callen became a tireless proponent of safer sex and took that message wherever he could. Even his singing was political. The song "Living in War Time" is a sobering summation of the lack of government and national resolve to adequately confront the epidemic. Callen and the Flirtations had a cameo spot in the AIDS-themed film *Philadelphia* (1993), and Callen himself played Miss HIV in the musical comedy film about AIDS, *Zero Patience* (1993). According to Jim Merrett, writing in the *Advocate,* "Callen appears as a drag Miss HIV in a role that apparently appealed to him because he got to hold a note longer than Barbra Streisand." And hold that note he did.

Michael Callen's solo album *Purple Heart* came out in 1988. With the Flirtations, which also formed in 1988, he released two albums: *The Flirtations* (1990) and *Live, Out on the Road* (1992).

Again, from *Surviving AIDS:* "AIDS forced me to take responsibility for my own life—for the choices I had made and the choices I could still make. For better or worse, AIDS has made me the man I am today." Michael Callen died 27 December 1993. He was thirty-eight.

Profile by
Lee Arnold

MARGARETHE CAMMERMEYER

In 1989, after a brilliant military career, Margarethe (Grethe)

Cammermeyer distinguished herself further when she became the na-

tion's highest-ranking officer to challenge the United States' longstanding

policy prohibiting gays and lesbians from serving in the armed forces. In

the years since, Cammermeyer has become an ardent though somewhat

reluctant activist. Her life and legal battles are documented in her 1994

autobiography Serving in Silence, *which served as the basis for an*

acclaimed film produced by Barbra Streisand and starring Glenn Close

as Cammermeyer.

1942– ·

American ·

military nurse

and activist

Cammermeyer was born 24 March 1942 in Oslo, Norway, which was at that time occupied by Nazi forces. Her father was a Norwegian doctor who had grown up in Africa, where his father operated a clinic, and her mother was a nurse and the daughter of a prominent psychia-

trist. The example of patriotic courage and opposition to tyranny came early in Cammermeyer's life: both her parents actively aided the Norwegian underground. They frequently sheltered members of the resistance movement in their apartment, which was across the street from Nazi headquarters, and in Cammermeyer's autobiography she recounts an incident in which her mother used her baby carriage to transport weapons to resistance fighters.

After the war, Cammermeyer's father's career as a neuropathology researcher required that he move frequently, and his family occupied a series of residences as Cammermeyer was growing up. In 1951, believing that the most challenging opportunities were to be found in the United States, he moved his family there. Cammermeyer was nine years old at the time, and she later noted that the transition was a difficult one. Throughout her adolescence, she was embarrassed by her foreignness and felt, for the most part, alienated from her classmates.

Cammermeyer was nevertheless an excellent student, interested in particular in science and math, and at the age of fifteen was invited to join a semi-professional baseball team. Throughout her childhood and adolescence she planned to become a physician, like her father. After a disastrous first semester at the University of Maryland, however, her self-confidence was shaken, and she transferred to the nursing program. She subsequently made up for her earlier poor performance, excelling at her studies, performing volunteer work in her free time, and working to pay her own expenses.

During her sophomore year, Cammermeyer discovered that if she agreed to join the army upon graduation, her remaining college tuition would be paid. Remembering the heroism of the American military during World War II, she also viewed serving as a nurse in the army as a way of augmenting what she viewed as the inferior status of her profession. In order to compensate for her failure to become a doctor, she hoped to become Chief Nurse of the Army Nurse Corps. Cammermeyer joined the army in July of 1961, before beginning her junior year at the university. After completing her degree, she was assigned to active duty at Fort Sam Houston in Texas, where she completed basic training and further instruction in practical nursing techniques.

After serving at Fort Houston and later Fort Benning, Cammermeyer applied for and was granted assignment to Germany, where she worked in a variety of nursing positions for the next two years. It was also in Germany that she met and married a young military officer named Harvey Hawken, despite some misgivings on her part about their compatibility. The couple subsequently served together in Vietnam in

Distinguished

Service

1967 and 1968, with Cammermeyer receiving the Bronze Star for her excellent performance at the 24th Evacuation Hospital in Long Binh.

Near the end of her assignment in Vietnam, Cammermeyer became pregnant with the couple's first child, and she was forced by regulations to resign from the army one month before her son was delivered. Her husband also left the service, and the couple settled near Hawken's hometown of Seattle, where they had purchased land a few years before. For the next several years, they worked toward a goal of self-sufficiency, building their own home, growing their own food, and raising a family that eventually included three more sons.

Shortly after the birth of her first child, Cammermeyer returned to nursing on a part-time basis. Then, in 1972, when the law prohibiting mothers with dependent children from serving in the military was repealed, she joined the Army Reserves and was assigned to be the nursing supervisor at the reserve hospital at Fort Lawton, Washington. She later wrote in her autobiography: "For the first time since my marriage, I felt that my dream to become a national chief nurse might one day be realized." Cammermeyer later accepted the post of Chief Nurse of the Washington State National Guard, and in 1987 she was promoted to the rank of colonel.

• *A Growing*

Awareness

Cammermeyer recounts in her autobiography that while she felt different from her peers at an early age, the idea that she might be homosexual did not occur to her until many years later. Nevertheless, she believes her feelings manifested themselves in a sense of alienation from her husband from the very beginning of their marriage. In addition, Hawken held traditional views of the role of women, resenting greatly Cammermeyer's professional ambitions, and, after several years of marital strife, the couple divorced in 1980. During the 1980s Cammermeyer devoted herself to her nursing career, moving in 1981 to San Francisco to work in the neuro-oncology unit of the Veterans Administration Hospital. In 1986 she returned to Washington State to be closer to her sons, who lived with their father, and to work at the veterans hospital in Tacoma.

It was in 1988, when she met and fell in love with an artist and teacher named Diane Divelbess, that Cammermeyer fully acknowledged her lesbianism. Shortly after their meeting, Cammermeyer and Divelbess developed a committed relationship, although Divelbess continued to maintain her own residence in California. The following year, still working toward her goal of becoming national Chief Nurse, Cammermeyer applied for the increased level of security clearance that would be necessary for her to attend the military's War College, and it was during the interview for this clearance that Cammermeyer revealed that she was a lesbian. She later noted that while she was aware of regulations against homosexuals in the military, she was not aware of the stringency of the rules, and she moreover believed that her rank and long record of achievements would make her an exception. "I didn't think that in America I would have to choose between being honest and serving my country," she wrote.

The regulations concerning homosexuals in the military were, however, specific and not subject to appeal; Cammermeyer's admission was cause for immediate discharge, and the army promptly instituted proceedings against her. Within a few months she was informed that she would be the subject of an investigation, and in 1991, when the investigation was finally completed, she was offered two options: she could resign from the military or request a hearing. Cammermeyer chose the latter, and sought help from the most prominent attorneys in the fields of civil rights and military law. Nevertheless, her appeal at the hearing was unsuccessful, and on 11 June 1992, she was discharged from the National Guard.

Although the exposure of the most intimate aspects of her life to wide public and media scrutiny was distasteful to Cammermeyer, she had come to believe that the military's policy must be challenged and defeated. As a result, she refused to accept the army's decision, and promptly filed suit in civil court, seeking to challenge the constitutionality of the military's ban on homosexuals. At the same time, she began making public appearances to rally support for her cause and rapidly moved to the forefront of the movement for gay and lesbian rights. In 1994, a federal judge ruled against the army, but the government has appealed the case. It may take a supreme court decision to finally return Cammermeyer to her position.

Meanwhile, Cammermeyer has become a most effective advocate for the civil rights of homosexuals. With her unblemished military record and professional credentials, which include a Ph.D. in nursing, she commands great respect among military officials, legislators, and the public at large. In 1992 she was awarded the Feminist of the Year Award by the Feminist Majority Foundation, and that same year she was named Woman of the Year by the National Organization of Women. In 1994 Cammermeyer was nominated for Woman of the Year by the American Biographical Institute, and she has since received a variety of other awards from political and professional organizations as well as the gay and lesbian community.

The Battle for •

Justice

Profile by
Joann Cerrito

DEBRA CHASNOFF

*T*he day after she won the 1992 Academy Award for Best Docu-

mentary—and also made film history at her acceptance speech by

publicly thanking her female lover—Debra Chasnoff finally decided

that filmmaking was "what I should do." Chasnoff had spent years

before this working for an assortment of progressive organizations, only

sporadically stopping to make movies. She's now a dedicated filmmaker,

producing powerful documentaries that address a variety of social

issues, from environmental crises to lesbian and gay rights.

1957– ·

American ·

filmmaker

Born 12 October 1957 in Philadelphia to Sue Prosen, a psychologist, and Joel Chasnoff, an attorney, Debra Chasnoff grew up in Maryland's liberal Montgomery County, where her father was elected to the Maryland State Legislature. Although her family was politically moderate, Chasnoff remembers being keenly aware of and sympathetic to the civil rights and the anti-war movements as a child.

Graduating a year early from high school, Chasnoff entered Wellesley College, where she majored in economics. She also helped organize a boycott, led by the human rights group INFACT, of the Nestle company, whose profits were soaring due to its sales of nutrition-poor infant formula to developing countries. In her sophomore year, Chasnoff fell in love for the first time—with a woman—and came out as a lesbian.

Chasnoff graduated from Wellesley in 1978 and moved to Somerville, Massachusetts, where she landed a job in a prestigious consulting firm, some of whose clients were telecommunications companies that promoted nuclear power. But Chasnoff, having become a part of the anti-nuclear movement, felt torn, and soon quit. By her own admission, she has not had a "straight" job since. She became an editor and co-publisher at *Dollars and Sense,* a progressive economics magazine, and went on to organize, administrate, and raise funds for other periodicals and for groups such as 9 to 5, an advocacy organization for clerical workers. About 1980, Chasnoff met Kim Klausner, then a union organizer at Boston University. The two began a primary relationship—and, on Klausner's suggestion, made a movie.

Choosing Children, a film about lesbians deciding to have children, was three years in production, and released in 1984 to positive reviews and top awards. In 1985, Chasnoff and Klausner moved to San Francisco, where Chasnoff was associate producer for *Acting Our Age,* an hour-long documentary on women and aging; advised Roberta Achtenberg on her campaign for State Assembly; and became cofounder and executive editor of the lesbian and gay quarterly *OUT/LOOK.* In 1988, the couple's first son, Noah Klausner Chasnoff, was born.

In 1990, INFACT hired Chasnoff to write and direct a documentary about its second corporate responsibility campaign, a boycott of the General Electric Company (GE). According to INFACT, GE, then a leader in the production and sale of nuclear weapons, had failed to clean up its Hanford Nuclear Reservation site in Washington state, and had knowingly poisoned its Knolls Atomic Power Plant workers in Schenectady, New York, with asbestos and nuclear radiation.

With a budget of only $65,000, Chasnoff finished her film in a little over nine months. *Deadly Deception: General Electric, Nuclear Weapons and Our Environment* lasts a mere twenty-nine minutes, yet its impact is harrowing, due to Chasnoff's decision to juxtapose scenes of birth defects and cancer suffered by citizens and GE workers, with the blithe corporate jingle: "GE: We bring good things to life." At the last minute, Chasnoff entered her film in the Academy Awards competition for Best Documentary Short Subject—and was astounded when it was nominated.

On 30 March 1992, Debra Chasnoff accepted her Oscar, and told a billion people worldwide to "boycott GE." She also thanked her "life partner," Kim, and their son Noah, "who reminds me on a daily basis why it is so important to keep working for peace and justice." Although GE assured the public that INFACT's boycott, *Deadly Deception,* and Chasnoff's speech had no effect on its earnings, the company nevertheless announced less than a year later that it was pulling out of the nuclear weapons industry.

Chasnoff won over twenty-five more awards for her film, then went on to direct *A Day in the Life of Continuum* (1993), a film about an HIV treatment center, and *Reflections Through a Social Change Prism* (1994), about progressive activists who gather to assess the state of their movements. In 1994 Chasnoff's and Klausner's second son, Oscar Chasnoff Klausner (named not for Chasnoff's Academy Award but for her great-grandfather and Klausner's great-uncle), was born.

It's Elementary, Chasnoff's latest project, is a feature-length documentary about elementary through middle school teachers addressing lesbian and gay issues with their students. The project was motivated, says Chasnoff, by the anti-gay rhetoric of the 1992 Republican convention and by the prospect of her own son entering school, "where the family he adores would be invisible." She is also developing a film about the Karen Thompson/Sharon Kowalski gay and disability case.

Whatever her project, Chasnoff is committed to building a world of equality and compassion. "It's very important," she says, "that my work be politically useful." With her intelligence, her artistry, and her political commitment, Chasnoff looks forward to many more years of provocative, insightful filmmaking. So can we.

Profile by
Susie Day

AARON COPLAND

*A*aron Copland, one of the United States' most honored cultural

figures, created a concert music uniquely American in sound and

spirit. Several of his works—including Appalachian Spring, Lincoln

Portrait, and Fanfare for the Common Man—*have become national*

classics. *Among his many honors were the Presidential Medal of Free-*

dom, the Congressional Gold Medal, and the Kennedy Center Award.

He won an Oscar for his movie score to The Heiress, *a Grammy for the*

Suite *from his opera* The Tender Land, *and a Pulitzer Prize for the ballet*

Appalachian Spring. *Hailed as the "Dean of American composers,"*

Copland was tireless in his support of American music and generous in

his encouragement of others.

1900–1990 ·

American ·

composer

Born in Brooklyn, New York, 14 November 1900, Aaron Copland was the fifth and youngest child of Harris Morris Copland and Sarah Mittenthal Copland. Harris Copland was born in Lithuania in 1860. At the age of seventeen, like many European Jewish boys of his generation, he immigrated to America. Somewhere in the transition the family name, "Koplan" or "Kaplan," was translated as "Copland."

When Sarah Mittenthal was six or seven, her family came to America from a small village on the Russian-Polish border. She was raised in Chillicothe and Peoria, Illinois, and later in Dallas, Texas. The Mittenthals moved to New York City when Sarah was nineteen, and she married Harris Copland in 1885. By the time Aaron was born, his father was proprietor of H. M. Copland's Department Store on Washington Avenue in Brooklyn. The family lived above the store, and Mrs. Copland and the children helped out in the business.

• *Musical*

Beginnings

As a child, Copland heard violin-and-piano duets played at home by his oldest brother Ralph and sister Laurine. Aaron coaxed Laurine into teaching him piano, then moved on to private lessons. After youthful attempts at songwriting, Copland in 1917 began the study of musical composition with Ruben Goldmark, his first important influence. Goldmark gave Copland a solid grounding in the fundamentals, but to Copland's dismay, his mentor was not fond of the new musical idioms and experiments of the day.

Copland studied with Goldmark until 1921. During this period he was an avid concert-goer, and read about the more controversial composers—Stravinsky, Schoenberg, Ornstein, Mahler, Sibelius—in Paul Rosenfeld's commentaries in *The Dial,* an avant garde monthly. By the time Copland graduated from Boys High School in 1918, he had already decided not to attend college, but to pursue a musical career instead. His studies were supplemented by various jobs playing piano, from Brooklyn's Finnish Socialist Hall to several hotels in the Catskills.

Copland's good friend Aaron Schaffer was studying at the Sorbonne in Paris and provided a steady correspondence detailing artistic life there, including accounts of contemporary musical events. When Copland read in *Musical America* magazine that the French government was planning to establish a summer school for American musicians at the Palace of Fountainbleau, he was the first to apply, and was awarded a scholarship.

Copland also arranged that at the end of the summer, he would share an apartment in Paris with a distant cousin. Thus began a lifelong friendship with Harold Clurman, later known as a writer, critic, and one of the founders of the Group Theatre.

Copland sailed for France in June 1921. At Fountainbleau he made an important connection. Upon the urging of a friend, he reluctantly agreed to sit in on a harmony class. The instructor, Nadia Boulanger, so impressed Copland that he determined to study with her when he returned to Paris.

Copland's stay at Fountainbleau also yielded the first sale of his work. At the intermission of a student concert, he was approached by Jacques Durand—Debussy's publisher—who expressed interest in *Le Chat et la souris (The Cat and the Mouse)*. For the piece, Copland received the grand total of 500 francs (about $32.50).

Nadia Boulanger's musical knowledge was vast and she had invaluable contacts. Her Wednesday teas would draw writers, painters, and the *crème de la crème* of composers: Stravinsky, Milhaud, Poulenc, Roussel, Ravel, Villa-Lobos, Saint-Saens. Copland flourished under her strict and caring discipline. Another of her American students, Virgil Thomson, became a longtime Copland colleague.

In 1924, when it was announced in Paris that the famous Russian conductor Serge Koussevitsky would be leading the Boston Symphony Orchestra the following season, "Mademoiselle" took Copland to see him. The composer was later fond of telling friends, including this author, that at the end of the meeting, the charismatic conductor declared with a flourish, "You vill write a concerto for organ, Mademoiselle Boulanger vill play it, and *I*, Koussevitsky, vill conduct!"

The Boston performance was preceded by the work's premiere with the New York Symphony in December 1924. As Copland noted in his eponymous autobiography (1984), conductor Walter Damrosch, aware that this modern piece might ruffle his audience's traditional sensibilities, declared from the stage: "If a gifted young man can write a symphony like this at twenty-three, within five years he will be ready to commit *murder!*"

A Tumultuous •

American Debut

Copland had made a sensational debut. But even in those early years, he was also interested in helping promote the cause of new music. In 1928, with composer Roger Sessions, he organized the Copland-Sessions Concerts of Contemporary Music. In the first of four successful seasons, works by eleven American composers were featured.

For several years in the 1930s, Copland wrote the "Scores and Records" column for *Modern Music* magazine. In 1937, his "opera for school children," *The Second Hurricane,* with libretto by Edwin Denby and directed by Orson Welles, was performed by a student cast at New York's Henry Street Settlement.

While one characteristic became evident in certain pieces (for example, *Piano Variations* and *Statements for Orchestra* both written about 1930)—they were "difficult"—another characteristic also began to emerge—Copland's use of indigenous folk themes. *Vitebsk* (1929) incorporated Jewish folk tunes; *El Salon Mexico* (1937), written at the request of Copland's great friend, composer Carlos Chavez, used themes heard in Mexican cantinas; cowboy songs were the inspiration for *Billy the Kid* (1938), commissioned for Lincoln Kirstein's Ballet Caravan. More Western tunes were used for *Rodeo* (1942), choreographed and danced by Agnes de Mille with the Ballet Russe de Monte Carlo. Dance rhythms heard in Havana influenced *Danzon Cubano* (1942). Copland's *Clarinet Concerto* (1948), written for Benny Goodman, was inspired by American jazz.

Copland's most famous use of folk themes was his adaptation of the Quaker hymn "Simple Gifts" in *Appalachian Spring,* the ballet he wrote for dancer/choreographer Martha Graham in 1944. This is perhaps his most enduring and popular work.

During the World War II years, Copland produced the dramatic *Lincoln Portrait* (1942), with its quotes from the Gettysburg Address, and the stirring *Fanfare for the Common Man* (1943). His important *Third Symphony* (1946) incorporated elements of *Fanfare*. Later quintessentially American pieces are two sets of *Old American Songs (Newly Arranged)* (1950 and 1952), as well as *Twelve Poems of Emily Dickinson* (1950).

Copland toured Latin America on behalf of the Coordinator of Inter-American Affairs (1941) and the State Department (1947). William W. Austin noted in the *New Grove Dictionary of American Music* that Copland "in many ways . . . exemplified the 'good neighbor policy' of Franklin Roosevelt—Copland's Americanism was always more neighborliness than chauvinism."

Though not a very political man, Copland was summoned in 1953 by the U.S. Senate Permanent Subcommittee on Investigations and interrogated by its chairman, Senator Joseph McCarthy, the infamous anti-Communist. The committee took no action against Copland, but as a result of the publicity, several concerts, commissions, and honors were cancelled, and his passport was tied up for some time.

Copland welcomed the opportunity to write for films, and enjoyed his brief stays in Hollywood working with the excellent studio orchestras. His feature-length scores, which set a new standard, were *Of Mice and Men* (1939), *Our Town* (1940), *The North Star* (1943), *The Red Pony* (1948), *The Heiress* (1949), and *Something Wild* (1961).

One of Copland's longest affiliations was with the Berkshire Music Center at Tanglewood in Lenox, Massachusetts. This largest and most famous of American summer music festivals was founded by Serge Koussevitsky. Beginning in 1940, Copland spent twenty-one out of twenty-five summers at Tanglewood, teaching, lecturing, conducting, and composing.

Also an integral part of Tanglewood was Copland's dear friend, composer and conductor Leonard Bernstein. They originally met in 1937 when Bernstein, a Harvard junior, had astonished Copland with a dazzling rendition of Copland's *Piano Variations*. They became close personal and professional friends. As a conductor, Bernstein championed Copland's music, and in the late 1960s when Copland's composing years were ending, Bernstein helped him establish a conducting career. In short, Bernstein adored Aaron, and Copland got a kick out of the flamboyant "Lenny."

In the 1960s, Copland's work took a new direction as he turned to serialism and a twelve-tone technique. His *Connotations for Orchestra* (1961–62) and *Inscape* (1967) have a harsher, more dissonant sound than his earlier works, and though not as popular, have been critically praised.

Copland served as president of the American Composers Alliance and the American Academy of Arts and Letters, and he was an early and important member of ASCAP, the American Society of Authors, Composers, and Publishers.

Teaching at the New School for Social Research in New York inspired Copland's first book, *What to Listen For in Music* (New York: McGraw-Hill, 1939). That was followed by *Our New Music* (New York: Whittlesey House, 1941), later revised and updated as *The New Music, 1900–1960* (New York: W.W. Norton, 1968). In 1951 Copland was appointed Norton Professor of Poetics at Harvard University, the first American composer to hold that position. His lectures there were later published as *Music and Imagination* (Cambridge: Harvard University Press, 1952). *Copland on Music* (New York: Doubleday, 1960) consisted of selected essays.

Copland also helped popularize serious music by appearing as speaker, pianist, or conductor on fifty-nine television programs between 1959 and 1972.

Well-spoken, with an easygoing yet droll sense of humor, Copland was an even-tempered man, a gentleman. While musically and intellectually he was open to new ideas, his personal style was simple and

A Good Citizen •

of the Republic

of Music

unpretentious. "Home" was a utilitarian studio in New York City, then a converted barn in Ossining, New York. In 1960 he bought a comfortable yet rustic house overlooking the Hudson River in Peekskill, New York. There, at "Rock Hill," he spent the next thirty years.

His long-term composer colleagues included William Schuman, Elliott Carter, David Diamond, Ned Rorem, and Paul Bowles. Boosey & Hawkes of London remained his music publisher from the day in 1938 when British composer Benjamin Britten introduced Copland to the firm. In his eighties, Copland published two volumes of autobiography, written with Vivian Perlis, director of the American Music Oral History Project at Yale University.

• **A Private Life**

Copland never officially came out, though he was quite relaxed and open with friends. His most important relationship was with photographer Victor Kraft, a younger, darkly handsome man who grew quite tempestuous. Kraft, who later married and fathered a son, died in 1976, after he and Copland had known each other for forty-four years. Copland's friend Paul Moor wrote in the *Advocate* in 1991, "One cannot question Victor's deep, lifelong love for Aaron and his sometimes fierce protectiveness of him. Over the years, Aaron did have other primary male relationships—in at least one, he even shared his house—but as long as Victor lived, he occupied a unique position in Aaron's cosmos."

Copland was a musical genius, perhaps the greatest composer the United States has ever produced. He traveled the world as an ambassador for new music, and was honored by many nations. Over forty colleges and universities granted him doctorates, and in 1982 Queens College of the City University of New York founded the Aaron Copland School of Music. Upon his death, his papers were presented to the Library of Congress. The bulk of his estate was used to establish the Aaron Copland Fund, for the support of young composers.

Profile by
Michael E. O'Connor

MICHAEL DENNENY

1943– •

American •

editor

*A*s an editor at St. Martin's Press and co-founder of Christopher Street *magazine and the Publishing Triangle, Michael Denneny has worked tirelessly and successfully to bring gay literature into the main-stream. Michael Leo Denneny was born 2 March 1943 in Providence, Rhode Island and was raised in Pawtucket, Rhode Island, where his mother, Dorothy, worked in a factory and his father, Leo, was a postman. Of his parents, Denneny said, "Both were avid readers when I was quite young, although neither had gone past high school, and this had an impact on me." Books were so important to the young Denneny that he spent his allowance joining eight book clubs. After attending public school, Denneny left Rhode Island in 1960 to attend the Universi-*

ty of Chicago, where he spent the next decade, first as a student and later as an instructor. Denneny was greatly influenced by his mentors at the university's Committee on Social Thought, renowned scholars Hannah Arendt and Harold Rosenberg, to whom he attributes much of his success in later years.

Denneny has always been politically active. During his teenage years he protested nuclear testing, participated in Woolworth's lunch counter sit-ins, and picketed for civil rights. While at the University of Chicago, he became increasingly involved in the anti–Vietnam War movement. His political activism led to Denneny's disenchantment with academia: "I'd always thought I'd end up an academic and didn't know what else to do." Denneny eventually found a job at the University of Chicago Press, "after being convinced that this wasn't technically part of the university."

It was during this time that Denneny came out. "From my early teenage years on, I knew I responded to male erotica yet I led a straight life (mostly) . . . until I was 27, when the events at Stonewall precipitated a crisis." To come to terms with his sexual identity, he joined a consciousness raising group, "which I learned to my surprise was being led by my last girlfriend," Denneny continued. "It was hard to be gay in Chicago. Most people just thought it was my latest political enthusiasm. So, in essence, I moved to N.Y.C. to try out being gay. (It worked!)"

When Denneny moved to New York City in 1972, he intended to work in the theater, but the only job he could find was as an editor at Macmillan. "I got into publishing by accident, to pay the rent," Denneny commented. While at Macmillan, Denneny worked with several notable authors, including Buckminster Fuller and Ntozake Shange. In 1975, Denneny published his first gay book, Allan Ebert's *The Homosexuals: Who Are What We Are,* a book of interviews with gay men. Around the same time, Denneny worked with Chuck Ortleb and others to found *Christopher Street,* a gay literary magazine modelled after the *New Yorker.* Finding material for the magazine was difficult at first: "Having no place to publish it, most gay writers we knew simply were not writing gay material. This we didn't figure out until we had done several issues and it created problems. I remember one issue where Ed White wrote something like five different articles under five different names to fill up the magazine," Denneny reminisces. "We had a great many friends who were (gay) writers and from the beginning *Christopher Street* was supposed to be a writers' magazine. It survived because this large and open-ended group of gay writers supported it."

A month after *Christopher Street* appeared, Denneny was fired from Macmillan. "When looking for jobs, I plopped the magazines down on the table, announced that I was involved with it and if that was a problem we should just enjoy the lunch (since this is a very expensive restaurant and you're paying)." He continued, "Although [the interviewers] said it didn't bother them, I only got one job offer, at St. Martin's (and none for the next 17 years)—which made me think being publicly gay had something to do with it."

During his seventeen years at St. Martin's Press, Denneny published over 500 books, one quarter of which were concerned with homosexuality. In 1987, Denneny launched Stonewall Inn Editions, the first trade paperback line to exclusively publish gay and lesbian books. Currently Stonewall Inn has eighty-four titles in print. While at St. Martin's Press, Denneny helped to found the Publishing Triangle "to encourage and support gay and lesbian writing in every way we could, as well as being a networking organization for gay/lesbian people in publishing." Denneny helped to establish the Bill Whitehead Award, honoring lifetime contribution to gay and lesbian writing, and to launch Gay and Lesbian Book Month, to encourage broader visibility for gay and lesbian titles. In 1994, the Lambda Literary Awards paid tribute to Denneny's immense contribution to gay and lesbian publishing by presenting him with the Publisher's Service Award. Later that year, Denneny moved to a new job as an editor at Crown Publishers, and shortly thereafter he was awarded the prestigious Literary Market Place Editor of the Year Award for 1994 for Individual Achievement in Trade Editorial. He has since returned to St. Martin's Press.

Denneny's staunch dedication has contributed enormously to the phenomenal increase in gay and lesbian titles available today. Publishing gay books "was in effect like holding down a second job, since I also had to keep a regular publishing list running," reflects Denneny. "When I started it was a rare thing for a mainstream house to publish a gay book and it caused a great hullabaloo. I wanted to normalize the publishing of gay books. Originally I thought it would take three to five years; it actually took about 15, but the effort was finally successful. Every major publishing house in the country now does gay books and it isn't considered extraordinary."

Profile by
R. Ellen Greenblatt

MARTIN DUBERMAN

Martin Duberman, a prolific and prize-winning historian, biographer, playwright, and critic, is one of America's most prominent gay scholars and educators. He emerged as a gay activist in 1973 after a twenty-five-year struggle to suppress his homosexuality. He later became a pioneer in the fledgling field of gay and lesbian studies.

1930– •

American writer •

and educator

Duberman was born in New York City on 6 August 1930. His father, Joseph M. Duberman, was a Ukrainian Jew who emigrated to the United States and became a successful dress manufacturer. Duberman's mother, Josephine (née Bauml) Duberman, was a second-generation Austrian American who became a homemaker after her marriage in 1923.

Competitive, intelligent, and linguistically gifted, Duberman steadily climbed the ladder of academic success. He graduated Phi Delta Kappa from Yale University in 1952 and received his M.A. in 1953 and Ph.D. in history in 1957 from Harvard University. He taught history at Yale for five years while he prepared his doctoral dissertation for publication. *Charles Francis Adams, 1807–1886* (1961) won him the prestigious Bancroft Prize and a faculty appointment at Princeton University in 1962. Through 1971 he was successively assistant professor, associate professor, and full professor at Princeton. He was the editor of, and a

contributor to, *The Antislavery Vanguard: New Essays on the Abolition-ists* (1965). His second biography, *James Russell Lowell* (1966), was a finalist for the National Book Award. He collected his writings for publication in *The Uncompleted Past: Collected Essays, 1961–1969* (1969). In 1971 he was appointed Distinguished Professor of History at Lehman College, City University of New York.

Meanwhile, Duberman had broadened his writings beyond the spheres of biography and history. He had been interested in the theater since his teenage years and began earnestly writing plays in the early 1960s. The first, and most commercially successful, of his many plays was *In White America* (Produced New York, 1963; Houghton, 1964). This dramatic piece reflected his interest in race relations and the civil rights movement. It won the 1964 Vernon Rice/Drama Desk Award for Best Off-Broadway Production of the season. After enjoying a long run, it was filmed for television in 1970. The success of *In White America* opened further opportunities for Duberman. He began to write articles and reviews for several national publications, appeared on PBS, and became loosely affiliated with some New Left organizations. He collect-ed many of his later plays in *Male Armor: Selected Plays, 1968–1975* (1975).

This period of growing acclaim, however, was marked by inner turmoil, as Duberman revealed in his memoir of his youth and early adult years, *Cures: A Gay Man's Odyssey* (1991). While still an under-graduate at Yale, he had begun to have sex with men. His discomfort with his homosexuality grew, even as he discovered the Boston—and later New York—parks, bars, bathhouses, and beaches where homo-sexual men congregated in the 1950s. His successive relationships were generally troubled and short-lived. In 1955 Duberman commenced fifteen years of intermittent therapy with a series of well-respected but homophobic psychotherapists to "cure" his "sickness." He explained in *Cures* that therapy only reinforced the societal homophobia that he had earlier internalized.

During the 1960s Duberman grew dissatisfied with academic life, particularly Princeton's smug milieu of privilege. Four factors contribut-ed to an inseparable gulf that developed between him and his Princeton colleagues: his play-writing, his 1964 change of residence from Prince-ton to Greenwich Village, his sympathy for student radicals, and the university's rejection of his proposed education reforms.

Duberman gradually broke from his troubled past in the early 1970s. After his last therapist terminated his sessions in 1970, he never again turned to psychoanalysis to "cure" his homosexuality. Gay themes increasingly permeated his plays, books, and essays. His 1971 play

Payments (produced in New York, 1971), for example, drew on his personal experiences with male hustlers. In *Black Mountain: An Exploration in Community* (1972), an innovative and controversial history of an experimental North Carolina college community, he publicly admitted his homosexuality. His essay on post-Stonewall gay male literature, one of the first of its kind to appear in a national publication, was published by the *New York Times Book Review* in its 10 December 1972 issue.

Duberman's emergence as an openly gay activist, writer, and scholar accelerated after the *Times* essay. In 1973 he was simultaneously on the originating boards of the Gay Academic Union, the Lambda Legal Defense and Education Fund, and the National Gay and Lesbian Task Force. He appeared as a gay spokesperson on television and on college campuses and frequently published articles on gay literature, theater, and news events. Frustrated by the commercial failure of his plays after *In White America,* Duberman redirected his energies in the late 1970s to researching gay and lesbian history. He published many historical documents that he discovered hidden in libraries and archives in a *New York Native* column that ran from 1981 to 1983. These documents, along with selections from his own writings and personal diaries, were published as *About Time: Exploring the Gay Past* (1986). Duberman was a co-editor of, and a contributor to, a ground-breaking collection of historical essays, *Hidden from History: Reclaiming the Gay and Lesbian Past* (1989). His widely praised *Stonewall* (1993), the first book-length examination of the watershed 1969 riots, traced the transformation of the homophile movement into gay liberation through the interlocking lives of six lesbians and gay men.

The research and writing of *Paul Robeson* (1989) drew on Duberman's lifelong interest in theater, civil rights, and left-wing politics. This life of the African American actor, singer, and political activist was critically acclaimed for its balance and documentation.

Duberman served as the Director of the Center for Lesbian and Gay Studies (CLAGS) at the Graduate Center, City University of New York in the early 1990s. Founded by Duberman in 1991, CLAGS is a model program that sponsors conferences and colloquia and provides research grants. He is also the general editor of two Chelsea House Publishers series of books, one on notable lesbians and gays and another on issues in gay and lesbian life, primarily aimed at teenagers. In 1996 Duberman's second autobiographical work, *Midlife Queer: Autobiography of a Decade, 1971–1981,* appeared.

Duberman, who was chosen by Paul Russell for inclusion in his book *The Gay 100: A Ranking of the Most Influential Gay Men and*

Lesbians, Past and Present (1995), has exerted a profound influence on gay and lesbian scholarship. His research, teaching, and writings have helped to shape a younger generation of queer academics, and CLAGS serves as a model for the integration of gay and lesbian studies into the higher education setting. Furthermore, Duberman's personal journey of liberation has inspired his readers in their individual lives.

**Profile by
Joseph M. Eagan**

MELISSA ETHERIDGE

*O*ne of the more popular rock and roll performers in the United

States, Melissa Etheridge has been steadily building a loyal following

throughout the 1990s. The return to grass-roots rock that Etheridge

practices, along with the raw emotion present in her music, is responsi-

ble for much of her popular appeal. As she told David Wild, "I come from

the heartland."

1961– •

American singer •

and songwriter

Melissa Lou Etheridge was born on 29 May 1961 in Leavenworth, Kansas, to John and Elizabeth Etheridge. John Etheridge taught psychology and government in addition to coaching basketball at the Leavenworth high school. Elizabeth Etheridge was an army computer specialist. Melissa was the couple's second child, following Jennifer, Etheridge's elder sister of four years. Etheridge was raised by her parents to be self-sufficient. As she told Fred Schruers, "My father grew up in poverty . . . it was sort of the same case for my mother. . . . My parents went through changes over time—they really evolved. But in the 1960s and 1970s, when I was growing up, they were hardworking, trying to just do good—but quite on their own." From an early age, Etheridge displayed a love of music. When Etheridge was three years old, as she told Patricia Smith, she was "hooked on radio." From there, it didn't take long for Etheridge to decide on a career.

Around the time of her eighth birthday, Etheridge's father gave Etheridge her first guitar. Shortly after, she began lessons with a local jazz musician named Don Raymond, and at the age of ten wrote her first song, "Don't Let It Fly Away (It's Love)." Two years later Etheridge began performing live at a variety of public functions, including bowling alleys, bars, and even supermarket openings. Etheridge began playing with her first band, a country-and-western group called the Wranglers, when she was thirteen. The group enjoyed a moderate amount of local success, performing in a variety of locales and situations. By this time Etheridge had become proficient not only on guitars but also on the saxophone, clarinet, and piano. Etheridge's father was extremely supportive of his daughter's endeavors during this period. As she told Maureen Littlejohn, "My father helped me when I was singing in bands. He took me around to the bars and sat there all night because I was underage."

It was around this time that Etheridge first made the discovery that she was a lesbian. "It wasn't until my seventeenth birthday that I kissed a girl and went, 'Whoa!'" she told Schruers. "All of a sudden everything just went boom inside. And then it was like, 'Oh, two plus two, that's it.' It added up. It made sense." But Etheridge's revelation only led to a continued sense of isolation at school. "Not only was I different because I was lesbian and had no interest in a lot of the things that the girls around me were interested in—boys, cheerleading—but I was a musician, and there were not too many of those around my high school either." Although her ability as a musician did bring her a few friends, Etheridge chose not to get too attached since she had no plans to spend the rest of her life, nor that much longer, in Leavenworth.

Upon graduation, Etheridge enrolled in the Berklee College of Music, in Boston. But, while hungering for the rock and roll lifestyle, she dropped out after only her second semester. She supported herself for the next year by working part time as a security guard at a Boston-area hospital while performing in local clubs in her off hours. Etheridge then returned to Leavenworth, where she worked at a restaurant for nine months to earn enough money to buy a car. On her twenty-first birthday she moved to Los Angeles to pursue her own identity. As she told Schruers, "A lot of it was [that] I wanted to get away from what I was in that town . . . and go to a place where I could make whatever I wanted to make and, yeah, be whoever I wanted."

For the next four years, Etheridge played the women's bar scene in Long Beach, California. During this period she played in various lesbian

- **"Whatever I**

Wanted"

clubs and at local women's festivals, all the while developing her distinctive songwriting style (which has been described as Springsteenesque). She first heard the music of Joni Mitchell, Janis Joplin, and Joan Armatrading while playing in Long Beach, and those influences figured prominently in establishing Etheridge's songwriting. Prior to this time Etheridge's act consisted primarily of cover songs, but these artists, and the burgeoning sense of self-worth that she was herself cultivating, allowed Etheridge to begin writing songs. She soon began doing predominantly original music in her act and then hired a manager.

In 1986, Chris Blackwell, the founder and chairman of Island Records, signed Etheridge to a recording contract. Blackwell had come to see her play at a club called Que Sera Sera. After hearing only five songs, he approached her with his offer and she quickly began work on her first album. *Melissa Etheridge* was released in 1988 and received favorable reviews. Several of these early reviews, such as the one by Ralph Novak, praised Etheridge's energy and emotion: "[Etheridge's] music has a rigorous vitality, and there's an edge to it." This was indicative of the critical reception that Etheridge would enjoy throughout her career. Although *Melissa Etheridge* did not sell well initially the sales picked up after she appeared on the Grammy Awards show in February of 1989, eventually earning Etheridge her first gold record. Her next album, *Brave and Crazy*, was released in 1989. The concert tour promoting the album prompted Jon Bream to write that Etheridge was "a remarkable, emotionally charged singer of the caliber of Bruce Springsteen and Janis Joplin." Etheridge continued that type of singer/songwriter approach to her music with her third album, *Never Enough*, in 1992. The album was immensely popular and earned Etheridge a Grammy Award for best female rock vocalist. When she accepted the award, according to *Current Biography*, "she dedicated the award to her father and thanked her lover, Julie Cypher."

Etheridge had met independent filmmaker Julie Cypher while shooting the video for "Bring Me Some Water" (a single from *Melissa Etheridge*) in 1988. Cypher was working as assistant director on the shoot when the two met and eventually, after Cypher's separation from her husband, actor Lou Diamond Phillips, fell in love and decided to spend their lives together. The couple have been together since and announced in late 1996 that Cypher was pregnant. The couple's baby girl, Bailey Jean Cypher, was born in Feburary of 1997.

Etheridge's announcement of her sexuality at the Grammys was not as shocking as it could have been since she had come out in January 1993 at the National Press Club in Washington, D.C., during the first lesbian and gay inaugural celebration. As Etheridge told Rich Cohen in

Rolling Stone, the announcement was spontaneous: "I had no plan to do it that night, no plan whatsoever. It was the atmosphere." Shortly after the announcement, Etheridge's next album, *Yes I Am,* was released. The title was widely, and wrongly, acknowledged as an affirmation of her lesbianism. It was rather, as Etheridge has stated in numerous interviews, simply the declaration of a lover's confidence in being the right partner for her lover. This double meaning in the album's title is indicative of the way in which all of Etheridge's work can be perceived. Her writing has always had a sort of androgynous style to it. As she has noted to Patricia Smith, "It's not a conscious effort on my part. I didn't realize I was doing a genderless thing, but then I saw how it made my music accessible to almost everyone."

Etheridge released her latest album, *Your Little Secret,* in 1995. The album came at the end of a triumphant year that saw performances at Woodstock, on "MTV Unplugged" with Bruce Springsteen, and at the grand opening of the Rock and Roll Hall of Fame in Cleveland, Ohio.

Profile by
Michael J. Tyrkus

LILLIAN FADERMAN

*L*illian Faderman is the foremost expert of lesbian history in the

United States. A professor of English at California State University,

Fresno, Faderman was born in the Bronx, New York on 18 July 1940.

Her parents were immigrants from Latvia and Poland and she was

raised by her unmarried mother, a garment worker. Faderman's first

professional aspirations were in theater, because actresses provided a

unique model of successful, independent women, and she took formal

acting training at the Theatre Arts Workshop in east Los Angeles from

1951 to 1955. This experience would lead, indirectly, to one of her many

books on the social history of lesbians.

1940– ·

American ·

professor and

writer

As a teenager, Faderman was initiated into the mostly underground gay world of the 1950s by a male friend who showed her the bar scene. She now considers herself fortunate to have interacted with such positive role models while she was still growing up. In a 1994 interview with *10 Percent* magazine, she says, "[T]hose women dancing together, talking together, and being what I assumed to be independent of men—that vision was like an epiphany. It showed me what I could do with my life, that I could be as ambitious as I wanted. I didn't have to cut eroticism out of my life." Her provocative theory that independence from men constitutes the crucial element of lesbianism, rather than sexuality alone, is a central theme in all of her writing.

At age seventeen Faderman married an older gay man as a way to escape from home. When the marriage ended soon after, she enrolled at the University of California at Berkeley, where she received a B.A. in English in 1962. Continuing her resistance to convention, she earned money for school by working as a stripper in San Francisco. The pay for women was higher, she recalls, than waiting tables or clerking, and the labor less intensive.

Faderman earned master's and doctoral degrees in English at UCLA, and an educational management certificate at Harvard. Her early academic publications include two co-edited volumes of American ethnic minority literature in 1969 and 1973, years before multiculturalism became popular on campuses nationwide. Her first book was *Lesbian Feminism in Turn-of-the-Century Germany* (1980), co-written with Brigitte Eriksson. Her next book, *Surpassing the Love of Men,* was more ambitious in scope, tracing women-loving women from the sixteenth century to the 1980s, in Europe and the United States. This book established Faderman as an important historian and theorist of lesbianism. When asked to take sides in the academic debate between essentialists, who credit heredity for sexual orientation, and social constructionists, who read history and culture as the forces shaping sexuality, Faderman identified with the latter. Despite its recognition with both gay and non-gay publishers' awards, *Surpassing the Love of Men* was attacked by some essentialists because it appeared to de-sexualize love between women before the twentieth century. But according to Faderman in the *10 Percent* interview, essentialist theories that inflate biology's role in sexuality are simplistic and misleading. "They don't account for the fact . . . that people often move in and out of sexualities; they could be heterosexual for one period of their lives and homosexual for another. . . . It seems to me the essentialists don't deal with the complexity of human sexuality."

Awards for •

First Book on

Lesbian History

In *Surpassing the Love of Men,* Faderman poses a significant question for lesbian history: Why were passionate romantic friendships between women socially accepted before the twentieth century, and how did they come to be stigmatized? Before the 1910s, women's love affairs—whether sexual in a contemporary sense or not—were considered normal, but since then they have been mostly viewed as pathetic at best and destructive at worst. While Faderman argues that pre–twentieth-century romances between women were generally devoid of genital sexual contact because women were taught to be passionless, she adds that "whether or not these relationships had a genital component, the novels and diaries and correspondence of these periods consistently showed romantic friends opening their souls to each other and speaking a language that was in no way different from the language of heterosexual love: They pledged to remain 'faithful' forever, to be in 'each other's thoughts constantly,' to live together and even to die together."

According to Faderman, the real challenge of lesbianism was economic rather than sexual: women who did not marry, for either financial security or love, threatened the patriarchal order that described women exclusively as mates for men. Either as titillation or dire warning, lesbianism of the kind we understand today has been around since at least the sixteenth century. In France, in the sixteenth and seventeenth centuries, lesbianism was considered a prelude to heterosexuality, not a threat but an aphrodisiac to men, as long as the women "lovers" did not take themselves seriously. All extant lesbian erotic literature before the eighteenth century was written by men. The typical formula was two conventionally beautiful women, the older of whom seduces the younger and whose relationship consists primarily of jealousy. Eventually a man rescues and converts the younger woman to her true heterosexual self.

For eighteenth- and nineteenth-century men, a woman who passed as a man was a greater criminal than a woman who merely loved another woman. Indeed, given conventions concerning women's great capacities for feeling over thinking, women were expected to love each other. But to dress, work, and live as a man was to appropriate masculine privilege in a radically unacceptable way. As Faderman writes, "Transvestites were, in a sense, among the first feminists. Mute as they were, without a formulated ideology to express their convictions, they saw the role of women to be dull and limiting. They craved to expand it—and the only way to alter that role in their day was to become a man." While many nineteenth-century transvestites engaged in erotic lesbian relations, their significance as gender outlaws is as great as their sexual rebellion.

In *Surpassing the Love of Men,* Faderman blames the rise of sexologists in the late nineteenth century for pathologizing love between women. Combined with Victorian anti-feminism, the decadent movement's voyeuristic interpretation of female sexuality led to a new suspicion of women's romantic friendships. The sexologists, who were doctors, scientists, or social philosophers, created a third sex, the invert, who neurotically rejected women's prescribed, passive role. As soon as love between women earned a sexual connotation, romantic friendships and lesbianism would never be separated again.

Faderman insists that lesbianism has more to do with affectional preference than with sex. Women loving women has been *made* a mostly sexual phenomenon by pseudo-science, not necessarily by lesbian experience. In her conclusion, Faderman imagines a time when all people will avoid the labelling performed by sexologists, and which has been so damaging to women who love women. She writes that in an ideal world, "potential or actual bisexuality, which is today [1981] looked on by lesbian-feminists as a political betrayal and by heterosexuals as an instability, would be normal, both emotionally and statistically."

Faderman's next book, *Scotch Verdict,* elaborates on the theme of women's relationships in the nineteenth century, by examining the transcript files of the court case that inspired Lillian Hellman's "lesbian" play, *The Children's Hour.* As a teen studying acting, Faderman played the role of "bad seed" Mary Tilford in Hellman's play and had her first serious crush on an adult, her drama coach. This experience gave Faderman a lifelong interest in the true story of the case, that of schoolmistresses Marianne Woods and Jane Pririe, who sued Dame Helen Cumming Gordon for libel in Scotland in 1810. *Scotch Verdict* is an idiosyncratic rendering of Faderman's research in Scotland, combining a condensation of the trial transcripts and Faderman's own diary entries. Romantic friends desirous of financial independence, Woods and Pririe opened a girls' school, and seemed to have succeeded when a local aristocrat sent her granddaughter to them. But the girl (Mary Tilford in Hellman's play), a half-caste, illegitimate Indian child, told her grandmother of strange behavior between the two teachers and the school was immediately closed. Woods and Pririe sued for libel, since the veiled accusations of sexual misconduct between them appeared so ludicrous in 1810, and while they eventually won their case, their careers and life together were over.

Although Faderman believes it would have been unlikely for the two women to have engaged in genital sexual activity, she argues that the crux of the case was its challenge to the convention that women's romantic friendships were completely asexual. Lesbians simply did not exist in nineteenth century Scotland. As one of the judges put it, "God forbid that the time should ever arrive when a lady in Scotland, standing at the side of another's bed in the night time, should be suspected of guilt because she was invited into it." All of the judges found the case particularly difficult, not only due to its prurient nature, but also to their own frank disbelief in the accusations.

Faderman ultimately takes the case of the girl, Jane Cumming, who initiated the rumor, calling her as much a victim of the Victorian class, race, and gender system as the two women whose lives she ruined. All of the women, but especially the servants, who participated in the trial (not a single man testified) were cross-examined for their veracity, emphasizing women's tenuous claims to citizenship, not to mention equality, at that time.

As Faderman puts it, "It must have been intimidating enough to be a woman examined and cross-examined by a room full of men—but to be examined and cross-examined on the subject of sex, and moreover a variety of sex that was not supposed to have existed, must have been terrifying." *Scotch Verdict* shows contemporary readers the price of invisibility for lesbians and all women living independently of men.

● **Odd Girls**

Nominated for

Pulitzer

In 1991 Faderman published another award-winning title, *Odd Girls and Twilight Lovers: A History of Lesbian Life in Twentieth-Century America,* which picks up historically where *Surpassing the Love of Men* concluded. Beginning with romantic friendships and their perversion by sexologists in the 1920s, *Odd Girls* moves through each decade of our century, focusing especially on working-class lesbians and their distinctive culture, and the conflict between them and the lesbian feminists of the 1960s and 1970s.

Odd Girls begins by reminding the reader that when the book was written in the 1980s, lesbianism was more accepted than it ever had been in this century, but it was still not considered as normal as romantic friendships were earlier. Faderman attributes four choices to the woman-loving woman in the twentieth century: she could see lesbians as the experts initially had—women trapped in men's bodies—and thus consider herself normal because she had no desire to be male; repress her feelings and deny the attraction she felt for women; live as a closeted lesbian; or define herself as a lesbian and thus show independence and a certain social radicalism.

Lesbianism, along with feminism and a radical struggle for women's rights, have always been connected by the dominant culture, but the same women have not necessarily been feminists and lesbians. Working-class lesbians from the 1940s and 1950s, for example, felt betrayed by radical lesbian-feminists in the 1960s and 1970s who equated women's liberation with lesbianism and ignored the struggles of earlier lesbians who either passed as men or lived closeted. Lesbian feminists, mostly middle class and college educated, often criticized non-feminist lesbians for their politics, without acknowledging the courage of merely surviving as a lesbian before the 1960s.

Such misunderstandings have occurred, and still do, based on ethnic as much as class background, and the splits over identity politics challenging the mainstream women's movement have been echoed in lesbian movements. But Faderman points out that the evolution of social acceptance, or at least tolerance, for lesbianism has allowed increasingly more women to "come out" and be themselves regardless of politics. Thus butch-femme couples, once relegated to the working-class, can co-exist with high-powered "lipstick lesbians" in mini-skirts. They can even, fantastically enough, be the same woman according to her mood.

Perhaps Lillian Faderman's most important contribution to the growing documentation of lesbian realities is the manner in which she presents her findings. Meticulously researched and referenced, her books are accessible to the non-academic reader; she has tried and succeeded in giving lesbians, as she says, a "useable history." The utility of such practical scholarship cannot be overestimated, especially considering the influence working-class lesbians have had and continue to have in shaping lesbian cultures. All women, equipped with the latest gender theories or not, should have a chance to read their own histories. One thinks, for example, of working-class writer and historian Leslie Feinberg, author of *Stone Butch Blues* and *Transgender Warriors,* whose work on blue-collar women passing as men in the 1950s might not have been possible without Lillian Faderman's pioneering scholarship.

Faderman's latest contribution to lesbian history is an anthology of men's and women's writing about lesbians from the seventeenth to the late-twentieth centuries. In *Chloe Plus Olivia,* stories, poems, and essays document first how men viewed women-loving women, and secondly how women viewed themselves, both in fantasy and in their daily lives. *Chloe Plus Olivia* continues Faderman's project of providing scholarship and literature useful to many women, with a biography and bibliography of each author before the entry. Her selections range from the detailed nature imagery of Emily Dickinson to the sado-masochistic details of Pat Califia, placing, for the first time, all varieties of lesbians and lesbian desire together.

Lillian Faderman lives in Fresno, California, with her partner of many years, retired music professor Phyllis Irwin. Faderman's nineteen-

Profile by
Catherine A. Wiley

year-old son, Avrom (she laughingly calls herself the first lesbian to use artificial insemination), is a doctoral student at Stanford.

BARNEY FRANK

*B*arney Frank has been involved in many key political issues during

his eight terms in Congress. An outspoken liberal, he led the legislative

struggle for the redress of Japanese Americans interned in camps during

World War II. In 1990 Frank fought against provisions of the immigra-

tion law barring HIV-positive persons from entering the United States.

He worked diligently and successfully for amendments to the Fair

Housing Bill, which included AIDS victims and HIV-positive persons

under its provisions. During House debate on allowing gays and

lesbians in the armed forces, Frank authored the "Don't ask, don't tell,

and don't listen, and don't investigate" policy as a more inclusive

alternative to Senator Sam Nunn's "Don't ask, don't tell" compromise.

1940– •

American •

politician

125 •

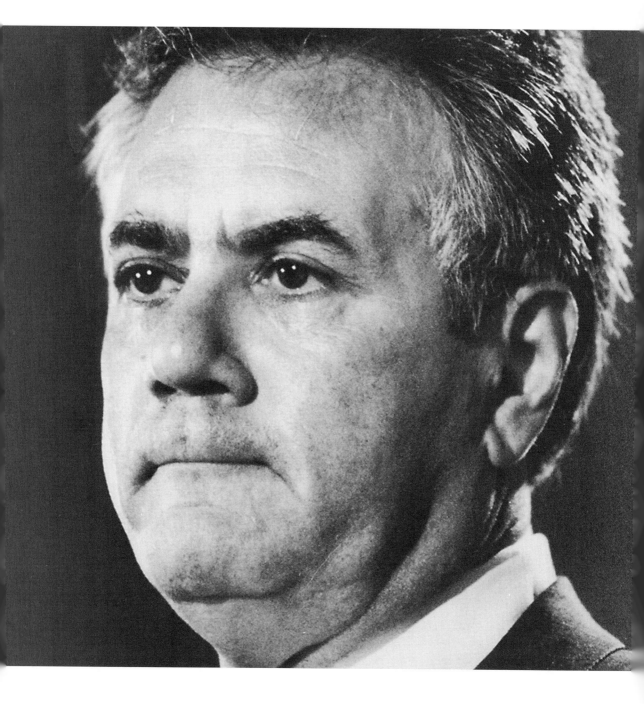

The proposal reflected Frank's propensity for matching liberalism with hard-nosed pragmatism in order to move the legislative agenda. While Frank vigorously debated and voted against Nunn's "Don't ask, don't tell," the policy was adopted into law.

Colleagues on Capitol Hill describe Frank as a natural politician who has the instinct for effectively framing issues and accomplishing the task at hand. He is noted as a "sharp-tongued and quick witted debater" by fellow congressmen. Frank is also considered to be a brilliant, honest, and strong deal-maker. While he listens intently to arguments, his rapid-fire delivery of questioning and debate has disarmed many opponents. He is less rigidly partisan than many members of Congress, openly considering the intellectual merits of legislation above the political fray, and viewing himself as a pragmatic zealot.

Barney Frank was born on 31 March 1940, to Samuel and Elsie Frank in Bayonne, New Jersey. He has one brother, David, and two sisters, Doris Breay and Ann F. Lewis. Growing up in Bayonne he often helped his father at the truck stop he owned and managed, pumping gas. While Frank describes his parents as not well educated, they put a premium on education and reading for the family. Following graduation from high school in 1957, Frank attended Harvard University. He took a year's leave when his father died, and graduated with an A.B. degree from Harvard in 1962.

From 1963 to 1967 Frank worked at Harvard as a teaching fellow in government, and in 1966–67 served as the assistant to the director of the Institute for Politics at Harvard's John F. Kennedy School of Government. He worked on the Mississippi Summer Project in 1964, and various political races in the Boston area. He abandoned pursuit of a Ph.D. degree at Harvard to assist Kevin White's successful mayoral election in Boston. Frank served as Mayor White's executive assistant from 1968 to 1971, familiarizing himself with the Boston political scene and its vital players. He then worked for one year as administrative assistant to U.S. Congressman Michael J. Harrington, from Massachusetts. Frank revealed in a July 1987 interview with the *Washington Post* that during his tenure in Congressman Harrington's office, he strongly believed he could never be an elected official because he was gay.

In 1972 Frank ran for election to the Massachusetts House of Representatives for a vacated seat in Boston's Back Bay district. He was elected by plurality to the State House due in large part to Boston University students in the district, who also supported the presidential bid of George McGovern. As a state legislator Frank targeted issues of women's rights, gay rights, and social services in his policy programs.

Elected to •

Massachusetts

House of

Representatives

His strident liberal agenda caught the attention of Massachusetts and national politicos. Despite his confrontational and unorthodox behavior he won three more terms as state legislator. During his tenure in the Massachusetts state legislature Frank was selected as "Legislator of the Year" by several state and national groups. By 1977 he earned a law degree from Harvard University and in 1979–80 taught public policy courses at Harvard's Kennedy School of Government.

Following Pope John Paul II's 1980 reaffirmation of church doctrine that prohibited Roman Catholic clergy from serving or seeking public office, liberal Jesuit priest Robert F. Drinan declined to seek a sixth term in Massachusetts' fourth congressional district. Within days of the papal decree the prospective number of candidates for Drinan's seat swelled to sixteen, including Barney Frank and John Kerry, a Middlesex prosecutor with no legislative experience. Frank was considered the "political heir apparent" for representative from the district, and Kerry quickly withdrew from the race. Frank declared his candidacy for the seat and moved from Boston's Back Bay neighborhood to outlying Newton. The archbishop of Boston, Humberto Cardinal Medeiros, warned parishioners of the fourth district's four hundred Catholic churches not to vote for Frank or candidates who approved the legalization of abortion. With the support of Drinan and the endorsement of the *Boston Globe* he defeated the conservative, anti-abortion challenger, Mayor Arthur Clark of Newton, by a small margin. In the general election he defeated Republican Richard Jones by a similar margin.

In his first term of office Frank was chosen to serve on the Government Operations Committee; the Select Committee on Aging; the Banking, Financing, and Urban Affairs Committee; and the Judiciary Committee. Frank rolled out a progressive program of action. He sponsored a bill to prevent new owners of low-income buildings from evicting current tenants. Frank vociferously fought the Reagan administration attempts to dismantle the Legal Services Corporation, and cut budgets in elderly social services programs.

The politically configured fourth congressional district encompassed affluent suburbs, depressed factory towns, and rural farms alike. Following the 1982 redistricting, Frank was left with a district that was 30% his own constituency and 70% from the district previously served by Representative Margaret Heckler. Heckler was a formidable and popular opponent. Most congressmen believed Frank would not survive this political battle.

Frank targeted Heckler's major weaknesses in the campaign. He exploited the considerable dissatisfaction of the low-income, blue-collar, and elderly voters with Heckler's term in Congress along with her support of President Reagan's economic policies. Overcoming political adversity, Frank carried the district with 60% of the vote in the 1982 general election. This adverse experience helped coalesce the public and private lives of Frank. Soon after being reelected to his second term he began to tell close political allies and college friends he was gay. He was seen at Washington, D.C.'s Gay Pride Day festivities, and most of the Massachusetts delegation knew or surmised he was gay.

In the 1984 election Frank defeated his Republican opponent, Jim Forte, by a wide margin. Two years later Republicans did not field a candidate, and Frank defeated the American Party candidate Thomas D. DeVisscher by an even wider margin, receiving 89% of the vote.

The liberal pragmatic side of Frank soon came to the forefront. While he vehemently supported obvious liberal measures, such as legislation that would make it easier for low-income and elderly persons to obtain generic drugs, he was on the opposing side of other liberal mainstays. Frank was among the few liberals who supported the Simpson-Mazzoli immigration reform bill and legislation that would give equal access to school facilities for student religious groups.

Supporter of •

Needy

With the 1986 publication of former congressman Robert Bauman's autobiography, *The Gentleman from Maryland,* Frank was publicly outed. In the book Bauman refers to Frank as the "witty liberal who appears at Washington's annual Gay Pride Day in a tank top with a young companion." Many reporters called and asked Frank directly if he was gay. Frank refused comment because of the scurrilous content of Bauman's autobiography. He added, though, that when he did talk about his life it would be through the *Boston Globe.*

During a May 1987 interview with the *Boston Globe* Frank publicly acknowledged he was gay. He stated: "I don't think my sex life is relevant to my job. . . . But on the other hand I don't want to leave the impression that I'm embarrassed by my life." Frank admitted later the ideal would have been if he didn't have to say the words, and it wouldn't be a front page story in the *Boston Globe* or the second story of the evening newscast following the Celtics. Nearly 90% of the correspondence Frank received afterward was supportive. Further evidence of his constituents support came in his 1988 landslide reelection. Even in Fall River, the stronghold of blue-collar Roman Catholicism, Frank carried a large vote plurality.

A 1989 Republican National Committee memo to two hundred Republican leaders brought Frank's sexual orientation into the spotlight again. The memo compared the voting record of the newly elected House Speaker Thomas S. Foley to that of Frank's voting record. The memo, which contained the headline "Tom Foley: Out of the Liberal Closet," was an attempt to depict Foley as a left-wing liberal who might be gay. Frank attacked the memo as a vicious unfounded attack, and if they didn't desist he would reveal names of Republican congressmen and other well known Republicans who were in the closet. As a result Mark Goodin, who had written and distributed the memo, resigned as communication director of the Republican National Committee.

• *Plagued by*

Embarrassing

Publicity

In less than three months Frank was again thrown into a whirlwind of embarrassing publicity. Stephen Gobie, a housekeeper and driver for Frank, revealed in a story in the *Washington Times* that he had run a male prostitution business out of Frank's townhouse with the full knowledge of the congressman. A convicted felon, Gobie was on probation when Frank met him through a personal ad. The same day Frank held a news conference and admitted he knew Gobie was a prostitute, but hoped he could help rehabilitate him. While Frank acknowledged the truth in some of Gobie's claims he stated he was unaware of the prostitution operation in his townhouse until the landlady reported to him suspicious activities, at which point Frank fired Gobie. Frank told *Newsweek* reporter Tom Morganthau: "Thinking I was going to be Henry Higgins and trying to turn him (Gobie) into Pygmalion was the biggest mistake I ever made. It turns out I was being suckered."

A number of congressman and journalists rose to Frank's defense. Speaker of the House Thomas Foley issued a statement asserting that Frank had provided exemplary service to his constituency and the country, and would continue doing so long after the Gobie issue had been forgotten. Morton Kondracke, a journalist for the *New Republic,* dismissed the idea that Frank had become a deadly political burden for the Democrats and his legislative effectiveness had been destroyed. On the same date the *Nation* declared, "What has been overlooked in all the to-do about his future is the true significance of his predicament, which is the predicament of all transgressors of our mythical sexual norms who desire to serve the government. . . . Nothing gets said about the intolerance ingrained in our culture that makes life hell for those like Frank who discover they are different."

Through the insistence of Herb Moses to fight the allegations, Frank called for an investigation by the House Ethics Committee. The committee launched an investigation into the Gobie charges. On 20 July 1990, five years after he met Gobie, the House Ethics Committee reported it found no evidence Frank knew of the prostitution ring being run in his townhouse, and extremely few facts to support Gobie's claim such activity occurred earlier. The committee further found several of Gobie's allegations untrue, and there was no evidence to substantiate the claim.

Frank was cited for misusing Congressional privilege in getting Gobie's parking tickets waived. Following four hours of heated floor debate, Frank accepted the committee's findings and apologized for his actions. The House of Representatives voted to reprimand Frank for his actions, following failure by vote of House members to expel or censure him.

Running for his sixth consecutive term in 1990, Frank was challenged by Republican nominee John Soto, an accountant and lawyer. Soto continually charged Frank with bad judgment, and asked him to submit to an HIV test and to make test results public. Soto's tactics were dismissed by constituents and Frank carried a resounding majority of the vote. Prior to the 1992 election the fourth district was again redistricted. Frank won reelection hands down. In seeking his eighth term of office Frank was challenged by minor party candidates and won easily. Frank's political comeback was due in large part to his perseverance, intelligence, and hard work.

Frank's political manifesto was published in 1992. The book, *Speaking Frankly: What's Wrong with the Democratic Party and How to Fix It,* argued the party had become too closely allied with the radical fringe, alienating mainstream voters. Liberal democrats suffered as a result of their close association and their defense of the protestors in the 1960s and 1970s. That was why the Democrats had lost five of six presidential elections by 1992. Now it was time for the Democrats to expose the radical right politics of the Republicans along with the issue of class warfare.

Frank played a leading role in the 1993 debate concerning lifting the ban on gays and lesbians in the military. He believed Congress was not politically ready to completely lift the ban, so he advocated a clear alternative to Senator Sam Nunn's policy: that service people could lead an openly homosexual lifestyle off-base, but were forbidden to reveal their sexual orientation while on duty; the so called "Don't ask, don't tell, and don't listen, don't investigate" policy. After much political debate and rancor the controversial Nunn compromise, "Don't ask, don't tell," was approved by Congress, minus Frank's vote, and signed into law by President Bill Clinton.

Following the Republican takeover of the U.S. House and Senate in the 1994 elections, Frank has served as the voice of the Democratic opposition. He declared that his mission is to shine the light where the Republicans don't want it shone.

While Frank describes himself as an often controversial, pragmatic liberal, he has consistently been a supporter of gay rights. He was one of the first Massachusetts legislators to sign a gay rights bill. He wrote a revision of the McCarran-Walter Act, which removed homosexuality as grounds for denying entry by foreigners into the United States. He has co-sponsored the Employment Non-Discrimination Act. Frank has also worked diligently for AIDS funding and housing programs for persons with AIDS. Working with the Clinton administration, Frank secured the establishment of non-discriminatory employment policies in all federal agencies. Further procedures were also instituted whereby gay, lesbian, and bisexual employees could file grievances for maltreatment. Most importantly, he was responsible for the rescision of the federal security clearance ban for gays issued during the Eisenhower presidency. Frank continues to reside in Washington, D.C. with his longtime companion, economist Herb Moses.

Profile by
Michael A. Lutes

ALLEN GINSBERG

*I*n a public career of more than forty years, Allen Ginsberg has been

a pioneer in broadening the range of American poetry, opening it up to

new influences, freeing it from convention and inhibition, and restor-

ing its appeal to a large public. From his first reading of "Howl" before a

wildly enthusiastic audience in San Francisco (1955) to the publication

of his major Collected Poems *(1985) and beyond, Ginsberg has*

championed individual freedom in his writing, performances, and

appearances, proclaiming his defiance of all forms of control, conformi-

ty, or spiritless materialism. He probably did more than any individual

to prepare the way for gay liberation, and as much as any when it

organized. His poetry celebrates homosexuality in frank terms, and

1926– •

American •

poet

challenges discrimination against it. As one of the founders of the Beat Generation, Ginsberg combined elements of revolt, liberation, and idealism that still hold a strong appeal for youth not just in the United States, but throughout the world. He may well be the most widely traveled artist of all time. While his refractory message may now be blunted by the self-deprecating irony of old age: "Drink your decaf Ginsberg old communist/*New York Times* addict, be glad you're not Trotsky" ("Not Dead Yet" in *Cosmopolitan Greetings,* 1994), he has remained engaged with the world, adapting to meet its challenges, refusing any compromise with the establishment against the disestablished.

Irwin Allen Ginsberg, who was named for his paternal grandfather S'rul Avrum Ginsberg, was born 3 June 1926, in Newark, New Jersey, the second son of Naomi and Louis Ginsberg. A poetic and artistic temperament was very much in evidence in the family. Naomi sang, played the mandolin, and made up stories colored by her communist sympathies. Louis, an accomplished poet, earned his living teaching English in Paterson, New Jersey. Allen's older brother, Eugene Brooks Ginsberg, eventually dropped his last name, and as Eugene Brooks, became a well-known attorney and poet in his own right.

Questions of identity haunt Ginsberg's poetry, and, given his family background, this is hardly surprising. Many differences came between his parents. Naomi's family arrived in the United States in 1905, fleeing the Russian pogroms. Whereas Louis was a socialist, a lifelong liberal, and agnostic, Naomi was a staunch communist and unrelenting atheist. Her passion for a workers' revolution and active part in local Communist Party politics fueled her aversion to Louis's liberalism and "bourgeois" poetry. Given Louis's modest income, money was always tight and caused tension. Above all, Naomi's health was precarious in the extreme. She had a first nervous breakdown before her marriage—a marriage opposed by his family—and another when Allen was three. She spent time in a private sanatorium that her husband could ill afford, causing him to go deeply into debt. Her delusions of persecution grew steadily worse and came to define her. The barbaric treatments she underwent, including some forty insulin shock treatments, did nothing to help. In 1948, by which time she and Louis had divorced, Allen had to sign the papers authorizing a prefrontal lobotomy. He had little choice, given her violent schizophrenic paranoia, but this action would haunt him for the rest of his life. Naomi died in a mental institution in 1956. Louis Ginsberg died twenty years later, in 1976.

While Allen Ginsberg was loved by both his parents, circumstances at home were painfully difficult. Even as a boy, he was increasingly called upon to look after Naomi. In his poem "Kaddish," a deeply moving commemoration of his mother, he describes an episode that occurred when he was fifteen. As she experienced an epileptic seizure in their bathroom at home, he could only stand by helplessly, a witness to her utter, hellish loss of bodily control.

In spite of the domestic arguments, the penury that led to frequent moves, the anti-semitism of other children, the frequent scenes of indignity at home, and the confusion and embarrassment caused by his awakening homosexuality, Ginsberg was a superior student. At East Side High School in Paterson, he was elected president of the Debating Society and the Talent Club, and when he was graduated in 1943, his excellent academic record earned him a university scholarship from the State of New Jersey.

Inevitably, Ginsberg's childhood marked him deeply. His willing acceptance of Naomi, and his attempt to understand and even identify with her, psychosis and all, fostered and forever shaped his extraordinary ability to identify with the victim or underdog—Australian aborigine, Indian pariah, or American homeless, for example—against the establishment, viewed as oppressive. Throughout the 1960s and 1970s, he played a major role in antiwar demonstrations and liberation movements. Having observed Naomi exposed in all her frailty and difference, he in turn elected to reveal himself and to try to understand himself more fully. Certainly his sense of personal identity was far from secure, with parents who placed different expectations upon him, a home environment that was anything but stable, and a sexual identity that for many years caused him shame and indeed self-rejection.

• Columbia University and the Beginnings of Beat

Ginsberg enrolled at Columbia University. He soon gave up plans to become a labor lawyer to concentrate instead on literature. Lionel Trilling and Mark Van Doren, nationally renowned men of letters and professors at Columbia, saw in the son the literary gifts of the father, whose poetry they admired. But if Trilling and Van Doren represented the academic pole of student life at Columbia, Ginsberg also discovered a far different world.

He became friendly with, and indeed fell in love with, Lucien Carr, a brilliant classmate from Saint Louis, worldly wise and widely read. Carr, a heterosexual, the first of many to whom Ginsberg would be attracted in a pattern of hopeless love, introduced him to a circle of friends that included William Burroughs, David Kammerer, Jack Kerouac, and others. Burroughs, a brilliant thirty-year-old Harvard graduate in English, knew Carr from their home town of Saint Louis. A homosexual, Burroughs had already embarked on his lifelong exploration of alternative visions ranging from Mayan civilization to Rimbaud's *Season in Hell* to a wide range of mind-altering drugs. He was fast becoming an authority on hallucinogens. Like Carr, he was fascinated by the low life of New York. David Kammerer, another of Carr's acquaintances from Saint Louis, was obsessed with Carr and followed him to New York. Carr could offer Kammerer no satisfaction beyond tolerating his presence. Finally, in the summer of 1944, Carr, importuned and threatened by the jealous Kammerer, stabbed him to death. He received a light sentence.

The brilliance of Kerouac stood out, even in this remarkable group. In his quest for a New Vision, a literature of spontaneous expression, he had written by far the most. In addition, he combined athletic prowess (he had attended Columbia briefly on a football scholarship) with unusual sensitivity. Ginsberg fell in love with him. Out of friendship or open-mindedness, Kerouac had several sexual encounters with Ginsberg, but Ginsberg, recognizing the lack of reciprocity in these relations, was left far from satisfied.

In the company of his friends, Ginsberg discovered the hidden New York world of drifters, panhandlers, addicts, and outcasts, a counterculture that slipped through the net cast by mainstream society. In their own quest for a new vision and an alternative form of expression, Kerouac, Burroughs, and the neophyte Ginsberg, the nucleus of what became the Beat Generation, found in the New York nether world inspiration and, ultimately, a perverse state of grace. In a flash of recognition, Kerouac grafted the notion of beatitude onto the earlier sense of *beat* as downcast.

The explosive mixture of artistic inventiveness, low-life experience, homosexual tension, and drug experimentation has no precedent in American literature, but it bears comparison with French precursors, in particular Rimbaud's affair with Verlaine around 1870, or, to a lesser extent, Cocteau's with Radiguet in the early 1920s. But, whereas Rimbaud stopped writing before he was twenty, and Radiguet died at twenty, Ginsberg found himself as a poet quite late, at close to thirty. By some miracle, he has been able not only to survive, but to keep on searching, to keep on finding, and to keep on writing into old age. Through it all, he maintained an extraordinary gift for friendship, even when that friendship was sorely tested, as by Kerouac's alcoholism or political conservatism, for example.

Kerouac was the first person to whom Ginsberg revealed his homosexuality. Ironically, Ginsberg was dismissed from Columbia in 1945 over an incident that partly involved Kerouac. A dean of students entered his room at night to investigate obscene remarks Ginsberg had written in the grime of his window. He found Kerouac sharing his friend's bed in real innocence—Kerouac needed a place for the night— but perceived perversity. Ginsberg was expelled for a year, moved in

Coming to •

Terms with

Homosexuality

with Burroughs, and immersed himself in the marginal life of the city under the homosexual and hallucinogenic guidance of the future author of *The Naked Lunch*. In 1948, after re-enrolling at Columbia, he completed his bachelor of arts degree with an A- average.

While at Columbia, Ginsberg was acutely embarrassed by his homosexuality and tried to conceal his feelings from Carr and Kerouac. As part of a course of psychotherapy he underwent in 1948, he admitted his sexual orientation to his father. Louis considered homosexuality a mental disorder and was especially upset when he learned of Allen's love for Neal Cassady. The two had met in 1947. Cassady, the prototype for Dean Moriarty of Kerouac's novel *On the Road,* became an icon of the Beat Generation, a legend for his nonstop talk, fast driving, sexual exuberance, and boundless energy. Born on the road in Salt Lake City, he seemed to embody the broad spirit of the West. He and Ginsberg became lovers and Ginsberg experienced with him an unprecedented intensity of passion. Ginsberg made him the subject of many poems and dedicated the collection *Planet News 1961–1967* (1968) to him. In "Elegy for Neal Cassady," Ginsberg celebrated Neal's memory with a tenderness reminiscent of Walt Whitman's homoerotic subtlety in, say, "Song of Myself." But Ginsberg was also the poet of undisguised carnality and deliberate provocation, as may be seen from his poem "Please Master" (1968). Even allowing for the violence of the period— the Vietnam War, demonstrations, counter-demonstrations, and extremes begetting opposing extremes—the language of *this* elegy to Cassady was unprecedented in its presentation of the details of gay sex.

If the image we now have of Ginsberg, colored by "Howl" and later poems to Cassady and others, is of a man at ease with his sexual identity, it is worth recalling that the pressures to conform with the heterosexual majority were so great that in 1950 he announced to Kerouac, after being discharged from the Psychiatric Institute, that he would give up homosexuality and try to lead a "straight" life. He had spent eight months in the psychiatric hospital as a condition for avoiding prison after naively receiving stolen goods for some petty burglars in New York. For a while, he did try to live the heterosexual life.

If Ginsberg's courage in speaking out proved to be a catalyst for the gay liberation movement, the spirit and substance of his relationship with Peter Orlovsky served as a prototype for many gay couples. Ginsberg saw a painting of Orlovsky and asked to meet him. Orlovsky struck Ginsberg not just with his beauty, but his gentleness. In February 1955, in San Francisco, the two formally exchanged vows, in a mutual giving of self, an agreement to seek whatever salvation they could find together. In spite of Orlovsky's recurring mental illness, drug addiction, and problem drinking, Ginsberg has honored this relationship and stood by his friend.

In 1948, in the first of several mystical revelations, hearing what he took to be the voice of William Blake, while reading Blake's "Ah Sunflower" after masturbating, Ginsberg saw himself as one in a line of visionary poets. His simple faith in poetry and in his role as a poet were strengthened, becoming quite exceptional in an unpoetic era. In the years immediately following, Ginsberg was far from inactive, accumulating life-experience and writing. But in many respects these were years of latency, maturation, and preparation. With "Howl," he and the Beat Generation found their poetic voice. In an evening organized by Ginsberg, he and Gary Snyder, Kenneth Rexroth, Michael McClure, Philip Lamantia, and Philip Whalen read to a capacity crowd at the Six Gallery in San Francisco, 13 October 1955. The event was of incomparable significance. With his one poem, Ginsberg crystallized the voiceless desperation of all those alienated by the materialism of American society, took pride in his own homosexuality, restored poetry's relevance to a large public, and re-inserted it in an oral tradition, while fulfilling the Beat dream of a free-flowing, spontaneous form of expression.

Howl and Other Poems (1956), published by San Francisco poet Lawrence Ferlinghetti's City Lights Books, reached a huge audience and enshrined Ginsberg as national poet and figure of controversy. Ferlinghetti was arrested and charged with publishing obscene material. Though he and Ginsberg won the trial and the volume was hailed by many as a groundbreaking work of genius, others condemned its lack of decorum. Not just "Howl," but companion poems such as "In the Baggage Room at Greyhound," "Sunflower Sutra," "America," and "A Supermarket in California," juxtaposing a critique of the United States with a search for beauty and meaning amid the shards of a debased reality, have lost none of their appeal.

From the heartrending demise of many that opened "Howl"—"I saw the best minds of my generation . . . destroyed by madness"— Ginsberg turned to one, his mother, in "Kaddish" (*Kaddish and Other Poems,* 1956), composed under the influence of hallucinogenic drugs. A terrible intimacy unites son to suffering mother. In other poems, as in the beautiful "At Apollinaire's Grave," a more tranquil intimacy prevails.

In his fascination with death and his pursuit of enlarged or altered consciousness—involving an astonishing range of experience from using the very potent hallucinogen yage in Peru, to living next to suffering, disease, and death in India—Ginsberg ran the risk of a complete loss of self in death or madness. But he came to turn away from this self-destructive bent. *Planet News, 1961–67* (1968) chronicles drug experiences with Kerouac and others and LSD "trips" with Timothy Leary, alongside an attack on the phantasmagoric jumble of images through which television conceals political realities and the horrors of the Vietnam war ("Television Was a Baby Crawling Toward That Deathchamber"), before outlining his ongoing search for expanded consciousness in the Orient. But in India, he met a Tibetan lama, Dudjom Rinpoche, who advised him to stop, renounce this search, accept his body, and look to himself. This reversal that came into perfect focus on a train ride from Kyoto to Tokyo is described in "The Change." At that point, Ginsberg understood with perfect clarity that he must let go of Blake and Beat and the drug-induced hallucinations that were now hounding him, ghosts barring the way to the future. In the second half of *Planet News,* Ginsberg's contact with quotidian reality becomes firmly grounded and quite ironic, a pattern that continued into later poetry.

• **Buddhist and**

More

The very title *Mind Breaths: Poems 1972–1977* (1978) reflects Ginsberg's interest in Oriental meditation, the oneness of mind with breath as it is expelled and dissolves in space. The title poem "Mind Breaths," in which the "stanzas" are a series of breath units, is serene and effective. In 1971, after a year of Hindu sitting meditation, he met Tibetan Lama Chogyam Trungpa Rinpoche, studied with him, and in 1972 took formal vows as a Buddhist, assuming the name Lion of Dharma. At Trungpa's request, he became a cofounder of the Jack Kerouac School of Disembodied Poetics at Naropa Institute in Boulder, Colorado, a Buddhism-based university. Ginsberg was co-administrator of the School for ten years, and taught there regularly. Trungpa himself, who died in 1987, was very controversial.

Eclectically gifted as ever, Ginsberg also composed, with encouragement from Bob Dylan, a number of blues songs that are included in *Mind Breaths.* He had sung them at his own recitals or during his long tour with the "Rolling Thunder Review" led by Dylan in late 1975. And, incorrigibly iconoclastic as ever, he includes in the collection "Sweet Boy, Gimme yr Ass," as forthright as the title suggests, and "Come All Ye Brave Boys," a homosexual *carpe diem* as explicit as any ever written.

Ginsberg's later collections, including *White Shroud, Poems 1980– 1985* (1986) and *Cosmopolitan Greetings, Poems 1986–1992* (1994) continue to reflect his Buddhist studies and practice. But of course, however proud he is of helping bring Buddhism to the United States, he cannot be defined by this alone. Dharma Lion, he is also "Yiddishe Kopf" *(Cosmopolitan Greetings)* and unrepentant Beat, bringing to his art a diversity of experience, a depth of compassion, and a power of indignation that assign him a unique position as America's leading poet.

Profile by
James P. McNab

JEWELLE GOMEZ

J ewelle Gomez, author and activist, has touched many lives through

both her writing and her community involvement. The author of two

books of poetry, a feminist vampire novel, and an autobiographical

book of essays, Gomez's work often explores the complexity of identities

and communities. She describes her own complex identity in her

collection of essays, Forty-Three Septembers, *as "African-American,*

Ioway, Wampanoag, Bostonian, lesbian, welfare-raised, artist, activ-

ist." Gomez connects her writing with her personal struggles; in a 1991

interview in Ms. Magazine, *she says, "Audre Lorde says poetry is not a*

luxury; poetry for me is the embracing of the difficulty of struggle in my

own personal life. Everybody can be doing that."

1948– •

American writer, •

activist, and

teacher

Jewelle Gomez was born on 11 September 1948 in Boston, Massachusetts, to John "Duke" Gomez, a bartender, and Dolores Minor, who would later become a nurse while in her fifties. Growing up, she lived with her great-grandmother, Grace A. Morandus, who had been born on an Indian reservation in Iowa of half-Ioway, half–African American parents. Gomez traces her desire to write back to her childhood: "I wanted to write ever since I was a kid, growing up with my great-grandmother in a cold-water flat in Boston," she recalls in a 1994 volume of *Contemporary Authors*.

Gomez describes her extended family in her book of essays, *Forty-Three Septembers*. She writes affectionately of her father, Duke, as a man known for his style and charm: "My father was magic." Duke maintained two households with two wives, neither of whom were Gomez's mother; as a child, Gomez visited these two homes each weekend. Gomez graduated from Northeastern University with a B.A. in 1971, and from Columbia University with an M.S. in 1973.

Gomez was employed as a production assistant for WGBH-TV in Boston on "Say Brother" from 1968 to 1971 and, in the 1970s, in New York City for Children's Television Workshop and WNET-TV. She also worked as a stage manager for various Off-Broadway theaters between 1975 and 1980. In *Contemporary Authors,* Gomez says, "My training in journalism was excellent grounding in writing for the feminist and gay press, and helped me to focus my own essay and fiction skills." In fact, she published her first book of poetry in 1980, *The Lipstick Papers,* with the lesbian press Firebrand Books.

Moving from her work in the theater and with television, Gomez worked as a New York State Council on the Arts program associate from 1983 to 1989. In 1989, she became the director of its Literature Program, a position she held until 1993. Gomez also began teaching as a lecturer of Women's Studies and English at Hunter College in New York City from 1989 to 1990. She became increasingly visible as an activist as a founding board member of the Gay and Lesbian Alliance Against Defamation (GLAAD) in 1985, and as a member of the Feminist Anti-Censorship Taskforce (FACT). Gomez's public involvement also included her service as a member on boards of advisors for several organizations, including the Cornell University Human Sexuality Archives, the National Center for Lesbian Rights, the *Multi-Cultural Review* magazine, Open Meadows Foundation, and the PEN American Center.

Gomez's second book of poetry, *Flamingos and Bears,* was published in 1986, also by Firebrand. Its title poem was later included in the 1992 anthology *The Persistent Desire: A Femme-Butch Reader.* Gomez won the Money for Women/Barbara Deming Award for fiction in 1990;

her novel *The Gilda Stories* was published the following year and received an enthusiastic public reaction. In *Belles Lettres,* Karen Crowley calls *The Gilda Stories* "one of the most imaginative novels in lesbian fiction . . . a rare reading experience." The novel traces a community of vampires from 1860s Louisiana to the twenty-first century, with a heroine whom Judith E. Johnson in *The Kenyon Review* appropriately describes as "a kind of American Everywoman engaged in a pilgrimage through our History, our society, and our changing ideas about life, love, responsibility, and the proper place of women." In her novel, Gomez set out to redefine the vampire, a mythological creature that exists in many cultures; in *Contemporary Authors,* Gomez reflects: "The novel is about the often overlooked interconnection between power and responsibility—how we create family for ourselves in extraordinary circumstances and how heroic any one of us can be." *The Gilda Stories* won Lambda Literary Awards for both fiction and science fiction in 1991. *The Gilda Stories* was also adapted for the stage in a production entitled *Bones and Ash: A Gilda Story.* A collaborative effort between Gomez and the dance company Urban Bush Women, the production also featured music by lesbian composer Toshi Reagon and toured the United States during the 1996 season.

Central to Gomez's writing is "continuity, a link to a past and a future, to a people, to all people," writes Susan Sherman in *New Directions for Women.* This concern with "continuity" can be seen both in *The Gilda Stories* and in her collection of essays, *Forty-Three Septembers,* which was published in 1993. In this book, Gomez writes her own history, and in doing so, describes both her family history and a history of feminist and lesbian communities with which she has been involved. Gomez's third book of poetry, *Oral Tradition,* was published in 1995.

Gomez has recently moved from New York to San Francisco and has become an active, vocal, and visible member of many communities in this new city. Gomez taught creative writing at New College of California, San Francisco, and has been researching material for a biography of Audre Lorde. In *Contemporary Authors,* Gomez declares, "What do I hope to achieve by writing? Changing the world!"

**Profile by
Elizabeth Hutchinson
Crocker**

MARGA GOMEZ

*S*uccessfully merging artistic genres and categories, Marga Gomez

is a multitalented entertainer who has forged a career as a stand-up

comic, actor, writer, and performance artist. The daughter of a

Cuban comedian and a Puerto Rican exotic dancer, Gomez bills

herself as an "exotic comedian"; like her comic idol, Lily Tomlin,

Gomez is adept at creating a bevy of outrageous characters onstage.

Gomez is known for her ability to shift easily from comic one-liners to

dramatic disclosure, and has received critical acclaim in the 1990s

as one of the outstanding purveyors of the dramatic monologue form.

She is also a recognized leader in the growing field of gay and lesbian

comedy.

Hispanic •

performer

and writer

Marga Gomez was born to two well-known New York City performers, Margo (who danced under the name Margo the Exotic) and Wilfredo Gomez (known onstage as Willy Chevalier). Growing up in the upper Manhattan neighborhood known as Washington Heights, Marga Gomez entered show business as a child performer, appearing onstage with her parents for the first time at the age of seven. The Latino theatrical world provided an unconventional and influential backdrop for Gomez's early years; she later chronicled her formative childhood experiences in performance pieces such as *Memory Tricks* and *A Line Around the Block*.

Gomez's parents divorced in the mid-1960s, at which time the fame and financial security they had previously earned in the theater began to dissolve. Gomez went to live with her mother in Massapequa, Long Island, and saw her father on weekends. Gomez had attended an inner-city Catholic school as a child; during her adolescence, she attended a high school where she was the only Latino student. Suburban Long Island felt isolating to Gomez, and she became shy and introverted. On graduating from high school, Gomez went to Oswego State College in upstate New York, where she first came out as a lesbian. After studying English and political science for two years, Gomez flunked out of college and moved to Binghamton, New York, where she became involved in a lesbian feminist community.

- ***Career Starts in***

San Francisco

Gomez moved to San Francisco in the early 1980s, where she attempted to get involved in acting. She joined Lilith, a feminist theater ensemble, and toured Europe and the West Coast extensively for three years. Gomez credits this experience with giving her theatrical monologues and stand-up material a feminist edge. Gomez also spent a season with the San Francisco Mime Troupe and was one of the original members of the Latino comedy group Culture Clash. During this time, Gomez developed her stand-up routine—a mixture of off-beat characterizations, quirky social commentary, and sexual politics.

By 1988 Gomez had acquired a loyal following and won the Cabaret Gold award as "Entertainer of the Year" from the San Francisco Council on Entertainment. Gomez has performed at countless events across the country and has been a featured performer on television shows such as "Rosie O'Donnell's Stand-Up Spotlight/VH-1," HBO's "COMIC RELIEF VI," and Comedy Central's "Out There." In addition to her work for television, Gomez made a brief appearance in the feature film *Batman Forever*.

In 1991, as a result of an offer from the University of California at San Diego's Multi-Cultural Theater Festival, Gomez created her first full-length performance monologue, *Memory Tricks*. The monologue was the first in a series of performance pieces written and performed by Gomez, along with *Marga Gomez Is Pretty, Witty & Gay* and *A Line Around the Block*. It is this body of work that has brought Gomez her greatest critical attention, including rave reviews, international media focus, honors, and awards. The tragicomic story of Marga's relationship with her flamboyant mother, *Memory Tricks* traces the emotional path from her mother's days as a showgirl to her struggle with aging and Alzheimer's disease. Gomez probes the difficult emotions surrounding the mother-daughter relationship—in this case, a relationship in which the child must play mother to her own parent.

Following its six-week, sold-out run at The Marsh Performance Space in San Francisco, *Memory Tricks* was twice chosen to be a part of the prestigious "Solo Mio" festival at Life on the Water Theater in San Francisco. Gomez was invited to perform a one-hour version of *Memory Tricks* as part of the New York Shakespeare Festival's Festival of New Voices in 1992, followed by a limited engagement of the complete piece in April 1993. It has since been performed all over the United States, Canada, and Europe.

Gomez's next performance piece, *Marga Gomez Is Pretty, Witty & Gay,* opened at Josie's Cabaret in San Francisco in October 1991 to packed houses. The work has played across the United States, and in March 1993 it was included as part of the Whitney Museum's Biennial Performance Series. The work's title is a send-up of the song "I Feel Pretty" from *West Side Story;* it also marks the fact that Gomez has been an out performer for most of her career. Although *Memory Tricks* only indirectly mentions Gomez's lesbianism, *Marga Gomez Is Pretty, Witty & Gay* is packed with lesbian humor, including a hilarious sketch describing a fantasy relationship between Anais Nin and Minnie Mouse. During the show, Gomez overturns a common stereotype of gays and lesbians with the line, "We do not recruit, we impress."

Gomez began performing *A Line Around the Block,* a companion piece to *Memory Tricks,* in 1994. The work was co-commissioned by the Mark Taper Forum in Los Angeles and The New World Theater at the University of Massachusetts in Amherst. *A Line Around the Block* had its creative beginnings in a sketch entitled "The 13 Minutos," which formed part of the theater group Culture Clash's show, *Carpa Clash,* at the Mark Taper Forum. Gomez won Theater LA's 1993–1994 Ovation Award as best featured actress in a play for her work in *Carpa Clash.*

A Line Around the Block is a remembrance of Gomez's father, Willy Chevalier, as well as a bittersweet look back at the Latino theatrical world of the 1950s and 1960s. Gomez has credited her father with giving her the desire and the determination to go into show business. In both *Memory Tricks* and *A Line Around the Block*, Gomez pays tribute to her parents by showing the limits placed on their talents by discrimination against Latinos and Latinas. Despite her own assimilated background, the immigrant experience of her parents and Latino/a culture have been major influences on Gomez's work. Gomez sees the strength of her writing coming from being an outsider in two worlds: a queer in the Latino world, a Latina in the gay world.

Playhouse International optioned Gomez's screenplay of *Memory Tricks*, which has been expanded to include several players in order to be made into a feature film. Gomez has also contributed written material to several books: *Out, Loud & Laughing; Out of Character;* and *Contemporary Plays by American Women of Color*. Currently, Marga Gomez is dividing her time between coasts as she continues with all her pursuits. With her many talents and powerful presence, this rising star—an inspiration to both the gay/lesbian and Latino/a communities—is just beginning to shine.

Profile by Teresa Ortega

BARBARA GRIER

1933– •

American •

publisher

*P*ublisher and editor Barbara Grier has spent four decades on the

frontline of lesbian publishing, originally as a contributor to and later

editor of the first national lesbian magazine, The Ladder, and currently

as the co-founder and publisher of Naiad Press, the world's largest

publisher of lesbian books.

Barbara Grier was born on 4 November 1933, in Cincinnati, Ohio to Dorothy Vernon Black and Philip Strang Grier. Her father was a physician and her mother worked as a secretary. She has two older half brothers, William and Brewster, and two younger sisters, Diane (who is also a lesbian) and Penelope. Her parents separated when Grier was ten and divorced when she was thirteen.

Throughout her childhood and youth, Grier traveled extensively, visiting every state in the union and several foreign countries. According to Grier, the travel "took the place of formal education. To the extent I have been successful, I owe it to being extremely well-read and well-traveled."

Grier remembers being "madly in love with my babysitter" at the age of eight and having several other crushes on other young women before she came out at age twelve. Relating her coming out process in the

lesbian classic, *The Coming Out Stories,* Grier states: "When I discovered behavior patterns in myself that I could tell were different from
behavior patterns in my friends . . . I investigated it in quite a sensible
way for a fairly bright child: I went to the library and started looking." In
the video *Lesbian Tongues,* Grier tells what happened when she returned from the library and told her mother that she was a homosexual.
"My mother answered, 'No, because you're a woman, you're a lesbian.
And since twelve years old is too young to make such a decision, let's
wait six months before we tell the newspapers.'"

From that time on, Grier has lived her life openly as a lesbian.
"What's hard about being out?" Grier asks and answers immediately,
"What's hard is *not* being out!" Grier credits her ease in coming out to her
mother: "She was very supportive. She didn't consider it unusual or
remarkable. She had come from a background in the performing arts
and had been around gays and lesbians all her life. If all people coming
out were as supported as I was by my parents, we would grow up
without any vestige of emotional pain."

Shortly after graduating from high school in 1951, Grier met Helen
Bennett in the literature and popular section of the Kansas City (Missouri) Public Library and began a relationship that was to last twenty years.
The couple moved to Denver, Colorado so that Bennett could attend
library school. "It was there I began to write and began to collect lesbian
literature. As it later turned out, that's what I was to spend my life doing,"
Grier reminisced in *Heartwomen.* Afterwards, they moved to Kansas
City, Kansas where they both got jobs at the local public library, Bennett
as a librarian and Grier as a clerical worker in the cataloging department.

Grier became involved with the legendary lesbian publication *The
Ladder* almost from its inception. *The Ladder,* the first national lesbian
magazine, was begun by the Daughters of Bilitis in San Francisco,
California in 1956. In an interview with Kate Brandt, Grier reflects:
"When I saw my first copy of an issue of *The Ladder* I realized what I was
going to spend my life doing." From 1957 to 1972, she was involved in
practically every aspect of the operation, from reviewing books to
contributing articles to writing columns to editing and eventually publishing the magazine.

Grier Works on •

The Ladder

Grier began her fifteen-year association with *The Ladder* by
submitting book reviews for its "Lesbiana" column. Since in the 1950s,
there could be serious repercussions for women writing openly as
lesbians, Phyllis Lyon, editor of *The Ladder* at that time, urged Barbara to
write under a pseudonym. She did so, thinking it was "romantic and
glamorous" and chose the name "Gene Damon: Gene, because I'd
always liked and wanted the name, and Damon, because it means,

literally, 'the devil' or 'demon'," Grier states in *Happy Endings*. She eventually took on several more pseudonyms, and wrote at least one entire issue of *The Ladder* herself "including letters both for and against a particular topic" using these various pen names.

She also submitted articles and reviews to other gay publications, including *ONE Magazine*, the *Mattachine Review*, and *Tangents*. Throughout her association with these publications and afterwards, Grier worked a series of clerical jobs to pay her expenses so she could devote herself to her lesbian volunteer work. She threw herself wholly into this work, spending all her free time writing and researching.

In 1967 Grier met Donna J. McBride, who had just joined the staff of the Kansas City Public Library. McBride had been warned about "that woman who collects *those* books." Recognizing her own lesbian feelings, McBride recalls that she would read every book that Grier requested and later even started following her around the library. In 1971, McBride began to volunteer at *The Ladder* and soon became involved with Grier, who ended her twenty-year relationship with Bennett. The couple moved in together on 22 January 1972. McBride continued working at the Kansas City Public Library, "rising through the ranks." She eventually abolished the literature department where both she and Bennett had met Grier. "She made certain that I couldn't hunt there anymore," quips Grier.

After taking on a succession of progressively more responsible positions at *The Ladder,* including fiction and poetry editor, Grier took over as editor-in-chief in 1968. The late 1960s was an era of social activism and Grier witnessed the birth of several liberation movements, most notably those demanding equity for women and gays. Reflecting on the times in *Heartwomen,* Grier comments, "as the new wave of the feminist movement became a powerful force it seemed obvious to me that that's where the magazine had to go." However, Grier's political activism ran contrary to the assimilationist philosophy of the Daughters of Bilitis (DOB). "In 1970, Rita [Laporte, national president of DOB] and I literally divorced *The Ladder* from DOB—i.e., we stole it. We took the magazine away and turned it into a very strongly women's liberation magazine, although it stayed purely lesbian," Grier told Kate Brandt in *Happy Endings*. The takeover was short-lived, however, because without the DOB's financial backing "*The Ladder* simply ran out of money." Its last issue appeared in the fall of 1972.

Much of the content of *The Ladder* was republished in book form during the United States bicentennial year (1976), including *The Lavender Herring: Lesbian Essays from The Ladder* (Diana Press), *Lesbian Lives: Biographies of Women from The Ladder* (Diana Press), and *The*

Lesbians Home Journal: Stories from The Ladder (Diana Press), all of which Grier co-edited with Coletta Reid; and *Lesbiana: Book Reviews from The Ladder, 1966–1972* (Naiad Press), edited by Grier herself.

Shortly after the demise of *The Ladder,* Anyda Marchant and Muriel Crawford lent Grier and McBride money to start a lesbian publishing company. In January of 1973, Naiad Press was founded, publishing its first book, *The Latecomer* by Sarah Aldridge (Anyda Marchant's pseudonym), the following year in January 1974. For the next eight years, both McBride and Grier worked full-time jobs in addition to running Naiad Press. In 1980, the couple moved Naiad from Kansas City to Tallahassee, Florida, where they ran the business out of their garage. Grier became Naiad's first full-time employee in January 1982 with McBride following as the second in June of that same year. From those modest beginnings, sole proprietors Grier and McBride have carefully cultivated Naiad Press, transforming it into the world's largest lesbian press, publishing altogether over 300 books. Commenting on Naiad's impressive growth in the video *Lesbian Tongues,* Grier says: "I love the idea that lesbian money literally is keeping Naiad Press growing like crazy."

Naiad Press, the oldest continuously publishing lesbian press in the United States, has supplied a generation of readers with romance, mystery, science fiction, fantasy, and humor books and has resuscitated many lesbian literary and pulp classics from past generations, including Margaret C. Anderson's *Forbidden Fires,* Gertrude Stein's *Lifting Belly,* Gale Wilhelm's *We Too Are Drifting,* and Ann Bannon's *Beebo Brinker* series. Additionally, Naiad has published such significant works of nonfiction as Clare Potter's *Lesbian Periodicals Index* and J. R. Roberts's *Black Lesbians: An Annotated Bibliography.*

Included among the diverse array of authors published by Naiad are Katherine V. Forrest, Jeannette Foster, Lee Lynch, Claire McNab, Isabel Miller, Jane Rule, Diane Salvatore, Ann Allen Shockley, Sheila Ortiz Taylor, and Valerie Taylor. Grier herself has contributed to Naiad's prolific output by co-editing several books herself, including *The Erotic Naiad* (1992), *The Romantic Naiad* (1993), and *The Mysterious Naiad* (1994), all edited with Katherine V. Forrest; and *The First Time Ever* (1995) and *Dancing in the Dark* (1996), both edited with Christine Cassidy.

Naiad Press books have been recognized in gay and lesbian literary circles, winning one American Library Association Gay, Lesbian, and Bisexual Book Award and six Lambda Literary Awards. Tribute has been paid to Grier as well for her unrelenting devotion to lesbian and gay concerns. In 1985, the prestigious Gay Academic Union paid homage to Grier by bestowing upon her its President's Award for Lifetime Service.

Grier •

co-founds

Naiad Press

And in 1992, both Grier and McBride were awarded the Publisher's Service Award at the fourth annual Lambda Literary Awards banquet.

Throughout her life Grier has been an avid collector and documenter of lesbian literature. She began "haunting" used book stores as a teenager collecting books with lesbian themes, an activity that "began as a search, and then it became a dream, and then it became an obsession," according to her account in *Happy Endings*. She became friends with Jeannette Foster, author of *Sex Variant Women in Literature,* who helped Grier find even more ways to identify lesbian-themed literature.

Along the way, Grier documented what she found. Throughout the early 1960s, she (under the pseudonym of Gene Damon) and noted author Marion Zimmer Bradley together compiled what they termed "a complete, cumulative checklist of lesbian, variant, and homosexual fiction, in English, or available in English translation, with supplements of related material, for the use of collectors, students, and librarians." She went on to compile, with the help of Lee Stuart and later Jan Watson (a pseudonym of Donna McBride) and Robin Jordan, the renowned bibliography *The Lesbian in Literature,* originally published in 1967 and updated twice.

Her obsession with these materials has resulted in one of the largest collections of its type, including manuscripts, personal papers, photographs, and other memorabilia, as well as books and periodicals. Grier donated this collection, valued at over $400,000, to the newly opened James C. Hormel Gay and Lesbian Center at the San Francisco Public Library.

Currently, Grier and McBride live "terribly middle class" lives in Tallahassee, Florida. "We are very good neighbors, yet very publicly and explicitly lesbian. We do not hide it. In other words, the grass is green, the sky is blue, and we're lesbians."

What most concerns Grier today is the issue of gay and lesbian marriage: "In the eyes of the law a man and a woman who are legally married are one person, one body. When one person dies, their possessions pass seamlessly to the other, like siamese twins, and no inheritance tax is assessed. We are not similarly protected in our relationships. It is a privilege granted solely to heterosexual married couples—one that is used for social control. If the State were to eliminate this privilege totally, its coffers would be soon be empty. What politicians are voting against is not against marrying a mate—they don't want us to take advantage of social security or to have disability acts kick in. It all has to do with money. Money is the decision making factor in this country."

Grier continues: "Another aspect of this issue is that marriage creates visibility. When we are banned from marrying, we are kept from doing publicly the ordinary and rational things that people do anyway—marry, settle down, get jobs, and live like everyone else."

Barbara Grier has brought lesbian culture and literature into the lives of two generations of lesbians. Through her work with *The Ladder* in the 1950s and 1960s and Naiad Press in the 1970s, 1980s, and 1990s, she has lived up to her goal of "making it possible that any lesbian, anywhere, any age, who comes out can walk into a bookstore and pick up a book that says, 'of course you're a lesbian and you're wonderful!'"

Profile by
R. Ellen Greenblatt

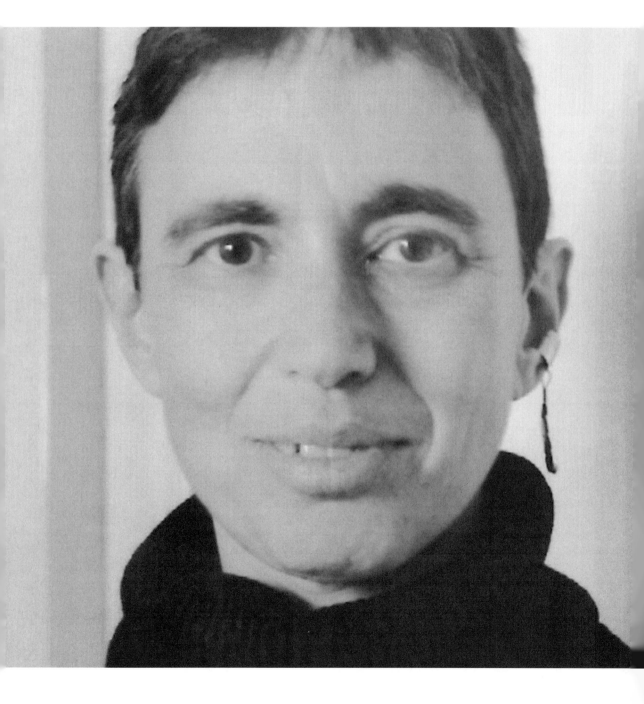

MARILYN HACKER

Marilyn Hacker has been writing poetry for at least thirty years.

1942– •

Since the private publication of The Terrible Children *(1967), Hacker*

has written ten books of poetry. All of them concentrate on two relation-

American •

ships: women's relationships with other women and their worlds, and

poet

women poets' relationships to literary forms. Her work is also known for

its graphic, yet lyrical, portrayals of women's bodies and for its frankness

about lesbian love. According to Felicia Mitchell in Dictionary of Literary

Biography, *"Marilyn Hacker fits into the contemporary poetry scene*

because of her unusual critical perspective, which bridges the tradition-

al and the feminist. . . . Hacker has insisted and shown that the

traditional poetic forms are as much women's as they are men's."

Hacker excels at writing the sonnet and the sonnet sequence. In her *Love, Death, and the Changing of Seasons* (1986), she brings the frankness of the forbidden—the love that should not speak its name as well as the vocabulary that should not make its presence known—to the sonnet:

> Well, damn, it's a relief to be a slut
> after such lengths of "Man delights not me,
> nor woman neither," that I honestly
> wondered if I'd outgrown it. Chocolate
> or wine, a cashmere scarf, a cigarette,
> had more to do with sensuality
> than what's between my belly and my butt
> that yearns toward you now unabashedly.
> I'd love to grip your head between my thighs
> while yours tense toward your moment on my ears,
> but I'll still be thankful for this surprise
> if things turn out entirely otherwise,
> and we're bar buddies who, in a few years,
> will giggle about this after two beers.

The head between the thighs nestled in the ninth line, especially designed to rhyme with "surprise," exemplifies Hacker's wit and impeccable sense of form. In Hacker's hands, this age-old form, a form that women have been using since its inception, makes way for lesbian lovemaking, twentieth-century style.

Ironically, what many critics refer to as her "graphic," "frank," or "honest" language, she refers to in an interview with Karla Hammond as "ordinary": "I like the tension in a poem that comes from the diction of ordinary speech playing against a form." Perhaps her lyrical strength and charm lie in her ability to assert the ordinariness of lesbian love language.

Marilyn Hacker was born 27 November 1942 to Jewish immigrants Albert Abraham Hacker and Hilda Rosengarten Hacker. She grew up in the Bronx and attained most of her formal education in New York, culminating in a bachelor of arts degree from New York University. Hacker tells Karla Hammond that her earliest education about women writers and feminism occurred through adolescent reading that she happened into on her own: "I've always been and continue to be a science fiction reader. When I was an adolescent, there wasn't very much science fiction by women. . . . Now, much of the most exciting new speculative fiction is being written by women. . . . Women writers are interested in writing about women enjoying all the human freedoms." Hacker's discovery of poetry also occurred quite early in her life: "When I was ten or eleven or twelve I thought of male poets as being 'poets' and thought, as one thought then, that it was the women poets who needed the qualifying adjective. . . . I wish now that I had been aware of the work of H.D. [Hilda Doolittle] when I was in my teens. Yet her work was largely out of print."

In an interview with Annie Finch in *American Poetry Review,* Hacker reveals that her earliest memories of writing have her writing in fixed forms: "I wrote little quatrains when I was five years old. I like to think that somebody read me Blake's *Songs of Innocence*—I didn't though come from a family where poetry of any kind was read out loud. . . . The first poem I can remember writing which was a bit more than doggerel was a sonnet."

Similar to many successful writers, Hacker discusses her education about poetry and writing as synonymous with reading from an early age. Along with her formal education, Hacker considers the reading of poetry as a great influence on the formation of herself as a writer. In her interview with Finch, she emphasizes this point when she discusses her methods of conducting poetry workshops: "When I teach writing, I'm always teaching reading as well. . . . Too many students enroll in writing courses in American universities as an alternative—not an enhancement—to taking literature courses. They want to write, but they've never read anything. That offends and perplexes me as an inveterate reader—but it's also a damned shame for them."

When asked by interviewer Karla Hammond to name the writers that she read and who she felt most influenced her, Hacker immediately named women writers: "Adrienne Rich is the one who first comes to mind. I've been reading her with great interest since about 1972. . . . Another writer with whom I've felt a strong affinity is Judy Grahn. I was lucky enough to know about her work since 1968 or 1969 when we were both in San Francisco. Audre Lorde is awfully good: both on the page and to hear aloud." Hacker reads mostly women poets, though she admits in her interview with Finch that there have been some touchy moments when she has felt at odds with the women writers she has most admired: "Adrienne Rich's love-hate relation with fixed forms touches me more directly. I'm a writer who's a woman, Jewish, lesbian, feminist, urban, as she is herself: there's no way I could not have felt implicated by her decision, in the early 1970s, not only to reject traditional prosody, but to state that she was doing so out of feminist convictions, out of her relationship, as a woman, with the language and the canon. But my own self-examination, as much visceral as rational, did not produce the same recoiling."

Although Hacker voices and acts on her commitments to women throughout her life, she never confuses this commitment with deference to their politics. She strives to establish and maintain her voice among the many women writers she cherishes, rather than to echo their concerns.

In 1961, Hacker married the African American novelist Samuel R. Delany. They had a child, Iva Alyxander Hacker-Delany, about whom Hacker writes continuously throughout their lives together. Hacker, a lesbian, and Delany, a gay man, were married for thirteen years. Since their divorce, Hacker has had love relationships with women. She writes about these relationships with a range of emotion throughout her poetry. She currently lives with her lover, Karyn London.

With the publication in 1974 of *Presentation Piece,* for which she won the Discovery/The Nation Award, the Lamont Poetry Book Award, and the National Book Award, Hacker achieved immediate acclaim and has remained a significant figure in poetry from that moment. She has authored eleven books: *The Terrible Children* (1967); *Highway Sand-wiches* (1970); *Presentation Piece* (1974); *Separations* (1976); *Taking Notice* (1980); *Assumptions* (1985); *Love, Death, and the Changing of Seasons* (1987); *Going Back to the River* (1990), which received a Lambda Literary Award; *The Hang-Glider's Daughter* (1990); *Winter Numbers* (1994), which received a Lambda Literary Award and the Academy of American Poets/The Nation Lenore Marshall Prize; and *Selected Poems 1965–1990* (1994), which received the 1996 Poets' Prize. Poetry is central to Hacker's life, as is commitment to women, she told Hammond: "Right now, primary commitment to women, on every possible level, is central to my life: politically, in my personal relation-ships, and with respect to what I'm attempting to do in my work and with other writers." From the moment she set out to write, Hacker has not swayed in her vision to be a superb writer of fixed form poetry and to write women's lives into these forms.

Marilyn Hacker lived in London and worked as a book dealer throughout the early seventies. In 1974, she became both mother to Iva and a National Book Award winner. *Presentation Piece* immediately established Marilyn Hacker as one of the most significant writers of the day. This book brings together the graphic images and forthright language about love that would become Hacker trademarks. As well, it attends to fixed forms and the gathering of intriguing, time-bound quotes that have resonance for all people of this generation. Lines such as "Take another little/piece of my heart now baby," from the title poem "Presentation Piece," resuscitate Janis Joplin's scratchy voice as if it were fraught with prophetic meaning. Joplin provides one of the multiple

- *Collection*

Establishes

Voice, Wins

National Book

Award

quotes residing in this poem that serves as part of a presentation piece for the times, a piece that tells us, "One of these messages may be for you."

Presentation Piece also includes feminist commentary. In the poem, the female persona gazes at the male's inadequacies in "She Bitches About Boys":

> Girls love a sick child or a healthy animal.
> A man who's both itches them like an incubus,
> but I, for one, have had a bellyful
> of giving reassurances and obvious
> advice with scrambled eggs and cereal

This gaze constitutes a flash of knowledge and resistance to come.

In "Sestina," Hacker displays the graphic language of sexuality that will become part and parcel of her expressive system of poetics throughout her career. Hacker portrays male genitalia: "Your cock whispers/ inside my thigh that there is language/without memory."

She includes in this book a number of fixed forms, including the sonnet sequence "A Christmas Crown." As well, she includes villanelles and sestinas. All of her skills are apparent and honestly delivered in this book. What comes thereafter is enhancement of these skills. Felicia Mitchell reminds us that "the images of the body, the harsh and honest sounds and words of common language, which are held by the form, and the sense of humor ensuring that disappointment never seems like despair constitute Hacker's mark." The book demanded attention for all the reasons that Hacker has proved worthwhile reading throughout her career.

Passionate •

Lesbian Sonnet

Sequence Finds

Audience

In the years following publication of *Presentation Piece,* Hacker has moved back and forth between the United States and Paris. She has held a variety of visiting creative-writing professorships; has edited a number of literary magazines, including the feminist literary magazine *13th Moon* (State Uiversity of New York, Albany) in the mid-1980s, an issue of *Ploughshares,* and a four-year stint as editor of the *Kenyon Review;* and has been a single mother.

Love, Death, and the Changing of the Seasons (1986) chronicles in sonnets the cycle of love between two lesbians. The cycle begins simply, with mere hugs: "Hug; hug; this time I brushed my lips/just across yours, and fire down below/in February flared," and ends one year— 212 pages—later: "I drank our one year out in brine instead/of honey from the seasons of your tongue." Throughout the sequence, Hacker captures emotions in the slowest, most minute details: mundane intimacies, out-of-control moments, heartwrenching rejections, warnings unheeded, ensuing neediness and suffocating clinginess, cooling off, loneliness, loss, absence, anger, and ultimate acceptance of a love ended. It reads like a narrative of people about whom you care deeply. She creates people with stunning emotional capacities, those that we see in ourselves, those from which we want to protect ourselves, and those we want to enjoy again. At times the reader wants to call out to the "I," "hold back," "be careful," and at other times, one wants to say: "call her," "take a risk." It is an incredibly interactive piece of writing, an engaging, humble, loving text, a text about human beings at their most vulnerable: Human beings in love.

Hacker's sense of love and poetic form is that it is fraught with humor. In the beginning of the relationship between Hacker and Rachel, she quips:

> I venture it's a trifle premature
> to sign the china-pattern registry
> before you are, at least, at liberty
> to hang your PJ's on my bathroom door.

In another sonnet, she depicts fantasizing about Rachel, her new lover, and masturbating on a friend's couch:

> Which didn't deter me then from lying down
> on Jackie's couch, for the first time in days,
> to let my hands and mind go back a ways,
> and forward, in, against, above, around,
> until I said your name (what corn) and came.
> (I didn't muck up the upholstery,
> Jax).

This humor is one that catches her laughing at herself and at the melodrama of sexual fantasy. Moaning Rachel's name and joking about the love stains on the furniture demonstrate Hacker's determination to bring the beauty of the sexual imagination to the fixed form and prescribed rhythms of the sonnet—what better form to contain the rhythms of love.

Hacker writes about her relationships with women, and she writes in fixed forms because it brings her pleasure. "I write the way I do," she told Finch, "because it's the way that gives me most pleasure, and which finds me my way into the poem."

Hacker told Hammond that "as a woman becomes more and more politicized, as a feminist, she realizes that her concerns are concrete, that while they apply to the world at large, her perceptions of them begin as perceptions of her own life. The political concerns express something that permeates her whole life, permeates *my* whole life." Hacker will continue to chronicle the process of women making changes and making connections in their own worlds and the world at large.

Sometimes women are unable to connect with one another. Hacker is especially compassionate about this inability, and she is not afraid to use her own experience as grounds for poetic musing: In the last poem included in *Selected Poems,* "August Silence," Hacker painfully and courageously resurrects the relationship she had with her dying mother-in-law, Iva's grandmother:

> Because you are
> my only daughter's only grandmother,
> because your only grandchild is my child
> I would have wished you to be reconciled
> to how and what
> I live. No name frames our connection, not
> "in-laws." I hoped, more than "your son's ex-
>   wife."
> I've known you now for two-thirds of my life.

Much of Hacker's life work has been to frame the nameless inside the names, to work on providing forms for the formless. She has already succeeded, and she has not yet run out of stamina for the future. Marilyn Hacker's importance to poetry is synonymous with her persistent contribution of her own life experiences to the feminist lesbian canon.

Selected Poems •

1965–1990: *A*

Lifetime of

Women

**Profile by
Renee R. Curry**

BARBARA J. HAMMER

*A*ppropriately termed "the mother of lesbian film" for her ground-

breaking experimental techniques and themes, Barbara Hammer is an

award-winning auteur/spokesperson for both lesbian and indepen-

dent, avant-garde film. She has made more than eighty films and videos

since 1968, consciously choosing to remain outside standard narrative

forms, opting instead for a more somatic, poetic, and often highly erotic

approach that involves the camera as "caresser." This prioritization of

her own aesthetics over traditional strictures has earned her films a

reputation for being sensual, intellectually stimulating, and always

challenging.

1939– •

American •

filmmaker

Born 15 May 1939 in Hollywood, California, Hammer traces her earliest artistic influences to her maternal grandmother, Anna Kusz. As Cathleen Rountree relates in her book *Coming Into Fullness: On Women Turning Forty,* Barbara learned from Anna early on "that art is anything you say it is, . . . the most important decision is to keep making it."

Barbara's mother, Marian Hammer, was likewise an early influence, albeit from the other end of the spectrum. Marian's immigrant, Ukrainian, working-class background fostered a desire to rise above her class, and Barbara's freckle-faced precociousness pointed toward a financial way upward following the twinkling, tapping lead of Shirley Temple. Lack of money for the right acting classes squelched the fantasy, but the seed of Barbara's love for the theater was planted. "It would be very curious for her [Marian] to see that I am involved in film," Hammer told Rountree in 1991, "but on the other side of the camera."

In 1961, Hammer received a bachelor's degree in psychology from the University of California, Los Angeles, married the day after graduation, and moved to San Francisco with her husband, where she enrolled in the master's program in English at San Francisco State University. A series of what she calls "social jobs" followed which, according to Raymond Murray's *Images in the Dark,* included "counseling for emotionally disturbed teenagers, playground supervision, and even a bank job."

It did not take long for Barbara to realize that a vital, yearning, creative part of her was being neglected. "I wanted to stay home and *make things,"* she told Rountree, "but I couldn't justify the self-indulgence." She was coming to terms with having overlooked that critically important period in a woman's life where "she can make her own way in the world, earn money, travel, have an experience as a solitary individual, rather than as a child of a family, or the wife of a husband." A brief attempt to try to get pregnant proved unsuccessful—which in the end, according to Hammer, was lucky "because what I really wanted was to be an artist."

Barbara Hammer did not come out as a lesbian or an artist until she was 30. Following a brief stint as a painter and a potter, she made her first Super-8mm short in 1968. The film, *Schizy,* deals with an individual's conflicting masculine/feminine feelings. Her first 16mm film *(A Gay Day)* playfully satirizes marriage by showing two women, both in bridal gowns, rolling down a hill together. Next came the groundbreaking *Dyketactics* (1974), a film encompassing how she feels her life changed since she began making love to women. It was hailed by many as the first truly erotic lesbian film to be made by a lesbian. *Superdyke* (1975) follows a gang of women in early guerilla-girl takeovers of San

Francisco institutions, while *Menses* (1974) and *Women I Love* (1976) work to reclaim a celebratory femininity that has been buried in a society dominated by men.

According to Holly Willis in *Film Quarterly* (1994), her work "is both stridently lesbian and boldly experimental . . . humorous stories which play with mythological images of women and critique the patriarchal world." At the same time, Hammer often forgoes formal filmmaking techniques with her disassembly of standard narrative, opting instead for animation, superimpositions, and optical printing techniques to appeal to a viewer's more experiential senses—like touch. "I began to connect touch and sight in my work in 1974" with *Dyketactics,* Hammer told Willis. "I think that my sight is connected to my sense of touch. . . . It was Aldous Huxley who pointed out that children know the world through touching before they can ever see. We are touching even when we are sleeping!"

The year 1993 marked the premiere of Hammer's fifty-first feature-length film, *Nitrate Kisses*. It was termed by some critics, including Canby and Ayscough, as a demanding, passionate, "heavy-hammering" documentary that examines the loss of queer history through the intercutting of newer and older experimental clips of lesbians and gay men—young and old—as they make love and talk of their experiences, both past and present. Most other reviews were less checkered, and *Nitrate Kisses* received acclaim at the Sundance Festival and won various awards at international festivals throughout 1993.

Hammer believes *Kisses* is her most intellectual film thus far. The experiential level of the camera caressing the couples throughout is still a major focus but, as Hammer told Willis, "I decided not to leave the research out of the film this time. I kept the quotes from the books that really influenced me . . . and shot them. Some people feel like it breaks, but again, that's what I want it to do—break the continuity that is part of commercial cinema."

In 1995, Hammer's Making Visible Productions released *Out in South Africa,* Hammer's pastiche of interviews with lesbians and gay men throughout that country over several weeks in 1994—in the townships, at her film workshops, and at a retrospective festival of her films. True to form, the film is neither a linear narrative nor a straight documentary, and was met with reviews that reflected Hammer's ongoing artistic motivation to keep viewers examining the efficacy of traditional filmmaking/storytelling structure. Terms like "disturbing and exhilarating," "fascinating and frustrating" were used to describe the work, but always with the stipulation that it was a "must-see." In a February 1995 review in the *Advocate,* Victoria A. Brownworth called

Out in South Africa "an uneven but intensely moving look at the personal and political struggles of an emerging lesbian and gay culture . . . [held together] by Hammer's keen eye for complementary visual imagery."

In the end, Barbara Hammer's ongoing success as a filmmaker and an artist centers on a dual desire: a striving to make her films accessible to an ever-widening audience, and to maintain a visionary edge. The autobiographical *Tender Fictions* (winter 1995) reaches for this goal by broadening the future landscape for lesbian autobiography even as it challenges a younger gay/lesbian generation to carve their own identities from the Americana mold.

Hammer continues to promote and document lesbian visibility/sensibility by inviting women around the world to share their dreams, fantasies, and aspirations via her Web Page on the Internet. "We don't want to always be looking at our own cultural product, we want to contribute to the general culture," Hammer told Owen Levy in *Moving Pictures Berlinale* in February 1996. "Our work shouldn't be closed off to the world at large and the world shouldn't close itself off."

**Profile by
Jerome Szymczak**

HARRY HAY

*H*arry Hay not only helped found gay liberation in the United States but also provided some of the most creative and influential ideas for lesbians and gay men. After a bohemian life in Hollywood and labor activism during the Depression, in 1950 Hay organized (with four others) the Mattachine Foundation that began the modern gay movement. In 1978 with a second wind he helped launch the Radical Faeries. Always struggling against conformities, Harry Hay continues developing further visions of sexual, social, and spiritual liberation.

1912– •

American •

activist

Born near Brighton Beach in Worthing, England, 7 April 1912, Henry "Little Harry" Hay Jr. early gloried in the delights of nature, particularly of the sea and the wild woods. In 1914 his mother Margaret Neall (born in Arizona Indian Territory) moved the family to join Henry Sr.—"Big Harry"—in the mountains of Chile at the Atacama Desert Copper Mine. In 1916 Big Harry suffered a disabling accident. The

family resettled in Orange County, California, and then in 1919 moved to Los Angeles.

Hay's mother, a magnificent female baritone, taught him to sing before he was a year old. As a three year old in the icy Andean night, he could hear Quechua villagers singing the traditional four-octave Inca Hymns to the Sun. Through a Woodcraft Ranger Boys' Group in Los Angeles, his love of music expanded to include Monteverdi, Handel, Wagner, Bruchner, and Mahler.

The Rangers developed Hay's interest in the mountainous West, a lifetime love affair. Learning horsemanship between ages eleven and thirteen, he had some preparation for work in the hayfields of western Nevada where his father sent him in the summer of 1925. An Indian teammate invited him to join his village Feast day where the Sacred Ghost-Dance Prophet Wovoka (1856–1932) appeared. Known to Anglos as "Jack Wilson," Wovoka's songs, dances, and sacred vestments had terrified the United States Army between 1885–1891. Hay's maternal uncle had fought against the Sioux and received a decoration for the slaughter committed at Wounded Knee in 1890 against followers of Wovoka. In 1925 Wovoka looked "into his heart" and blessed the grand-nephew as one "who will someday be a Friend."

In the fall of 1930, Hay entered Stanford University's experimental independent studies program, but he pursued lovers, poetry, and drama more than medicine, law, or engineering. Hay had several affairs at Stanford with fellow soloists in the Glee Club, a college actor, a swimming team diver, and filmmaker/poet classmate James Broughton. In the winter of 1932 a severe sinus infection forced him to leave school.

In the Hollywood of the 1930s he worked in many jobs: a "bit" part actor in B movies, in repertory stage companies, in portraying the first "Gay" part in professional theater (May 1935), and ghostwriting the 1943 Academy Award winning *Heavenly Music*. His sometime lover Will Geer found him "very believable" as an actor. Some years after Geer's death in 1974, Hay said to his widow, "I had him first," to which she replied, "I had him longest."

Hay first learned about radical politics from the Wobbly (IWW) migratory workers during the Nevada summers of 1925 to 1932. Geer encouraged Hay's political bent, which developed into a lifelong struggle against oppression. The Communist Party USA taught Hay every possible organizing technique. In the 1930s they represented a vital progressive force, promoting popular art, literature, music, and theater. Hay married another Party member for whom he felt and would always feel immense affection.

The party offered two essential skills for oppressed groups: organization and theory. In 1941 Hay worked with the New Theater League in New York, which carried Stanislavsky's theater technique to Trade Union requirements. At the Southern California Labor School and at the People's Educational Center in Hollywood, he taught the legendary course "The Historical Development of Folk Music." Folk music provided a vital link between the radicalism of the 1930s and later years. Both guests in the Hay household, Woody Guthrie in the 1930s and Pete Seeger in the 1950s inspired Joan Baez, Judy Collins, Bob Dylan, and a host of others.

• Founding the Mattachine Society

Researching medieval music, Hay found references to confraternities of peasant monks who performed forbidden fertility songs and dances in the Vernal Equinox Festival Dance (now called April Fools Day). "Mattachine" was the name of one of the performing confraternities. "The Mattachine troupes conveyed vital information to the oppressed in the countryside of 13th–15th century France, and perhaps," Hay recalled, "I hoped that such a society of modern homosexual men, living in disguise in 20th century America, could do similarly for us oppressed Queers."

Lovers and acquaintances had brought stories of Magnus Hirschfeld's group in Berlin and of Henry Gerber's corporation in Chicago, but the former had been destroyed by the Nazis and the latter by the Chicago police. On 10 August 1948, Hay interested others in presenting an anti-entrapment plank for Henry Wallace's Progressive Party platform. Nothing came of that proposal, but the "Bachelors for Wallace" provided a basis for further organization. On 11 November 1950, a group gathered to discuss Hay's call to form discussion groups on Alfred Kinsey's *Sexual Behavior of the Human Male* (1948). The five founders included Hay and his then lover Rudi Gernreich, Dale Jennings, Bob Hull, and Chuck Rowland. From the *Kinsey Report* (1948), Hay had extrapolated that ten percent of the population was gay and from that he had argued that gays formed a cultural minority since there was a common language, "a psychological make-up in common, and in the cruise-necessities of the double entendres of CAMP . . . a common culture." Most lesbian and gay organizations and culture even now continue to work through these ideas.

In February 1952, the Los Angeles police accosted Dale Jennings, arrested him, and charged him with "lewd and dissolute behavior." A defense committee quickly organized, and in June the court dismissed all charges against Jennings after the jury deadlocked (eleven believed Jennings; one supported the policeman). In effect, the community had won the first U.S. court victory. In a single year the Mattachine grew from a few hundred to a few thousand members. Feeling the new awakening, the Los Angeles Mattachine Society Steering Committee sent a letter to city council candidates asking their views on the rights of homophiles.

The authorities struck back quickly. As part of the red-baiting of the times, a Los Angeles columnist charged that Mattachine represented a threat to the city: "a well-trained subversive could move in and forge [sexual deviates] into a dangerous political weapon." Another newspaper fingered Harry Hay as a Marxist. Groups within Mattachine, meanwhile, organized to normalize the group. They attacked both the idea of a gay culture and any agitation. Hoping to paint themselves as acceptable, they praised all institutions of "home, church, and state." They threatened to turn anyone in to the F.B.I. who opposed such institutions. In 1955 the House Un-American Activities Committee visited Los Angeles and called Harry Hay to testify. While his testimony seems to have successfully befuddled the committee, he remained largely excluded from gay groups until the end of the 1950s.

Between July 1952 and May 1962, Hay lived with a beautiful young Danish hatmaker. He plunged himself into a multi-level historical materialist research into the roots of what is now called "gay consciousness." ONE Institute (an independent offshoot of Mattachine) published his "The Moral Climate of Canaan in the Time of Judges" in the premier issue of *ONE Institute Quarterly of Homophile Studies* (1958), the first scholarly lesbian/gay publication in the United States. Hay explored the mother goddess traditions of the Canaanites as an early expression of gay sensibility.

In 1963 Hay lived for four months with Jim Kepner, another of the great pioneers in the Los Angeles gay liberation struggle. In October 1963 he met John Burnside, who had invented the teleidoscope, a wonderful instrument that made it possible for the viewer to perceive the world kaleidoscopically. Together Burnside and Hay developed a projector, called a symmetricon, which—using color-slides as well as bits of Venetian glass—could project "healing patterns" into an infinity of delight.

In 1965 they formed the Circle of Loving Companions in Los Angeles to provide at all lesbian and gay meetings an "open mike" for dissenters. Early in the Vietnam War, Hay and Don Slater in Los Angeles and others in San Francisco set up networks of gay draft resistance. In 1966 Hay and Burnside helped establish the North American Committee of Homophile Organizations (NACHO). Meeting in San Francisco in May 1966, the western branch inaugurated the first zap of the American Psychiatric Association.

In May 1970 Hay and Burnside moved their teleidoscope factory to New Mexico. They brought a small industry to the Tewa Indian Pueblo of Oke Owinge (known as San Juan Pueblo) and promoted gay liberation to both the Chicano and Tewa pueblos. Hay found gay life in Santa Fe and Albuquerque very conservative. The Circle of Loving Companions set about grass-roots organizing and began self-examination workshops in the gay and lesbian group at the University of New Mexico. Together with Katherine Davenport, they got the Lambdas de Santa Fe organized in 1977, hosted the first openly Lesbian-Gay dance in Santa Fe, and won first prize for the handsomest booth at the Santa Fe Fiesta. In 1976, the crew for the documentary *Word Is Out* (1978) caught the couple picking rosehips on the banks of the Rio Grande. In a 1989 "Valentine for Harry" Burnside wrote, "Hand in hand we walk, as wing tip to wing tip our spirits roam the universe, finding lovers everywhere. Sex is music. Time is not real. All things are imbued with spirit."

Having retired from the city, the two settled in the desert. Jonathan Katz published a long interview with Hay in *Gay American History* (1976) and John D'Emilio featured him in *Sexual Politics, Sexual Communities* (1983). Hay in the meantime remained active with groups such as the Committee for Traditional Indian Land and Life and worked with Rarihokwats of the Mohawk Nation *Akwesasne Notes*. Hay helped organize the Nation-Wide Friends of the Rio Grand, which successfully stopped developers from diverting water from agriculture.

In New Mexico, Hay pursued his lifelong study of Native American life. His researches into the berdache (man/woman or more properly "two spirit") tradition have inspired and paralleled the works of Sue Ellen Jacobs, Judy Grahn, Arthur Evans, Mitch Walker, Walter Williams, Starhawk, Will Roscoe, and many others.

• **Radical Faeries**

In the fall of 1978, Don Kilhefner and Harry Hay invited Mitch Walker to join them in hosting a workshop around these new sensibilities at the UCLA meeting of the Gay Academic Union. The workshop led to further organization. Harry Hay and John Burnside moved to Los Angeles the following July where, with Kilhefner, they issued "A Call to Gay Brothers" for "A Spiritual Conference for Radical Faeries." Over two hundred faeries answered the call Labor Day weekend, 1979, at a desert sanctuary near Tucson, Arizona. They explored "breakthroughs in gay consciousness," shared gay visions, and awakened "the spiritual dimensions of their lovely sexual gayness."

That gathering and subsequent ones, on both local and national levels, mushroomed much as the early Mattachine Society had. A wide network of rural communes already existed; *RFD, a Male Journal for Gay Brothers,* begun in 1974, already provided communication among groups and individuals. In the summer 1975 issue of *RFD*, Burnside and Hay contributed an essay on the emerging Faerie sensibility. The relationships among individuals and groups remained flexible and occasionally contentious. Nonetheless, together they sought to reassert a gay liberation overwhelmed by academics, politicians, business groups, and others who sought to confine the movement to no more than a behavioral variation. In July 1995 the first Euro-faerie gathering convened, involving Faeries from eight countries.

Some of Hay's original ideas have now become so accepted within the lesbian and gay movement that they now seem commonplace, such as the idea of gays as a cultural minority and the importance of organizing as a minority and fighting back with education, protest, litigation, and other strategies. Even activists who denounce what they call "essentialist" theory continue to attend conferences, offer courses, write books, and develop lesbian/gay/bisexual study programs—all within the parameters set out by the early Mattachine Society.

Other of his ideas await further development—for instance, what he calls "the right to appreciation." Every lesbian or gay man feels a constant erasure of their lives by family, fellow workers, and society in general. That erasure is really a form of extermination. Hay has always argued that gays share a different consciousness, a consciousness that offers additional gifts to the rest of society, who do not share these gifts. Using a "gay window" that is both developed and inherited, queers can illuminate the whole society.

Hay has stressed the peculiar subject-subject nature of gay male relationships. For him homosexual love does not serve some exterior purpose as marriage, family, property, or reproduction. Instead, beyond the exuberances of the pleasure principle, we find a possibility of a new "love for fellows equally dedicated and devoted" to each other that carries with it a special consciousness "of transcendent sexual wholeness."

Because of weakly developed gay groups in France, many French theorists—Foucault, Derrida, Deluze, Cioux—have had some envy of the United States' capacity to materialize ideas into organizations. As early as 1835, de Tocqueville in *Democracy in America* commented on the American tendency to create associations. Some organizations have remained quite parochial without much thought behind them, but none of them has been without effect. Many groups, in particular groups in which Hay participated, have provided rich stores of ideas: the early Mattachine, the Gay Liberation Fronts, and the Radical Faeries. They have preserved and developed a different consciousness that can be a common heritage for all.

Harry Hay has never rested on his many past triumphs or long mourned his losses. For the twenty-fifth anniversary of Stonewall in New York City in 1995, he was one of the organizers for the Spirit of Stonewall (SOS) counter-parade. At the Stonewall Inn, he joined representatives of drag queens, hustlers, sexologists, AIDS activists, boy lovers, and other liberationists to rally another parade in which the whole community could march. Arm and arm with Jim Kepner and John Burnside, Hay led off the demonstrators (estimated by the press as 70,000, in comparison to 700,000 at the official parade). With Hay, the Radical Faeries, Nambla, Act Up, the American Civil Liberties Union, and a vast assemblage of demonstrators marched from the original Stonewall site to Central Park. When he organized Mattachine in 1950 Hay was two decades before Stonewall. In 1995, he remained out of step—decades if not centuries ahead of the mainstream.

Profile by
Charley Shively

ESSEX HEMPHILL

c. 1956–1995 •

African American •

writer

W hen Essex Hemphill began his writing career, there was little if any voice credited to the gay community. Through his poetry and the compilation of various anthologies, Hemphill was instrumental in bringing such issues as gay identity and community to the attention of mainstream society. Hemphill, however, was not content with merely establishing a gay voice in his writing; he also sought to promote an African American voice as well.

Essex Hemphill was born in Chicago but grew up in Washington, D.C. The second of five children born to what he has called "very strong parents," Hemphill was very close to his mother. As he grew up, he found the racism around him to be all too apparent. As an adolescent, Hemphill became equally aware of his homosexuality and of the oppression of homophobia:

> My sexual curiosity would have blossomed in any context, but in Southeast Washington ... I had to carefully allow my petals to unfold. If I had revealed

them too soon they would have been snatched away, brutalized, and scattered down alleys. I was already alert enough to know what happened to the flamboyant boys at school who were called "sissies" and "faggots."

While still in his twenties, Hemphill began exploring his identity. He was impressed by the black nationalist movement that was popular in the 1960s and 1970s, but as Hemphill got older, he found that the doctrine of that movement "proved too narrow a politic" for his interests. The politics of the gay and lesbian movement also proved too narrow for Hemphill, who sought a comfortable space for his blackness and for his gayness.

Hemphill's search for a voice for the black gay male was made increasingly difficult by the effects slavery had had on the culture of America. According to Michael Broder in his essay on Hemphill in *Black Writers,* "Slavery and racism often encouraged white men to bolster their own sense of masculinity by asserting their dominance over black men. In response to this violent and abusive history, the black community placed a high premium on strong male images." Consequently, Hemphill understood that homosexuality, particularly effeminacy, was definitely taboo. Finding it difficult to be gay within the black community, and as equally difficult to be black within the racist gay community, Hemphill found the challenge to forge his own identity compounded and his efforts to do so frustrated.

For Hemphill, the theme of "being a minority within a minority" was a recurring one. That much is clear not only from his own work, but from the selections he includes in works like *Brother to Brother,* the controversial anthology of black gay poets he agreed to complete when its editor, his dear friend Joseph Beam, died in 1988. The anthology succeeded in giving black homosexual writers a literary identity. Not only did Hemphill support a distinct black voice, he also believed there was a need for a black gay sensibility. "There is a sensibility," he maintained in a 1988 *Village Voice* interview, "that heightens the flamboyance and drama of language, dance, and music."

In a continuing effort to identify a distinct black gay voice and a gay sensibility, Hemphill has noted the particular gifts or blessings of individuals. "Take care of your blessings," he said in a 1990 interview. "Some of us bake wonderfully, write, paint, do any number of things, have facilities with numbers that others don't have. Those," he explains, "are your blessings. . . . Just be aware of what your particular things are and nurture them and use them toward a positive way of living. Take care of your blessings."

The poet, who took very good care of his own blessings, in 1985 published two chapbooks, entitled *Earth Life* and *Conditions*. Selections from these and more recent works are included in later anthologies. Hemphill's poetry has also been included in a number of anthologies, and a selection of his own poetry is included in *Brother to Brother*. The exploration of being a black gay man was continued in *Ceremonies,* an anthology of Hemphill's own writings, published in 1992. In a *Village Voice Literary Supplement* review of the book, David Trinidad asserted that Hemphill "has forged—with few role models to emulate, and with little or no support from the white gay literary establishment—an identity and a style."

In addition, Hemphill wrote and performed his own monologues—gathered in the collection *So Many Dreams*—and then co-founded the *Nethula Journal of Contemporary Literature*. Hemphill, who also contributed to Isaac Julien's film *Looking for Langston Hughes* and Marlon Riggs's *Tongues Untied,* was, according to Broder, "a key figure in the emergence of a distinctive African American perspective in the overall field of gay literature." He became extremely vocal about AIDS in his speaking and in his writing. He even voiced skepticism about the "natural" origins of the virus that has successfully left its mark on two minorities of which Hemphill, as a black gay man, was a member.

Hemphill died on 5 November 1995, from AIDS-related complications. He was very much aware that he had no closet to go back to, and he was unable to understand how, once out, anyone could try to go back. In his own writing, Hemphill tried to "be very real" with himself when "alone with that paper."

DAVID HOCKNEY

David Hockney is one of the best-known and most popular living

artists in the world today. He has worked in a variety of traditional

media—painting, sketching, and etching—and has been quick to take

up new technological methods—the Polaroid camera, the color photo-

copier, the digital paintbox, the fax. His set designs for opera are widely

celebrated. Hockney combines great ability as a draftsman and colorist

with an endless pictorial curiosity and inventiveness. A vigorous de-

fender of the human element in art, he is also aware of the challenges

and opportunities created by modernism. From his student days in

London, he has incorporated gay images and concerns into his work,

and has proved himself to be a staunch supporter of gay rights and an

1937– •

British artist and •

stage designer

implacable opponent of censorship.

David Hockney, the fourth of five children, was born in the northern city of Bradford, England, on 9 July 1937. His father, Kenneth, who worked as an accountant's clerk, was a man of independent mind, a pacifist, and himself an amateur artist, whose painting of Laurel and Hardy always hangs on his son's studio wall; his mother, Laura, was a strict Methodist, a teetotaller, nonsmoker, and vegetarian. Hockney won a scholarship to Bradford City Grammar School and in 1953 entered Bradford School of Art. He first sold a painting, *Portrait of My Father,* for £10 in 1955. At art school, his sexual preference was not evident; he had become conscious of his orientation in his mid-teens, but in 1950s Britain, homosexual acts were still illegal and bore a strong social stigma.

From 1957 to 1959, Hockney, exempted from military service as a conscientious objector, worked in hospitals in Bradford and Hastings, and did little painting. In September of 1959 he became a postgraduate student at London's Royal College of Art. There, he began to tackle gay themes in his painting and to acknowledge his sexual preference more openly. The painting *Erection* (1959–60) was the first sign of his new openness, and he carried it further in *Doll Boy* (1960), the title of which referred to a recent record by the pop singer Cliff Richard, on whom Hockney had a crush. In his first autobiographical volume, *David Hockney by David Hockney* (1976), he says that some of his pictures at this time "were partly propaganda of something I felt hadn't been propagandized, especially among students, as a subject: homosexuality."

Hockney was impressed by the power of the male nudes in a London exhibition of Francis Bacon's paintings in the spring of 1960. In his second year at the Royal College of Art, he made friends with Mark Berger, an American fellow student. Berger introduced him to gay places and people, and they discussed the poetry of Whitman and Cavafy. Hockney had read Whitman's complete poems in the summer of 1960, and Whitman's words started to figure significantly in his painting. *Adhesiveness* (1960) takes its title from Whitman's term for friendship between two men, while Whitman's *Leaves of Grass* provides the title and some lines, which are incorporated into the actual painting, of *We Two Boys Together Clinging* (1961). This title is also, however, a joking reference to a newspaper headline about a climbing accident that could be taken to refer to a homoerotic idyll with Cliff Richard: "TWO BOYS CLING TO CLIFF ALL NIGHT LONG."

In 1961 Hockney made his first visit to the United States, to New York City, where he dyed his hair blond, thus creating a key feature of what was soon to be his public image as a star of "Swinging London." On his return from New York, he painted a large picture called *A Grand*

First Exhibition •

Sells Out

Procession of Dignitaries in the Semi-Egyptian Style, inspired by Cavafy's poem "Waiting for the Barbarians." The sight of a friend juxtaposed with an Egyptian statue in an East Berlin museum sparked off a further important painting of this period—*The First Marriage* (1962). As well as painting, Hockney also produced, between 1961 and 1963, his first major series of etchings: *A Rake's Progress,* a witty and stylish modern version of William Hogarth's pictorial warnings of the dangers of loose living. In September of 1963 he accepted a *Sunday Times* invitation to travel to Egypt to make drawings for its color supplement, although these were not published as the Kennedy assassination took precedence. His most notable triumph in 1963 was his first solo exhibition at the London gallery of his dealer John Kasmin: all his paintings were sold.

Hockney was starting to dream of California. Early in 1963, he painted *Domestic Scene, Los Angeles,* working from his imagination and from photographs in the magazine *Physique Pictorial.* John Rechy's novel of Californian gay life, *City of Night* (1963), excited him. In December of 1963 he went to New York again, where he met artist Andy Warhol and Henry Geldzahler, a curator of twentieth-century art at the Metropolitan Museum, who was to become a friend and a subject of several paintings and drawings. He flew to California in January of 1964. In his book *David Hockney* (1987), Marco Livingstone quotes a *Listener* interview of 22 May 1975 in which Hockney recalls that in his first week on the West Coast, the sight of a freeway ramp rising into the air made him think: "My God, this place needs its Piranesi; Los Angeles could have a Piranesi, so here I am!"

Hockney rented a studio in Santa Monica and started to use acrylic paint. He taught at the University of Iowa in the summer and traveled extensively in the United States, through New Mexico, Oklahoma, and Kansas to Chicago, and by the Grand Canyon to New Orleans and then to New York. There his first one-man American exhibition was held, and, like his London exhibition the year before, it was a success. In December he returned to London but was back in the United States the following year, teaching at the University of Colorado in the summer, visiting Los Angeles and New York again, and producing the set of six lithographs called *A Hollywood Collection.* He returned to London in October for a further one-man exhibition at the Kasmin Gallery. By now, he had made a reputation in both Britain and the United States as a talented young artist and as an embodiment of what was seen as the vibrant, hedonistic "Swinging London" of the 1960s.

In January of 1966, Hockney traveled to Beirut and produced drawings for what became his *Illustrations for Fourteen Poems from C.*

P. Cavafy, his first major series of etchings since *A Rake's Progress.* He then accepted a commission from London's Royal Court Theatre to design a production of Alfred Jarry's absurdist play *Ubu Roi.* After finishing these, he returned to California to teach painting for six weeks at the summer school of the University of California, Los Angeles. To Hockney's disappointment, his students were mainly housewives; there was, however, one deeply attractive young man, Peter Schlesinger. Hockney and Schlesinger became partners for six years, living together in both California and London. Schlesinger started to figure prominently in Hockney's work, for example in the paintings *Peter Getting Out of Nick's Pool* (1966) and *The Room, Tarzana* (1967). But Hockney's most memorable painting of this period was one in which the human figure was only implied: the quintessential Californian painting *A Bigger Splash* (1967) captures the immediate aftermath of a dive into a swimming pool in such a way as to transform an instant of hectic activity into an image of hypnotic stillness.

Hockney's interest in photography increased from 1967; he started to mount his photographs in large albums, and he bought a 35mm Pentax camera. The following year, making some use of photographs, he painted *American Collectors: Fred and Marcia Wiseman,* the first of a number of double portraits that formed a significant strand of his work: these included *Henry Geldzahler and Christopher Scott,* and *Christopher Isherwood and Don Bachardy,* both in 1968, and, in 1971, *Mr and Mrs Clark and Percy,* which became the most popular picture at London's Tate Gallery.

Photography, •

Portraiture,

and Opera

In 1970, at the age of thirty-two, Hockney enjoyed the accolade of a large retrospective exhibition, first at London's Whitechapel Gallery and subsequently in Hanover, Rotterdam, and Belgrade. But his personal life was unhappy during this period. His relationship with Peter Schlesinger broke up in 1971, plunging him into deep depression. In 1972, he put in six months' work on another double portrait, that of the ballet dancer Wayne Sleep and his partner George Scott, but he was dissatisfied with it and would finally abandon it. The year 1972 also saw, however, an increase in his activity as a photographer. In preparation for the painting *Portrait of an Artist (Pool with Two Figures)* (1972), he took about 200 photographs, using a new Pentax camera with automatic exposure.

When Pablo Picasso died in 1973, a Berlin publisher commissioned a number of artists, including Hockney, to produce a print for a portfolio called *Homage to Picasso.* Hockney went to Paris to work on this etching with the master printer Aldo Crommelynck, who had been Picasso's close associate for twenty years. Crommelynck introduced Hockney to sugar lift and color etching techniques, and Hockney, characteristically, became fascinated with this new medium. Another new field opened up to him in 1974, when he was asked to design the sets for a production of Stravinsky's *The Rake's Progress* at Glyndebourne, the rural opera house in the English county of Sussex. Hockney had loved opera since his father had taken him to see Puccini's *La Bohème* in Bradford when he was about ten, and the design of operatic sets became a major aspect of his work. The year 1974 also saw the release of Jack Hazan's film *A Bigger Splash* and the start of Hockney's relationship with Gregory Evans.

• *Fighting for*

Figurative Art

In 1976, Hockney, at Henry Geldzahler's suggestion, read Wallace Stevens's long poem "The Man with the Blue Guitar," a meditation on the transformative power of art that alludes to Picasso's Blue Period painting *The Old Guitarist* (1903). The poem fascinated him, and he produced first a set of drawings, and then a series of colored etchings using the technique that Crommelynck had developed for Picasso. These were published in the spring of 1977. By then, Hockney was embroiled in controversy about the relative merits of abstract and figurative art. The January/February issue of the London magazine *The New Review* carried on its front cover a photograph of Hockney and his friend and fellow artist R. B. Kitaj in the nude. In a conversation published inside the magazine, they affirmed the importance of figurative art and attacked what they saw as the sterility of abstraction. Hockney enjoyed pointing out later that the outraged reactions to the cover photograph proved the point about the importance of the human image.

Hockney started work in New York in mid-1977 on designing *The Magic Flute* for Glyndebourne, and worked extensively in gouache for the first time. In the same year, he also painted the restrained and moving double portrait *My Parents; Model with Unfinished Self-Portrait,* which shows Hockney himself drawing and Gregory Evans curled up asleep; and *Looking at Pictures on a Screen,* in which Henry Geldzahler is looking at paintings by Vermeer, Piero della Francesca, Van Gogh, and Degas. The following year he completed, in six weeks, twenty-nine pressed color paper pulp pictures called *Paper Pools,* which explore his fascination with water and light.

On 4 March 1979, the British Sunday newspaper *The Observer* carried an interview with Hockney headed "No Joy at the Tate," which attacked the acquisitions policy of Norman Reid, then the director of London's Tate Gallery, for its emphasis on abstract art at the expense of modern figurative work. A major controversy ensued. Meanwhile, Hockney went on with his work in theater design, producing, early in 1980, set and costume designs for a triple bill of Satie, Poulenc, and

Ravel, which was staged the following year at the Metropolitan Opera in New York. In his painting, he was now concerned to escape from what he saw as the trap of naturalism and to explore further the possibilities opened up by cubism. Over three weeks in November of 1980, he painted *Mulholland Drive,* which offers a montage of multiple views of the road that led down into Los Angeles from his Californian home.

For two years from 1982, photography became Hockney's chief preoccupation. He produced over 140 montages of Polaroid pictures, a selection of which was exhibited in Paris, and many "photo-joins," collages of 35mm prints intended to create multi-perspective images. Meanwhile, his work in theater design was the subject of an exhibition called *Hockney Paints the Stage,* shown in a range of venues in the United States, and in Mexico and London. He started painting again in 1984; he also began to produce lithographs in 1984 and 1985, some of them in large formats, and these were exhibited at Kasmin's gallery in London in 1985. The December 1985 issue of *Vogue* magazine featured forty-one pages of Hockney's photographs and drawings.

From Photo- •

Joins to Very

New Paintings

In 1986 his interest in the artistic potential of the color photocopier resulted in the *Home Made Prints.* In his stage work, he took on the task of designing the sets for the Los Angeles Music Center Opera's production of Wagner's *Tristan und Isolde,* and in 1987 he also designed the Waltz Pavilion for Andre Heller's Luna-Luna Park in Hamburg. The year 1988 saw a major Hockney retrospective, first at the Los Angeles County Museum of Art, and then at New York's Metropolitan Museum and London's Tate Gallery. He bought a house next to the sea at Malibu, where he set up a studio, producing a set of small portraits and, in October, his first fax-machine works. These works were shown in 1989 at the Sao Paulo Biennale and a range of other venues. Toward the end of the year, he produced his first computer drawings.

In the 1990s, Hockney's energies show no sign of flagging. He has designed sets for Puccini's *Turandot* for the San Francisco Opera and Chicago Lyric Opera, and for Strauss's *Die Frau ohne Schatten* at London's Royal Opera House; he has drawn portraits and collages, and has done further work in gouache; he has made drawings on his Macintosh PC, such as *Beach House Inside* (1991); and, above all, he has painted the series of abstract *Very New* (or *V. N.*) Paintings (1992–93), which are remarkable for their exuberance of color and their energy and grace of form. Most recently, he has exhibited inkjet prints of photographs exploring the relationship between photography, painting, and reality. In the London *Times* of 3 June 1996, he says that inkjet technology produces "the most beautiful printing of photography I have ever seen." Hockney is still a very active artist, and it is impossible, as yet, to attempt a conclusive assessment of his achievement. The chief criticism of his work has been that it fails to grapple with the darker side of life, and it is true that suffering—the anguish of AIDS, for example—finds no echo in his art. But he has amply demonstrated his capacity to provide rich and stimulating feasts of visual pleasure.

Profile by
Nicolas Tredell

HOLLY HUGHES

1955– •

American play- •

wright and per-

formance artist

*I*n the introduction to her collection of plays and performances, Clit

Notes: A Sapphic Sampler, *Holly Hughes encourages her audience to*

resist what she describes as "the epidemic of easy answers." She writes

that "the truth is fine for some people, but a lot of us need more. We need

a story." The complex, controversial, and necessary stories that Hughes

performs are rooted in questions without easy answers—questions like:

What does it mean to speak of lesbian sexual desire? What language(s)

can you use—create, borrow, or steal? What iconography? How does

your family of origin influence/ disrupt/ resist/ encourage those desires?

What kind of theater can accommodate them? How will public perform-

ance of such questions affect your reception and funding? This last

question was met with some frightening answers in 1990, when the National Endowment of the Arts (NEA) canceled the grants awarded four controversial artists, including Hughes. Though the "NEA Four" sued the endowment and the denied grants were reinstated in 1993, the ugly, resonating "easy answer" was that some stories—especially the "obscene" stories of homosexual desire—were too threatening to be shared.

Born 10 March 1955 in the navy bean capital of the world—Saginaw, Michigan—Holly Hughes grew up in a Republican upper-middle class family. Her mother was unhappy. Her father was often absent. She and her younger sister were raised with traditional values, but that did not mean she was doomed to lead a "normal life," meaning a life like her parents'. Perhaps without even meaning to, her parents encouraged the life of an escape artist. "It was my parents who taught me how to imagine a life different from theirs," says Hughes. "They gave me stories." As a child, Hughes imagined alternate stories, ones that "opened places for [her] to disappear, where no one could follow." The ability to create such places was a skill that she would use later, in her writing and performance, with a more extroverted purpose. Hughes attended Kalamazoo College, graduating in 1977. Soon after, she moved to New York City to take classes at the New York Feminist Art Institute. But her aspirations of becoming a painter were frustrated after the first few months of exposure to the overabundance of disappointing minimalist art in SoHo. Between shifts as a waitress, she searched for other outlets for her creativity. Such wanderings eventually led her to the East Village's WOW (Women's One World) Cafe, a collective perform-ance space run by a group of women who were, as Hughes puts it, primarily "refugees from lesbian feminism who had gone AWOL from other collectives." A butch/femme dynamic was at home with them. Sex was not enemy territory. Hughes' curiosity about the women and events at WOW seduced her into volunteering at the cafe. That was the beginning.

In the encouraging environment of WOW, Hughes began making theater in 1983. As she writes in *Clit Notes*, "The kind of theater I make is generally and often pejoratively called performance art." Further, as she explained to Joe Brown and Kara Swisher of the *Washington Post* in 1995, "The term 'performance artist' exists primarily because main-stream theater is so conservative and married to naturalism and so uncomfortable with autobiography that they had to create this whole other category." Whatever the name for the kind of theater that she was creating, Hughes began using it as a vehicle to explore and articulate her desire for women. The audience at WOW was listening and watching. Her first evening of performance there, called *Shrimp in a Basket*, contained the first part of what was to become her first major play, *The Well of Horniness.*

Filled with illusive, campy, dyke sexiness, Hughes' first play used some of the same parodic strategies that were a feature of WOW productions. Mining the imagery of pulp novels, soap opera TV culture, and the butch-femme dynamics of lesbian subculture, *The Well of Horniness* introduces Garnet McClit, lady dick, a stock figure for Hughes of the tough, girl-clue-watching detective. Late in the play, Hughes offers this useful stage direction, which seems to speak as a prime directive for the production: "Feel free to go too far; it's the only way to go in this play." The play was performed several times in the East Village and in several different forms, including a production as a radio-show for WBAI in New York City. Hughes was on her way.

The Lady Dick (1985) reintroduces the she-dick Garnet McClit. In the headnote accompanying the piece in *Clit Notes,* Hughes offers a tribute to the pulp murder mystery novels that her mother used to read and that she also picked up—the stuff she found sexy, even though she was not supposed to. In *The Lady Dick* Hughes transforms the iconography of such novels and their attendant mystery into a different sort of mystery, one that can puzzle over questions of identification such as "I still don't get how you can be a dick and a lady at the same time," while challenging assumptions about what it means to be either.

• **Hughes Takes**

Dress Suits *on*

the Road

Dress Suits to Hire, which Hughes wrote for Lois Weaver and Peggy Shaw of The Split Britches theater troupe, marked a turning point for her because it was written with the intention of being performed outside WOW, at the East Village's Performance Space 122—not primarily a lesbian space. After opening at P.S. 122 in May 1987, the play moved to midtown Manhattan's Women's Interart Center and then on tour to Milwaukee, Wisconsin, and to the University of Michigan. Several theater critics and scholars have addressed the complications and concerns of performing "lesbian theater" in a larger venue, questioning whether a more conventional theater setting and a heterosexual appropriation undermines its subversive methods and content. But Hughes, in a spring 1989 interview with Rebecca Schneider of the *Drama Review,* insists that it is important to put the work out there in a larger context, even if that move can be scary. As for the issue of "heterosexual appropriation," Hughes resists the idea of some particular correct (lesbian) reading. She says, "People will approach my work in different ways. . . . People have thought all sorts of things. And those things could be there! I really believe in art and I believe in allowing the audience to have their own personal subjective view."

In addition to stirring up scholarly conflict on the state(s) of lesbian theater, *Dress Suits* also earned Hughes authorship of her own genre, "Dyke Noir." In a review for the *Village Voice,* C. Carr uses this term to describe the world of Hughes' play—the tough talkers and "the shady, shifty operators" from hard-boiled fiction as well as the kind of gallows humor her work employs. *Dress Suits to Hire* begins with Deeluxe's strangling by her own right hand, which is inhabited by Little Peter. So there is a dead body and a mystery from the first scene. As the character Michigan questions and answers the authorities via a disconnected plastic phone, ". . . did I discover it? Many years ago. I first discovered the body in the Hotel Universal in Salamanca." Has there been a crime? And, if so, who has committed it? As Carr puts it in her review, "the *characters* are the crime—women who drive each other to emotional extremes, who put their sexuality upfront where everyone has to acknowledge it." These are the kinds of crimes and mysteries and dicey territories that Hughes relishes exploring in her work.

After the success of *Dress Suits,* Hughes continued to write and perform and to garner attention. In 1988 at P.S. 122 she introduced a version of her next major work, *World Without End,* which is in the form of a monologue. In it Hughes speaks from the point of view of the daughter who, after her mother's death, interrogates her own sexuality and the complex legacy of her mother. Hughes' own mother had died in 1987. The daughter asks those burning questions that remain after the body is gone, and in asking, tells a powerful story of origins.

In the late 1980s, public funding of art became a battleground of ideologies. Work that addressed the body was especially vulnerable to attacks, particularly if that body was queer. Artists such as Hughes, who had received NEA funding for "out" work performed in spaces that were publicly funded, began to expect trouble in 1989 when Congress passed a restrictive language code that equated homosexuality with obscenity. Work that was deemed "obscene" would not receive public funding. In 1990 John Frohnmayer, then chairperson of the NEA, vetoed funding for Hughes and three other performance artists, Tim Miller, Karen Finley, and John Fleck. The NEA Four, as they were called, were attacked in Congress by Jesse Helms and other conservatives, and in the press, often by people who had never even seen their work. Hughes and the other artists became symbols of the "art wars."

Though the artists sued the NEA, challenged the political grounds on which the defunding was made, and eventually won back their grants, an atmosphere of homophobia loomed large. The negative publicity also took a personal toll on the artists. In a June 1994 article for the *New York Times* on the four-year anniversary of the NEA symbolhood,

The NEA •

Controversy

and Its

Aftermath

Hughes told William Harris that basically she lost two years of her life. She endured public humiliation, death threats, and pressure from the anti-censorship movement not to bring up the issue of homophobia because it would turn off straight people and threaten the success of the campaign. She was depressed and felt a hopelessness that kept her from writing. The public nature of the debate also affected her family of origin; a section of her performance *Clit Notes* addresses their hurtful response to her ordeal.

After several years of difficulties, including the illness and death of her father in the summer of 1993, Hughes, with the support of her friends and colleagues, began writing, performing, and teaching again, with a vengeance, in New York and across the country. Her solo work *Clit Notes* was commissioned by the New York Shakespeare Festival, opened at P.S. 122 in February 1994, and went on tour in 1994 and 1995, after having been performed in progress around the United States and England in the fall of 1993. In a March 1994 review for the *Village Voice*, Laurie Stone wrote the following: "Blistering and poignant, *Clit Notes* is an apologia, a kind of letter to her dead father, chronicling how she came to be a lesbian and how sex, the out life, and solo performance merged into a calling." The piece won a prestigious Obie Award, which honors the best Off-Broadway work in New York.

- **Clit Notes** *Hits*

the Shelves

In April 1996 Grove Press published *Clit Notes: A Sapphic Sampler,* Hughes' first collection of plays. The collection includes the major pieces discussed above and is a testament to her craft as a storyteller. Part of Hughes' introduction to the collection also exists in her current work in progress, tentatively titled *Cat O'Nine Tales,* which was performed in the winter of 1996 at P.S. 122. Laurie Stone's February 1996 review for the *Village Voice* of this latest incarnation includes Hughes' comments on the changing nature of her work: "The earlier work showed the escapades of an escape artist. Now I'm writing as an exile. There is no complete escape from the original family."

Profile by
Karen Helfrich

As Holly Hughes' work continues to grapple with difficult questions from many different vantage points, her audience continues to benefit from her astute observations and her resistance to the easy answers. Her stories are intimate, vital, and human; the telling is magical.

ALBERTA HUNTER

*A*lberta Hunter's long life and marvelously varied career reads like a

chronicle of twentieth-century blues and jazz. From Memphis to

Chicago to New York—and then to London, Paris, and Copenhagen—

Hunter was living proof that drive, determination, and a desire to sing

"like a million dollars" can lift one up from poverty and discrimination

to heights undreamed of, especially for a black woman in whose mind

lesbianism tarnished the image of respectability she so desperately

sought. Hunter sang with and composed for the likes of Louis Armstrong,

Ethel Waters, Fats Waller, Bessie Smith, Josephine Baker, and Paul

Robeson, and crossed paths with presidents, prime ministers, and

princes around the world. Yet, somehow she always maintained a

1895–1984 •

African American •

songwriter and

performer

197 •

down-home dignity and common sense, balanced by the sparkling wit and naughtiness of her lyrics. As her nephew Sam Sharpe told biographers Frank C. Taylor and Gerald Cook, "going to see her was like going to an old-time faith healer."

Alberta Hunter was born on April Fool's Day in 1895 in Memphis, Tennessee. She was the second of two girls, and claimed her older sister, La Tosca, was always preferred by her mother because she was lighter-skinned and prettier. Her father, a Pullman porter, abandoned the family soon after Alberta's birth, although her mother insisted for years that he had died of pneumonia. After he left, Alberta's mother was forced to take a job as a maid in a white bordello. Starting when she was ten, Alberta was molested by both a family friend and her school principal, traumas she later realized instilled in her a resentment for most men.

From early on, it was obvious Alberta was going places. Her strict mother taught her to respect herself, while her beloved Granny gave her "the sweets while Mama was slapping out the discipline," according to Taylor and Cook. Every time Granny would bathe Alberta, she would touch the three moles on the bottoms of her feet and say: "This child is going to be a wanderer." "She was right, too," Alberta said decades later after circling the globe many times. "I've been more places accidentally than most people have been on purpose."

Alberta showed no signs of being a musical prodigy. She was shrewd with money and "always jiving," she claimed. Stuck with Granny at church each and every Sunday "from the minute they opened the doors to the time they closed them," she and a friend would mug the kids at church for the pennies they had brought for the offering and sneak off to buy ice cream. Years later, she would surreptitiously slip tips intended for all the musicians in her cleavage (feigning an itch) and was even caught with her hand in the tip jar during club raids. Near the end of her life, she had numerous tax problems, claiming she could never understand why anyone like herself should have to pay more than $7,000 a year.

What early musical education she did get came from Beale Street and the flashy blues bands that would parade up and down it. Between 1890 and 1900, the population in Memphis doubled, primarily because blacks from the South were drawn to job opportunities and the comparatively open sociability this new black capital of the mid-South evidenced. The reputed father of the blues, W. C. Handy, moved from Alabama to Memphis in 1905, and Alberta would run down to Beale Street the minute she heard the brassy Handy band. Years later, when Alberta was making a name for herself in Chicago, Handy would come and look *her* up.

When she was eleven, Alberta's mother remarried, and she got even less attention when her half-sister Josephine was born. In school, things were not much better. "I was never playful like a child," she told Taylor and Cook. "I was always like you'd expect a grown woman to be." Truth was, she was also avoiding any of the boys' sexual advances. She claimed every boyfriend she ever had was soon stolen by some other girl, and years later she waxed philosophical on this point when she exclaimed to Taylor and Cook: "Oh Lord, God is good! They got the marriage, and I got the fame."

At sixteen, Hunter made her way to Chicago, hoping to get a job singing like the daughter of a friend of her mother, who was making a whopping $10 a week. After spending some time as a cook in a boarding house and dutifully sending money home to her mother, she finally wore down the owners of Dago Frank's, one of the city's wilder whorehouses, and got a job there as a singer. She stayed on for two years, honing her performance skills and earning both admiration and good tips from the girls, pimps, and customers.

Over the next few years, she worked her way up through a succession of both black and white clubs and cabarets, earning respect as both a singer and a composer, and gained a following. Soon she was known as the "south-side's sweetheart," and songwriters were flocking to her to try to get exposure for their new blues material. When her step-father and mother separated, she moved her mother up to Chicago.

Alberta got her first taste of the big time with an extended engagement at Chicago's Dreamland Cafe in 1917. There she sang with Joe "King" Oliver's band and earned $17.59 week. Within a few years, she was making $35 a week and an unheard-of $400–$500 in tips. It was around this time that she also premiered her most famous composition, "Down-Hearted Blues," which was recorded and made a "signature" song by Bessie Smith in 1923. In six months, the record sold 800,000 copies, and Hunter never saw any royalty payments.

• **Propriety and**

Lesbianism

In the 1920s and early 1930s, Alberta Hunter and Bessie Smith found themselves recording some of the same songs, "'Taint Nobody's Business If I Do" and "Aggravatin' Papa," among them. Yet there was no animosity between them, and Alberta always said she admired Bessie's singing, just as she did that of her other contemporaries, like Ethel Waters. She would never, of course, try to sing like them, but she also avoided them partly because of their sometimes-public problems with lovers, Smith with her men and Waters with her women. Alberta was always closeted about her lesbianism, concerned with propriety and the progression of her singing career. She simply never discussed it.

While singing at a club in Cincinnati in 1919, she set her sights on a handsome waiter named Willard Townsend. The two impulsively crossed the border into Kentucky and were married, partly to squelch the gossip that Alberta was a lesbian, according to Taylor and Cook, and partly because Willard represented the respectability Hunter longed for. The couple returned to Chicago, but Alberta could not bring herself to sacrifice her career for the marriage and would not even sleep with Townsend under her mother's roof. They stayed together only two months, though Alberta did not divorce him till four years later. "Lord, I treated him awful," she confessed years later.

The closest Alberta came to coming out of the closet was when she applied for a passport in 1920. She had moved to New York to further her career, and listed her address for the U.S. Department of Commerce as 109 West 139th Street, c/o Miss Lottie Tyler. Lottie, a maid to a touring white actress, had handed her card to Alberta after one of her performances in Chicago, whispering, according to Taylor and Cook: "If you ever come to New York, come and see me." She must have made an impression for, although one or both of them eventually changed their mind about traveling to Europe, they remained, according to Taylor and Cook, "friends and lovers for many years." Alberta's strong, independent will to travel and pursue her career no doubt accounted for the fact that they did not live together for long, though they did meet whenever their conflicting schedules permitted, and actually did travel to Europe a few years later.

Alberta's ambition was beginning to pay off. Traveling between New York and Chicago, she met and worked with Louis Armstrong, Sidney Bechet, Eubie Blake, Fletcher Henderson, and Fats Waller. Sophie Tucker even asked her to teach her how to sing "A Good Man Is Hard to Find," but Alberta wasn't about to give away any of her secrets. Besides, as she told Taylor and Cook, "nobody can learn my style because I don't even know it myself. It's always changing."

She started landing roles in various musicals both on and off Broadway. She also began recording under contract with the Gennett label, which was making a nice little profit with so-called "race" recordings. Ever the shrewd businesswoman, she also recorded for other labels under pseudonyms to maximize her own profits, using names like Mae Alix, Helen Roberts, Monette Moore, and (perhaps with a little vengeance in mind) that of her half-sister Josephine Beatty.

Feeling she had conquered the Big Apple, she set her sights on Europe, following in the footsteps of Josephine Baker. In 1927, she and Lottie headed for Paris, ostensibly on vacation but, at least in Alberta's mind, also to look for work. Two months after their arrival, Lottie returned to the States with another woman, but Alberta stayed on. "I tore the place up," she told Taylor and Clark. "I put my foot down and went to town," she recalled, as she moved both socially and professionally to the Riviera and finally to London in 1928. Oscar Hammerstein and Jerome Kern saw her there and offered her the part of Queenie opposite Paul Robeson in the London production of *Showboat* in 1928.

Between 1927 and 1937, Hunter worked chiefly in Europe, eventually traveling with her own musical company to enormous success in Stockholm, Copenhagen, and even Alexandria, Egypt. She returned briefly to New York and Chicago during this decade, but was now labeled too sophisticated for a black entertainer in the ever-racist States. "They do not want refinement and finesse in a Negro performer," she later said. "All they want is niggerism, a whole lot of foot-stomping and shouting." Biographers Taylor and Cook righteously label this period in Alberta's life as her "commute between pride and prejudice." Alas, in 1938, while in Paris, she received a letter from the American Consulate advising her—like scores of other Americans—to return home. War loomed on the horizon, and even Hunter's courage was no match for Hitler's bellicose aims.

Where Is

Home?

But home was both not what it used to be . . . and ever the same. Spoiled by the more egalitarian Europeans, she found it painful and demeaning to step back onto America's racist shores. Moreover, the blues was being supplanted by the more romantic melodies of the burgeoning big-band era. With lucrative engagements scarce, she savvily softened both her look and style and signed on for a series of tours with the USO, traveling extensively to perform for the troops during World War II, and again in the early 1950s in Korea. She continued to perform sporadically both stateside and in London, but by 1954 she fell on increasingly hard times and retired from show business.

By now, Alberta Hunter was nearly sixty and had enjoyed a full and exciting career well beyond her wildest Memphis-girlhood dreams. Many would have been content to rest on such substantial laurels well into their old age, but not Alberta Hunter.

In 1954 she went back to school and studied to be a nurse. Three years later she got a job at Goldwater Hospital in New York City, but only after she lied about her age, saying she was only fifty when she was already sixty-two. "I wanted to give something back to my fellow man," she said of this period in her life. "I learned more about compassion during this time than in my whole life previous." Twenty years later, after the hospital believed it had allowed her to work a full five years beyond mandatory retirement at sixty-five, she retired at the age of eighty-two.

In May of 1977, Alberta was persuaded to go to a party at jazz pianist Bobby Short's Manhattan apartment. Barney Josephson, the owner of New York's popular jazz club the Cookery, was amazed and delighted to learn she was still alive, and invited her to perform "provided she still had all her teeth and would not whistle into the microphone," according to Taylor and Cook. When she opened there in October of that same year, she was an instant success, even after twenty years of not singing. The *New York Times* said she was "as relaxed as a bag of bones," and the following spring, the *Toronto Globe* described her—with her husky, risqué renditions of songs like "Handyman"—as "a contralto that wears boots."

Though she was now in her eighties, there was no slowing Alberta Hunter down. She had her audience back in her sure, delicately iron hand. Through the late 1970s and into the 1980s, she made numerous television appearances, appeared at Carnegie Hall, sang for President Jimmy and Roslynn Carter (wearing her coat in the reception line "just so he could see I had one"), wrote the title song and recorded the soundtrack for Alan Rudolph's film *Remember My Name,* and recorded two albums featuring her favorite hits, *Amtrak Blues* in 1980, and *Look for the Silver Lining* in 1983. She also received an award from the city of Memphis "for her immense contribution to the development of an important art form, the blues." In accepting it, Alberta wasted no time reminding city fathers that as a child, she wasn't even allowed to walk on the sidewalks because of her color.

In 1983, Alberta fell ill and required colon surgery; but ever the crowd-pleaser, she still managed to complete a scheduled concert in Brazil. In the summer of 1984, her health still failing, she cut short a concert in Denver and was rushed back to New York. She died at home soon after.

In the end, the woman who was always stingy with money but generous in spirit and song had stipulated only $700 be spent on her funeral. So, though a prominent undertaker picked up her body, a cut-rate Staten Island company cremated it. According to Taylor and Cook, Alberta's thoughts on death mirrored those of her longtime English friend Lady Mendl, whose thoughts were reported in an article Alberta had clipped and saved from the *Montreal Herald* in 1950. "No funeral, no flowers, please and above all no exhibition even from the most loving friends. I want their memories of me to be in their hearts. If I have been of any help to any living being, let them think of that the day they hear I am dead."

Alberta closed many a show with the following sentiment: "If you came in with a troubled mind or heart and I have erased some of it, then I

Coming Back •

with All Her

Teeth

Power, •

Conviction,

Compassion

203 •

feel that my living has not been in vain." It is for these sentiments of power, conviction, and compassion—this triad of strengths that fired her contralto voice and fueled her life—that Alberta Hunter is best remembered.

Profile by
Jerome Szymczak

KARLA JAY

1947– •

Educator, •

writer, editor,

and activist

*K*arla Jay is a leading scholar in the field of gay and lesbian studies,

dedicated specifically to promoting lesbian visibility in all of its "won-

derful diversity." Most recently, Jay has devoted her scholarly pursuits to

documenting the historical, material, erotic, and psychic vicissitudes of

lesbian life. As the series editor of New York University Press's The Cutting

Edge: Lesbian Life and Literature, *the only lesbian studies series in the*

world published by a university press, she is responsible for selecting new

scholarship and biography in lesbian studies as well for reprinting lost or

never-published lesbian texts. She has written for numerous popular

periodicals, including Ms. *magazine, the* New York Times Book Re-

view, *and the* Village Voice, *and is currently professor of English and*

director of Women's Studies at Pace University in New York City.

The second of two children, Karla Jay was born on 22 February 1947, in Brooklyn, New York. Jay's parents placed a high value on education and, subsequently, from eighth-grade on she attended an all-girls academy which she credits with fostering her intellectual development. Excelling both in the classroom and on the playing field, she won a Regent's Scholarship, which enabled her to attend Barnard College in New York City, where she majored in French.

According to her profile in Martin Duberman's cultural history *Stonewall,* Jay's social consciousness was awakened during her senior year at Barnard. At this time, she witnessed and participated in the student protest at Columbia University in April 1968, over the administration's insensitive policies toward its black neighbors, its involvement with government-sponsored weapons research, and its complicity with the Vietnam War. For Jay, the Columbia fracas marked the starting point of her political and feminist struggles.

With a sharpened political awareness resulting from the events at Columbia, Jay joined the Redstockings (a radical feminist and Marxist group) shortly after its founding in 1969. Other prominent members of this organization include Ellen Willis, Alix Kates Shulman, and Rita Mae Brown. Jay spoke widely at this time on feminist consciousness-raising and participated in the second protest of the Miss America contest in Atlantic City. While not directly embroiled in the events at Stonewall in 1969, she enthusiastically joined the Gay Liberation Front (GLF), embracing its credo for substantive social change through political action. Jay spent the early 1970s committed to the feminist and gay and lesbian liberation movements, working between New York and California—the 1995 documentary *A Question of Equality* features her activist experiences and insights on the era. Awarded a teaching assistantship in the French department at New York University in the mid-1970s, Jay eventually settled on the East Coast, earning a master's degree in 1978 and a doctorate in 1984 in comparative literature.

A prolific scholar and full professor at Pace University since 1990, teaching courses ranging from "Introduction to Women's Studies" to "Modernism and Gender," Jay has also edited, written, or translated over nine volumes. She researches extensively on lesbian modernism and has produced the first in-depth, feminist biographical and literary study of Natalie Clifford Barney and Renée Vivien entitled *The Amazon and the Page* (1988). This work recovers Barney and Vivien, two lesbian expatriates living in Paris at the turn of the century, from literary obscurity and establishes for them a position in a continuing female tradition.

Jay's most recent endeavors clearly translate her activist principles into scholarship. As editor of *Dyke Life: From Growing Up to Growing Old: A Celebration of Lesbian Experience* (1995) and *Lesbian Erotics* (1995) and as co-editor with Joanne Glasgow of *Lesbian Texts and Contexts: Radical Revisions* (1990), Jay validates lesbian existence and literature as worthy areas of analysis. These volumes investigate the heterogeneity of lesbian communities, the history of lesbian eroticism, and the methodologies of lesbian interpretation. Covering topics such as lesbian parenting, femme sexualities, and lesbian narrative space, these anthologies fortify the richness of lesbian studies as an academic field.

The Lambda Literary Awards have recognized Jay's written work on three separate occasions. Most recently, *Dyke Life* was a Lambda Literary Awards finalist in the categories of anthologies and lesbian studies. Both *Lesbian Texts and Contexts* and *The Amazon and the Page* were finalists in the best anthology and best non-fiction categories respectively in 1991 and 1989.

Jay's dynamic publishing history is complemented by the active role she has taken in academia. Besides co-chairing the Lesbian and Gay Caucus of the Modern Language Association from 1993 to 1995, Jay serves on the editorial boards of the *Lesbian Studies Journal* and the *Lesbian Review of Books*. Her prolific publishing career, committed to representing the diversity of lesbian lives, places Karla Jay on the "cutting-edge" of gay and lesbian studies.

**Profile by
Annmarie Pinarski**

BILL T. JONES

*G*enius, iconoclast, romantic, post-modernist, preacher, hero, vic-

tim, and survivor are just a few nouns used to describe Bill T. Jones.

Brilliant, fearless, arrogant, defensive, offensive, frightening, generous,

humble—just a few adjectives. His work summons similar reaction. In

addition to having choreographed over fifty works, Jones is artistic

director of Bill T. Jones/Arnie Zane Dance Company and associate

artistic director of the Lyon Opera Ballet, with works in the repertories of

Alvin Ailey American Dance Theater, Boston Ballet, and Berlin Opera

Ballet, among others. He has directed theater—for the Guthrie Theater

in Minneapolis, Minnesota—and opera—for Glynbourne Festival

Opera, New York City Opera, and the Houston Grand Opera. He is a

1952– •

African American •

choreographer

and writer

209 •

1994 recipient of the MacArthur Genius Fellowship, numerous NEA fellowships, two New York Dance and Performance (Bessie) Awards, and a *Dance Magazine* Award. He co-authored *Body Against Body* with his late partner and lover Arnie Zane and is the author of an autobiography, *Last Night on Earth*. He is also African American and HIV-positive, which he discusses with zeal, eloquence, pathos, and violence, in performances that often move audiences to tears.

William Tass Jones was born in Bunnell, Florida, April 1952, the tenth of twelve children. His parents, Estella and Augustus Jones, were migrant farm workers who picked their way north or south depending on the season. In 1959, the family settled in Wayland in the Finger Lakes region of upstate New York, allowing the children continuity and the family a home base. There his parents variously harvested crops, managed a camp of migrating farm workers, and operated a restaurant/juke joint. In the shadow of the juke joint, the seeds for Jones' artistic imagination sprouted. He and his siblings, especially his sister Rhodessa, a performance artist, entertained themselves by singing while they harvested crops in the fields together. In school, Jones distinguished himself as an actor and athlete, graduating with the dubious self-congratulation of having not written a single paper.

At the State University of New York at Binghamton, in fall 1970, Jones discovered dance. Martha Graham had come to town, and seeing her company perform was a life-changing experience. In high school he had performed in theater and with a rock band called Wretched Souls, and so was no stranger to performance. But dance spoke to him in ways unexpected and deep, allowing him to see the potential of merging his athleticism with a more theatrical expression. Completely won over, he went immediately to dance class, where he encountered body-type prejudice. He realized the necessity of developing, defining, and articulating a movement vocabulary of his own, one which countenanced all body types—high buttocks and low, feet arched or flat, body corpulent or rail thin—and which didn't rely solely on the articulation of the pointed toe or turned-out foot, but on dancing itself as a partner to language. In addition to Graham (modern dance) and Jerome Robbins *(West Side Story),* his early influences were Percival Borde (African dance), George Balanchine (classical ballet), and Yvonne Rainer (post-modern choreographer and filmmaker).

That same year Jones met Arnie Zane and had another life-changing experience. A small Jewish-Italian man, Zane caught Jones' eye at a campus pub in Binghamton. Sexually curious and very much a product of the 1960s, Jones desired to experience another man and made no secret of his sexual interest in Zane. The two went back to Jones' room in the Third World corridor of the university dorm and spent the night together. For the next seventeen years, they would be called *BillandArnie* or *ArnieandBill*. Or described by the media as "tall and black with an animal quality of movement" (Jones) and "short and white, with a nervous, pugnacious demeanor" (Zane). Together they would define a new audacious dance that was nontraditional, athletic, provocatively homoerotic, and often personal. Together they would become perhaps the most celebrated, if not the most notorious, *out* gay couple in America.

Less than a year after meeting, the two moved to Amsterdam. Before packing up and leaving, they hitchhiked to Wayland to visit Jones' parents. Estella Jones was more alarmed by the possibility that her son would be lost in Europe beyond her reach and protection, than by the fact that he was having sex with a man. A deeply religious woman, she was first and foremost a mother and ruled her family with fiery love. Once gaining assurance that Zane would not leave Jones behind in Europe, she offered her blessings, and from that moment on, as long as her son was all right, she stayed clear of the relationship between the two men, neither discussing nor acknowledging it.

In Amsterdam the young lovers supported themselves with menial employment while indulging in the liberties of the city. Chatting over tea and opium, they visited with artists, composers, and designers, gathering ideas and observing life abroad as Bohemians. Though still very much driven by the 1960s' sexual ethos, Jones was quite taken by the casualness of sex, and became involved with a mutual friend of Zane's and nearly ruined his relationship. Neither accomplished much creatively during this time, though Zane, who was well on his way to establishing a career as a photographer, was actively taking pictures. Still, as exciting as it was, Amsterdam was not what they thought it would be, so the decision to leave was easily arrived at.

On their return, Jones met Zane's parents, who owned a bakery in the Bronx. The occasion ended violently, and five years passed before the couple saw Zane's parents again. Jones fell back into dance with fever and fervor. After the long months of physical and creative inactivity abroad, he was determined to make something artistically important. He re-enrolled at Binghamton, and soon after created with Zane their first duet. Called "Begin the Beguine" after a Benny Goodman record, the piece was a romping parody of 1930s-style dancing and earned them a bit of notoriety on campus. Afterward, Zane, who still mostly considered himself a photographer, began choreographing.

Jones felt he needed to learn more. In the dance department, under the mercilessly critical eye of Percival Borde, Jones determined that he was missing a more formal dance education, with which he would have the vocabulary to create his own movement language. Zane and Jones moved to Brockport, where Jones enrolled at the university as a dance major. The antecedents of his formal ideas about dance begin here. In a contact improvisation class taught by dancer/choreographer Richard Bull, Jones began to see dance as solving problems with movement. Jones and Zane explored the idea further when they met choreographer/contact improvisationist Lois Welk. Physical awareness was heightened with contact improvisation, and Jones, with comparatively pedestrian movements, was finding his voice and defining a vocabulary. This was a remarkably rich period, threatened only by his interest in the Krishna Consciousness Movement and missing his family.

In the summer of 1972, Lois Welk moved to San Francisco to revitalize the American Dance Asylum, a collective of former Brockport choreographers Welk had founded. Azel, Jones' closest brother, had moved to the Bay Area several years before and most of the East Coast family had since followed him there, including his sister Rhodessa. Without Welk, there was no reason to stay in New York, so Jones and Zane followed her, moving into Rhodessa Jones' home—Tomato— which she shared with her partner and their child. The experience of San Francisco underscored Jones' need for family more than it inspired creativity. The social climate, still very much tinged with the anti-materialism resistance of the 1960s, sneered at success of all kinds, and Jones, Zane, and Welk soon found themselves very frustrated. After a year and the tragic death of a niece, Jones, along with Zane and Welk, moved back to Binghamton, and the business of making art began.

The American Dance Asylum put roots in an old, dilapidated Elk's Club, with its members—the trio plus another dancer and a poet—living in contented poverty eating pancakes, peanut butter, and apples picked from a nearby tree. Each artist experimented with form and presentation, often showing works in their large, open home to an audience of just themselves or to a few intrepid people from the university. Shortly after his return, Jones began to have success. The work that put him on the map was called "Everybody Works/All Beasts Count," an imaginative dance which he and sixteen other dancers dramatized with vocals. It earned him a 1976 Creative Artist Public Service Award (CAPS). Soon after, he appeared at the Clark Center Dance Festival at CUNY Mall and received very encouraging reviews. "Everybody Works" was performed in Central Park, then at Dance Theater Workshop and the Kitchen.

The first reviews came in: the *New York Times* said Jones was a "performer worth watching." The *Soho News* said that he had "an

Learning the •

Language of Art

engaging stage presence." The duets Jones and Zane did together grabbed attention and critical acclaim. Jones was on his way.

In 1980 Jones and Zane broke away from the American Dance Asylum. Their sights were set on New York City, but neither felt comfortable living in Manhattan so settled in Valley Cottage, New York, some forty-five minutes away. There they created their first major work. Inspired by non-narrative cinema and visual arts, "Blauvelt Mountain" is a seventy-minute-long tour de force, involving a number of different activities, from *a capella* singing to talking to pedestrianisms like standing, sitting, and walking, all arranged and rearranged for perceptual effect. It premiered at the Dance Theater Workshop in 1980 and toured Europe with the Kitchen Center for Dance, Music, and Video.

"Social Intercourse: Pilgrim's Progress," Jones' next major work, appeared the following year at the American Dance Festival, with Jones billed as an "Emerging Choreographer" and Zane as Jones' administrator and artistic consultant. The work was a melange of oppositional ideas, traditional versus new wave, formal gestures versus informal. It included an improvised solo, in which Jones by turns told the audience, "I love women," then, "I hate women."

> I love white people. I hate white people. I'd like to kiss you. I'd like to tear your fucking heart out. Why didn't you leave us in Africa? I'm so thankful for the opportunity to be here.

The audience was shocked. This one performance tagged Jones with the reputation of being angry and unpredictable. Not surprisingly, another invitation from the American Dance Festival was not forthcoming—not for ten years.

At the 1982 New York premiere, at Downstairs at City Center, dance critic Arlene Croce was in the audience. "Bill T. Jones has marched the New Narcissism right into the fever swamp," she wrote in the *New Yorker*. Jones and Zane were offended. Previously she had taken exception to a prayerlike solo Jones had done in performance, dismissing it. When Jones was offered a commission for a new work by Alvin Ailey for his dance company, Jones named his new work "Fever Swamp." Croce was not amused and would later be at the center of a storm of controversy surrounding Jones.

Artistic success, though, had been brokered and Bill T. Jones/Arnie Zane and Company, which officially incorporated in 1982, was in demand. In 1984 they created "Freedom of Information" for the Théâtre de Ville in Paris. The work was loosely based on an air crash in

Washington, D.C., and featured a man recounting the tragedy while dancers wildly and variously barked, crawled, tumbled and turned, and fell. The scandalous work was well received and the company, through the United States Information Agency, was invited to tour Asia in 1986.

Success was not the only change in their lives. AIDS had settled among them. In 1984 Zane began to show signs of illness and in 1986 was diagnosed with lymphoma. A terrible two-year battle began of slow deterioration, with Zane fighting against it until he could not fight anymore. During Zane's illness he created "The Gift/No God Logic," and finished what would become their last collaboration, "A History of Collage." The company continued touring, more often than not without Zane. Then touring stopped, art stopped. Zane was near death. Jones, himself diagnosed HIV positive but asymptomatic, stayed by his lover until Zane died 30 March 1988. Now alone, Jones was devastated.

Almost immediately, a remarkable period of creativity supplanted the apathy of tragedy, and Jones rebounded, driven by both loss and fear of his own mortality, and in the midst of a management crisis. Since 1988 he has created over twenty new works, two of them full-evening in length. Both evening-length works—"Last Supper at Uncle Tom's Cabin/The Promised Land" and "Still/Here"—and two comparatively smaller ballets—"D-Man in the Water" and "Absence"— are, by all standards, considered American masterpieces. Each fixates on an element of disorienting tragedy, and finds ground and centeredness in humanity. Each is the apotheosis of faith.

Tragedy, •

Creativity, and

Survival

"Absence" (1989) was the first work Jones created after Zane's death. Using pantomime and the rituals of weddings, the ballet is an almost Zenlike study of death. While posing before the camera and dancing with his bride, the groom, without warning or cause, is chosen. Before everyone's eyes, he is taken away. Devastated, the bride struggles with loss, but eventually is able to move away from her grief and live. Alone and lost, the groom struggles among the dead but eventually, like his widowed wife, is resigned.

"D-Man in the Water" has roots in a daydream in which Jones envisioned living and dead friends trapped in a lake, futilely swimming against a current, many of them already drowned. Remarkably, everyone tries to save everyone else. Inspired by and wedded to Felix Mendelssohn's *Octet in E-flat major,* the ballet is considered by many to be Jones' signature repertory work. The work garnered two Bessie Awards.

"Last Supper at Uncle Tom's Cabin/The Promised Land" (1990) is a virtuosic, albeit rambling, dissecting work on American racial violence, racial history, marginality, and commonality. Three and one-half hours long, the opus retells (via libretto by poet Ann T. Greene) the story of Harriet Beecher Stowe's famous slave tract, *Uncle Tom's Cabin,* with comically painful tableaux; segments the tragedy of slavery into parts corresponding to the terrifying ordeal of Stowe's runaway slave, Eliza; interrogates faith and Christianity by asking of a clergyman questions like, "Is Christianity a slave religion? Is AIDS God's punishment?"; and realizes humanity in its purest, most vulnerable state. From each community where the work was performed, fifty people, one-thousand in all, participated in this last section, "The Promised Land," standing naked, hand-in-hand, on stage. The work, denounced by the Vatican, was often unfairly criticized, but even so, was an enormous success. Julius Hemphill, the composer, was awarded a Bessie for his original score.

"Still/Here" (1994), Jones' most controversial work to date, is about survival with life-threatening illness. For theatrical fodder and movement inspiration, Jones conducted around the country what he called "Survival Workshops"—group interviews and movement exercises directed by him and set designer Gretchen Bender with terminally ill women and men, geriatrics, children, and African-, Asian-, Latin-, and Caucasian-Americans. These sessions were videotaped and used as the visual background for the staged work, and shaped the libretto/compositions of Kenneth Frazelle and rock/musician Vernon Reid. "My intention has been to create a work, not as a rumination on death and decline, but on the resourcefulness and courage necessary to perform the act of living," said Jones of his drama.

Almost immediately the work was at the center of a storm of controversy. At its New York premiere, the work was attacked in the *New Yorker* by its dance critic, Arlene Croce, who refused to see the work on the grounds that victimization as art renders the work undiscussable by critics. Suddenly the work was grist for newspaper and radio debate, largely carried on by people who, like Croce, had not even seen the work. Controversy followed the project on its tour to London and Edinburgh, where an effort had been mounted to prevent the work from being shown. The attacks were in vain; the work's integrity and originality were unassailable, "its place among the landmarks of twentieth century dance [is] assured," proclaimed *Newsweek* magazine.

True to form, Jones moved on to the next projects, including a collaboration with Nobel Laureate Toni Morrison and legendary drummer Max Roach, called "Dega," (1995), a world premiere with the Lyon Opera Ballet called "24 Frames Per Second," and a 1996 season of repertory works in New York. With his new companion, Bjorn Amelan,

Jones lives a life unimaginable when Arnie Zane died in 1988. The last lines of his autobiography *Last Night on Earth* are, "Tomorrow will come. It always has. It will be all right."

Profile by
Shawn Stewart Ruff

CLEVE JONES

A co-founder of the San Francisco AIDS Foundation in 1982 and

originator of the NAMES Project AIDS Memorial Quilt, Cleve Jones is a

long-term survivor of AIDS. Among his many accomplishments, Jones

was an administrative assistant to California State Assemblyman Art

Agnos (who eventually became Mayor of San Francisco), served three

terms on the San Francisco County Democratic Central Committee, and

lobbied for the Quaker-sponsored Friends Committee on Legislation.

AIDS Quilt •

founder

Through the NAMES project, Jones conveyed the personal side of the AIDS pandemic: a dimension beyond statistics and scientific theories. At a time when AIDS was often perceived as a disease affecting mostly gays and intravenous drug users, Jones heightened the American consciousness about a virus that knows no bounds.

Cleve Jones was born on 11 October 1954 in West Lafayette, Indiana, to Austin and Marion Jones. Both his parents are professors at Arizona State University. Jones moved to San Francisco in the early 1970s.

Following the 1978 assassination of Jones' friend, openly gay San Francisco Supervisor Harvey Milk, Jones participated in each annual candlelit march commemorating Milk. By November 1985, with the AIDS epidemic having taken more than 1,000 lives in San Francisco, Jones asked each of the march's participants to make placards showing the names of friends and family who had died of AIDS. Despite the death toll, Jones felt the subject of AIDS remained shrouded in confusion and denial. "We could all die without anyone really knowing," he said in the summer 1993 issue of *Critical Inquiry*.

After the march ended, Jones and many others taped the placards to the San Francisco Federal Building's facade. Jones compared the sight to that of a patchwork quilt passed down over many generations. "I thought of my grandmother, and my great-grandmother, and it was such a warm, middle-class, traditional values kind of feeling," Jones told the *Desert Sun* in February 1996.

- *Quilt Grows*

from One Panel

to 32,000

With this image in mind, Jones created the first panel for the NAMES Project Memorial Quilt in memory of his best friend Marvin Feldman. Completed in February 1987, the panel's abstract design consists of five stars of David—each dominated by a pink-red triangle—and Feldman's full name spray-painted on a white sheet. Four months later, the quilt's 2,000 panels were shown in Washington, D.C., an event that drew about 500,000 people.

By the mid 1990s, the AIDS Memorial Quilt comprised 32,000 panels from all fifty states and twenty-eight countries, and there were thirty-eight NAMES Project chapters in the United States and thirty-two independent Quilt initiatives worldwide.

In the January 1989 issue of *Mother Jones,* Jones called the AIDS Quilt an internal and external strategy. "I needed to take care of myself, to make changes that would keep me strong and able to fight. And needed a strategy that would affect the outside world, which clearly is going to decide whether we're going to survive."

Unlike organizations such as ACT-UP, the AIDS Quilt relies on mainstream appeal. Jones said in *Mother Jones,* "Our posture just isn't going to be angry. We're not a political organization."

Jones further explained: "We're not lobbying or endorsing candidates. We want the grandmother from Iowa who hand-stitched her boy's flannel shirts together to be comfortable enough with us to come and see the panel. We don't use the rhetoric of the gay liberation movement or the Left or the 'New Age.' We don't allow ourselves to be defined in a way that will exclude anyone."

Jones has collected many awards. He was named "Person of the Week" by ABC News following the Quilt's inaugural display in Washington, D.C. in October 1987. In 1993 he received Harvard AIDS Institute's second annual AIDS Leadership Award. In February 1996, he received a Steve Chase Humanitarian Award.

He has many admirers. "60 Minutes" aired a favorable story on him. Randy Shilts, who wrote the best-selling book *And The Band Played On,* once described his friend in a *Mother Jones* interview as "rare among political types, in that he doesn't take himself very seriously. He promotes himself, but he promotes a larger cause. He understands politics with a capital P: the point is to change people, not just to campaign or get elected."

In the 1990s, the AIDS Quilt has become a teaching tool for educating young adults. According to a December 1995 article in *The San Francisco Chronicle,* "Follow-up surveys at schools that display pieces of the quilt show that more than two-thirds thought more about their own chances of being infected after viewing it; nearly 90 percent said they would be more willing to take steps to avoid contracting the AIDS virus."

Jones sees another purpose for the AIDS Quilt: to encourage the federal government to increase its research endeavors and clinical trials programs. In a November 1995 article in the *San Francisco Examiner* he wrote, "I am a long-term survivor of AIDS. . . . Ten years ago, I never imagined that I would be alive today." But he also acknowledged that only more research can save his life or any other infected with HIV.

Instrument for •

Behavioral

Change

Profile by
David Levine

FRANK KAMENY

*F*rank Kameny's quiet scientific career abruptly ended in the late

1950s when he was fired for being a homosexual. He promptly chal-

lenged the federal government's ban on the employment of homosexuals

and later took on federal policies on security clearances for homosexu-

als and the nation's perception of gays as sick people, among other

battles. His 1968 slogan "Gay Is Good" helped change the gay move-

ment's self-perception, paving the way for gay pride.

1925– •

American •

astronomer and

activist

Franklin Edward Kameny was born on 21 May 1925 in Queens, New York. By the age of four, he had taught himself to read, and he aspired to be an astronomer at six years old. As a pre-teen he was aware of homosexual feelings, but he assumed they were temporary.

He entered Queens College at sixteen, but World War II interrupted his education. In 1945, he served in an armored infantry battalion in Germany, where he survived dangerous combat. After returning to the United States in 1946, he earned his B.S. degree in physics.

Kameny dutifully dated young women throughout high school and college, though his attractions to men never subsided. In 1954, while studying astronomy at the graduate level, Kameny acknowledged his homosexuality. In 1957, a year after earning his Ph.D. from Harvard, he landed a Civil Service job with the Army Map Service in Washington, D.C., where he received superior performance ratings. At the end of that year, however, he was discharged because of homosexuality. This moment, Kameny admits, catalyzed a shy astronomer into a full-time advocate for gay civil rights.

He contested the dismissal through every possible channel. His lawyer abandoned the fight after a few years, but Kameny personally petitioned the United States Supreme Court. By the time the high court refused to hear his case in 1961, his drive and intelligence had rendered him an amateur lawyer. With a few dedicated peers, he started the Mattachine Society of Washington (MSW), the nation's first "civil-liberties, social-action organization dedicated to improving the status of the homosexual citizen through a vigorous program of action," according to an MSW brochure. The group targeted employment discrimination in the government, and Kameny, recognized as the authority on security clearances for gay people, personally worked on hundreds of cases against the Civil Service Commission and the Pentagon during the next three decades.

Kameny also attacked the assumptions that pervaded society and damaged many gays. "We are the experts on our homosexuality," he declared in the early 1960s, refuting countless psychiatrists, ministers, and others. This view became more influential after his article for *Psychiatric Opinion* (February 1971), in which he assailed the unscientific nature of psychiatric "sickness" claims that reinforced society's bigotry. He followed with protests of the American Psychiatric Association, calling for it to strike homosexuality from its list of pathologies (which it finally did in 1973).

Inspired by the "Black Is Beautiful" rallying cry in the late 1960s, Kameny coined the phrase "Gay Is Good," which became the slogan in 1968 for the North American Conference of Homophile Organizations. The phrase helped to augment the confidence that began after the 1969 Stonewall uprising, and thousands joined in fighting military discharges, employment discrimination, and sodomy laws.

In 1971, several friends persuaded Kameny to become the first self-declared gay man to run for Congress. He campaigned against five other candidates for the District of Columbia's nonvoting post in the House of Representatives, championing personal freedom and gay rights in every appearance. Though he finished fourth, some of his rhetoric—published in *The Gay Crusaders*—reads like a prophecy: "As homosexuals, we are fed up with a government that wages a relentless war against us and others of its citizens, instead of against the bigotry of our society. This is our country, our society, our government—for homosexuals quite as much as for heterosexuals. . . . You will be hearing much from us in the next thirty days—and long thereafter!"

His activist achievements include the reversal of the Civil Service Commission's anti-gay policy on 3 July 1975, and the repeal of D.C.'s sodomy law on 13 September 1993. The latter feat represents a three-decade battle for Kameny, who personally drafted the new law at the request of a city council member.

In a 1995 interview with the *Washington Blade* before his seventieth birthday, Kameny said that he has not had many long-lasting committed relationships. "I'm emotionally independent," he said, "and I'm not looking for the love of my life."

After reflecting on a long career of activism, he told the *Blade* interviewer: "If I had to choose one particular thing I've done and put it at the pinnacle of all of which I'm proud, it would be 'Gay Is Good.' It encapsulates, in a way that has been taken up by others, everything that I stand for and have worked for."

**Profile by
Tom Musbach**

JONATHAN NED KATZ

*"T*he learned and constitutionally irreverent" Jonathan Ned

Katz, in the words of Gore Vidal, has played a central and decisive role

in creating the field of gay and lesbian history. Galvanized by the gay

liberation movement that followed the Stonewall uprising of 1969, Katz,

in his early work, captured the personal and collective shift in the sense

of self, from the shamefully "homosexual" to the affirmatively "gay" and

"lesbian." As an independent scholar, without academic affiliation or

outside funding, Katz manifested his vision through his seminal Gay

American History, *published in 1976. From the start Katz's vision has*

been one of inclusive diversity, among lesbians and gay men and ethnic

groupings in America. While uncovering previously hidden gay

1938– •

American •

historian and

activist

and lesbian history, Katz realized that the "homosexual" and "heterosexual" categories were an historically recent development. First in *The Gay/Lesbian Almanac* (1983), and more substantially in *The Invention of Heterosexuality* (1995), Katz develops the idea of "heterosexuality" and "homosexuality" as social-historical constructions.

Jonathan Ned Katz was born in New York City on 2 February 1938, to Phyllis B. and Bernard Katz, and grew up in Greenwich Village. His mother supported his scholarly endeavors in a professional manner (as an editor), and his father, according to Katz, taught him "to be outraged at social injustice, and about the need for united action toward radical change"—which his life's work bears out. Jonathan Katz changed his name in the public record to Jonathan *Ned* Katz in the mid 1980s, after another Jonathan Katz publicly advertised his conversion to heterosexuality through a cult philosophy. Katz has lived in a companionate relationship with David Barton Gibson in Manhattan since June 1976.

- *Katz "Comes*

Out" as a Gay

Man

Katz grew up in the 1950s, a time of conformity, anxiety, and McCarthyism—Senator Joe McCarthy seemed to find "un-American" communists and homosexuals under every other bed—when "homosexual" was one of the worst things anyone could be. In *The Invention of Heterosexuality* Katz reports, "with a new and dawning horror, I had first consciously applied the word 'homosexual' to my feelings for men. . . . Even now, after all these years, I still recall the dread that the word 'homosexual' evoked on that conformist fifties morn."

He spent the next fifteen years in a state of isolation and shame, reading a great deal. He participated in marches against the war in Vietnam and "applauded (from the sidelines) the black civil rights struggle and, later, the rise of the black power movement." Katz researched and wrote two radio scripts for WBAI-FM in New York City, "The Dispute Over the Ownership of Anthony Burns" (1968) about a fugitive slave case and "Resistance at Christiana" (1969) about a fugitive slave rebellion, and the script for two volumes of educational recordings, "Black Pioneers."

Although Katz was oblivious to the Stonewall uprising while it was taking place, virtually under his nose, its import reached him a year later when a friend in his therapy group gave him an article to read, "Homo/Hetero: The Struggle for Sexual Identity," by Joseph Epstein. "I experienced with new and stunning force the depth of antihomosexual hatred. . . . I understood: My homosexual feelings made me and others objects of 'prejudice'—subject to stigma, as a group, like black people, like women." In the winter of 1971 he began attending Gay Activist Alliance meetings. He found himself "exhausted and reeling from the intense, abrupt shift in understanding and emotion I was so quickly undergoing," an experience common to many middle-class homosexuals who had become adults before Stonewall.

In the early 1970s Katz read voraciously, and to gain insights into oppressed social groups—blacks, women, and gays. He turned one of his radio plays into a book, *Resistance at Christiana;* published a book for young people about a black pioneer woman; reviewed Dennis Altman's 1971 *Homosexual Oppression and Liberation* for the *Nation;* and participated in the founding of the Gay Academic Union in 1973. As a gay activist scholar Katz has played founding roles in numerous gay academic groups, and was on the founding committee of the organization now known as the National Writers Union.

Katz sought to capture the exuberance of "gay liberation" and to spread the word. Borrowing from the black, women's, and anti-war movements, he conceived an agit-prop documentary play. Katz envisioned *Coming Out!* as part historical, part literary, itself a document of the historic changing times. It is a two-act play with ten actors who speak many more voices of characters in situations of historic importance to the new movement. It premiered in June 1972.

"*Coming Out!* is intended to express," commented Katz in *Coming Out!,* "the sense of justified outrage at our oppression; a new militant determinism to subvert the heterosexual dictatorship by organized, united action; a new sense of ourselves as a social group with a history not only of persecution, but also of resistance." In her review of a 1973 performance on the SUNY/Albany campus, Nancy Miller observed that "the value of *Coming Out!* is not . . . primarily as a theatrical piece, but in its expression of the bitterness and resentment and the hopes and aspirations of homosexuals in the U.S." Identifying the gay liberationist strategy, Miller concludes, "the process of 'Coming Out' as a force quite apart from the play is not only *not* ending, but, on the contrary, is just beginning."

Martin Duberman's comments on *Coming Out!,* on the front page of the *New York Times* Sunday drama section, brought Katz to prominence unexpectedly, and he accepted a publisher's small advance to write a book of documents on homosexual history; *Gay American History* was published three years later. During this period Katz oversaw the Arno Press Series on Homosexuality, reprinting over fifty titles of mostly forgotten works (such as novels by Ann Bannon, the Daughters of Bilitis' *The Ladder,* and Ford and Tyler's novel *The Young and Evil*) and a few new titles, notably James Steakley's *The Homosexual Emancipation Movement in Germany.*

Katz's vision took definite, if massive shape. The documents he unearthed revealed "evidence of a vast, subterranean world of same-sex relations, coexistent with the ordinary historical universe." Mainstream academic scholars of the day direly warned any would-be "gay" scholar against pursuing such activities as "professional suicide." Non-affiliation with academia ultimately gave Katz the intellectual freedom to pursue his ideas unhampered by professional politics. "The aim of my research," Katz asserted, "was intellectually quite modest—to simply recover and present a significantly large, wide-ranging collection of historical documents . . . of Gay American history."

Gay American History: Lesbians and Gay Men in the U.S.A. was massive, but hardly exhaustive. Katz organized the documents into six categories: "Trouble" (legal persecution), "Treatment" (homosexuality as medical pathology), "Passing Women" (female cross-dressing, lesbians), "Native Americans/Gay Americans" (same-sex affection among indigenous peoples), "Resistance" (political action), and "Love." Katz reprinted some rare, original documents—some first-time translations (especially from the German); records from insane asylums, universities, and churches; articles from psychiatric, psychological, and legal journals; court records, diaries, literary sources—most of which focused on "ordinary" gay and lesbian people and how they had lived their lives. Katz acknowledged that his book represented but one of many possible "authentic gay" views.

It seems impossible to overestimate the impact, direct or indirect, of Katz's *Gay American History*. Its publication triggered an explosion of research across academic disciplines (including history, sociology, anthropology, and literature), leading to new interdisciplinary work and competing theories, and a major boom in gay publishing, first in the small presses, and increasingly in the major houses. This boom has undergone several permutations in twenty years, but has yet to show signs of slowing down. Katz had started out to counter "the prevailing notion of homosexuality as a purely psychological phenomenon" that focused discussion and research "almost exclusively on three areas: the causation, character, and treatment of homosexuality as a psychosexual orientation disturbance," and to conceive the notion "as a historical, social, political, and economic phenomenon, as well."

In his introduction, Katz stated that he intended *Gay American History* as a catalyst for gay liberationist social change, "part of that national and worldwide organization and activity for radical social change in which each group, starting from a sense of its own particular oppression, is struggling for the democratic control of that society in which all work, live, and try to love." In 1977, Katz read Jeffrey Weeks'

Coming Out: Homosexual Politics in Britain, From the Nineteenth Century to the Present, which confirmed the direction of Katz's own thinking. Immediately, he wrote to Weeks "eager to contact a like-minded gay historian of the left, pleased that a small international group of gay and lesbian conspirators was quietly starting homosexual history recovery work."

Discovering the •

Through the rest of the 1970s and into the early 1980s Katz continued assimilating new insights and adjusting his theories to accord with what he and others were discovering to be the unstable, shifting historical nature of sexual categorizing. He incorporated these ideas in the second volume of documents, published in 1983 as *Gay/Lesbian Almanac: A New Documentary.* Foremost was the idea that "heterosexuality" is a modern fabrication with a history of changing, contested meanings. In America since the late nineteenth century, "the heterosexual and homosexual have danced in close dialectical embrace," Katz wrote. Katz stressed again his own focus on eroticism and erotic feelings (including genital, erotic, and/or emotional intimacy), rather than social identities or persons, and cautioned against the false and ahistoric tendency in modern society to universalize "sexualities." Historical analysis, Katz concludes, reveals that the way we lust is not a "scientific" matter, and therefore does not have a "scientific" answer.

Dialectical

Embrace

By the 1980s Katz had established himself as a public scholar, speaking, giving lectures at major universities, and receiving an occasional teaching appointment and small grants. Over a two-year period (1988–1990), Katz penned nineteen monthly "Katz on History" columns for the *Advocate.* In 1989 he scripted a theater piece on Walt Whitman, "Comrades and Lovers" (produced in several places between 1989 and 1992), and in 1992 a committee sponsored by the Rockefeller Foundation invited Katz and others to help plan the twenty-fifth anniversary exhibit commemorating Stonewall.

The Invention •

Reading Mary P. Ryan's *Womanhood in American: From Colonial Times to the Present* and Lisa Duggan's work on women and American society in the 1920s spurred Katz to get to the bottom of "the social enforcement of heterosexuality." His initial inquiry into the history of heterosexuality as a social institution appeared in the January–March 1990 issue of *Socialist Review.* Five years later, Dutton published the book-length *The Invention of Heterosexuality.* Katz's work has never wandered far from the feminist tenet that "the personal is political." *The Invention of Heterosexuality* is the first extended, explicit history of "heterosexuality" as a normalizing social institution. It is also, in part, an autobiography and an intellectual history of recent feminism.

of

Heterosexuality

In seven chapters, Katz roams from the personal to the collective, demonstrating the dialectical process of change. Starting from a personal account of his development as an activist scholar and historian, Katz returns to the late nineteenth century, when the sexologist Krafft-Ebing and his contemporaries made "sexuality" a scientific concern. From here, Katz summarizes and synthesizes several developments in the history of sexuality. The earliest, transitional "medical model" of sexuality distinguished between sexual acts as "perverted" because they "turned away from" procreation and "sex-love" as good and healthy, as long as it occurred within the context of "true love" and marriage.

Earlier, in the early nineteenth century, society drew distinctions not between different- and same-sex eroticism, but between true love and false love, and distinguished between sexual acts that maximized procreation or "sinfully" wasted human seed. When the middle class generally adopted contraception, non-reproductive intercourse was normalized as "heterosexual." "The making of the middle class and the invention of heterosexuality went hand in hand," observes Katz. Freud is presented by Katz as both the "major modern maker of heterosexuality's ahistorical medical model *and* as subversive theorist of heterosexuality's social construction—its historical invention." Freud, says Katz, would play an important role in transmuting sex from productive duty to acts of pleasurable consumption. But if non-reproductive sex was now "normal," the deviant could no longer be defined simply as the non-procreative. Homosexuals had to represent a neurotic failure of emotional development. The purpose of "the homosexual" in this was to validate the middle class's assertion of being "normal" in contrast, and to naturalize and universalize the dominance of the middle class social order. Katz then connects Freud's (and others') idea of normative heterosexuality to the larger social project of normalizing and standardizing everything, from the gauge of railroad tracks to train schedules, time zones, and even intelligence (the "IQ test"). Kinsey's six-point scale gave the bipolarity of sexual social identity a more nuanced range of differentiation.

Katz now reviews developments in modern feminist thought. In *The Feminine Mystique* (1963) Betty Friedan demonstrated how the personal and sexual are linked with power and politics. Ti-Grace Atkinson targeted heterosexual society as a culturally enforced, inequitable arrangement. Kate Millet introduced the concept of *Sexual Politics*. In "The Traffic in Women" (1975), Gayle Rubin theorized the "sex/gender system" (gender is the socially imposed division of the sexes). Katz notes the 1970 Radicalesbians' "zap" confronting feminists with their own fear of lesbians, and dominance of heterosexual assumptions. He also observes that the operation of a powerful taboo continues to keep heterosexuality outside of analysis to this day. Katz confesses to finding Michel Foucault's work rich with suggestion for his own understanding of the changing social-historical organization of eroticism and gender.

As Lisa Duggan says in her afterword, "In putting the arguments of historians of sexuality, that the categories heterosexual/homosexual are historical and changeable, into public discourse, Katz has done us a very significant service. If such arguments remain confined to the university classroom and academic conference, they won't push public debate and policy the way we need them to."

In 1995, Jonathan Ned Katz received the Publishing Triangle's Bill Whitehead Award for Lifetime Achievement in Lesbian and Gay Literature. His papers are collected in the manuscript division of the Research Libraries of the New York Public Library.

**Profile by
Les K. Wright**

LARRY KRAMER

*L*arry Kramer is best known for his leadership in the gay communi-

ty's fight against AIDS. Throughout the 1980s, as the disease spread from

a few isolated cases into a plague that decimated the gay male commu-

nity, Kramer unrelentingly prodded gays—and all Americans—to

action through his political and theatrical writings and speeches. He has

often been called the angriest man in America.

1935– •

American writer •

and activist

Kramer was born 25 June 1935, in Bridgeport, Connecticut, to George L. and Rea W. (Wishengrad) Kramer. He attended Yale University, graduating with a B.A. in 1957. After a stint in the army and an attempt to find theater work, Kramer started working at the William Morris Agency, the training ground for many a show business career, in 1958. He was an assistant story editor at Columbia Pictures in New York from 1960 to 1961 and a production executive in London until 1965, when he became an assistant to the president of United Artists in New York. In 1967, he was the associate producer for the film *Here We Go Round the Mulberry Bush*.

His most significant contribution to film was 1969's *Women in Love*, which he adapted from D. H. Lawrence's novel and produced. It earned him Best Screenplay nominations in 1970 from both the Academy of Motion Picture Arts and Sciences and the British Film Academy. *Women in Love* represents Kramer's first attempt to address homosexuality in his work, and his efforts to interpret Lawrence's thinly veiled portrayals of homosexual love were critically well regarded.

- ***La vie New***

York

After the success of *Women in Love,* Kramer went through a period of self-discovery as a gay man. He knew he was gay during the 1960s, but he spent that time concentrating on his career, not his sexuality. Now, as a thirtysomething gay man living in the midst of the burgeoning gay movement, Kramer wished to portray that aspect of his life further in his work.

Kramer started writing a novel in 1975. His life in the mid-1970s was typical of that of many upper-class Manhattan gay men at the time: discos, drugs, bathhouses, Fire Island weekends, and a new promiscuity engendered by the gay sexual revolution. Kramer dove into the gay scene but remained unfulfilled, seeking love but finding only sex. His disenchantment was all too evident when his autobiographical novel, *Faggots,* was published in 1978 at the apex of gay sexual freedom. The novel, which graphically depicts the lifestyle of Fire Island's gay male community, features Fred Lemish, a gay man who vainly searches for true love, family, and stability in a world bent on momentary sexual pleasure. Kramer was ravaged by many gay critics, who accused him of sacrificing hard-won sexual liberation. Nevertheless, the book became a best seller, has remained in print for two decades, and is now considered a ground breaking portrayal of modern gay history.

After *Faggots,* Kramer found himself in the gay public eye, where he has remained ever since. He reflects on the genesis of his public life in *Reports from the holocaust: The Making of an AIDS Activist:* "I learned that if one is going to speak one's mind, best be prepared to get as good as you give. This was a lesson—violent, vocal, vociferous—I was to learn a thousand times over with the appearance of *Faggots.* I thought I'd written a satirical novel about the gay life I and most of my friends were living. I'd meant it to be funny. . . . It never occurred to me that *Faggots* would be *controversial.* I was completely unprepared for its hostile reception in certain political quarters." It was a lesson that would be useful in the tumultuous decade to come.

- ***The AIDS Years***

In 1981, when a few dozen gay men in New York and San Francisco were found to be suffering from a rare form of cancer called Kaposi's sarcoma, it was not long before Larry Kramer was warning the gay community of the impending danger in the pages of the *New York Native.* Most gays were either indifferent or hostile. With memories of

Faggots still fresh, critics accused him of inciting panic and of instilling gay homophobia and anti-eroticism.

By 1982, when it was clear to Kramer and some of his friends that gay men with AIDS could not rely on their local or national governments to provide the health care services they needed, let alone a cure, they formed Gay Men's Health Crisis. Kramer helped supervise the daily running of the organization. He recalls in *holocaust* that "it became a consuming passion—helping, urging, nurturing, watching this small group develop, at first falteringly, but then beginning to grow as increasing numbers of dedicated men and women came to join us. It was one of those rare moments in life when one felt completely utilized, useful, with a true reason to be alive."

In early 1983, the AIDS infection and death rates continued escalating, no answers were forthcoming from the medical and governmental establishments, and most gays still considered AIDS a temporary problem. A frustrated Kramer made one of his most fervent calls to action in his now-famous article "1,112 and Counting" in the 14–17 March 1983 *New York Native*. At that time there were 1,112 documented cases of AIDS, with 418 deaths, so he implored the gay community to fight:

> If this article doesn't scare the shit out of you, we're in real trouble. If this article doesn't rouse you to anger, fury, rage, and action, gay men may have no future on this earth. Our continued existence depends on just how angry you can get. . . . Unless we fight for our lives, we shall die. In all the history of homosexuality we have never before been so close to death and extinction. Many of us are dying or close to dead.

The article, which called for more money for AIDS research, better treatment of AIDS patients, better media coverage of AIDS, and better political representation, was reprinted by gay newspapers around the country. It caused the final break in Kramer's already-strained relationship with the Gay Men's Health Crisis board. He reluctantly resigned.

Suddenly having little to do, he wrote a play as an outlet for his activist voice. *The Normal Heart* opened in early 1985 to positive reviews and ran for more than a year. It has been restaged around the world. The play was a vehicle for Kramer's anger at the government, the medical establishment, and the media for not acting to combat AIDS.

By 1987, Kramer had been at the forefront of AIDS activism for six years but was still frustrated by the lack of progress in battling the epidemic. On 10 March 1987, he gave a speech at New York's Gay and

Lesbian Community Center detailing the incredible difficulties doctors were experiencing in getting new AIDS drugs. He pleaded for his audience to take responsibility for themselves and to demand immediate action from the Food and Drug Administration (FDA) and other government agencies charged with AIDS research. The emotional speech inspired the formation of the AIDS Coalition to Unleash Power, or ACT UP. ACT UP used civil disobedience, protests, sit-ins, and other public demonstrations to convince the FDA to release experimental AIDS drugs. The organization proved remarkably effective in bringing AIDS to the forefront of America's consciousness. Soon, ACT UP chapters opened across the country, and the organization's motto, "Silence = Death," became a rallying cry for its young activists.

In 1988, Kramer himself discovered that he was HIV-positive and that he suffered from a liver disorder that threatened his life as much as AIDS. He was told he had two years to live, but he has remained healthy much longer than he or his doctors expected. In 1992, *The Destiny of Me,* the sequel to *The Normal Heart,* opened in New York. In an October 1992 *New York Times* essay about *Destiny,* Kramer said:

> I further complicated my task by determining to write a personal history: a journey to acceptance of one's own homosexuality. . . . This journey, from discovery through guilt to momentary joy and toward AIDS, has been my longest, most important journey. . . . Indeed, my homosexuality . . . has been the single most important defining characteristic of my life. . . . I think the lives that many gay men have been forced to lead, with AIDS awaiting them after the decades-long journey from self-hate, is the stuff of tragedy.

By 1996, Kramer was at work on "a very long novel about the plague," tentatively titled *The American People,* and was preparing to film *The Normal Heart,* directed by John Schlesinger, commencing fall 1996. He lives with his partner, David Webster, an architect and designer, in New York and Warren, Connecticut, where they are currently restoring a house.

Kramer's contributions to the gay community are testament to the power of words. His endless diatribes in the form of essays, books, speeches, and plays served to galvanize gay men and lesbians as no individual ever has. As much as anything, his angry activism proves that, when faced with death and indifference, one individual can effect change. Kramer summed it up in the June 1994 *Progressive:* "There are very few voices as loud as mine. And I don't think I'm doing anything special. I'm fighting for my own life as well as everybody else's. I don't want to die."

Profile by
Joseph E. DeMatio

k. d. lang

k. d. lang is a vocalist, an avant-garde performance artist, and a

songwriter who has made valid contributions in the areas of western

music, pop, and jazz. Perhaps "alternative" would better describe her

musical style. She certainly gives one plenty of choices. Her earliest

performances could be best classed as alternative, but she quickly began

to evidence a more traditionally western music style, clearly influenced

by Patsy Cline. Her performances, however, remained more energetic

and fantastic than is usual on a western stage. In other words, she

entertains her audiences. She has said that her vocal style is dictated by

her voice. Just as one does not play Gregorian chants on a piccolo, she

cannot sing truly alternative music with her "instrument."

1961– ·

Canadian ·

singer

241 •

Kathy Dawn Lang was born in Edmonton, Alberta, Canada on 2 November 1961, the fourth and last child of Audrey and Adam Lang. Her brother John is eleven years her senior, her sister Jo Ann is six years older, and her sister Keltie only three at the time of her birth. Her ancestry is Icelandic, Dutch, Irish, Scottish, English, and German Jewish; she has been known to claim Sioux as well. In other words, she is a typical mixture of the many people who came to settle in North America. In 1962 the family moved to Consort, Alberta, where lang grew up.

Consort is a small town, with a population of fewer than 1,000 people. The area is farm and ranch country with wheat as the major crop, and cattle as the most popular range animal. Despite her reputed comment that "it was the kind of place where you knew everyone from the day you were born until the day you could get yourself out of there," she was able to gain from her childhood the kind of knowledge and experience that were important to her development as a performer.

Her mother, Audrey Lang, bought the family a used piano and saw to it that her children had music lessons. She drove them to a convent in Castor, Alberta, fifty-two miles west of Consort, once a week for many years. At the age of seven, lang was being instructed in the mysteries of the piano by a nun. Sister Xavier taught the little girl music basics and soon had her singing, encouraging her to compete in a number of talent contests during her childhood. At the age of ten, lang picked up her brother's guitar and started learning to play. When she was twelve her parents divorced and her father moved away. Her mother continued with her teaching job, and took over the running of the family business, a local drug store.

Lang joined the Consort High School volleyball team at fourteen and tackled that sport with the determination that later lead her to a successful music career. An interest in music wasn't all that unusual in her hometown but she often took her guitar, as well as her gym bag, when the volleyball team played out of town. She graduated from the local high school in 1979, having won the Athlete of the Year award in tenth, eleventh, and twelfth grades, an unusual honor. She was popular, well-liked by her classmates, and her friends included both boys and girls.

Apparently she knew she was a lesbian while still in her teens, and was able to accept herself. She expects that same acceptance in return in a style that has since become famous. That attitude hasn't been achieved with any more ease than most people experience, but the point is that it has been achieved. From her 1992 interview with the *Advocate,* where she stated that she was a lesbian, to the current time, she has been

- *Lang Comes*

Out

publicly matter-of-fact about her sexuality. She keeps her private life quiet, anticipating and receiving respect.

Not that she doesn't have a sense of humor about all the furor. She appeared on a *Vanity Fair* cover wearing a man's suit, sitting in a barber's chair, and pretending to be shaved by barely clothed super-model Cindy Crawford. A good-humored appearance on *The Tonight Show* with host Jay Leno and the little green muppet, Kermit the Frog, gave further evidence. When the talking frog seemed about to descend into the swamp of sexism, lang warned him that he "didn't want to go there." A warning which caused him, apparently, to gulp. In a publicity announcement for a cosmetic company during the spring of 1996, she and drag queen RuPaul had fun as the spokespersons. Good humor makes for good promotions, both for cosmetic companies and singing careers.

She and her band, The Reclines, first appeared on the album scene back in 1984 with *A Truly Western Experience* (Homestead). It was independently released, an eight-track recording made with $2,000 borrowed from her mother. The budgets have gone up since then. After being on the road, paying their dues one night at a time, and building a backlog of fans, they were ready for bigger and better experiences. The album was released at the same time lang and The Reclines had achieved a coveted spot at the Edmonton Folk Festival, an important event in the Canadian western music world.

Country and •

Western, Torch

and Twang

From there they took their music, and lang's high-energy, vocally superb performances to the professionals. Her manager, Larry Wanagas and Richard Flohil, a publicist and concert promoter from Toronto, booked "k.d. lang and the reclines" into a Toronto blues bar called Albert's Hall for the end of October of 1984. It was their East Coast debut. From there she became a celebrity.

By her second album, *Angel With a Lariat* (Sire, 1987), she'd gone international, wooing the American audience. The audience was more appreciative than the male establishment of the country and western music hierarchy. Other performers were more interested in her talent than her lesbianism, as evidenced by the number of collaborations of which she has been part. It was difficult getting air time, however. This marriage of lang and country and western couldn't last forever.

Ready to experiment with different styles of music, and looking, perhaps, for some room to stretch her talent, lang broke away from country with her fifth album, *Ingenue* (Sire, 1992). Reinventing her career? Not really; her popularity depends more upon her enduring talent than upon a style of music. Just as it was when she announced her

Le Jazz Hot •

homosexuality, nobody was all that surprised, except for a few odd minds that live in ivory towers.

Now, more than thirteen years after making a start with a little band, and hoping for success, lang is an established star in the business of music. She has also established a place in the public eye for the straightforward acceptance of gay performers. Those are about the only certain things in her career, because she has a talent for reinventing herself. At this point, no one can be certain what the next step will be, but it's sure to seem logical once she takes us there.

Profile by
Sandra Brandenburg

AUDRE LORDE

*A*n international political and social activist, Audre Lorde used

transforming incidents in her life to craft her essays and poetry and, in

turn, to recreate herself; hence, the truth of her often quoted, "I cannot

be categorized." Nonetheless, recognizing through experience the reali-

ty of worldwide societal categorizations that serve to marginalize, Lorde

confronted racism, sexism, and homophobia, empowering those many

women experiencing personal violence or battling cancer—most espe-

cially women of color and lesbians. A "sister/outsider" as a black

lesbian, Lorde's dialogue insisted on inclusion and breaking silences;

she contributed generously to build a global women's collective. In 1991

after receiving the Walt Whitman Citation of Merit in Albany, Lorde,

1934–1992 •

African American •

writer and

activist

speaking as state poet for New York, raised her familiar question, "What does it mean for a Black, lesbian, feminist, Warrior, poet, mother to live in a world full of the most intense contradictions?" The documentary *A Litany for Survival,* filmed from 1986 to 1992, conceived by Ada Gay Griffin and directed by Michelle Parkerson, records Audre Lorde's own life and work as one answer.

Born 18 February 1934, in New York City, Audre Geraldine Lorde was the third daughter born to Linda Balmar and Frederic Byron Lorde, a police officer and real estate owner. Her parents were West Indians who emigrated from Grenada to Harlem where, Robert Ridinger asserts in *The Gay & Lesbian Literary Companion,* the young Audre was raised "to fit the mold of many young woman maturing in that metropolitan area." That upbringing included Catholic schools, where Lorde says, "being smart was sometimes not as important as being good, and I was really bad" *(Litany).* Nevertheless, Lorde, whose near blindness until she was fitted with glasses at age three or four forced her to observe the world at close range, early on discovered a love of language, especially of poetry. "Words would get me high"; she especially liked the love poems of Edna St. Vincent Millay and would often quote lines of memorized poetry in response to others' questions.

She began writing poetry at twelve or thirteen "because I had a need inside of me to create something that was not here" *(Litany).* At Hunter High School, one poem was considered "much too romantic" for inclusion in the school paper. She triumphed when the poem was published in *Seventeen* (April 1951).

Two weeks after high school graduation, Lorde moved to her own apartment on the Lower East Side; she started classes at Hunter College, had a brief affair that resulted in a terminated pregnancy, and tried various jobs, including factory worker, nurse's aide, and domestic cleaner. In 1954, Lorde abandoned the very white "gay girl" scene in Greenwich Village to study at the National University of Mexico, where for the first time she was surrounded by brown-skinned people and, most important for her poetry, discovered that words could re-create rather than create her emotional world. Returning to New York, Lorde published "La Llorono" in *Venture* under the pseudonym Rey Domini (Audre Lorde in Latin). The mythical story captures the complex relationship with her mother, which is also evident in "Black Mother Woman" in *From a Land Where Other People Live* (1973). With *Zami: A New Spelling of My Name; A Biomythography* (1982), Lorde acknowledges the strong influence of her mother's recounts of her island life ("Zami" is "a Carriacou name for women who work together as friends and lovers," Lorde writes) and stresses the importance of learning from the continuity of historical roots, particularly from other cultures. In this autobiographical novel infused with myth, Lorde traces her adolescence and growing self-awareness, and with her lyrical, vivid descriptions breaks the silence about lesbian lovemaking. In *Contemporary Lesbian Writers of the United States,* Elaine Upton identifies "Martha" in *Cables to Rage* (1970) as "an early overtly lesbian poem." In 1972, Lorde read "Love Poem" in an Upper West Side coffeehouse no longer worrying who knew that she had always loved women, as she told Adrienne Rich in "An Interview" first published in *Signs* (1981); after the poem's publication in *Ms.,* she posted it on the English Department bulletin board at John Jay College of Criminal Justice, where she was teaching. But Lorde was not always overtly a lesbian.

By 1959, Lorde had earned a B.A. in literature and philosophy from Hunter College, where she edited the student magazine *Echo* and met a lifelong friend, historian Blanche Wiesen Cook. By the late 1960s, Cook and her partner Clare Coss formed part of Lorde's women's support network, joining her in numerous political and personal activities. After earning an M.L.S. at Columbia University, Lorde served as a librarian at the Mount Vernon Public Library and the Town School Library in New York City.

- *"Learning from*

the 60s"

Lorde's marriage in 1962 to attorney Edwin Ashley Rollins shocked the women who loved her. But as Cook suggests in *Litany,* women, especially lesbians, married at that time. As Lorde says, "to be a black woman poet in the 60s was to be invisible, really invisible . . . triple invisible as black, lesbian and feminist." Before the interracial couple divorced in 1970, two children, Elizabeth and Jonathan, added "lesbian mother" to Lorde's many dimensions. She raised her children "as warriors, not cannon fodder," Jonathan attests in *Litany,* "she never let us get away with not fighting." Lorde's essay "Man Child: A Black Lesbian Feminist's Response" collected in *Sister Outsider: Essays and Speeches* (1984) offered understanding to other lesbian mothers facing their sons' manhood. In "Turning the Beat Around: Lesbian Parenting 1986" *(A Burst of Light),* she reflects on learning to control her black woman's pent-up anger and guide her children toward self definition. The dialogue continued in the 1993 *Ms.* article "Raising Sons."

Earlier, however, in 1968, amidst her collapsing marriage, Lorde began to achieve some recognition: she won an NEA grant and her first book of poetry, *The First Cities* (1968), was published just after she spent six weeks as poet-in-residence at Tougaloo College, a black college in Mississippi. Despite her fears, Tougaloo's nurturing environment provided Lorde with her first opportunity to work with black people. She identified their need for "strong Black people" under their own definitions and offered them her strength and honesty. Most of the poems in *Cables to Rage* were written at Tougaloo. When Lorde left Tougaloo she knew that being a librarian was not enough—she had to teach. She also knew that Frances Clayton, whom she met there, would be a permanent part of her life. For nineteen years, Clayton shared Lorde's house on Staten Island as lover and co-mother to Lorde's children. Martin Luther King Jr.'s assassination, announced while she listened to her former Tougaloo students in a concert at Lincoln Center, galvanized her resolve to become more involved.

The publication of her first poetry collection *The First Cities* precipitated another important decision: Lorde began teaching, at first holding several part-time positions. She accepted Mina Shaughnessy's invitation to teach in the pre-baccalaureate SEEK writing program at City College. Again terrified, Lorde taught her students as well as herself; with them, she learned prose writing. Teaching "Race and the Urban Situation" in the education department at mostly white Herbert H. Lehman College of the City University of New York helped Lorde clarify her responsibility to black students, especially to black women.

Next, she successfully petitioned John Jay College to offer a course on racism as well as a remedial writing course using creative writing. At John Jay, as an open lesbian in the black community, Lorde again used honesty and openness in heading off her critics. In "Learning from the 60s" *(Sister Outsider)* and again in *Litany,* Lorde stresses that differences must be respected and used for change, a directive she followed in and out of the classroom. With her induction into the Hunter College Hall of Fame in 1980 Lorde capped a distinguished teaching career within the City University of New York. After a decade at John Jay, she moved to Hunter College and subsequently held the Thomas Hunter Professorship; in 1985 students and friends dedicated the Audre Lorde Women's Center on her alma mater's campus.

Over the next decade Lorde's work as teacher, contributor to journals, and poetry editor of *Chrysalis* and *Amazon Quarterly* placed her in the forefront of feminist voices within the academy. In 1972 and again in 1976, she won Creative Artists Public Service Grants. The first supported preparation of *From a Land Where Other People Live,* nominated for the National Book Award along with work by Alice Walker and Adrienne Rich. When Rich received the award she accepted for all three "in the name of all women whose voices have gone and still go unheard in a patriarchal world." In 1975 Lorde won the Broadside Press Poet's Award, and Staten Island Community College named her Woman of the Year. Continuing to teach at John Jay College, Lorde published additional volumes of poetry and essays, including the political poetry in *New York Head Shop and Museum* (1974); *Between Ourselves* (1976); *Coal* (1976); and *The Black Unicorn* (1978). She delivered papers, such as "The Transformation of Silence Into Language and Action" at the Modern Language Association's "Lesbian and Literature" panel in 1977. The *Out and Out* pamphlet *Uses of the Erotic: The Erotic as Power*, first delivered at the Fourth Berkshire Conference on the History of Women at Mount Holyoke in 1978, asserts the erotic as "the nurturer or nursemaid of all our deepest knowledge" *(Sister Outsider)*. In the late 1970s, Lorde and Barbara Smith co-founded Kitchen Table: Women of Color Press in a fusion of politics and art to further the liberation of women of color.

Lorde kept personal journals; they provided "seeds" for poems, such as "Harriet," "Suckle," and "The Litany for Survival," all found in *Black Unicorn*. Considered Lorde's most mature poetry, the volume has as central motifs the ancient women of Dahomey and repression as a means of control. "Notes From a Trip to Russia" records her observations from the 1976 African-Asian Writers Conference in Moscow. This and others of her essays and addresses from 1976 to 1983 are collected in *Sister Outsider: Essays and Speeches* (1984). The book is a classic in women's studies courses and takes its name from a poem in *Black Unicorn*, "Sister Outsider," which, as Barbara Christian notes in *The Women's Review of Books*, is a compression of most of Lorde's concerns.

• *Breaks Another*

Taboo

The journal entries also proved the source for another book. In 1978 Lorde was diagnosed with breast cancer, and thus began a fourteen-year battle. *The Cancer Journals* (1980), even with its title, meets the disease and the medical profession head on. Lorde documents her mastectomy and subsequent decision not to implant a prosthesis. By now, the formerly "tongue-tied" Lorde could skillfully use language to record the roller coaster ride of her emotions and her outrage at medical assumptions and women's lack of choices. The book won Book of the Year for 1981 from the American Library Association's Gay Task Force. Again Lorde's honest voice led the way in writing about taboo subjects. Her courage and forthrightness about cancer empowered other women in similar circumstances. Paul Russell, in *The Gay 100*, accurately notes, "Lorde was a fierce truth speaker who influenced a whole generation to see with new eyes."

As one expects, cancer did not slow Audre Lorde. If anything, as Jonathan Rollins says of his mother, her "life took on a kind of immediacy; there was a change in the tone of her writing" *(Litany)*. On her fiftieth birthday, she wrote in her journal essay "A Burst of Light: Living With Cancer," "Cheers to the years! Doing what I like to do best" *(A Burst of Light)*; she was at the University of Ohio addressing the black students. With Gloria I. Joseph, Lorde co-mothered Sisters in Support of Sisters in South Africa (SISA). By March 1984, however, doctors were urging a liver biopsy; she refused the invasive surgery.

In "Living on the Line," Gloria T. Hull observes that "place is central in Lorde's work." Indeed, Audre cared deeply about people and the global environment. She traveled to reach across differences, especially internationally. May and June 1984 found her in Berlin teaching a course on Black American women poets and leading a workshop in English. She introduced German women of the Diaspora to the word "Afro-German" and encouraged them to organize. Eventually they published *Farabe Bekennen (Showing Our Colors)*. She read her poetry in Switzerland. While in Berlin she sought advice and treatment from an anthroposophic doctor, which continued yearly until shortly before her death. In 1984 Lorde was awarded the Borough of Manhattan President's Award for Literary Excellence. Indefatigable, she visited women writers in Cuba, and in August 1985 delivered "The Language of Difference" as the keynote address at a Woman's Writing Conference in Melbourne, Australia, incorporated in the journal essay "A Burst of Light," published in the 1989 book of the same name, which won the American Book Award.

By November 1985, however, a second anthroposophic doctor recommended Lorde seek treatment at the Lukas Klinik in Arlesheim, Switzerland, where, accompanied by Frances Clayton, Lorde accepted the diagnosis and challenge of living with metastasized cancer. As she said, "Battling cancer is very, very much to me like battling racism, like battling sexism. I often visualize it in very political terms. . . . [I visualize] cancer cells as white South African policemen" *(Litany)*.

In 1986 in St. Croix, Lorde participated in "The Ties That Bind," a conference on Caribbean women, and in Bonnieux, France, she met with the Zamani Soweto Sisters from South Africa as part of her ongoing work with SISA. As guest professor at the University of Berlin in 1989, Lorde continued her work with Afro-German women. In 1990 Lorde's life and work were honored and celebrated when over a thousand women from twenty-three countries gathered for the "I Am Your Sister" conference in Boston. Nnosing Ellen Kuzwayo, a member of the South African Parliament, addressed Audre: "You have sent your message just through your love, your warmth and everything a human being in the leadership should have" *(Litany)*. Other accolades included the Walt Whitman Citation of Merit in 1991 and appointment as the Poet Laureate of New York State by then-Governor Mario Cuomo. In St. Croix, the Pan African Support Group organized the ceremony at which Lorde received the name Gamba Adisa, meaning "warrior, one who gives meaning to her words." She continued to write poems, many collected in *The Marvelous Arithmetics of Distance: Poems 1987–1992* (1993), for as she wrote to women, "Poetry is not a luxury. It is a vital necessity of our experience" *(Sister Outsider)*.

She danced until the end; the final poem in the collection is "The Electric Slide Boogie," dated 3 January 1992.

Audre Lorde died on 17 November 1992, in St. Croix where she lived with her companion Dr. Gloria I. Joseph. Since then, the documentary "A Litany for Survival" has been released, and in the summer of 1994 the Caribbean Cultural Center African Diaspora Institute saluted her with the exhibit "Transcending Silence: The Life and Poetic Legacy of Audre Lorde." The political legacy of Audre Lorde, as friend Blanche Wiesen Cook reminded at the memorial service held 18 January 1993, is for "each of us to dedicate our lives to activism . . . so that we may reclaim and re-vision the world" *(Transcending Silence)*.

Profile by
Judith C. Kohl

GREG LOUGANIS

*G*reg Louganis is considered by sportswriters, fellow athletes, and

fans to be the greatest diver in world history. For over a decade he was

unbeatable in diving competitions. He found comfort in the natural

athletic finesse of acrobatics and the springboard. The pool was a

sanctuary where he could be himself and do what he most enjoyed.

1960– ·

American ·

Olympic athlete

Gregory Efthimios Louganis was born on 29 January 1960, in San Diego, California. His biological parents of Samoan and Northern European ancestry were fifteen at the time of Louganis' birth and placed him up for adoption. He was adopted by Peter and Frances Louganis of El Cajon, California. His father, Peter, was a controller for the American Tuna Boat Association in San Diego. Reared in a middle-class neighborhood, Louganis had a difficult childhood. Because of dyslexia and his dark Samoan complexion he was often ridiculed as a child. Adolescence was a time of confused sexuality, and being adopted, he was unsure of parental affection.

Louganis and his adopted sister, Despina, took dance lessons as young children. During the dance lessons he was taught to visualize and think through complex routines—a practice that would later assist him in performing highly technical dives in competition.

Dr. Sammy Lee, a two-time Olympic diving gold medalist, watched Greg Louganis' 1971 AAU Junior Olympics performance at Colorado Springs, Colorado. Afterward Lee stated: "His spring was so much higher than that of any child his age. . . . He was years ahead of his group." Coached by Dr. Lee in the 1976 Olympics in Montreal, Quebec, Canada, Louganis captured the silver medal in the platform diving finals and finished sixth in springboard diving.

In 1978, Louganis emerged as a preeminent diver, winning the platform championship at the World Aquatic Championship and the U.S. Diving indoor 1-meter and 10-meter titles. He entered Florida's University of Miami the same year. While attending the university, Louganis captured numerous titles. Since the NCAA had no platform diving event Louganis was restricted to springboard diving, forcing him to concentrate and improve his technique in this area.

The following year Louganis won gold medals in the springboard and platform events at the Pan American Games. He was favored to win both competitions at the 1980 Olympic Games in Moscow, but was prevented from participating by the United States boycott of the games. Louganis transferred to the University of California at Irvine in 1981 to train under coach Ron O'Brien, of the Mission Viejo Nadadores Diving Club.

Under O'Brien's direction Louganis repeated winning both springboard and platform titles in the 1982 World Championships. At the meet he became the first diver in international competition to be awarded scores of a perfect 10 from all seven judges, performing an inward one-and-one-half pike. His front three-and-one-half pike received 92.07 points, the highest score ever awarded a single dive.

At the 1984 Olympic Games in Los Angeles Louganis captured gold medals in both the platform and springboard diving events—the first time since 1928 that a male diver captured the title in both events. His score of 710.91 points in the platform diving event made him the first diver to break the 700 point barrier in championship competition. This same year Louganis was given the Sullivan Award, naming him the country's amateur athlete of the year. He graduated from the University of California at Irvine in 1983 with a bachelor of arts degree in drama. In 1986 he was awarded the Jesse Owens International Trophy, and in the following year was named the 1987 USCO Sportsman of the Year.

Louganis held an undefeated string of 3-meter springboard titles from 1981 to 1987 until he took second place at the U.S. Diving Indoor Championships. Louganis won the springboard and platform diving events six years straight at the U.S. Olympic Festival from 1982 through

1987. He repeated as double gold medal winner in both platform and springboard diving at the 1986 Worlds and the 1987 Pan American Games. By August 1988 Louganis had garnered an impressive record of diving victories. He had won forty-seven of sixty-seven U.S. indoor or outdoor U.S. Diving National Championships, went undefeated in Olympic Trials from 1976–88, and won Pan American gold medals a record ten times from 1979–87.

O'Brien trained Greg Louganis for the 1988 Olympic Games in Seoul, South Korea. O'Brien, like Dr. Lee, believed that Louganis was the best diver in the history of the sport. Louganis had the rare talent to combine strength, power, and grace in a unique blend that was his trademark. He captured gold medals in both the springboard and platform events for a second consecutive time. In order to capture the gold in platform diving Louganis had to successfully complete a reverse three-and-one-half somersault in the tuck position, the "dive of death." The dive had a degree of difficulty of 3.4, compounded by the fact that a Russian diver had died striking his head on the platform, while attempting the dive at the World University Games in Edmonton, Canada. Louganis skillfully hit the dive and won the gold medal.

But the Seoul Olympics would not be one without controversy for Louganis. Early in 1988 he tested HIV-positive and Coach O'Brien was the only person at the games who knew of his HIV status. On the ninth of his eleven qualifying springboard dives Louganis struck his head on the diving board, leaving an open wound. While the risk of HIV transmission was extremely negligible, the attending physician Dr. Puffer was not informed of his status and stitched Louganis' head wound without gloves or adequate precautions.

Following the 1988 Olympic Games, Louganis "lost the water," in diver's terminology. His personal life had been marred by an abusive relationship in the mid 1980s. His manager quickly took over managing Louganis' career and their life, at the same time embezzling most of his money. While Louganis' homosexuality was an open secret in diving circles and his HIV status a guarded secret, it wasn't until the 1994 Gay Games IV in New York that he came out publicly.

In 1994 Louganis met author Eric Marcus. He collaborated with Marcus on his autobiography, *Breaking the Surface,* which was a cathartic event for Louganis. In over seventy hours of taped interviews Louganis revealed his bouts of depression, attempted suicide, drug abuse, rape at knife-point by a lover, abusive relationships, loss of a loved one to AIDS, and the revelation of his own HIV status. His autobiography showed how he overcame these obstacles with the same grace, prowess, and beauty that signified his diving career. The book

- *Autobiography*

Proved

Cathartic

soon appeared on the *New York Times* bestseller list and negotiations were underway for a television movie based on the book. Louganis then went on to star in the 1995 off-Broadway solo show, *The Only Thing Worse You Could Have Told Me*. He also appeared as Darius in the New York production of *Jeffrey,* a play about gay dating and HIV in the 1990s. Delivering the most poignant line in the play, Darius states to Jeffrey, "Hate AIDS, Jeffrey, not life."

Louganis has set the mark in athletic competition that few other athletes have achieved. He has overcome adversity in his personal life with the same skill and finesse that was the trademark of his diving career. And he has lead the way for a greater understanding of the personal side of AIDS.

Profile by Michael A. Lutes

PHYLLIS ANN LYON and DEL MARTIN

*F*or well over forty years, Phyllis Lyon and Del Martin have stood for

much that is insightful, brave, pioneering, and progressive in the

development of a successful lesbian community in the United States.

Though born in 1924 in Tulsa, Oklahoma, Lyon was raised and

educated primarily in the San Francisco area. Martin, born in 1921, is

a San Francisco native. Both concentrated on journalism as a career,

with courses and newspaper posts at both San Francisco State and the

University of California at Berkeley. At both institutions, they held

editorial positions at the campus newspapers. There followed work

on trade publications in architecture and building in both Seattle

and San Francisco. Additionally, Lyon attained a doctor of

American ·

writers and

activists

259 ·

education degree in human sexuality at Berkeley.

When she was just nineteen, Martin married James Martin. They had one daughter and were subsequently divorced. Lyon has never married. From the time when they really formed their lesbian partnership, on 14 February 1953, Lyon and Martin have been unceasing in their activities to change the self-understanding of lesbians from the perverted, guilt-ridden, oppressed persona that most homosexual women of that time maintained to that of the healthful, proud, assertive lesbians of today. In the process of their own self-revision, Lyon and Martin led other women out of the closet, gradually eliminating the stigma stamped on them by a homophobic society and replacing it with a new identity of pride and social validity.

• **Organized the**

Daughters of

Bilitis

It must be remembered, however, that the beginning of the change was small, informal, and even somewhat furtive. In the early 1950s, when the scourge of McCarthyism was rampant in the nation, exposure of any gay person's homosexuality was as sought after as a revelation of association with communism. Gay groups such as the early Mattachine often felt only marginally safe even behind drawn shades in supposedly private homes. In this atmosphere, the beginning of a secret society of lesbians was a little party of eight women meeting in Lyon and Martin's apartment in a Castro neighborhood that was still far from being an internationally famous gay enclave.

By the fourth meeting, a name for the group was seen as necessary, and one member suggested Daughters of Bilitis. Bilitis was identified from a long love poem by the French writer Piere Louys (1870–1925). She was supposed to have lived on the island of Lesbos at the time of lesbian poet Sappho (600 B.C.). The name had an appropriateness for the group and could also be thought a sly screen because it sounded as innocuous as any other "ladies' lodge." The organization became familiarly known as DOB.

After a first year of working out rules and regulations, the DOB brought out the first issue of the *Ladder,* a twelve-page mimeographed magazine, with Lyon as editor. This publication asserted the DOB's purpose: to help lesbians discover their potential and place in society. Specifically, it would assist the lesbian in her search for her personal, interpersonal, social, economic, and vocational identity.

The fame of the *Ladder* and the DOB spread. At the crest of its fame and influence, there were chapters of the DOB in Chicago, Boston, New Orleans, Reno, Portland, San Diego, Cleveland, Denver, Detroit, Philadelphia, and even Melbourne, Australia. In the early

1960s, the DOB gained greater notice throughout the country, beginning with its first national convention in San Francisco in 1960.

In the immediately following years, the DOB was active everywhere in encouraging lesbians to come out and in preparing for legal changes, enlisting support from such politicos as Philip Burton, at that time a member of the California legislature. Lyon and Martin today believe that the first convention and the later founding of the Council on Religion and the Homosexual are among the highest points in their careers in the advancement of lesbian status.

The protest of the CRH against the police conduct at the New Year's Ball on 1 January 1965, where such tactics as the photographing of all entering and other acts of intimidation were utilized, marked a powerful first in organized condemnation of the harassment of gay and lesbian people. The spectacle of organized religion rebuking the police was an astonishing development.

Episcopal Bishop James A. Pike named Martin and Don Lucas of the Mattachine Society to a Joint Committee on Homosexuality from the Diocesan Departments of Ministry and Social Relations. A major result was an endorsement of homosexual law reform, along with a denouncement of entrapment procedures and an assertion of the need for a broad sex education program for clergy and laity alike. Another important consequence was support from the Northern California Council of Churches for the elimination of the anti-sodomy law.

A recurring irritant to active lesbians during the 1960s and 1970s was the tendency of gay male groups to marginalize lesbians. Such groups as the DOB were ignored, their achievements disregarded. Martin points out that even such reputable figures as the historian Martin Duberman gave next to no attention to such events as the first DOB convention. Finally, in some disgust, Martin published an article called "Goodbye, My Alienated Brothers" in an autumn 1970 *Advocate,* the national gay news magazine. The following statement was typical: "Goodbye the male chauvinists of the homophile movement who are so wrapped up in the 'cause' they represent that they have lost sight of the people for whom the cause came into being."

Today, Martin feels that the piece was quite true at the time of publication and is, even now, not without relevance, though relations between the gay sexes have improved. "The situation now," she stated in interview, "is that in times of crisis, the two sexes unite in effort. And since 1980, the accepted practice of using the phrase 'gay and lesbian' has diminished the assumption that 'gay' is all inclusive."

Clashes •

Between Gay

and Feminist

Movements

Lyon and Martin have also seen through difficult relations between lesbians and the National Organization for Women. DOB's leaders did not find an immediate response for the women's movement even from lesbians themselves. Lyon and Martin point out that many members of the homophile movement and the women's movement found themselves torn between the two, citing Barbara Gittings and Kay Tobin especially. But the most adamant single opponent to lesbians in the women's movement was NOW's original leader and longtime reigning high priestess, Betty Friedan. When in 1969 Martin wrote to Friedan suggesting that NOW take a definite stand on the lesbian issue in its March national conference, Friedan did not reply.

Lyon and Martin point out that this reticence was, in a way, to be expected, given the long history of male rejection of NOW or any other effort of women to achieve equality by simply calling such women "dykes." But gradually, the women of NOW came to realize that many of the members, including some in leadership positions, were lesbians.

Resolution of the conflict came when some 750 delegates to the 1971 conference of the National Organization for Women in Los Angeles voted overwhelmingly that "a woman's right to her own person includes the right to define and express her own sexuality and to choose her own life style" and that "the oppression of Lesbians is a legitimate concern of feminism."

• *Expanding*

Public

Understanding

of Lesbian

Issues

Such statements reflect the change that swept the gay movement for both men and women in the post-Stonewall period. From the drive for rights and decent tolerance, the more militant activists of both sexes demanded liberation. This difference is strong in Lyon and Martin's 1973 book, *Lesbian Love and Liberation*. They state now that this volume should be thought of as "The Yes Book on Sex." Also an advancement was the inclusion of pictures.

Other developments demonstrated that Lyon and Martin were involved in a wider variety of feminist issues. Martin's 1976 book *Battered Wives* asserts that liberation of women must include recognition of injustice against spouses, including those in both heterosexual and lesbian unions.

But the work that remains their greatest contribution to lesbianism is *Lesbian/Woman,* which first appeared in 1972 and was re-published with updates in a special twentieth-anniversary edition in 1992. In the introduction, Lyon and Martin are emphatic that while there can probably never be a definitive or a truly objective book on the Lesbian, they believe that a representation of the experiences of lesbian life, expressed in lesbians' own terms and in the context of lesbians' own self-awareness, is the best single means for bringing understanding of lesbian nature to all who need to know it.

They set about accomplishing this goal by first differentiating between myth and reality through describing their own discoveries and then showing how diverse lesbians can be in our own society and other cultures of the world, correcting stereotypes and misinterpretations en route.

Similarly, descriptions of the development of self-image in Martin's own experience, compared with those of other lesbians, demonstrates how the growth of a lesbian's psychological self is little different from that of a heterosexual. But here too, those influences that distort and therefore warp the psyche are excoriated. The authors conclude this chapter on the lesbian's evolution of her own identity with this observation: "She must find her own destiny out of her own guts."

"What do Lesbians do sexually?" With that arresting question, the authors open their chapter on sexuality and sex roles. Their multifaceted answer is candid and helpful, including a blunt warning against such chauvinist distortions as those of Dr. David Reuben in his *Everything You Always Wanted to Know About Sex but Were Afraid to Ask*. As for social stereotypes of "butch" and "femme," Lyon and Martin's familiarity with many different lesbians in a wide variety of situations, including therapeutic ones, affirm that such role playing is followed in only a minority of pairings.

The chapter "Life Styles" explores the relationships of major life components, such as matings, vocations, families, races, and scenes for socialization. After a review of all influential aspects, Lyon and Martin conclude that "Lesbians are pretty much the same around the world." But the reader is well prepared for that statement by a thorough and often vivid depiction of individual cases. The next chapter extends the life styles consideration to include the role of mothering.

In "Growing Up Gay," Lyon and Martin delineate the needs and problems of girls realizing their lesbianism and trying to act on it in a fulfilling way. The most difficult hurdles facing emerging lesbian young women involve their family relationships. Much of this chapter is straightforward advice to both the girls and their parents. A major warning for parents is to not immediately run to a psychiatrist, especially since many of these therapists are ill-informed and ill-suited to be truly therapeutic to such troubled young women.

In "Lesbian Paranoia—Real and Imagined" Lyon and Martin explore the differences between the two states of mind, carefully advising the use of a positive self-image coupled with a growing understanding of how the individual can change. The concluding advice is to be "honest about yourself" and make decisions on that basis.

One of the main advantages for lesbians today, Lyon and Martin affirm, is that organizations exist that provide a social-psychological context to give strength to a developing identity. While they hold to the civilized processes vital to a democratic society, they certainly do not devalue the defiant militancy that appeared after Stonewall, citing the example of an eastern U.S. group called the Lesbian Avengers, who marshalled lesbian power to defeat a statewide anti-gay initiative in Idaho.

For the twentieth-anniversary edition of *Lesbian/Woman,* Lyon and Martin have wisely added an update that combines carefully selected anecdotal pieces and mini-histories of developments showing the presence of lesbian influence in many fields of endeavor. Typical is the story of Miriam Ben-Shalom, who made blazingly clear her self identity as a "radical Lesbian feminist" in the U.S. Army Reserve and fought court battles to stay in the service as a constitutional right. Similarly, the growth of lesbian influence in the arts of comedy, music, theater, film, and video is well documented. Health matters, such as a discussion of Chronic Fatigue Syndrome and cancer, the latter as a "silent crisis," are also reviewed. Important to both lesbians and gay men, the AIDS epidemic and its consequences are discussed.

Gay and lesbian events that have become international institutions are traced in genesis, development, and preservation. The Gay Olympics is a prime example, with the authors recapitulating how the games originated in the vision and drive of Dr. Tom Waddell, were extended in four-year intervals, and had to suffer the ignominy of being refused the use of the term 'Olympic' by U.S. court order because Congress had made the term the property of the U.S. Olympic Committee. Nevertheless, the Gay Games go on in much the same spirit as the original. The authors captured this spirit when they described the feelings of the spectators when the participants were formed on the field of Kezar Stadium at the 1982 games: "Everyone at the ceremonies was moved emotionally by the pride of belonging to a Lesbian/Gay extended family that encompasses the planet."

Concluding their update, Lyon and Martin outline a "Lesbian Agenda for the 1990s." Applauding the growing movement to come out, the authors see the appearance of new leaders among many groups, ethnic and youth organizations especially, as a great harbinger, advising followers and supporters to "develop and treasure our new leaders."

Far from diminishing their activities, Lyon and Martin remain busy as ever in the mid-1990s. They have their own company, LyMar Associates, an agency for consultation, writing, and lecture sponsorship. Reflecting their own age, but also pioneering for the lesbian movement as a whole, they now are deeply involved in what they call "old lesbians organizing for change."

**Profile by
Marvin S. Shaw**

265 •

IAN McKELLEN

Sir Ian McKellen has long been considered one of the theater's finest

1939– •

classical actors, particularly for his roles in a variety of Shakespeare

productions. Apart from his acting career, however, McKellen has also

British actor, •

worked as an activist. Because of his distinction of being the first openly

writer, and

gay British actor to have been recognized by his country's government,

activist

McKellen has succeeded in gaining considerable public attention for the

cause of gay rights.

Ian Murray McKellen was born in Burnley, England, on 25 May 1939. He attended Wigan Grammar School and the Bolton School. By the age of twelve he was acting regularly in productions at Bolton. But, while he was aware of his attraction to men long before adolescence, his life was focused on his acting, not on his libido. McKellen later attended St. Catharine's College, Cambridge, where he earned his bachelor of arts degree in 1962.

During his time at Cambridge—nine terms in all—McKellen began his acting career, playing twenty-one parts over the years. He made his stage debut in 1961 in *A Man for All Seasons* at the Belgrade Theater, Coventry. McKellen's London debut came in 1964 in the role of Godfrey in *A Scent of Flowers,* for which he won a Clarence Derwent Award. His performance was sufficiently impressive and, as a result, landed him a season with the National Theatre, thereby beginning to cultivate a professional reputation. In 1967, McKellen made his New York debut. He performed in *The Promise,* and in 1968 his performances in *White Liars* and *Black Comedy* earned him rave reviews. By 1970, McKellen had established himself as one of the contemporary theater's finest performers with title roles in *Richard II* and *Edward II.*

In addition to his acting, McKellen has helped to found and establish his own theater companies. Most notable of these was the Actor's Company, founded in 1972. In the Actor's Company all of the performers were equal, sharing in choosing plays, receiving equal pay, billing, and lead roles. In 1974 McKellen joined the Royal Shakespeare Company, where he performed in a number of acclaimed productions over a four-year period. McKellen left the Royal Shakespeare Company in 1978 when he accepted a role in *Bent,* a drama about gays in Nazi concentration camps, for which he was given the Laurence Olivier Award for best actor. Around this time he began touring with his extremely popular one-man show, *Acting Shakespeare,* which also garnered several awards, including the Edinburgh Festival's Drama Desk, Elliot Norton, and Antionette Perry awards.

In 1988, McKellen decided to come out and thus became the first major actor in England to do so. At that time, Great Britain—or rather, Margaret Thatcher's conservative party—was considering an anti-gay measure known as Clause 28. Clause 28 would have once again made gay behavior between consenting adults illegal in addition to, according to Ephraim Katz, forbidding the government "from allocating monies that would in any way 'promote' homosexuality." Because of this, McKellen received much criticism in 1991 for accepting knighthood from Thatcher, especially from the now-deceased Derek Jarman who saw Thatcher as an enemy of the gay and lesbian community. McKellen didn't see these incidents in the same way. As England's preeminent interpreter of Shakespeare, and the first actor of his generation to be knighted, McKellen believes that he, as part of the establishment, is in a strategic position to "dismantle it."

Others, arguing in favor of McKellen's knighthood, saw it as the recognition and acceptance of an openly gay actor by the government and the beginning of the end of the need for public figures to keep their sexual preference secret. McKellen, they argued, made no secret of his contempt for the government's policies concerning gays. As a gay man who has been successfully functioning in straight society for more than thirty years, McKellen considers himself a "gay communicator with the straight population." Since coming out, McKellen has become a vocal spokesperson for gay rights, and a regular visitor to Prime Minister John Major's residence at 10 Downing Street to lobby for lesbian and gay rights. McKellen regrets that so many gays and lesbians live in what they believe is the safety of the closet. Many, he says, do as he did when he was their age; but frankly lying about their sexuality, pretending to wait for the right woman or man, or entering into sham marriages is not anything he encourages. "In my own defense," he says, "I never lied."

Although McKellen speaks of two committed relationships, each eight years long, the theater is the one place where he has consistently devoted himself and where he feels he is most at home and in control of himself. When judged solely on his success in that medium, it would seem that he is correct.

Profile by
Andrea L. T. Peterson

CHERRIE MORAGA

*A*s a playwright, poet, and essayist who gained mainstream acclaim

in the late 1970s and 1980s, Cherrie Moraga was among the first to

break through the suffocating boundaries of Chicana/lesbian/feminist

writing. Her work not only embodies and speaks to the Chicana

experience in general—domestic violence, immigrant rights, male and

Catholic domination—but throws open the closet door for lesbian

Chicanas to embrace their unique status as newly radicalized voices for

their own culture within a culture. "My lesbianism is the avenue

through which I have learned the most about silence and oppression,"

she told interviewer Skye Ward in 1991, "and it continues to be the most

tactile reminder to me that we are not free human beings."

1952– •

Chicana •

writer and

activist

Cherrie Moraga was born on 25 September 1952 in Whittier, California to a Chicana mother and an Anglo father of British-Canadian descent. Her childhood was thus defined by a dichotomy of cultures; she was surrounded by the Spanish language and Mexican traditions of her mother's family, yet she avoided alienation by being able to blend in easily with her white schoolmates. Her mother and aunts were passionate storytellers, and her paternal grandmother was a vaudeville actress who also instilled in her a love for theater. Countless childhood hours were spent in the family kitchen listening to stories, giving Moraga an early appreciation for writing and drama. "The oppositions of race collide inside of me," she told Ward, "(and) my writing is always an attempt at reconciliation."

In 1974, Moraga received a bachelor of arts degree from a private college in Hollywood, becoming one of the few college-educated people in her family. She then taught English at a private high school in Los Angeles for two years, a period she credits with solidifying her need to write. After enrolling in a creative writing class at the Women's Building, she began the tentative process of coming out both as a Chicana and as a lesbian, spurred by the dual injustice of heterosexism and the fact that lesbian literature at the time largely reflected the experiences of white women. "Fundamentally," she told *Art in America* in 1990, "I started writing to save my life. Yes, my own life first."

"Writing to Save •

My Life"

Her first works were lesbian love poems, and Moraga cites her discovery of Judy Grahn's poem "A Woman Is Talking to Death" as instrumental in cementing her need to write not only as a lesbian, but as a Chicana as well. In 1977, she left the comfort of her teaching position and her extended family in Los Angeles to move to San Francisco, where she pursued an education in feminist/lesbian/Chicana literature at San Francisco State, in coffeehouses, and among a rich variety of like-minded women.

In 1979, Moraga met writer Gloria Anzaldua, and together they edited the groundbreaking anthology *This Bridge Called My Back: Writings by Radical Women of Color* (1981). The collection was precedent-setting because it gave voice to women of color, and expressed their rage at racism and oppression not only in general society, but in the women's movement as well. *Bridge* was a testament to Moraga's drive and vision. After being rejected by dozens of squeamish publishers, Moraga, African American lesbian activist Barbara Smith, and writer/ poet Audre Lorde co-founded Kitchen Table/Women of Color Press to publish it. The book went on to win the American Book Award from the Before Columbus Foundation and is widely used in women's studies courses around the country.

In the preface to *Bridge,* Moraga politicized her literary stance by identifying these women as "the revolutionary forces who bridge the divisions within society." Moraga's own contributions, an essay titled "La Guera" and two poems called "The Welder" and "For the Color of My Mother," launched her work into a political orbit with pressures of its own. "After *Bridge,*" she told Ward, "I felt my communities were standing over my shoulders whenever I tried to write. . . . When one has to represent a community, you can lose the integrity and freedom of your own individual perspective."

• *"The Woman I*

Was Raised to

Be"

Loving in the War Years (1983) followed soon after, revolutionary as well because it was the first collection of celebratory, passionate poems and journal entries written by a Chicana lesbian, and written in Spanish and English. But in *Loving,* Moraga also includes two essays that take Chicano culture to task for its verbal and sexual silencing of Chicanas. "I am a Chicana lesbian," she writes. "My own particular relationship to being a sexual person, and a radical, stands in direct contradiction to, and violation of, the woman I was raised to be." The seed of Moraga's yearning to speak to her larger community was planted.

In 1983, Moraga co-edited and contributed to *Cuentos: Stories by Latinas,* also published by Kitchen Table/Women of Color Press and, like *Bridge,* a standard text in women's studies courses across the country. In her review of *Cuentos* for the magazine *Third Woman,* Ana Castillo summed up the sentiments of many Chicanas when she said that "the book resounds with the exhilarated breath of the degagged."

In 1984, Moraga presented her first play, *Giving Up the Ghost,* at the Minneapolis women's theater Foot of the Mountain. In moving monologues, her three main characters explode myths of sexual isolation, challenge claims that defiant Chicanas are traitors to their race, and underscore the complexities of women's relationships in Chicana culture. According to Ward, *Ghost* points out "the salvation and liberation of Chicanas (as) realized through Chicana sisterhood—women loving women as sisters, mothers, daughters, and lovers."

Perhaps one of Moraga's most moving tributes to Chicano, Indian, homosexual, and half-breed culture in general is *The Last Generation,* a collection of her poems and essays dedicated to Audre Lorde and Cesar Chavez which was published in 1986. There she describes her work as "a prayer at a time when I no longer remember how to pray . . . (a recognition of) the violent collision between the European and the Indigenous, the birth of a colonization that would give birth to me."

Moraga herself describes her shift to playwrighting as a reunion with her people. "It was a great revelation," she told *Art in America* in 1990, "that a much larger community of people could inhabit me and speak through me." Her second play, *Shadow of a Man* (1990), examines the relationship between a mother straightjacketed by tradition and a daughter bent on making her own rules. Generational struggles within the Chicano family are made analogous to those between Chicanos and the dominant Anglo culture. After cavalierly losing her virginity, the daughter exclaims: "I wanted it to be worthless, Mama . . . not for me to be worthless, but to know that my worth had nothing to do with it."

Moraga's third play, *Heroes and Saints,* also dramatizes a Chicana woman's struggle for freedom and individuation, but from a more mythic perspective. Here, the main character, Cerezita, is a head without a body, confined to a wheelchair because of her mother's pesticide exposure in the fields, who dreams of liberation for herself and her people.

"Just as we have been radicalized in the process of writing this book," Moraga and Anzaldua wrote in the preface to *Bridge,* "we hope it will radicalize others into action." And just as Moraga has found a recuperative voice within her own struggle for identity, she imparts a wish for that same sense of recuperation and reunion among her readers. "If in the long run," she writes in her poem *If,* "we weep together/ hold each other/ wipe the other's mouth/ dry the kiss pressed there/ to seal the touch/ of spirits separated/ by something as necessary/ as time/ we will have done enough."

Reunion and •

Recuperation

Profile by
Jerome Szymczak

MARTINA NAVRATILOVA

1956– •

*F*rom *1970s apolitical athlete to 1990s lesbian and gay activist/*

spokesperson, Martina Navratilova has held steadfast to the often brutal

Naturalized •

roller-coaster ride of fame. From the tennis court to the palimony court,

American

from the painful decision to defect from Czechoslovakia for her beloved

tennis player

America to an outright rejection by a homophobic tabloid and sports

press, Martina has courageously held out for true acceptance—not mere

tolerance—on her own terms. "What our movement needs most," she

told a crowd of hundreds of thousands at the Gay and Lesbian March on

Washington in 1993, "is for us to come out of the closet."

"I don't like labels," she wrote in her 1985 autobiography *Martina*. "Just call me Martina." Now retired from tennis at forty, Martina is devoting her considerable energy to the fight for gay and lesbian rights—working for the National Gay and Lesbian Task Force and the

American Civil Liberties Union, among others. When a reporter at the March on Washington asked her why she was doing all this, she simply said that it felt right.

Martina has always led with her heart it seems, both on the court and off—a stance that has cost her considerably in both prestige and endorsements (albeit rarely among her gay, lesbian, and straight-but-sensitive admirers). The fact that she and Greg Louganis are still the only two major athletes out of the closet is a testament to the ingrained homophobia still prevalent in the world of sports. "Because she is comfortable in her own skin," author Neil Miller quotes mentor Billie Jean King as saying, "she helps all of us be more comfortable in ours."

• *"Too Small" to*

Compete

Martina was born to play tennis. Her grandmother was a highly ranked player in Czechoslovakia in the 1940s, both her parents served as tennis coaches for the government, and her sister Jana was also something of an amateur champion in Eastern Europe. All of which is more remarkable given that the Communist-controlled Czechoslovakian Tennis Federation (CTF) discouraged sports over education—"frivolity" over political indoctrination—throughout most of Martina's young life.

She grew up skiing in the Krkonose Mountains, and when her family moved to a suburb of Prague in 1961, she spent her summers watching her parents play in one amateur tennis tournament after another. "They took me with them every day," Martina recalled in an interview for *Sports Illustrated* in 1975. "I had an old racket my father cut down and I hit a ball against a wall. I could do it for hours. They would make me stop and sit me in a chair, but whenever they didn't watch me I would go to the wall again." Recognizing her dedication, her father started coaching her, and did so until she turned professional in 1973.

By the time Martina was fourteen she had captured her first national title, despite the fact that Czech officials said she was "too small" to compete. In an effort to strengthen her legs and arms, she took up ice hockey, swimming, and soccer off the courts. By age sixteen, inspired by her idols Margaret Court and Billie Jean King, she had won two more national women's championships and a junior title to become Czechoslovakia's ranking female player. Thumbing her nose at official pressure and finding less and less time to study anyway, she nonetheless excelled academically. "I never studied" she told *Sports Illustrated,* "but I loved geography, and I imagined myself in places like Chicago and New York."

In 1973, the CTF allowed her to play in an eight-week circuit sponsored by the United States Lawn Tennis Association. She failed to win any of the tournaments—thanks to champion Chris Evert—but played well enough to earn a standing in regular tournament draws. Despite her promise, all the media could focus on was her weight gain and "addiction" to junk food. In true Western fashion, she admittedly devoured Big Macs, pizzas, and pancakes like they were going out of style. "I was really fat and really slow," she told the *New York Times* years later with some amusement, "but I didn't know it."

Back in Europe the following year, Martina lost the weight and fought her way to the doubles finals in Italy and Germany, won the Junior Girls' Championship at Wimbledon, trounced expert clay player Nancy Gunter in the French Open, and won a spot on the lucrative U.S. Virginia Slims tour. The former "fatty" astounded the cynical American press with astounding victories in thirteen out of twenty-two matches against some of the toughest competition in the world. By the end of the circuit, she was the tenth-leading money winner in the world, and ranked as Rookie of the Year for *Tennis* magazine.

She was undoubtedly the strongest woman athlete in the game, and often displayed a force and determination on the court that rivaled that of the men. "My father taught me to play aggressively," she said in her autobiography *Martina,* "like a boy. Rush the net. Put it past them. Take a chance. Invent shots." By the summer of 1975, she had made it to the singles finals of seven major international tournaments, captured four doubles championships with partner Chris Evert, and led Czechoslova-kia to its first international women's cup victory since 1963. Her winnings totaled over $200,000, second only to Evert's.

Even as her career continued to skyrocket, the CTF watched with trepidation, claiming she was "getting too Americanized." After she "snubbed" Czech officials during the 1975 tournament at Wimbledon, and extended her stays in America as long as she dared, they clamped down on her commercial endorsements and refused to approve her request to sign up for World Team Tennis. At one point, they actually asked her to quit tennis and finish school. "That's when I realized I would never have the psychological freedom to play the best tennis as long as I was under their control," she said in a 1976 interview for *Sport* magazine.

In September of 1975, she asked the U.S. Naturalization and Immigration Service for asylum, claiming she had no interest in politics but simply wanted to play tennis wherever and whenever she wanted. Two weeks later she asserted her new-found independence by signing a $300,000 three-year contract as a World Team player with the Cleveland Nets, and agreeing to endorse tennis products for another $100,000 a year. "This country was waiting for me," she said in *Martina.* "It would give me the friends and the space and the freedom and the courts and the sneakers and the weight machines and the right food to let me become a tennis champion, to play the best tennis any woman ever played."

All the same, Martina recalls this period as the most lonely in her life. Here was a twenty-year-old world champion thrust into the unrelenting media spotlight, unable to share her success with the parents so supportive of and instrumental to her earlier achievements. "I wanted them up there in the stand," author Trent Frayne quotes her as saying after her Wimbledon win in 1976. "It's practically impossible for me to go back. The only way I can see them again is if they leave." She did not become a naturalized citizen until 1981, and therefore lived those six years under constant fear of some retaliation against her family. When it was necessary to fly over Communist airspace, she would even make appeals to pilots to alter the flight-path for fear that some mechanical breakdown would force them to land and trap her back behind the Iron Curtain.

This life-wrenching decision was unfortunately not without its consequences on the court. The next two years found her generally floundering, impatient, and out-of-control, even sometimes breaking into tears following a loss or a difficult call by the line-judge. What saved her was her friendship with retired golf champion Sandra Haynie, who represented professional athletes in business. "I tried to assure her she was in the sort of a slump that overtakes everybody," Haynie told Frayne. "When she couldn't understand her bad year, I kept telling her it was normal."

The huge ranch house in Dallas, Texas that Martina shared with Haynie soon became her refuge—the "power-spot" from which she gathered her wits and bounced back as competent on the courts as ever. Haynie encouraged Martina to regain control of her weight and her temper. The slightest gesture from Haynie on the sidelines would calm the volatile star, but if the two women were ever more than just good friends, it was never publicly acknowledged.

Not that Martina had ever been coy about her sexuality. Her new-found American freedom and confidence on the court enabled her to fully explore her lesbianism. But given the high profile of women's tennis in the late 1970s and early 1980s, the rabid pursuit of a now-global tabloid press, and the fact that her family's livelihood back in Czechoslovakia was largely dependent on her notoriety, Martina culti-vated a low profile. "Looking back to when I was sixteen or seventeen," she wrote in *Martina*, "I can see I had some crushes on women players and didn't really know it. I just liked being with them. By the time I was eighteen I knew I always had these feelings." But a political Martina was yet to be born. She did not want, according to author Neil Miller, "the sport to be tarred with the brush of lesbianism (any more than it was already)."

Back on top of her game and temperament, Martina won seven straight Virginia Slims tournaments beginning in 1978, setting a record by winning thirty-seven consecutive matches and losing only six sets. As her game improved, her confidence swelled, and she overtook close friends Chris Evert and Billie Jean King both on the court and as the "media darling." Between 1979 and 1982, her romance with author Rita Mae Brown was as hot a tabloid topic as her burning left serve. The couple bought a house together in Charlottesville, Virginia and even a Rolls-Royce Silver Cloud II with, according to author Neil Miller, a quote from Virgil—*Amor Vincet Omnia* (Love conquers all)—written on the side. Martina found it refreshing finally to be involved with someone who did not really care about her tennis game—someone who in fact did not think much of sports altogether. By Martina's own admission, Brown was simply the most interesting, literary person the twenty-three year old had ever met. And Brown was obviously smitten beyond the mere "research" for a Czech character in an upcoming novel that originally brought them together.

According to Neil Miller, it was Martina who broke off the relationship in the early 1980s, just as her career began to founder, suggesting that tennis still took precedence in her life. Indeed, as a result of Martina's openness, she was forced to resign as head of the Women's Tennis Association. Brown got her revenge, Miller speculates, by portraying Martina "as a temperamental Argentine tennis player in her satirical novel about the women's tennis circuit, *Sudden Death*." Nonetheless, the spilt was amicable, the Rolls-Royce was sold, and Martina and Brown remain friends.

Back on the court, Martina continued to thrive, capturing nine Wimbledon singles titles and four U.S. Open championships between 1978 and 1990. Yet now that her sexuality was public knowledge, a cowardly press and squeamish advertisers cost her millions in commercial endorsements. Tennis "fans" were even sometimes heard yelling "dyke" and "Martina is really a man" from the stands.

In 1984, Martina embarked on a relationship with Judy Nelson, a former Southern model and "Cotton Maid" queen who actually left her husband and two children to move in with Martina. In love, but cautious and aware of the pitfalls of fame and fortune, Martina and Judy videotaped a financial agreement in Texas in 1986, essentially promising Judy

Romance with •

Rita Mae

Brown

Palimony and •

Southern

"Divorce"

half of everything Martina was to earn during the run of the "marriage" should they eventually split up.

In 1992, when they broke up and Judy sued, Martina was livid over what she saw as Judy's betrayal and what she characterized to the press as a premeditated attempt to line her pockets with "Martina's millions." "I thought I was paying Judy a certain amount of money for every year we were together," Martina told Barbara Walters in an interview that year. "But certainly not if I go out and win a tournament and make $100,000 that $50,000 of that should go to Judy."

Obviously Judy thought otherwise, and a rather healthy "palimony" settlement (rumored to be nearly $2,000,000) was finally reached out of court. "I did everything for Martina but hit the tennis ball," Judy Nelson was known to remark. But from Martina's viewpoint, her only "crime" was that she did not love Judy anymore. "Should you have to pay for that?" author Sandra Faulkner quotes her as asking.

In an ironic turn of events, former lover Rita Mae Brown was asked to comment on the breakup in the introduction to Sandra Faulkner's book *Love Match—Nelson vs. Navratilova*. There were even rumors that Nelson and Brown had since become lovers. "Martina hasn't been trained to feel responsible for a partner once the bloom is off the rose," wrote Brown. "As far as I know, no woman has ever been inculcated into this way of thinking toward another woman." In the end, Martina was generally and unfairly "miscast" by the press as the predatory lesbian who had led Nelson astray.

• *Celebratory*

Love

"Martina wears her heart on her sleeve," notes Faulkner, "but once it has been broken, she conceals the pain quickly." Such is the perhaps understandable behavior of a champion who has faced off squarely and resolutely with adversity all her life—hiding from Russian tanks as a young girl in Prague, facing continual harassment by Czech secret police, making an emotionally wrenching decision to "abandon" her family for her treasured America, and then facing rejection and homophobia in her adopted homeland by many of the same people who cheered her lightening performances on the tennis court. "Only life itself is extraordinary enough to tolerate the story of Martina Navratilova," notes author Trent Frayne. "Put it on the silver screen and audiences would figure the (unlikely) plot an insult."

No doubt it is the very circumnavigation of this sometimes-thorny path that has led Martina to feel comfortable in the public spotlight of gay activism. In 1996 at age forty, she is learning to apply the same stamina that distinguished her on the tennis court to the fight for gay and lesbian rights and the endorsement of gay- and lesbian-owned businesses.

Finally, as she told the *International Herald Tribune* in the summer of 1996, she is in love "in a way I haven't loved before" with Hunter Reno, L'Oreal model and niece of U.S. Attorney General Janet Reno. It is Martina's lifelong outspokenness and determination to be accepted on her own terms that has elevated such a pubic declaration of love above the merely "tolerable" and into the realm of the celebratory. Such stands make declarations of love and pleas for full acceptance all the more possible for all the rest of us. "Don't worry," she remembers her father telling her as a young girl. "You're a late bloomer."

**Profile by
Jerome Szymczak**

JOAN NESTLE

*F*or Joan Nestle, history and literature are inextricably connected.

For over thirty years, she has written political essays, poetry, and erotic

short stories designed to address common assumptions and misconcep-

tions surrounding lesbian sexuality, butch-femme relationships, por-

nography, censorship, and the often-shaky camaraderie among lesbi-

ans as that community continues to flex its diversity. She has published

her work in dozens of wide-ranging women's periodicals and antholo-

gies, edited several more on female sexuality and femme-butch desire,

explored the rich relationships between gay brothers and sisters, and

lectured at hundreds of university campuses and forums on the impor-

tance of not marginalizing "traditional," pre-Stonewall gays and

1940– •

American •

archivist and

writer

lesbians and consequently "losing" them in the current politically-correct shuffle.

As a result of her outspokenness, Nestle has tackled issues of prejudice and what she terms "sexual bigotry" not only from heterosexuals, but from within lesbian/feminist communities as well. Only the most unflinching look at the diverse history of lesbian life is valid, she asserts, even if such rebel sexuality as butch-femme identification—not mere role-playing—is now considered taboo. Members of Women Against Pornography (WAP) have even called for censorship of what they feel are Nestle's pornographic depictions of lesbian sex—but Nestle holds fast. "I wanted people," she told *Advocate* interviewer Victoria A. Brownworth in 1992, "especially lesbians, to see that the butch-femme relationship isn't just some negative heterosexual aping." "If I wrote about flowers," she told writer Holly Metz in the *Progressive* in 1989, "if I used metaphors, it would be okay. But I couldn't."

• *Pre-Stonewall*

Pioneers

Joan Nestle was born on 12 May 1940 in New York City. Her father died before her birth, so she was raised by her mother Regina who, according to Nestle in her own collection of writings titled *A Restricted Country,* "left her with two satchels of scribbled writings" and a "belief in a woman's undeniable right to enjoy sex." (See "My Mother Liked to Fuck.")

In 1957 Nestle graduated from Martin Van Buren High School in Queens. In 1963 she got her B.A. in English from Queens College in Flushing, New York, where she still teaches English and creative writing. In 1968 she received her M.A. in English from New York University, and spent the next two years as a doctoral candidate in English, where she completed all her doctoral work except for her thesis.

Nestle's academic education was augmented by her visits to the gay and lesbian bars in Greenwich Village during the late 1950s and throughout the 1960s. From adolescence on, Nestle was aware of her attraction to women. She readily identified her teenage self as a "femme" and soaked up the edgy, furtive experiences—the sharply delineated and courageous butch/femme characters, and frequent raids by the vice squad—that defined Village lesbian bar-life in mid-century America.

These were women with pre-Stonewall fearlessness, struggling for acceptance and social connectedness in a time when their lifestyles were considered criminal. They were "pioneers" whose struggles Nestle determined should never be forgotten. In short, it was an era that has animated Nestle's political work and writing ever since. "My writing life began in the smoky backroom bars of the 1950s," she told Deborah A. Stanley in *Gay & Lesbian Literature,* "where as a young femme I witnessed both the glory of individual courage and the terror of institutionalized oppression. The work I do is in memory of their courage."

At the same time, however, Nestle's beliefs in equal rights overall were broadening. A life "in the shadows" was to prove inadequate for the challenges she saw looming ahead. Her political passion was formalized when she joined in the civil rights march from Selma to Montgomery, Alabama in 1965. In the mid-sixties, she also became involved with the Congress of Racial Equality (CORE) and went South to assist in voter registration drives. In 1971, she became officially active in the feminist movement by joining the Lesbian Liberation Committee. And in 1972, she helped establish the Gay Academic Union (GAU) to speak to and for lesbians and gays on college campuses across the country. Even in post-Stonewall times, Nestle contends, butch-femme lesbians shoulder a growing contempt for who they are; and now it also comes from their own sisters and brothers who want them to assimilate for the "political progress" of the cause.

In 1973, Nestle and a group of lesbians she had met via the GAU decided to chronicle and document the lesbian experience in the United States prior to the feminist movement. The result was the Lesbian Herstory Archives, first housed in a room in Nestle's apartment and, by 1992, large enough to fill a three-story house in Park Slope, Brooklyn, which is still the archives' permanent home. "To live without history is to live like an infant," Nestle wrote in *A Restricted Country,* "constantly amazed and challenged by a strange and unnamed world."

The thousands of books, letters, photographs, and private journal entries that comprise the still-growing archives are an effort to define the lesbian experience on both an individual and a communal level. "I see literature as the expression of history," Nestle told writer Susan Rochman in *Contemporary Lesbian Writers of the United States,* "and history as a form of literature." According to Nestle, history allows us to examine what went wrong and what went right, and documenting it allows us to experience the changes we observe both as individuals and as a community. What results is a certain "complication of issues" that defy simplistic analysis—an unwillingness on the part of the young to believe some stories of oppression are even real. "My roots lie in the history of a people who were called freaks," Nestle says in *A Restricted Country.* "I need to keep alive the memory that in the 1940s doctors measured the clitorises and nipples of lesbians to prove our strangeness . . . [and that] transvestites and transsexuals [were routinely] beaten by the police."

Even in the so-called "progressive" 1980s, Nestle recalls an article appearing in the *Journal of Homosexuality* in 1981—provocatively titled "Sexual Preference or Personal Style: Why Are Lesbians Disliked?"—which recommended that queer women "tone-down" their butch/femme personalities for a more placating androgynous one in order to find "greater homosexual acceptance." Such respectability and safety is not, according to Nestle, worth the price of separating ourselves from what she calls in *A Restricted Country* "the easily recognizable other."

• *"Deviant,*

Outcast, Other"

Overall, Nestle strives to speak for all "lesbian rebels" in the same way she has always proudly presented all of who she is in her writings. What is or is not permissible, the testing of boundaries, the stigma and strength of being an outsider—all of these are intertwining themes in her work. Just as she proudly presents all of herself—feminist, lesbian, Jewish, femme—she also describes, according to Rochman, "how her body—strong, defiant, and sexual—provided her with the ability to take part in and define history, and how it became a living marker for others' definitions: deviant, outcast, other."

What results, particularly in *A Restricted Country* and essays like "The Fem Question," is a challenge to the oppressors and "mainstreamed lesbians" alike. Individual memory is elevated above that of mere autobiography and into the realm of collective history, which, in Nestle's focus, becomes a history of lesbian passion, discrimination, and sometimes censorship and criticism from within her own community. "History will betray us if we betray it," she writes in *A Restricted Country*. "I write [erotica] to celebrate the fineness and richness of sexuality, the complexity of women's desire, because it is at the center of our history as it is at the center of our oppression as gay people."

One of Nestle's most notorious works—*Esther's Story*—is often held up as a prime example of her "pornographic" bent. It's about a one-night stand Nestle had with a woman passing as a man in the straight world. Feminists on all sides have attacked it and other stories (including her account of her mother's free spirit in *Country*) as "offensive." Others have praised these as revelatory and revolutionary for breaking long-held silences on women's sexuality in general.

"I listen very quietly to their expressions of pain, fear, or anger," Nestle told Metz, "and I have to pay it respect if I'm going to have any kind of dialogue at all." In her defense, however, Nestle notes that women have long enjoyed a variety of ways to be sexual that is beyond the label of victimization. Anti-pornographers must be willing to recognize that women have varied sexual experiences—both celebratory and "dangerous"—of their own free will. "Politically," Nestle told Metz, "the [anti-pornography] setting is one that will NOT save women, and in fact will do terrible damage to sexual minorities." In the end, Nestle sides with those who believe sexual experimentation and independence should never be regulated or silenced. New sexual territories should always—indeed, HAVE always—been open to and explored by women, as her unflinching look at lesbian history proves.

In 1990, Nestle joined with Naomi Holoch to co-edit an anthology of American lesbian short stories called *Women on Women*. By 1996, Holoch and Nestle were publishing a popular third edition designed to overturn the notion that lesbian writing is somehow a homogeneous, predictable genre. Their goal was to provide lesbians with an outlet "to see their lives in a different way," as they note in the introduction.

Women on •

Women

But beyond this, the collections stand out because they capture the magic of women's similarities and differences with one another in socioeconomic, historical, and familial terms—areas of distinction and difference too long ignored and unspoken. Contributions by Barbara Smith, Sheila Ortiz Taylor, Frankie Hucklenbroich, and Lu Vicker, for example, attest to the vastly different ethnic and intergenerational experiences among American lesbians who were "coming of age." "Most of my friends have such passionate, complicated relationships with their mothers," writes Smith, for example, in her contribution to *Women on Women 3* titled "Home Story." "Since they don't get married and dragged off into other families, they don't have to automatically cut off their ties, be grown-up heterosexuals. I think their mothers help them to be lesbians. . . . I still want what they have, what they have taken for granted."

In 1994, Nestle and fellow editor John Preston set out to explore gay and lesbian sibling similarities and differences in a collection of thirty-three stories titled *Sister & Brother: Lesbians and Gay Men Write About Their Lives*. What may at first have seemed a departure for Nestle was, in reality, not one at all. Here she was setting out to expose another intricate and complicated, heretofore unexplored history and culture—only this time of the kind brothers and sisters share when they both realize they are gay . . . are both alone and not alone in the family.

Can We Talk? •

When contributor Joyce Zonana writes, for example, of her relationship with her gay brother, she seems to reflect what Nestle has strived to do for decades with her own political essays on butch-femme marginalization. "Suddenly," Zonana says, "I knew that he was one kind of child, that I was another. . . . He was at the center; I was at the margin. [Now] Victor's still the one with the penis, I'm still the one in the dress. But we're also both the ones who are queer. . . . We've left behind the roles assigned to us . . . having found places to stand where we are equally at the center or at the margin, each simultaneously speaking or silent, each simultaneously nurturing or nurtured."

Nestle no doubt appreciates the sentiment, the re-examination of different ways of "being" lesbian, and the re-establishment of a certain erotic responsibility for who we are. "If the personal is political [as the women's movement taught us]," she says in *A Restricted Country,* "the more personal is historical. [It] demands attention be paid to how we fill our days and nights in any given economic system, how our flesh survives under different political systems, how we humanize gender tyranny, how we experience womanness and maleness in all the superstructures of class and race."

Profile by
Jerome Szymczak

SIMON NKOLI

Simon Nkoli is the first black South African to have gained national

1957– •

and international attention for coming out as a gay man. Nkoli's arrest

and trial as a member of the anti-apartheid movement—combined

South African •

with the efforts of like-minded gay and lesbian nonracialists—forced

activist and

South African white gay men and lesbians to take positions about

AIDS educator

apartheid, propelled the anti-apartheid movement to include gay and

lesbian rights within its vision of a more just society, and contributed

strategically to a worldwide discussion of the place of sexual liberation

within the politics of social justice.

Tseko Simon Nkoli (last name pronounced Ni-*ko*-dy) was born in the South African township of Phiri, in Soweto, the area that the apartheid-era Group Areas Act designated for African and mixed-race residence outside of Johannesburg, which was reserved by law for those of European descent. His parents separated while he was young and at age two he was sent to live with his grandparents, tenants on the property of a white farmer in the rural Orange Free State. Nkoli walked fourteen kilometers a day for schooling and worked on the farm as required by the landowner.

In an interview published in the anthology *The Invisible Ghetto,* Nkoli recalls, "I would leave the work and run to school, and then I would quickly return to the farm at playtime. . . . I used to reap the mealies, which was quite a heavy thing for a child. . . . Once a child had completed 10 bags, it would get 10 cents. . . . And if you hadn't done anything by a certain time, . . . [the farmer would] chase us on his horse, and then we would get flogged with his whip."

At age thirteen, Nkoli ran away from the farm because his grandparents and the farmer agreed that his schooling should end. Traveling by foot and train and by hitchhiking, Nkoli managed to make his way back to the Johannesburg township of Bophelong where his mother, step-father, and two younger half-sisters lived. Nkoli's mother, Elizabeth Nkoli, worked as a domestic, later as a sales clerk; his step-father, Elias Nkoli, was a hotel chef.

• *Fighting*

Apartheid and

Coming Out

While a high school student, Nkoli became a member of the United Democratic Front (UDF), the leading legally permitted anti-apartheid group. Nkoli's position as a student leader during the Soweto uprising of 1976 led to his imprisonment for three months. By 1981, Nkoli earned the position of secretary of the Johannesburg regional branch of the Congress of South African Students.

Like many gay men, Nkoli became aware of his homosexuality during his teen years. His first gay relationship began at age nineteen with Andre Van Zyl, a twenty-two-year-old white bus driver who had placed an ad in *Hit Magazine* for teens, requesting black pen pals. At Nkoli's twentieth birthday party, he came out to his parents, who reacted with anger and bewilderment. Though they eventually accepted his homosexuality, they first took Nkoli to all manner of "healers," including traditional African *sangomas,* their parish priest, and finally a psychiatrist. Ironically, the psychiatrist turned out to be gay himself and gave the lovers the idea of living together under the pretense that Nkoli was his lover's domestic servant.

In an interview published in the *Advocate,* Nkoli talked about this relationship, "It was not a comfortable relationship because of the political climate of the time. We didn't live together until we both decided to go to college. . . . The problem was with our parents. His family accepted his being gay, but not the fact that he was having a relationship with a black." From his political associates at the time, Nkoli experienced mixed reactions. He told the *Advocate,* "Some people did not believe that I was gay, and some people did reject me. There were those who were actually afraid to walk down the street with me. But I was lucky because the majority of people I was working with did not shun me."

Nkoli joined GASA (the Gay Association of South Africa) in 1980, but quickly became frustrated by its lack of black members and lack of attention to political issues. Nkoli told the *Advocate,* "I tried to go to GASA functions, but I couldn't attend those in the evening because of the Group Areas Act. I then tried to go to some gay nightclubs but was chased out or told they were for members only. I'd write letters to gay newspapers, telling them I was discriminated against and that GASA didn't seem interested in taking up political issues." In 1983, Nkoli began organizing an explicitly nonracial subgroup of GASA. "I decided to reach out to the black community. I wrote an article in the *City Press* [a major black newspaper], calling on gay black people, if there were any, to contact me. I gave my address even though I could have been bashed. I got lots of responses, not only from Johannesburg, but from all around South Africa," Nkoli recalled for the *Advocate.* This led to the formation of the Saturday Group, the first predominantly black gay organization in South Africa.

Soon after the formation of the Saturday Group in 1984, Nkoli was arrested with twenty-one other prominent leaders of the UDF and charged with treason and murder for deaths following a protest march against rent hikes in the townships. The Delmas Treason Trial became the most important rallying point for the liberation movement since Nelson Mandela's treason trial in 1962. Nkoli spent three years in jail, was released on bail 30 June 1987, and was finally acquitted on 17 November 1987.

Imprisoned for •

Treason

Gay and lesbian activists in South Africa and in the international anti-apartheid movement focused great attention on Nkoli's confinement and trial. In an interview published in the anthology *Defiant Desire,* Nkoli credited this worldwide support with helping to sway his codefendants to accepting him as a gay man: "What helped me most was that I received so many letters. I was the focus of attention in the trial, especially because of my homosexuality. . . . And so I would say to the others, 'Look, people won't be against us [because of my homosexuality]. Look how much support I'm getting.'"

GASA's lack of effort on Nkoli's behalf resulted in its expulsion from ILGA (the International Lesbian and Gay Association) and to the formation of more politically involved gay/lesbian organizations in South Africa, including Lesbians and Gays Against Oppression and the Organization of Lesbian and Gay Activists (OLGA) in Cape Town. Soon after his release from prison, Nkoli co-founded GLOW (Gay and Lesbian Organization of Witwatersrand, in the Johannesburg area), a predominantly black group that became the leading gay activist group in the region. He also made a twenty-six-city tour of Europe and North America speaking about his experiences during the trial and solidifying the bridge between anti-apartheid activists and gay men and lesbians.

• *The New South*

Africa

The formation of GLOW marked a watershed in the gay/lesbian movement in South Africa, from a white middle-class male leadership and constituency aligned with the apartheid system to a predominantly black, working-class male and female leadership and mixed constituency aligned with the liberation movement. In 1990 GLOW recognized the dawning of the new South Africa—signaled by the release that year of Nelson Mandela from prison—by organizing the first annual Lesbian and Gay Pride March in Johannesburg. GLOW and OLGA consistently called on the liberation movement to embrace the cause of gay/lesbian rights, and in 1993 the ANC endorsed such a platform in their draft constitution.

Realizing the dearth of AIDS information reaching the townships, GLOW initiated the Township AIDS Project (TAP), employing Nkoli in its efforts to reach black gay men and lesbians. Nkoli told the *Progressive,* "When we go to the townships and try to explain to the people what AIDS is all about, black people are not convinced that they can get it, because they have never heard of AIDS. . . . I believe there are many unreported cases [among township residents]. There are 4.5 million people living in Soweto and only about 600,000 in Johannesburg. Maybe seventy white people have died of AIDS in Johannesburg. But there are no statistics about us." In 1996 TAP will sponsor its fourth annual conference in Soweto on AIDS. In contrast to more affluent white South Africans, the African community continues to lack basic infrastructure to support people living with AIDS. TAP is working to address this lack.

Also in 1996, Simon Nkoli has came out as HIV-positive in articles in the *Sowetan* and the *Sunday Independent.* He has known his antibody status since 1985 while he was imprisoned. Fortunately, his most serious infection—tuberculosis—was successfully treated in 1992. Nkoli is grateful to have a supportive work environment where he has been able to work part time in order to conserve his strength, as well as the support of key friends and lovers, including Rod Sharp in South Africa, Roy Trevelion in England, and Chuck Goldfarb and Matt Brosius in Washington, D.C. Nkoli remains committed to the struggle for justice.

He told this writer, "While life is still there, there is lots of work to be done."

Nkoli's lifetime has spanned a remarkable four decades in the life of his country and the history of the international movements for gay and lesbian liberation—from the earliest signs of progress to the defeat of apartheid and the worldwide acknowledgment that gay men and lesbians exist and will not quietly accept second-class status. Unfortunately our lifetimes will remain a time of struggle, as the battles for liberation are fought on increasingly intimate and systemic levels. To progressive gay men and lesbians around the world, Tseko Simon Nkoli remains an icon, setting an example for all people to be who we are with dignity and power.

Profile by
Loie Hayes

RUDOLF NUREYEV

*E*verything about Rudolf Nureyev, who defected to the West from the

Soviet Union in 1961, seems larger than life. While his legend was

nourished by the media—Nureyev became instantly newsworthy—the

fact is that his life and art defy understanding. In an age of television, jet

travel, and mass adulation, Nureyev, a tireless performer and world

traveler, stimulated an interest in ballet that was without precedent. For

a long period he gave close to 200 performances per year, while also

working as a choreographer. He displayed a unique range of abilities,

including extraordinary athleticism, superb musicality, unusual intel-

ligence, and above all a commanding, indeed charismatic stage pres-

ence. It is no exaggeration to say that he reinstated the male dancer as a

1938–1993 ·

Russian ·

dancer and

choreographer

central figure. After the death of Diaghilev in 1929, this centrality had largely been lost. Balanchine's remark that "ballet is woman" held sway. Nureyev changed that, bringing to the male role a prominence, visibility, and electrifying erotic charge that it had either lost or never possessed. His longstanding partnership with the English ballerina Margot Fonteyn was uniquely beautiful and exciting to a wider audience than had ever before seen ballet. The tenacity of will that brought Nureyev from desperate poverty to extraordinary riches and world renown was never more in evidence than in his long, courageous fight against AIDS, of which he died 6 January 1993.

• *Childbood in*

Stalin's U.S.S.R.

Rudolf Hametovich Nureyev was born near Irkutsk, by Lake Baikal, 17 March 1938, on a train on the Trans-Siberian railroad going from Moscow to Vladivostock. His mother Farida and his three sisters had undertaken this perilous, twelve-day journey to meet up with his father, Hamnet, a soldier stationed in Manchuria. Both his parents were Tatars of Muslim origin. After some years of moving about, the family settled in Ufa, some two thousand miles from Leningrad and the Kirov Ballet, but near to where Rudolf's father had been born. The father remained on active service as a political instructor with the army, and did not come home for good until Rudolf was eight. The family lived in extreme poverty in a one-room shack, often going hungry, barely surviving. His mother would barter what remaining civilian clothes she had belonging to her husband for food.

In the midst of this grinding poverty, Nureyev was loved by his mother and very close to his sister Rosa, but there could be no bond between father and son. The father, a decorated war hero, fond of hunting, wanted Rudolf to become an engineer or doctor, and join the Communist Party. He could not abide the idea that his son wanted to become a dancer, and tried by all means possible to prevent it. Rudolf had joined a local Bashkir folk dance group, but when his mother was able to smuggle all her children into the ballet *The Song of the Cranes* at the Ufa Opera with just one ticket, the magic of the theater hardened his resolve to become a ballet dancer. Nureyev felt possessed from the age of eight by the single passion to dance ballet.

At the age of eleven Nureyev met in his hometown Madame Udeltsova, a woman who had once danced with Diaghilev. She helped him as best she could, then introduced him to her friend Madame Vaitovich, who had been a soloist with the Kirov. For several years, Vaitovich gave him lessons, while recognizing that he really needed to be with the Kirov. When he was seventeen, on a trip to Moscow with the Ufa Opera to appear with Bashkir Republic artists, he summoned up the courage to audition for the Bolshoi and was accepted into the school.

But he turned down the invitation, and with money owed to him by the Ufa Opera, he bought a one-way train ticket to Leningrad. He was able to obtain an audition at the Kirov and was accepted into the Kirov school, where he started in August 1955. His success in being admitted is astonishing, given that he was not young, and had relatively little training. Years later, the dancer Peter Martins would comment on how unpolished Nureyev was. But at the Kirov, they saw his passion and potential for greatness.

Brash as ever, Nureyev was unhappy with his first teacher and at being placed in a lower-level class. He asked to be moved up and, in a stroke of unusual good fortune, was placed in the class of Alexander Pushkin. Pushkin, teacher to Nureyev, Valery Panov, and Mikhail Baryshnikov, each very different from the others, has become a legend as a teacher, bringing out the best in his dancers without forcing them into one regimented style. Nureyev spent three years as a student at the Kirov. He was allowed—or took—liberties that no other had ever dared to take. But his brilliance was recognized. As a student in his final year, when much of the company was on tour, he danced the male lead in such standards as *Le Corsaire, Swan Lake,* and many others, an unprecedented honor. By the time of his graduation in the summer of 1958, he had made many enemies—including, especially, the director of the school, Chelkov. But his growing national reputation was confirmed at the end of his last year in school with his performances in a national competition in Moscow, and his graduation performance of the *Corsaire* pas de deux with Alla Sizova. He was offered contracts with the Bolshoi, with the Stanislavsky (the other leading Moscow company), and the Kirov. He chose the Kirov. In a signal honor, Dudinskaya, the prima ballerina of the Kirov and wife of its director, Sergeyev, intimated that she wished to have Nureyev as her partner.

In November 1958, Nureyev danced his first official role at the Kirov, opposite Dudinskaya, in *Laurencia.* The performance was a stunning success, and over the next three years with the Kirov, Nureyev became a cult figure in the U.S.S.R., recognized as the most brilliant dancer of his generation, given the male lead in both experimental ballets and standard classics such as *Don Quixote, Swan Lake, La Bayadère, The Sleeping Beauty,* and *Giselle* with the Kirov's finest ballerinas, almost all much older than he, and allowed to change the choreography to suit his own abilities. On the other hand, his flouting of the rules, independent spirit, and uncompromising arrogance, as well as the secrecy of his private life, caused him to be viewed with distrust. Stalin had declared homosexuality a crime, and, of necessity, Nureyev had to keep his private life to himself. He was given very little opportunity to dance outside Leningrad, or to meet with foreigners visiting the city.

Nureyev was a last-minute addition to the Kirov troupe invited to perform in Paris and London in May and June of 1961. He did not dance until the fifth evening of their booking at the Paris Opéra. If the Kirov at large was dazzling, Nureyev in particular proved to be a sensation. When he was not performing he refused to be herded around with the other members of the company, but went his own way, making friends in Paris, trailed by two KGB agents.

<table>
<tr><td>

• **Escape to the**

West

</td><td>

Nureyev's decision to go over to the West can be interpreted in many ways. Given that his family remained behind under a tyrannical regime, subject to reprisals, Nureyev never spoke out against conditions in the Soviet Union. But it seems clear that he found in the West a level of personal and professional freedom undreamed of at home. Certainly the actual decision does appear to have been rather spontaneous, although he had more than likely anticipated that it would happen sometime. On June 16, while the company was waiting at Le Bourget airport to take a flight to London, Nureyev was told that he would not be going to London but instead, as a special honor, to Moscow, to dance at a function at the Kremlin. He was told that he would be able to join up with the Kirov in London. He understood immediately that this was a ploy to return him to the Soviet Union as a virtual prisoner. Nureyev informed a friend of his wish to seek asylum, and the friend in turn informed the French police. After a scuffle, and over the objections of KGB agents, he was able to stay.

</td></tr>
</table>

Nureyev had always been willing to take risks, and generally his daring had been rewarded. In choosing to cross to the West, he took the greatest risk of his career, giving up the security of the Soviet system for a leap into an uncertain future. The Soviet authorities persisted in trying to bring him back, and he received pleading telephone calls and letters from his mother and father, and his favorite sister Rosa, as well as from his teacher Pushkin and his wife. The pleas and promises did not let up, but Nureyev, distrustful, preferred exile to return. Again, Nureyev's daring was to be rewarded.

He received an offer almost immediately. On June 23, he made his debut with the Marquis de Cuevas ballet, as the prince and the Bluebird in a new production of *The Sleeping Beauty,* alongside the great French ballerina Nina Vyroubova. Many in the audience at the Théâtre des Champs-Elysées, Soviet sympathizers, jeered him, calling him a traitor. The Cuevas offered Nureyev a six-year contract, but he refused a long-term commitment, since he wished to study in Copenhagen with Russian expatriate Vera Volkova, ballet-mistress of the Royal Danish Ballet, and Erik Bruhn, the premier male dancer of the period. Nureyev went to Copenhagen at the end of the summer. Bruhn and Nureyev fell in love, and their passionate friendship was to continue through much of the 1960s.

Inevitably, Nureyev's background of poverty and deprivation marked him deeply. In the West, he acquired sybaritic tastes, a vast personal fortune, and seven homes in various parts of the world, including an Italian island that once belonged to Massine. Related to this restless acquisitiveness was a compulsive sexuality, a constant in his life.

At the Kirov, the authorities had resented his need for secrecy, and suspected him of being a homosexual. Consensual sex between two adult males was a crime, severely punished. Of necessity, therefore, Nureyev's homosexuality could only be expressed within a private club or in a friend's apartment, with the risk of arrest by the KGB. Nureyev enjoyed greater freedom than any student before him, but even for him there were limits to what would be tolerated.

In the 1960s and 1970s, the contrast between the closed life-style of Leningrad and, say, Paris, London, or New York was enormous. In these Western cities and others, Nureyev became part of local gay legend. He was remembered for his prodigious sexual appetites in the bath houses, his picking up of "butch boys" (boy prostitutes), his alleged sexual encounter with Mick Jagger, and even (in Melbourne, Australia) for rushing out of the theater during intermission to have sex, only to be caught by the vice squad and let go to return and dance his final act.

But for all the flamboyance and all the stories that grew up around him, Nureyev never lost his need for privacy and secrecy. Coming from the Soviet Union, he never learned to accept the profligate intrusion of the Western press into his private life, though he was a master at manipulating that same press.

There will always be conjecture about the true nature of his private relationship with Margot Fonteyn, and it is clear that in their way each loved the other, There has been speculation that she had a miscarriage while carrying his child. He was deeply affected by her death from cancer in 1991. While quite misogynistic, and unambiguously homosexual, he was involved sexually with many women, including no doubt Madame Pushkin of the Kirov (as well as with her husband), and the dancer Maria Tallchief in his first months in Paris.

Alongside the numberless brief encounters that marked Nureyev's passage from city to city, there were lasting relationships of real love. The first and greatest was that shared with Erik Bruhn in the 1960s. In many respects, Bruhn, an elegant, smooth, and flawless dancer, was

From Closed to •

(Partially)

Open Society

299 •

Nureyev's polar opposite. Nureyev admired him greatly. Until Nureyev's arrival, Bruhn was the premier male dancer in Europe, and he came to suffer greatly, though without temperament, from the inevitable comparisons with his friend. Later, Nureyev would have two long-term relationships. The first, with Wallace Potts, a young American southerner, lasted through the late 1960s and early 1970s, though Potts remained a loyal friend until the end. The other, with Robert Tracy, a young dancer whom Nureyev met in 1979, was long-lasting but ended in acrimony.

Although Nureyev never declared his homosexuality candidly, it was hardly a secret. Quite apart from the specifics of his sexual orientation, his sheer sexuality was readily apparent—literally as well as figuratively, given his choice of revealing costumes—in his diverse roles, from *Le Corsaire* to his resurrection of Nijinsky's faun in *L'Après-midi d'un faune,* to Martha Graham's *Lucifer,* to many others. With Margot Fonteyn, that sexuality would capture the attention of the world.

• ***A Stellar***

Partnership:

Nureyev and

Margot Fonteyn

It was while he was in Denmark, with Volkova, that Nureyev received a call from Margot Fonteyn, inviting him to dance at the annual gala for the British Royal Academy of Dance in London in November 1962. He danced the solo *Poème tragique* to music by Scriabin, choreographed especially for him by Frederick Ashton, and the Black Swan pas de deux from *Swan Lake* with Rosella Hightower. Margot Fonteyn was not at first eager to dance with him. The frenzy unleashed by Nureyev had no precedent in the annals of British ballet. Most members of the audience—and this would continue to be true for a long time to come—simply suspended critical judgment and were caught up in the sheer excitement of the spectacle.

From the beginning, Ninette de Valois, founder of London's Royal Ballet, championed Nureyev, and encouraged Margot Fonteyn, its prima ballerina, to dance with him. Although Nureyev would always be just a guest artist at the Royal—he was not British—for many years, he was closely connected to it. After some hesitation, she joined him in a performance of *Giselle* at Covent Garden in February 1962. In every respect this was a major balletic event: a captivating performance in itself by both dancers, it was also the beginning of a partnership that is without equal in the history of ballet. Shortly before, Fonteyn, almost twenty years Nureyev's senior, was about to retire. Now, infused with a new vitality and radiance, she traveled extensively with him, often taking on very demanding roles. In just the first two years of their collaboration, they put on close to 200 performances. They helped spark a new interest in ballet in many parts of the world, playing to sold-out houses, both with the classics and with such new productions as *Marguerite and Armand,* created for them by Frederick Ashton, and

Kenneth MacMillan's *Romeo and Juliet,* which, after Nureyev and Fonteyn danced it, became in effect the Royal Ballet's standard *Romeo.*

From early on, Nureyev evinced an interest in the choreography of Balanchine and Martha Graham, and other masters of modern dance. Balanchine discouraged this interest when they first met in 1962. No one understood better than he that modern dance would require an unlearning of much of the splendid classical ballet training of the Kirov. But Nureyev did eventually achieve considerable success dancing in modern works by Paul Taylor, Maurice Béjart, Glen Tetley, and many others. His ten-year association with Martha Graham, beginning with her *Lucifer* in 1975, which she created for him and Fonteyn, provided a new source of inspiration. His ongoing fascination with Balanchine was crowned with success when Balanchine asked him to dance with Patricia McBride in an adaptation of Molière's *Bourgeois Gentilhomme* (1979), from which he learned, belatedly, to be a modernist in modesty and simplicity.

From 1983 to 1989, Nureyev assumed a new role as artistic director of the Paris Opéra Ballet, a notoriously difficult assignment, complicated by his increasingly ill health, the first signs of what was later recognized as AIDS. Three ballet directors had come and gone in the decade before. In spite of the many obstacles, through sheer force of will, Nureyev imposed a personal vision on the Opéra that shook it out of its lethargy and transformed its lackluster company. He overthrew the hierarchy that stifled young talent; changed the repertory, adding many new ballets, a good number of which, including *Swan Lake,* he choreographed himself; and fought the unions over their impossible demands. In his years as director his own strength was failing, and, defying reason, he continued to insist on dancing a full schedule. But now the achievement was not the personal one of Rudolf Nureyev, but that of the Paris Opéra Ballet, which could hold its head high anywhere in the world. In 1986, on its first visit to the United States in close to forty years, it enjoyed huge success in a three-week engagement at the Metropolitan Opera House.

Fittingly, Nureyev made his last public appearance where his career in the West had begun, at the Paris Opéra. It was the premiere, 8 October 1992, of his production of *La Bayadare.* Dressed in red satin, he watched from a couch in a box. He died two months later, after losing a twelve-year fight against AIDS.

Nureyev's influence has proved long lasting, not just in Paris, but in many parts of the world. He breathed new life into ballet, conquered a vast new public for it, and restored the male dancer to a position of prominence.

The Paris •

Opéra

**Profile by
James P. McNab**

PRATIBHA PARMAR

*W*hen Pratibha Parmar's family immigrated to England from

India, the young schoolgirl experienced firsthand the rampant racism of

the mid-1960s. Parmar and her family, along with immigrants from

the Caribbean and Africa, were labelled "black," and as such, as

Parmar describes in Queer Looks: Perspectives on Lesbian and Gay

Film and Video, *were "perceived as 'marginal,' 'peripheral,' and 'oth-*

er.'" In her films and videos, Parmar attempts to reflect the struggle of

those perceived by others as being "marginal" to confront and challenge

prejudice, be it based on race, gender, or sexual orientation.

Indian British •

video artist and

filmmaker

Parmar describes one of her first excursions into activism in the article "Other Kinds of Dreams" in the spring 1989 issue of *Feminist Review:* In 1978 she had co-written an article concerning the failure of the women's movement in Britain to address racial issues of importance to black women, which was to be discussed at that year's Socialist-Feminist conference. Acting on a suggestion from women who had participated in the discussion, the authors sent the article to the feminist publication *Spare Rib*. The resulting three-page letter of rejection made Parmar feel that black women were regarded by white feminists as outsiders, and that the opinions and concerns of black women were not central to the "white" women's movement.

While a postgraduate student at the Centre for Contemporary Cultural Studies at the University of Birmingham in 1982, Parmar was one of a group of students involved in writing and publishing the book *The Empire Strikes Back: Race and Racism in 70s Britain*. In the article "That Moment of Emergence," Parmar describes herself and her fellow contributors to this project as "the new generation that saw ourselves as both black and British." *The Empire Strikes Back,* she continues, "examines the everyday lived experiences of black British people as culture," and presents critical analyses of such topics as race relations, white feminism, and sexual identity.

Parmar served as guest ediotr of the July 1984 issue of *Feminist Review,* a special issue on the subject of black women in Britain. With this issue she and three other black lesbians "come out" in a very public way in the article "Becoming Visible: Black Lesbian Discussions." The four women express their doubts and fears about the wisdom of coming out in print, and Parmar herself reveals that her "greatest fear is total rejection from my family, who I am really close to." She makes the point that losing family as a support group would be far more devastating for a black than for a white lesbian, since the family represents the security and support not otherwise readily available to black women living in a racist society. Parmar's fear of being identified as a lesbian, however, is counterbalanced by her conviction that "the more of us that come out the stronger we are going to be, and the more other women are going to feel they are able to come out, because we are creating that kind of a situation where it is possible."

In the same article, Parmar reveals a situation in her life that had made a lasting impression on her and helped her form her identity as a black lesbian. In 1981, Parmar attended the OWAAD (Organisation of Women of African and Asian Descent) conference. The dissention among the women at the conference over whether or not black lesbians should have the right to hold their own independent workshop resulted in feelings of anger and alienation among homosexual and heterosexual women alike. In spite of the uproar, about forty black lesbians, including Parmar, did meet. Parmar credits the "horrible things" that happened at the OWAAD conference with the birth of the Black Lesbian Group (BLG). This was the first group for black lesbians in Britain, and Parmar states that it "gave me the confidence and support of other lesbians to be able to come out in ways that I'd not been able to before and be much stronger in myself about my own lesbianism."

Also in that same issue of *Feminist Review,* Parmar and Valerie Amos wrote the article "Challenging Imperial Feminism." In it, the authors set out "to show that white, mainstream feminist theory . . . does not speak to the experiences of Black women and where it attempts to do so it is often from a racist perspective and reasoning." The article offers a critique of white feminist literature and scholarship, and the "white feminists' failure to acknowledge the differences between themselves and Black and Third World women." The authors discuss the effects of imperialism on white feminist attitudes towards the family, sexuality, and the women's peace movement. In the area of sexuality, for example, Parmar and Amos point out that the feminist debates concerning gender roles, rape, pornography, homo- and heterosexuality, etc., are simply not as central to the black experience in a racist society as are other, more survival-oriented issues. As black women become more confident, the area of sexuality will become a more important topic of discussion. The authors also mention the difficulties black lesbians face in expressing their sexual identities, as they must endure the homophobic reactions not only of the white community, but of the black community as well.

Parmar and Amos conclude the article with a statement of rejection of the "white" women's liberation movement's theories and practices on the grounds that white feminists have not come to grips with the problems of imperialism and racism. They state that it is necessary for black feminists to treat "the totality of our oppression. . . . Only a synthesis of class, race, gender and sexuality can lead us forward, as these form the matrix of Black women's lives."

In the mid-1980s Parmar began making films and videos, commencing this career without having art or film school training. In the article "Filling the Lack in Everyone Is Quite Hard Work, Really. . .," which appears in *Queer Looks,* she relates that she did interview with the head of documentary at the National Film School, but the two did not see eye-to-eye on theories of documentary filmmaking, and "a very heated discussion" ensued. Without any training, then, Parmar found herself learning "on the job," a process that she describes in "Filling the Lack" as "frightening and scary": "It's scary because you're judged on what the audience sees. They don't know that you

• *Expresses*

Herself

Through Film

had to do the camera at one point, or you had to do the production managing and the off-line editing and everything else that you did on your own. And it's the first time you've ever done it, and you've had to learn it as you go along."

Parmar's early documentaries have themes that are reflective of her activities as a black feminist activist. The 1986 video *Emergence* examines the problems of alienation and loss of identity facing black and Third World women artists. Among those featured are African American poet Audre Lorde, and Palestinian performance artist Mona Hatoum. *Sari Red,* Parmar's second documentary, addresses the threats of racism and violence faced by South Asian women. It was made in memory of Kalbinder Kaue Hayre, who was the victim of a deadly racially motivated attack in Britain in 1985.

The homophobic tone of Britain's AIDS-awareness campaigns inspired *A Plague on You,* which was produced by London's Lesbian and Gay Media Group and appeared on British television in 1987. Parmar continued her exploration of AIDS and its effect on the gay community in 1988. *ReFraming AIDS* features interviews with AIDS-stricken gays and lesbians of different races, and shows how the lesbian and gay community has been affected not only by the disease itself, but by the myths surrounding it and the resulting anti-gay backlash. One of the topics covered was how AIDS was being used as a reason for restricting black immigration to Britain.

Parmar was criticized for including black and white gay men in *ReFraming AIDS,* and not limiting herself to black lesbians. This attitude, Parmar claims in "That Moment of Emergence," "reinforced my criticism of an essentialist identity politics as being divisive, exclusionary, and retrogressive. I would assert that our territories should be as broad as we choose."

Parmar continued the exploration of this broader territory in her next three works, examining, as she states in the above-mentioned article, "our histories of diaspora, the memories of migration and upheaval, the search for an integration of our many selves, and the celebration of 'us,' our differences, and our eroticisms." The 1989 video *Memory Pictures* treats the effects of racism and sexual identity on the life of gay Indian-born photographer Sunil Gupta. *Flesh and Paper,* a documentary made for British television in 1990, has as its subject the Indian-born lesbian poet and writer Suniti Namjoshi, author of "Feminist Fables" and "Conversations with a Cow." Parmar, in "Filling the Lack," tells of her satisfaction in presenting for the first time on British television, for nearly a million viewers, "an Indian woman in a sari talking about being a lesbian and Indian in a way which was not apologetic or explanatory." The half-hour film was made for Channel Four's gay and lesbian series *Out on Tuesday*.

• *Wins Frameline*

Award

The title of Parmar's 1991 film *Khush* is the Urdu word meaning "ecstatic pleasure." This film explores the difficulties, as well as the joys, of South Asian gays and lesbians living in India, Britain, and North America, and documents their "coming out." *Khush* originally was made for *Out on Tuesday,* and also has been shown at lesbian and gay film festivals. It won an award for Best Documentary Short at the Frameline Festival in San Francisco. Parmar recalls in "Filling the Lack" the thrill of that evening: "It was a very special moment. To get that kind of validation from your own peer group mattered much more than getting a great review from a critic. That kind of nurturing is very important. It's what's kept me going."

Double the Trouble, Twice the Fun was also made for *Out on Tuesday* and is a docudrama featuring the gay writer Firdaus Kanga. It deals in a positive way with the challenges faced by disabled lesbians and gays.

Parmar has found inspiration in the writings and achievements of black American feminists. In the 1991 documentary *A Place of Rage,* she interviews black activist Angela Davis, poet June Jordon, and writer Alice Walker. She went on to collaborate with the Pulitzer Prize–winning Walker in the creation of the film *Warrior Marks,* a 1993 documentary that treats the subject of female circumcision. This "initiation ritual," which involves the excising of all or part of the exterior female genitalia, is often performed under unsanitary conditions using the crudest of instruments and often ends in death. The filming required travel to The Gambia, Senegal, Burkina Faso, Britain, and the United States. The documentary features interviews with those who defend as well as those who condemn the practice, and also includes interviews with children who have themselves endured the procedure. Parmar and Walker also have collaborated on a book, *Warrior Marks: Female Genital Mutilation and the Sexual Blinding of Women,* which chronicles the making of the film.

• *The Future of*

"Queer Cinema"

In the article "Queer Questions" in the September 1992 issue of *Sight and Sound,* Parmar gives her views on the current state of "queer cinema." She points out that queer cinema is not just white, gay cinema, and expresses her dismay that it is still difficult for lesbian filmmakers to get funding. She emphasizes the positive benefits of gay and lesbian film festivals. Although these festivals do tend to be organized by white gays and lesbians, and white films predominate, they still often represent the only opportunity available to gay and lesbian filmmakers to get their works before the public.

There may be a hint of the future direction of Parmar's films given in the roundtable discussion that took place at her home in North London, as chronicled in the article "Filling the Lack." In the article, Parmar and her fellow filmmakers discuss the differences between fictional works and documentaries. Parmar expresses her occasional frustration with the documentary, in that it limits the filmmaker's artistic freedom. She explains, "As a fiction filmmaker, you can say what you want to say through your characters, whereas with documentary you've got the subject matter but you've also got the subjects, and you can't put words in their mouths." Parmar has already introduced dramatic elements into her films. In *Khush,* for example, she describes using "dramatic scenarios, performance, dance, and archive footage, used not as wallpaper but in and for themselves, as different kinds of voices and different modes of telling." In whatever direction Parmar's creativity takes her, it is certain that her dedication to fighting racism, sexism, and homophobia will continue to provide the heart of her work.

**Profile by
Jean Edmunds**

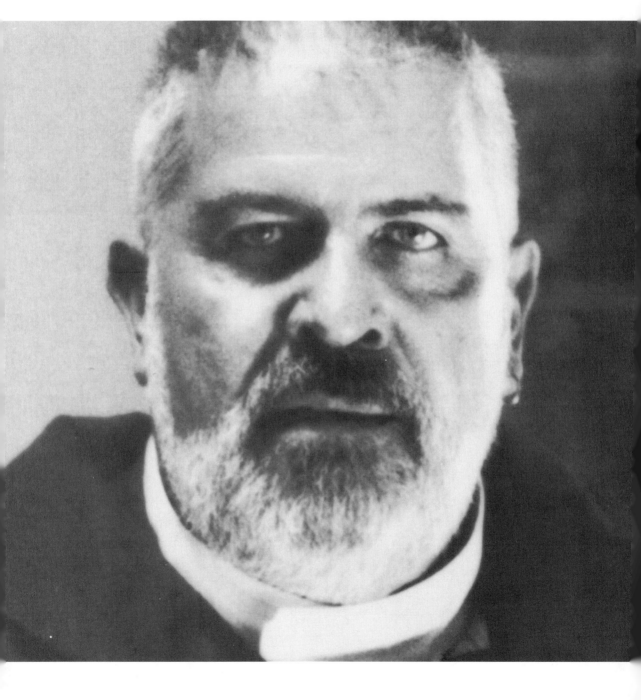

TROY D. PERRY

*T*he Reverend Troy D. Perry founded the Universal Fellowship of
Metropolitan Community Churches (UFMCC), the largest Christian
church for lesbians and gay men, in 1968. Besides his work as a
minister, he is also a prominent gay rights activist and author. Perry was
born in Tallahassee, Florida on 27 July 1940, the eldest of five sons of
Troy D. Perry Sr. and Edith Allen Perry. Troy Sr. owned a gasoline
station and a farm, but derived most of his income from bootlegging in
"dry" Leon County, Florida. When Troy Jr. was only a boy his father was
killed when, chased by the police, his automobile crashed. Edith Perry, a
homemaker with no job skills, soon remarried, but the marriage was
short-lived. Her new husband, an abusive alcoholic, dissipated his

1940– •

American •

religious

leader

wife's estate after moving the family to Daytona Beach, Florida. When Troy was thirteen, one of his stepfather's acquaintances sexually molested him. The next day Troy ran away to live with relatives in Georgia and Texas, and he returned to his family only after his mother left his stepfather.

The fundamentalist Christianity that Troy's extended family practiced provided him with opportunities during his teenage years. Licensed to preach at fifteen, he dropped out of high school after the eleventh grade to become an evangelist. He married a minister's daughter at age eighteen and they had two sons. After five years of marriage, Perry and his wife separated because of his homosexuality. He has already been excommunicated from two denominations, the last one occurring while he was pastor of a church in Santa Ana, California.

With the exception of his U.S. Army service from 1965 to 1967, Perry has lived in the Los Angeles area since the early 1960s. For a period both before and after his military service, he worked for Sears, Roebuck and Company and shared a Huntington Park house with another gay man, Willie Smith. During this period Perry was often deeply troubled and attempted suicide after a failed love affair.

On 6 October 1968, a twelve-person congregation met in the Perry-Smith living room for the first Metropolitan Community Church service. Perry officiated as minister, while Smith led the singing of hymns. Perry envisioned a Christian church to provide salvation, community, and social action for Los Angeles homosexuals. To promote attendance at his weekly services, he placed advertisements in a local gay newspaper, the *Advocate,* which subsequently provided favorable reports on his endeavors. Perry, who appointed the church's first board of directors and deacons, organized a range of social services and religious programs to serve the homosexual community. Quickly outgrowing the Perry-Smith living room, the congregation worshipped next in a local civic hall and then in the Encore Theater, where Willie Smith worked.

Perry dedicated the congregation's first permanent site in Los Angeles, the Mother Church, on 7 March 1971. During the next twenty-five years, he frequently traveled around the world to promote the church, which adopted the name of the Universal Fellowship of Metropolitan Community Churches (UFMCC).

Gay rights activism, one of the early hallmarks of the church, helped to swell its membership throughout the United States. In 1969 Perry and some followers joined a San Francisco picket line to protest the firing of a gay employee of the State Steamship Lines. He also helped to organize the first Los Angeles gay pride parade on Hollywood

Boulevard in June 1970. After the parade he was arrested as he began a prayer vigil and fast to protest California's anti-homosexual laws. Following a night in jail, he continued his ten-day fast amidst considerable press coverage.

Perry's role as a California gay leader was strengthened further when he became allied with liberal California politicians such as Assemblyman Willie Brown.

Although UFMCC membership multiplied throughout the United States and abroad in its early years, it faced many hurdles. Many of its worship sites, including the original Mother Church, were destroyed by arson. Perry's leadership, especially his emphasis on political and social action, was challenged on several occasions. Furthermore, in 1983 the National Council of Churches indefinitely tabled UFMCC's membership application and rejected its 1993 bid for observer status.

Although Perry's theology has usually been termed conservative, his social and political views are decidedly progressive. He performed holy union ceremonies for same-sex couples as early as 1970 and accepted the ordination of women ministers in UFMCC in 1972. In 1984 a majority of the UFMCC board of directors, as well as many of its ministers, were women.

Perry worked hard in 1977 to defeat Anita Bryant's successful Save Our Children crusade in Dade County, Florida. He was also a leading opponent of John Brigg's anti-gay ballot measure, Proposition 6, which was defeated in California in 1978. He served on the boards of the National Gay Task Force and the Gay Rights National Lobby and was a principal organizer of both the 1979 and 1987 national gay rights marches in Washington, D.C.

Perry's two autobiographical books, *The Lord Is My Shepherd and He Knows I'm Gay: The Autobiography of the Reverend Troy D. Perry* (Nash, 1972) and *Don't Be Afraid Anymore: The Story of Reverend Troy Perry and the Metropolitan Community Churches* (St. Martin's, 1990) testified to the powerful combination of religion and gay liberation in his life.

Perry continues to lead the UFMCC in the 1990s. By 1996 the church had over 39,000 members and 301 congregations in nineteen countries, and owned a five-story office building in Los Angeles that serves as UFMCC Global Headquarters.

**Profile by
Joseph M. Eagan**

DEB PRICE

J ournalist Deb Price writes the first nationally syndicated lesbian

and gay column published by the mainstream press. Deborah Jane Price

was born in Lubbock, Texas on 27 February 1958 and grew up in

Colorado. Her father, Allen Price, then an Episcopal priest, is now a

psychologist. Her mother, Jane Price, is a receptionist in a law firm. "As a

child, I was always 'different' in the way that gay adults often describe

looking back. I hated dolls, dresses and pretty much anything that girls

were supposed to crave. I loved to play and often found myself in play

rescuing women! As I grew older, I had major crushes on women

teachers and other girls," Price reflects.

1958– ·

American ·

journalist

When her parents divorced in 1973, Price, her brother Steve, and their mother moved to the East Coast. Price maintains a close relationship with her mother, asserting, "My mother has always been enormously supportive of me. She has always encouraged me, loved me and been a close friend as well as my mother. She has been remarkable since the column came out and outed her to her work colleagues and friends. She has marched in gay pride parades and is a tremendous source of strength for me. I never doubt her complete love for me. And that is something I have always drawn on to make it through the rough times."

Price had her first "romantic relationship" at the National Cathedral School for Girls in Washington, D.C., but did not really deal with being gay until she went to college. "I fully accepted myself in that I knew for certain I was a lesbian. But I was terrified of how other people might use that to hurt me. As a result, I dated men occasionally and was closeted even to gay friends," Price recollects.

Earning a B.A. and M.A. in literature at Stanford University, Price discovered a scarcity of academic positions and chose a career in journalism. She credits noted author Charles Dickens with influencing her choice: "In addition to being a novelist, he spoke out through the news periodicals against the horrible injustices of his day and he used his novels as well to educate readers about these terrible injustices. In hindsight, I am grateful that my path led me to where I am today. I feel tremendous gratitude that I was given the opportunity on a weekly basis to do something similar to what Charles Dickens did. Journalism combines a lot of my passions—writing, reading, thinking, debating, learning, exploring, talking, listening, caring, reaching out, growing."

Beginning her career at the *Northern Virginia Sun* in 1982, Price later moved to the States News Service, a Washington-based wire service covering Capitol Hill. In 1985 she became the news editor at the *Washington Post,* where she met her "lovemate," Joyce Murdoch. Price asserts, "I wasn't able to put it completely all together—be who I am and be truthful about it to everyone—until I met Joyce who was totally at ease with being gay. She was just getting ready to start a process of coming out professionally. But she had the personal acceptance down perfectly! And that was the kind of role model and friend I had desperately needed my whole life. We've really helped one another get to the place where we are today—totally out and trying to help other gay people. We work as a team. And we always have."

In 1989, Price became Deputy Washington Bureau Chief for the *Detroit News.* While working for the *News,* she successfully pitched the idea of writing a column on gay and lesbian issues, and on 8 May 1992 her column made its debut. Syndicated today in over 100 newspapers throughout the country, Price's columns add a human dimension to current gay and lesbian issues because she discusses them within the context of peoples' lives, often her own and Murdoch's. In a friendly, humorous manner, Price deftly educates her readers about commonly held misconceptions about gays and lesbians. Reflecting on the column's success, Price says, "Without a doubt, we both feel the most important thing we have accomplished professionally has been all the good that has come about through the column. We most love hearing from readers that the column helped bring their family back together. Sometimes, it's a letter from a parent; sometimes, it's from an adult child. But nothing gives us more joy than having been part of the process of healing in a family. We also love hearing from readers who find the column helpful in their journey of coming out."

Price and Murdoch collaborated on a book, *And Say Hi to Joyce,* the title of which derives from a concluding remark often found in Price's fan mail. Dedicated to "all the gay readers who've put twenty-five cents in a newspaper and found nothing reflecting their own lives inside," the book juxtaposes the first eighteen months of Price's columns against Murdoch's commentary on their impact. Comments Price, "We've been most pleased that the book makes people happy, that it makes people feel good about themselves and about other people. We like tapping into the good in ourselves and in others. And we like sharing the joy we've experienced through the column."

**Profile by
R. Ellen Greenblatt**

ADRIENNE RICH

Over the past three decades the writings of Adrienne Rich have

1929– •

helped to transform the current understanding of women's experiences

of such facets of identity as motherhood, lesbianism, and ethnicity.

American writer •

Rich's highly acclaimed poetry, which offers illuminating meditations

and educator

on her personal experiences of womanhood, has contributed to the

critical acceptance of the politicization of poetry. A self-identified

lesbian-feminist, Rich is a prolific writer of influential essays on the

position of women. Her work has helped to give a language to aspects of

women's experiences that have been previously considered "unspeak-

able," and also to shape the practice of feminist cultural studies today.

Rich was born in Baltimore, Maryland in 1929, to white southern Protestant Helen Jones and Dr. Arnold Rich, an assimilated Jew. As Rich explains in her essay *Split at the Root: An Essay on Jewish Identity,* Helen Rich was a composer and pianist who had sacrificed her artistic career to her domestic role as wife and mother according to the ideal of white, heterosexual femininity. It was by this ideal that she also raised her daughter. Arnold Rich, who became a professor in the department of pathology at Johns Hopkins Medical School, was brought up to aspire to acceptance by the white American professional class. As he guided his daughter's education through her childhood and adolescence, Arnold Rich tacitly communicated the importance of acceptance by this class to her.

Rich was educated at home by her mother until the fourth grade. She first began writing poetry as a child under the supervision of her father who, she recalled in *Split at the Root,* "made me feel, at a very young age, the power of language and that I could share it." Her first, childhood publications were plays: *Ariadne: A Play in Three Acts and Poems* (1939) and *Not I, But Death, a Play in One Act* (1941). As Rich notes in *Split at the Root,* the world in which she grew up was one of "white social christianity": she attended the Episcopalian church for five years and heard Episcopalian hymns and prayers in her school every morning.

In 1947 Rich left Baltimore to attend Radcliffe College. As she recalls in *Split at the Root,* there she met young Jewish women amongst whom she "was doing something that *is* dangerous: I was flirting with identity." She graduated from Radcliffe in 1951; in the same year her collection of poems, *A Change of World,* was chosen for the Yale Series of Younger Poets award by W. H. Auden. In her 1971 essay *When We Dead Awaken: Writing as Re-Vision,* Rich observes that her "style was formed first by male poets: by the men that I was reading as an undergraduate—Frost, Dylan Thomas, Donne, Auden, MacNiece, Yeats." She explains that looking back at the poems she wrote before she was twenty-one, she saw revealed beneath the carefully crafted style "the split I even then experienced between the girl who wrote the poems, who defined herself in writing poems and the girl who was to define herself by her relationships with men." She had not yet consciously recognized "the suppressed lesbian" whom, as she explains in *Split at the Root,* she had been "carrying in [her] since adolescence." The following year Rich was awarded a Guggenheim fellowship, which enabled her to travel in Europe and England. In the same year, the onset of rheumatoid arthritis began, for which Rich has continued to undergo surgery periodically throughout her life.

In 1953 Rich married the economist Alfred H. Conrad, and for the next thirteen years they lived in what Rich has described in *Split at the Root* as "the predominantly gentile Yankee academic world of Cambridge, Massachusetts." In the same essay, Rich reflects: "Like many women I knew in the fifties living under a then-unquestioned heterosexual imperative, I married in part because I knew no better way to disconnect myself from my first family." Her parents refused to attend the wedding because she had connected herself to an orthodox Jewish husband and family of eastern European origin. Rich did not see her parents for several years after her marriage. By the time she was thirty, she and Conrad had three sons, David, Paul, and Jacob. During these years of undergoing difficult pregnancies and taking care of three small sons, she was struggling to conform with the "feminine mystique" of the 1950s, trying to be a "good" mother and the ideal faculty wife and hostess. This was compounded by her relation to her husband's family, whom she sought to please by conforming with the role expected of a Jewish wife and mother. She had little time or energy for writing during this time, publishing only *The Diamond Cutters and Other Poems* in 1955. Another eight years passed before she published another book. During these years, Rich was torn by the conflict between writing and motherhood, which she experienced as a failure of love in herself. Retrospectively, she came to understand this conflict as social, not simply personal. "The experience of motherhood," she observes in *Split at the Root,* "was eventually to radicalize me."

It was during the 1960s that the "radicalization" of Rich gathered impetus. In 1966 she separated from her husband, left Cambridge, and moved to New York. From the late 1950s she had supported the Civil Rights Movement and yet she was still at this time "very politically ignorant," as she later explained to David Montenegro in an interview published in *American Poetry Review* in 1991. In New York, however, she became increasingly active in radical politics, especially in protests against the war in Vietnam. As she told David Montenegro, she was also persistently questioning "something that wasn't being talked about at the time very much. I was thinking about where sexuality belonged in all this." The relation between the personal and the political was further underscored for Rich in 1968, at a time when she was involved with work on racial issues, teaching in the SEEK and Open Admissions programs at City College of the City University of New York. The year saw for her not only momentous events on the larger political scene, but also the death of her father after a long illness. Following the suicide of Conrad two years later, Rich was to spend years disentangling her relations with the two men.

Rich's poetry of the 1960s is also marked by an awareness of the political dimension of personal experience. She had first discovered a dialogue between art and politics in the work of W. B. Yeats, which she read as an undergraduate at Radcliffe. Rich's *Snapshots of a Daughter-in-Law: Poems, 1954–62,* published in 1963, marks a shift from the detached formal elegance of her earlier work to a poetry informed by a conscious sexual politics whose voice is personal and immediate. The next four collections, which Rich published between 1966 and 1971, show her involvement in black civil rights and anti-war protest and her increasing identification with women's experiences.

• *Rich Gives a*

Voice to

Silenced Women

In her interview with David Montenegro for *American Poetry Review,* Rich commented that "where connections are being made always feels to me like the point of interest life" and that for her "the point of interest life is where I write poetry." Another important connection for her, she comments, was where the women's movement began to emerge out of the Left and the Civil Rights Movement at the end of the 1960s. From this time, Rich increasingly dedicated herself to feminism, whose aim as she understands it is "the creation of a society without domination," as she explained in a 1984 speech, *Notes Toward a Politics of Location.* Politics, for Rich, has always involved a regeneration of the self as well as a revolution of society. Her work attends particularly to women's sense of self as this is experienced through a female body, whose meaning is culturally determined and circumscribed. In her poetry, Rich seeks to create a language that will achieve a synthesis between the traditionally separated realms of art and politics, the self and the world. This is exemplified by *Diving into the Wreck,* which expresses personal anger and political principal relating to Rich's experience of womanhood. The book was awarded the National Book Award in 1974, which Rich accepted on behalf of women with Audre Lorde and Alice Walker.

As she became increasingly more involved with politics, Rich also began to write more prose. From the 1960s, she had been writing essays about the ways in which women's experiences have been made invisible, omitted from history and misrepresented in literature. In her influential 1971 essay, *When We Dead Awaken: Writing as Re-vision,* she argues that women must look back "with fresh eyes" at representations of themselves by male writers in order to understand how they have been placed in male-dominated society. Such an act of re-vision is, for women, Rich suggests, "an act of survival." Rich's exploration of women's experiences in male-dominated cultures was extended in her 1976 book *Of Woman Born: Motherhood as Experience and Institution,* a composite of autobiography, history, and anthropology. Here, Rich showed how the experience of motherhood, seemingly a natural condition, is in fact created by myths which are fostered by medical, social, religious, and political institutions. One of the main questions Rich asked in this book was why, "if heterosexuality was so natural," was it necessary for various cultures to control women through their prescriptive ideas about femininity and motherhood?

This was a question Rich asked again in a 1976 speech, *It Is the Lesbian in Us. . .*, where she recalled how her first love for women had been suppressed. This silencing, she discovered, had also taken place in literature, where lesbian identity was scarcely represented. Moreover, Rich argued, "it is the lesbian in us" who is creative: the woman who is submissive to male authority will always be a "hack." Rich's best-known contribution to thought about lesbian identity is her 1980 essay, *Compulsory Heterosexuality and the Lesbian Existence.* Here she sought to bridge the gap that she perceived between "lesbian" and "feminist" and was at pains to provide a new category and language through which to discuss lesbians. To this end, she coined the phrases "lesbian existence" and "lesbian continuum." By "lesbian existence" she designated the presence of lesbians in history and the way lesbians continue to "create the meaning of that existence." By "lesbian continuum," she drew attention to the importance and "primary intensity" of "woman-identified experience" in all women's lives. Through this specifically female experience, she argued, all women can be located at a point on the spectrum of lesbian identity, whether or not they choose to identify themselves as lesbians. Rich's argument has provoked controversy among lesbian critics, some of whom argue that the concept of a "lesbian continuum" negates the uniqueness of lesbian existence in which women relate to women sexually and form communities around this choice. For Rich, lesbian identity continues to embrace the woman who frees herself from the constraints of male images of women to become one who "has a sense of desiring oneself; above all, of choosing oneself," as she first put it in *It Is the Lesbian in Us. . . .* Through her writing about lesbian identity, Rich seeks to create a way of seeing that no longer needs men and heterosexuality at the center of all women's relationships and activities.

In 1976, Rich began her life with Michelle Cliff, the Jamaican-American novelist and poet, and she published *Twenty-One Love Poems,* where she expressed her lesbian sensibility through such lines as "I choose to love this time for once/ with all my intelligence" in "Splitting." Her 1981 collection, *A Wild Patience Has Taken Me This Far: Poems 1978–1981,* in which she continues to represent silenced women, was awarded the National Gay Task Force Fund for Human Dignity Award. From 1981 to 1983, she edited, with Cliff, the influential lesbian/feminist journal *Sinister Wisdom.*

Throughout the 1980s and into the 1990s, Rich continued to reflect on the position of women and the social factors that determine women's experiences, both in general terms and with reference to her own life. In two companion pieces, the 1983 poem sequence *Sources,* and her essay *Split at the Root,* Rich began to disentangle her complicated relations with her Jewish father and husband, in this way addressing her own ethnicity and trying to "become free of all the ghosts and shadows of my childhood, named and unnamed," as she comments in *Split at the Root.* Remaining committed to her exploration of the question, "What did it mean to be a Jewish lesbian?," as she asks in *Split at the Root,* in 1990 Rich became a member of the founding editorial group *Bridges: A Journal for Jewish Feminists and Our Friends.* Rich's involvement with the feminist debates over race since the 1980s has led her to examine her own position as a white woman through her poetry and prose.

Throughout the 1980s and 1990s, Rich has continued to teach in universities across America and has been awarded honorary doctorates by several universities in recognition of her work. Her ongoing attention to the need to highlight the importance of gender, race, class, nationality, and sexual orientation in the development of new ideas and knowledge continues to contribute to the directions taken by feminists working in the field today.

Profile by
Joanna Price

MARLON RIGGS

1957–1994 •

*B*rilliant, articulate, fearless, a consummate artist, a bright flame in

the world of documentary film—all of these accolades and more have

been used to describe the mere handful of documentaries Marlon Riggs

African American •

made in his too-short life. From his chronicling of black stereotypes

filmmaker

throughout our culture, to his unflinchingly homoerotic "riff" on black

gay men in our society, Riggs challenged his audience with his clear,

passionate voice—a voice that demanded full inclusion. "I loathe what

has been routine in our culture," he told journalist Barry Walters in

1993, "that level of disclosure that is really narcissism. There's often no

acknowledgment that one's struggle is part of a historical, social strug-

gle. So I tend to go overboard to compensate."

323 •

Even as a child, Texas-born Riggs was a fighter, a leader—well ahead of the pack. In an article for the *San Francisco Chronicle* shortly after Riggs' death from AIDS complications in April 1994, longtime friend and co-producer of *Color Adjustment* Vivian Kleiman recalls that "he was something of a child preacher. When he was a kid at church he would often be asked to get up and discuss the scripture, and I think that the sense of leadership and speaking to large groups was something he was comfortable with, and film is a logical extension of that." Riggs' mother Jean adds that, from early on, "he was very much an intellectual . . . he did all the things that other kids do, but he talked very early, walked very early, and read very early. He seemed always to be very wise." Finally, in an interview for the *San Francisco Examiner* in 1992, Riggs himself offered that he had "always been more cerebral and got teased tremendously about it as a kid."

Although best known for his films, Riggs was also a powerful writer and a natural teacher. In 1991, for example, he astonished participants at an Oakland poetry reading by getting up and reciting a fierce sexual fantasia about a black man's encounter with a white, racist skinhead. In the broadest sense then, all his work struggles to bridge the social and cultural chasms he experienced throughout his life—gay *vs.* straight, black *vs.* white, the poetic *vs.* the professorial—not to mention the more complex interweaving of "priorities" that multi-cultural identification "affords." "Are we *black* gay men, or *gay* black men?" he once asked fellow black, gay, and British filmmaker Isaac Julien, a question further complicated by the fact that both men had white lovers at the time.

Riggs received his master's degree from Harvard in the early 1980s and taught documentary filmmaking at the University of California at Berkeley in the final few years before his death. In addition to his films, he edited and contributed to the book *Brother to Brother: New Writings of Black Gay Men* and added his insights on living with HIV to a number of publications. "There was his academic side and his wild side," film editor and collaborator Deborah Hoffmann said in 1994, "and both sides were there every day. One minute he was this dry academic using billion dollar words and the next he was dancing down the hallway." "He was multi-voiced," said Essex Hemphill, a Philadelphia poet who figured prominently in Riggs' *Tongues Untied*. "Marlon's gift was his ability to weave together so many disparate elements and aspects of himself into his work."

Riggs' first important work was *Ethnic Notions* (1987), a documentary surveying 150 years of racial stereotyping in popular American culture—a look at "Negro-bilia" from Aunt Jemima dolls to cartoon "darkies." But his most controversial and autobiographical work—the first in which he appears himself—followed in 1988. That work, *Tongues Untied,* was lauded by critics as the first unflinching look at the black gay male sexuality in America in all its complexity. For once, the juxtaposition of black and male was not equated with rampant, predatory heterosexuality, but rather with a lyrical, randy, soulful reaching-out of brother to brother. The process of making the film was completely cathartic, Riggs told author Andrea Vaucher in 1993:

> So much of my life had been about effacement, self-effacement, pretense, masquerading, concealment, and indirection. When you are seeking empowerment and enfranchisement in the society, it requires that you negotiate with dominant cultures, whether straight, or mainstream African American. . . . That is why the documentary is called *Tongues Untied.* It was almost earth-shattering in what it taught me psychically about the power of speech . . . of self-affirmation . . . of an articulated self-identity.

Not surprisingly, *Tongues* was lambasted by the political right, most notably in 1992 when presidential candidate Patrick Buchanan shuffled clips from the film and inserted them into television spots accusing the Bush administration and the National Endowment for the Arts (NEA) of abusing government funds. (Never mind that the film received a meager $5,000 from the NEA.)

Riggs was quick to fire back, charging Buchanan with copyright infringement and tearing into him in a *New York Times* op-ed piece "because my film affirms the lives and dignity of black gay men . . . presidential politics have thus been injected with a new poison: the persecution of racial and sexual difference." A year later, Riggs provided a more academic but nonetheless burning insight into the controversy when he was interviewed by the *Examiner:*

> Our culture has reached the point where we can have some level of intelligent discourse on the subject of race without forcing one to be labeled as an extremist or polemic or militant or subversive. However, anyone who attempts to look at our sexualities, and simply doesn't privilege heterosexuality as the only model to which we should all aspire, gets labeled and discredited.

Riggs' *Color Adjustment* (1992)—which received the prestigious George Foster Peabody award—complemented *Ethnic Notions* with a look at the way African Americans have been depicted on television, juxtaposing situation comedy life with harsh realities outside the tube.

Even as *The Cosby Show* grew in popularity, Riggs showed in *Color Adjustment*, crack cocaine was decimating an entire generation of young black men.

In 1990, Riggs released his nine-minute film *Anthem*, a poetic rap exploration of gay African American love and desire. In 1991, he appeared in Peter Adair's film *Absolutely Positive*, a moving documentary about people living with HIV.

In 1992, Riggs released *No, Je Ne Regrette Rien (No Regrets)*, a video that explores the impact of AIDS on the African American male by mixing the testimony of five very different men with music and poetry. The visual metaphor for coming out of the AIDS closet is powerful, as critic Edward Guthmann noted in a *San Francisco Chronicle* review. "At first, we see them in isolated body fragments as they speak," he wrote. "One man's mouth, another's eyes, another's hands. Gradually they emerge in whole . . . their tales of survival are told, each is identified by name."

Riggs worked right up to the time of his death from AIDS complications in the spring of 1994, filming but not completing a searing look into contemporary notions of "authentic blackness" entitled *Black Is . . . Black Ain't*. Seven months later the film was completed by colleagues Christiane Badgley, Bob Paris, and Nicole Atkinson. The result is a highly personal, even playful, "deathbed confession" on Riggs' part about what it means to be called black, Negro, colored, African American, whatever, in this culture. "Even while he was dying," one critic wrote in the *Nation*, "Riggs apparently could look into the mirror of his American self and see the beginnings of a good party gathering. The man had his eyes open."

Toward the end, Riggs described his too-short body of work to author Thomas Avena as an epiphany, a series of "lights" along the path toward "our own personal novas." "In the illumination of my own struggle around being black and gay and now HIV-positive," he told author Vaucher in late 1993, "I wanted to connect to the communal struggle and to an historic struggle so that my story was not simply my story, but our story . . . for liberation, and redemption, and self-love." Perhaps this is why, as fellow filmmaker Michele Wallace wrote soon after Marlon's death, "his flame was high and his art was not cool. He was burning up."

Profile by
Jerome Szymczak

RuPAUL

1960– •

R uPaul Andre Charles was born in 1960, the only son in a family of

mostly women. It is to the strong women in his life that RuPaul dedicates

his love of the feminine principle. He grew up in San Diego, and

African American •

developed a fascination with the theatre early in life. His introduction to

entertainer

drag occurred when a girlfriend took him to see The Rocky Horror

Picture Show and when, in 1978, he met his first drag queens.

After dropping out of high school in the eleventh grade RuPaul sold cars for his brother-in-law and traveled around the country. In 1981 he saw a cable comedy show called *The American Music Show* and wrote to the producer, telling him how much he would like to appear on the show. When he did, it was with some female friends in an impromptu band called RuPaul and the U-Hauls. He became a regular on the show, but didn't appear in drag until there was an on-air drag wedding.

From the U-Hauls he went on to an all-male band called Wee Wee Pole, and played with them for about a year. In the mid-1980s RuPaul appeared in a series of underground films directed by John Witherspoon, the first three being *Trilogy of Terror*. He also published a series of pamphlets, which were mostly photographs of himself. But in 1984 RuPaul found himself broke and evicted from his apartment.

RuPaul then took off for New York with three other fledgling drag queens and put together a revue at the Pyramid in Greenwich Village. Being homeless in New York was a little rougher than in Atlanta, but RuPaul and his gang managed to stay alive and relatively unscathed. He returned to Atlanta for Christmas and recorded his first album, *Sex Freak,* for Funtone Records. The following summer he played Riff Raff in *The Rocky Horror Picture Show.*

In January 1986 RuPaul created a new persona for himself called Starrbooty. This led to another trilogy of underground films of the same name. He then went back to New York to promote the album at the New Music Seminar. After that he starred in *Mahogany II* (playing Diana Ross in drag), *American Porn Star, Psycho Bitch,* and *Voyeur.*

When he went back to New York he had to start over, and by the beginning of 1987 was working as a coat check boy at the Amazon Hotel. In 1988 he went to Los Angeles and landed a spot on *The Gong Show;* he lost to an Elvis impersonator. When he turned twenty-eight and found himself homeless again, he returned to Atlanta to live with his mother.

Upon returning to New York in 1989, RuPaul found that the drag scene had changed—it now demanded realism over style. RuPaul managed the transformation in fine form, and became a regular at a club called the Love Machine. It was then that he developed his signature perfume, Whore. This was really the springboard of his career, and later that year he appeared in the B-52's "Love Shack" video.

In January 1990 he was crowned "Queen of Manhattan" and appeared on *Geraldo.* But RuPaul was also on his way to becoming a serious alcoholic, and when he was fired from a video shoot for being inebriated, he decided it was time to rethink his life. After kicking his alcohol and drug habits RuPaul made his album, *Supermodel of the World,* and performed the album's single for the first time at Wigstock in 1992. This was followed by the Supermodel tour, which lasted until January 1994 when he opened for Duran Duran in Hartford, Connecticut. The video was nominated for best dance video at the MTV Video Music Awards that year. He also toured Europe and performed at the Cannes film festival. From there he hit Hollywood, appearing on *Arsenio Hall,* and was an award presenter at the Video Music Awards.

The straight media discovered RuPaul in 1995. Everybody wanted to interview him, review him, and get his advice on life. He sang a duet with Elton John—a remake of "Don't Go Breaking My Heart"—and filmed a video to go with it. He appeared in *Crooklyn, The Brady Bunch Movie,* and *To Wong Foo—Thanks for Everything, Julie Newmar.* He became the spokesmodel for MAC cosmetics, and in February 1996 was interviewed for *Harper's Bazaar* as the only male on a panel of supermodels, effectively announcing the impact RuPaul has had on the worlds of performance art.

**Profile by
Debora Hill**

BAYARD RUSTIN

1910–1987 •

African American •

activist

T hough often called "Mr. March" for his prime organizational role

in one of the most important nonviolent protests in American history—

the 1963 March on Washington—Bayard Rustin is still something of an

unsung hero in the history of the American Civil Rights Movement. The

ongoing specter of homophobia and fear of "red menace" Communism

that shadowed his career of over five decades reached a zenith in the

middle part of this century and forced him to step behind the scenes at

the height of his political power. Still, once his accomplishments are

noted, Rustin is easily categorized as one of the most influential

political, nonviolent strategists who fought not only for the rights of

African Americans, but for the dignity of all oppressed minorities. From his early labor union years to his "senior statesman" lectures at colleges and gay organizations around the country, Rustin held fast to the belief that the rights of African Americans were best secured and maintained in the long run as an integral part of deeper social reforms for everyone.

In the 1930s and 1940s, a youthful, radicalized Bayard Rustin worked with and recruited for the Communist Party, the War Resisters League, and various labor unions. He teamed with Martin Luther King Jr. in the 1950s and was a confidant, advisor, and speech writer until King's tragic death in the spring of 1968. He helped create both the Congress of Racial Equality (CORE) and the Southern Christian Leadership Conference (SCLC). In the 1980s, he urged gays and lesbians to follow his example and embrace their role in furthering social equity for *all* minorities. It was this wholistic focus on broader social objectives that spotlights Rustin as unique among twentieth-century social activists, black or white, gay or straight. "I reject the idea of working for the Negro as being impractical as well as immoral, if one does that alone," he said in a 1965 interview. To the end of his life, Rustin maintained this world view—the political was ever the personal, and vice versa.

- *"Fated"*

Activism

Bayard Rustin grew up in a poor section of West Chester, Pennsylvania, one of nine children supported by parents in the catering business. At the age of eleven, he was told that the woman he thought was his sister was actually his mother, and that his "parents" were actually his grandparents. His father was a West Indian man whom his mother had never married, and Rustin's grandmother was a devout Quaker. It was this combination of hard work, extended familial responsibility, and a commitment to social justice that formed the heart of Rustin's lifelong moral/activist code.

West Chester had been an important stop on the underground railroad, a fact that Rustin, in retrospect, felt fated his future as an activist. As he noted in his 1976 *Strategies for Freedom,* "The antislavery sentiment of the inhabitants was revealed in the town's architecture, for beneath its aging, Colonial homes ran hidden passageways which had concealed runaway slaves from (their) southern plantation owners."

The beginning of Rustin's college career coincided with the onset of the Great Depression, so Rustin, gifted as he was, had to drop out. In 1931 he moved in with a relative in Greenwich Village and put himself through classes at New York City College by occasionally singing at local clubs with singers like Josh White and Leadbelly. Strictly enforced segregation in places of public entertainment was still the norm for most of New York, except in those integrated clubs operated by Communist organizers. It was during this time that Rustin, like many black intellectuals of his day, embraced the Communist promise of racial equality and a cure for economic ills. He was soon traveling to colleges and union halls throughout the United States to speak out against segregation and social injustice. With the outbreak of World War II and the subsequent shift by the Party away from domestic reforms, Rustin was asked to stop his anti-segregation work. He quickly resigned.

By the mid-1940s, an undaunted Rustin was principal aide to labor leader A. Philip Randolph, an originator of the 1941 March on Washington. One of Rustin's first tasks was to target racial discrimination in the defense industry. It was Randolph who had been instrumental in pressuring Franklin Delano Roosevelt into creating the Fair Employment Practices Commission, and it was Randolph who, according to Rustin in his *Strategies for Freedom,* used "careful daring, (and a) sense of timing and strategy" to get Truman to sign an executive order in 1948 that finally ended racial discrimination in the military.

Randolph was Rustin's most beloved mentor. Shortly after Randolph's death in 1979, Rustin wrote that Randolph had unearthed for him the critical *economic* roots of racism, and had taught him above all "that the struggle for the freedom of black people is intertwined with the struggle to free all mankind."

In 1942, Rustin was hired by radical reformer A. J. Muste, founder of the international pacifist organization Fellowship for Reconciliation (FOR), to spearhead a Department of Race Relations. From this committee emerged the interracial Congress of Racial Equality (CORE), whose philosophy was patterned after the nonviolent direct action as exercised by Indian leader Mohandas Gandhi, and whose focus was on challenging racial discrimination in public accommodation and transportation through nonviolent mass protest. Here, Rustin found the heart of lasting, truly forward-moving success for the civil rights movement. CORE strategies satisfied his progressive agenda, utilized the energy and talents of both blacks and sympathetic whites, and salved his Quaker-bred sensibilities for nonviolence.

Ironically, it was in the years during and immediately following the war that Rustin faced the most grueling mental and physical challenges to these ideologies. His life's work became a roller coaster ride of peaks and valleys. In 1942, he worked in California on behalf of the interned Japanese and, as a conscientious objector in 1943, served three years in the Lewisburg Penitentiary rather than perform hospital duties. On his release in 1946, he resumed his CORE duties and traveled to India as chairman of the Free India Committee and a guest of Ghandi's Congress Party. In 1947, he served twenty-two days on a North Carolina chain gang (just one of dozens of beatings and arrests he was to suffer in his life) for joining one of the first Freedom Rides through the South—dubbed the "Journey of Reconciliation"—designed to test the U.S. Supreme Court prohibition against segregation in interstate travel.

In the early 1950s, Rustin fought for self rule in West Africa, assumed a leading role in the Aldermason Peace March in England, and joined the All African People's Conference in Addis Ababa. Yet despite his growing worldwide success, Rustin now also faced the ongoing, career-crippling isolation of homophobia, despite the "all encompassing" rhetoric of the political organizations he worked for. He had long been nonchalant and open about his homosexuality in private, and always discreet professionally. Yet, given the political/sexual hysteria and hypocrisy of the 1950s, he was now considered a potential liability by many of his colleagues.

According to *Contemporary Black Biography* (1993), "when Rustin began to run into trouble with laws against homosexual activity, FOR chairman Muste warned him that any such further actions would cause his dismissal." When he was arrested and sentenced to thirty days in jail on a morals charge in Pasadena, California in early 1953, a dispirited Rustin was forced to resign from FOR. It was a tragically humbling step behind the scenes that was to shadow his life and career to the end.

In December of 1955, the civil rights struggle in America reached a watershed when Rosa Parks refused to move to the back of the bus in segregated Montgomery, Alabama. The resulting bus boycott received nationwide attention and was viewed by Rustin as an opportunity to rejoin the fight and regain some lost political influence. He traveled to Montgomery, but was soon reproached by several black political leaders who feared that his personal life and past Communist connections would prove a liability to the cause. Led by A. P. Randolph, they convinced him to leave Montgomery.

Rustin had come too far to simply withdraw, however. As he wrote in his diary in 1956, "I had a feeling that no force on earth (could) stop this movement. It has all the elements to touch the hearts of men." Martin Luther King Jr., then head of the Montgomery movement, was quick to recognize Rustin's talents, and thus initiated a lifelong professional liaison. Rustin became ghostwriter, confidant, and tireless promoter of the "cult of personality" that was growing around King. Recognizing the movement's need for a charismatic, younger leader (by now, Rustin was twenty years King's senior), and reluctantly acquiescent to his personal "liabilities," Rustin helped the emerging leader behind the scenes by briefing him for meetings, drafting speeches and press releases, and introducing him to wealthy civil rights supporters.

- *Career-*

Crippling

Homophobia

With the arrival of desegregation orders from the Supreme Court in December 1956, the Montgomery boycott ended. Strategies for expanding the campaign throughout the South were just beginning though, as was Rustin's role as senior statesman. But once again, the potential for scandal loomed large. In 1960, the powerful black congressman Adam Clayton Powell threatened to expose Rustin's personal and political past, which precipitated Rustin's resignation from the SCLC. He was forced to forfeit his role as official head of the 1963 March on Washington. However, his long association with King nonetheless assured his central role as a behind the curtain organizer of one of the most important nonviolent protests in American history, best remembered as the march at which King delivered his riveting "I Have a Dream" speech.

It is important to note the fear that political segregationists wielded at the time. Right down to the eve of the march, Rustin's most stalwart supporters were afraid that conservatives and liberals alike would exploit Rustin's homosexuality and former Communist ties to "taint and dilute" the purpose of the protest—which was, for the first time in history, designed to draw attention to the *economic* roots of racism in America. But seventy-three-year-old Randolph, considered the most politically safe figurehead to lead the march, was by then vesting responsibility for the day-to-day planning and logistics almost completely to Rustin. In the end, thanks largely to King's intervention, Randolph appointed Rustin as his official march deputy and he was back on board.

In a last-ditch effort to derail the march, Senator Strom Thurmond told the press about Rustin's 1953 morals arrest and denounced him on the floor of the Senate as a draft dodger and Communist. The sabotage backfired and the attack served to rally black leaders around Rustin all the more. Throughout, Rustin himself kept a cool head, answering Thurmond's charges with prideful proof that he knew quite a bit more about morals and decency than the cagey Senator. "With regard to Senator Thurmond's attack on my morality," he wrote just prior to the march in 1963, "I have no comment. By religious training and fundamental philosophy, I am disinclined to put myself in the position of having to defend my own moral character. Questions in this area should properly be directed to those who have entrusted me with my present responsibilities."

By 1964, Rustin had grown disillusioned with nonviolent action as means of change. He turned his focus to the political arena, and from 1965 to 1979, he headed the A. P. Randolph Institute, a liberal think-tank sponsored by the AFL-CIO and designed to address social and economic ills. In 1975, he founded the Organization for Black Americans to Support Israel, a group that continues to this day.

From his "senior statesman" vantage point later in life, Rustin witnessed the violence, factionalism, and frustration that characterized the movement for racial equality well into the 1980s. His allegiance to radical reforms—total restructuring of political, economic, and social institutions—remained intact, and he continued to stress the importance of strong labor unions, coalition politics, and the vote. To those who advocated racial separatism, he answered that without equality for all, there simply is no equality for the few—no political base or ideology from which to take a stand. "The real radical," he wrote in a speech to black students in 1970, "is that person who has a vision of equality and is willing to do those things that will bring reality closer to that vision. And by equality I do not mean 'separate but equal,' a phrase created by segregationists in order to prevent the attainment of equality. I mean equality based upon an integrated social order."

Toward the end of his life, Rustin often spoke to gay organizations, emphasizing the importance of including gays and lesbians of all colors and backgrounds in the ongoing struggle for racial equality. Integration and "crossover" radicalism were the keys to true progress, he would argue; one group's gain against oppression is a step forward for all. Radicals "of all stripes" were needed.

Another common theme when he spoke to lesbian and gay groups was the importance of coming out. "Although its going to make problems," the *Alyson Almanac* quotes him as saying, "those problems are not so dangerous as the problems of lying to yourself, to your friends, and missing many opportunities."

Profile by
Jerome Szymczak

Bayard Rustin held fast to his dreams and his truths all his life, and consequently, never missed an opportunity to throw himself into the thick of this century's social struggles for equality.

ASSOTTO SAINT

A man of diverse talents, Assotto Saint was a dancer, choreographer,

1957–1994 •

writer, editor, publisher, and outspoken representative for victims of

AIDS. After his premature death from the disease, his friend Franklin

African American •

Abbott remembered him as "an intense character and fine performer."

writer and

Abbott continued, "he was quite a beautiful human being. Losing him is

performer

just one of our tragedies."

Born Yves Francois Lubin on 2 October 1957 in Haiti, Saint was raised by his mother and never met his father until many years after his birth. "I must have been seven when I realized my attraction to men," wrote Saint in his autobiographical essay "Haiti: A Memory Journey." But knowing he was gay and being gay in his native Haiti were not easy. It wasn't until 1970, on the heels of Stonewall, when he came to New York to visit—then to stay permanently—with his mother that Saint saw there was such a thing as a gay world.

Saint attended college, pursuing a pre-med course of study before being seduced into the world of dance. In the early 1970s he secured a place as a dancer with the Martha Graham Dance Company, but his involvement in the performing arts quickly broadened and he began to write for the stage as well. He subsequently founded the Metamorphosis Theater in New York, where he also served as artistic director. Saint collaborated with his life partner, Jan Holmgren, on several theatrical works that dealt with the lives of black gay men: *Risin' to the Love We Need, New Love Song, Black Fag,* and *Nuclear Lovers.*

During this period Saint was also writing poetry, and his works were widely anthologized during the 1980s. His work was included in *In the Life: A Black Gay Anthology* (Alyson Publications, 1986), *New Men, New Minds* (Crossing Press, 1987); *Gay & Lesbian Poetry in Our Time* (St. Martin's Press, 1988); *Sojourner: Black Gay Voices in the Age of AIDS* (Other Countries Press, 1993); and *Jugular Defenses* (Oscars Press). In addition, he served as poetry editor of the anthology *Other Countries: Black Gay Voices.* Perceiving the need for wider dissemination of black gay literature, Saint also founded the Galiens Press, which published, among other things, two seminal anthologies of black gay poetry. One Galiens publication, *Here to Dare: A Collection of 10 Gay Black Poets,* was nominated for a Lambda Literary Award. "Galiens" is derived from the two words "gay" and "aliens."

Collections of Saint's own work include a chapbook, *Triple Trouble* (published in *Tongues Untied;* GMP; 1987), and two collections of poetry: *Stations* (Galiens Press, 1989) and the posthumously published *Wishing for Wings.* His manuscripts and personal papers are archived at the the New York Public Library's Schomberg Museum in the Bronx.

Saint made his voice and presence heard not only in his written and performed work, but also in his activism. He was an impassioned spokesman and one of a growing number of advocates for gay artists suffering from AIDS. According to his friend, Walter Holland, "Assotto was determined to appear as an out HIV-positive artist. He was most concerned about the fact that many black artists went to their deaths in complete secrecy." Holland says that Saint was "fierce in his politics. He told it like it was and he was very astute." He also fiercely advocated the need for black gay writers to be nurtured and for poetry in general to be supported and encouraged. However, he was not ethnocentric in his advocacy, and he fiercely defended his involvement with Holmgren, a Caucasian. Holland has tried to write about Saint in the novel *The March* (Masquerade Books, 1996), but Saint was as complex as he was intense and fascinating, and capturing his essence is no easy task.

Exactly why Saint took on a new name is not clear. However, according to a close friend, the name Assotto Saint is far from randomly selected. "Assotto" is derived from a type of African ceremonial drum that presumably has a ritualistic connection as well as a practical function as a form of communication. The name "Saint" is believed to have been taken from the Haitian general and liberator Toussaint L'Ouverture (a.k.a. Pierre Dominique). Toussaint is a great symbol of liberation in Haiti, and it is thought that it tied Saint to his roots while at the same time being reminiscent of his own rebellious nature and his commitment to civil disobedience and civil insurrection.

In the mid 1980s, Saint returned to Haiti to meet the father he "never met, never saw pictures of, never heard mention of and accepted as a non-entity in my life." The meeting was not particularly successful—his father was unable to accept his son's homosexuality, and Saint was greatly frustrated over his father's rude and abrupt manner. The two parted with a handshake. Saint decided to phone his father one last time before leaving Haiti. His half-brother claimed that his father was not in. While Saint and Holmgren ate breakfast, a handwritten note was delivered to him. In the note, his father maintained that it was good that they finally met. He wished his son "good luck," a safe journey, and good health. "I crushed that note in my hand," says Saint in "Haiti: A Memory Journey," "and imagined it was his heart." No great reunion between son and long-lost father would take place, and dreams of having at last a loving father were shattered. Saint returned home to live the final and most productive decade of his young life.

**Profile by
Andrea L. T. Peterson**

CAROL SEAJAY

C arol Seajay's work as a publisher and writer is informed by a sense   **American** •

of activism that has created a powerful network of women and informa-   ***publisher***

tion for the past twenty years. In 1976, she co-founded the feminist   ***and writer***

bookstore Old Wives Tales; she is also the publisher and editor of Feminist

Bookstore News *and has contributed to* Ms. *magazine on the topic of*

feminist books and bookstores.

The women-in-print movement is both a social and political part of the feminist movement, which recognizes that women need to control the entire means of production in order to get the truth about women's lives into print. Seajay describes the drive of the movement as "a vision that if you gathered this information and put it in women's hands, the whole world would change."

This movement grew out of the necessity to gather and print the truth about women's lives and to connect women through print. As Seajay explains in an interview with Kate Brandt, "Fifteen, twenty years ago, there was such a clear sense that women were *not* in print. Women existed in print in the male image only—which is hard to

343 •

imagine at this point in time, that there really were not lesbian novels with happy endings."

While working for the feminist bookstore A Woman's Place in Oakland, California, Seajay attended the first annual Women in Print Conference. When the women attending the conference realized that they could benefit from the regular communication of a newsletter, Seajay volunteered to help. Since 1976, she has published and edited *Feminist Bookstore News,* a bimonthly magazine based in San Francisco. It represents over 100 bookstores and is distributed to presses and booksellers around the world.

To begin producing the newsletter, the five largest bookstores each invested $100. As Seajay said in her interview with Kate Brandt, "There was always an understanding that those stores that could afford to, put in more, and the stores that are tiny and [staffed by] volunteers, or are just surviving, put in less." The newsletter is funded in such a way that both large and small bookstores can participate.

Seajay runs *Feminist Bookstore News* full time. The newsletter has grown to include book reviews, discussions, debates, searches for out-of-print books, announcements, profiles of feminist bookstores, tips on new product lines, conferences, and related trends.

Seajay is a writer as well as editor and publisher of *Feminist Bookstore News.* Her contributions to *Ms.* magazine include "20 Years of Feminist Bookstores," an essay describing the growth of feminist bookstores and the relationship of bookstores to the women's movement. In this essay she says of the women who enter these bookstores, "Once they made it through the doorway, they took what they found and changed their lives—left abusive relationships, found new self-images, came out, found sisterhood and a community."

In a more recent essay, "Feminist Bookstores Fight Back," Seajay describes the changing market for feminist bookstores as large chain bookstores have begun to target feminist book buyers and have tried to edge smaller bookstores out of the market. The Feminist Bookstore Network held a Strategic Planning Conference to discuss the future of feminist bookstores and created a strategy to combat the large book chains. Strategies include celebrating National Feminist Bookstore Week, sponsoring Feminist Book Awards, and developing a catalogue of feminist books, which also includes a list of feminist bookstores in the United States and Canada.

Seajay's short story, "As Important as a Lamp," is included in *Dykescapes,* a collection of lesbian short stores edited by Tina Portillo.

The story is told from the perspective of Jean, a woman involved in a relationship with an abusive lesbian partner. During a violent attack by her partner, Jean processes the messages of survival that she has gotten from women at a battered women's shelter. The story ends as Jean walks away from the house and the abusive partner.

Seajay's involvement in the vision of the women in print movement is reflected in the many ways that she herself is involved with women's words. Through her bookstore, the Feminist Bookstore Network, her essays, and her fiction, she creates and promotes positive images for all women.

Profile by
Danielle M. DeMuth

345 •

RANDY SHILTS

*R*andy Shilts, an openly gay television and print journalist, wrote

three acclaimed books that chronicled contemporary gay and lesbian

political, health, and social issues. He was one of the first journalists to

recognize AIDS as a critical health issue, and his second book, And the

Band Played On: Politics, People, and the AIDS Epidemic *(St. Martin's,*

1987), is the definitive study of the epidemic's spread in the early 1980s.

1951–1994 •

American •

journalist

and writer

Born on 8 August 1951, in Davenport, Iowa, Randy Martin Shilts grew up in the Chicago suburb of Aurora, Illinois. His father, Bud Shilts, was a salesman, and his mother, Norma Shilts, was a homemaker. Both were Methodists and political conservatives.

At age twenty, Shilts announced that he was gay to his family and friends while attending Portland Community College in Portland, Oregon. He completed his education at the University of Oregon in Eugene, majoring first in English and later in journalism. He was the managing editor of the campus newspaper and became the head of the Eugene Gay People's Alliance.

After receiving his B.S. degree in 1975, Shilts became the Northwest correspondent for the *Advocate,* a gay publication. He moved to San Francisco shortly thereafter, where, as a staff writer with good research and writing skills, he reinvigorated the *Advocate*'s news coverage. In retrospect, among his most important articles were several detailing the alarming spread of sexually transmitted diseases among gay men amidst the indifference of government, medical, and gay leaders. He resigned from the *Advocate* in 1978, partly because of editorial differences with its owner and publisher, David Goodstein.

Shilts, meanwhile, contributed freelance reports about San Francisco's burgeoning homosexual community and about local politics to the city's public television station, KQED, from 1977 to 1980, and to Oakland's independent station, KTVU, from 1979 to 1980. The income from these reports enabled him to commence an extensive career as a freelance writer on gay and lesbian issues for several major American newspapers and magazines. His first book, *The Mayor of Castro Street: The Life and Times of Harvey Milk* (St. Martin's, 1982), intertwined the story of the slain gay leader with the emergence of gay political power in San Francisco in the 1970s. Shilts received national attention as his book was critically acclaimed by both mainstream and gay publications.

The *San Francisco Chronicle* hired Shilts as a staff reporter in 1981, making him the first openly gay journalist to write for a major daily newspaper. Initially assigned to cover the gay community, his articles about an alarming new disease striking gay men were among the first reports on AIDS in the mainstream press. He eventually exposed the indifference of the Reagan administration and the slow response of the medical and scientific communities to AIDS. But he also faulted anonymous sex commonly practiced in gay bathhouses for the spread of the disease, and criticized some gay leaders for viewing AIDS primarily as a public relations problem rather than as a medical crisis. Shilts was detested by many homosexuals for his early advocacy of lifestyle changes and safe sex practices, which many gay men initially saw as infringements on their hard-won cultural and sexual freedoms.

Based on Shilts' years of investigative journalism, *And the Band Played On: Politics, People, and the AIDS Epidemic,* documented the spread of AIDS from its possible origins to its global impact. Widely praised in the mainstream press, it was a finalist for the National Book Award in the nonfiction category, and won its author the American Society of Journalists and Authors Outstanding Author Award of 1988. It was adapted for a movie that was initially aired by the Home Box Office cable network in September 1993. Despite its commercial success, Shilts remained disappointed that his book failed to reverse government policies and personal lifestyle changes that would curtail the epidemic. In 1986 he himself had tested positive for antibodies to HIV, the virus that causes AIDS.

Shilts' final book, *Conduct Unbecoming: Lesbians and Gays in the U.S. Military, Vietnam to the Persian Gulf* (St. Martin's, 1993), was an exhaustive history of an explosive public issue at the time of its publication. It exposed the military's homophobia and hypocrisy, documenting its selective enforcement of its ban on homosexuals in its ranks. The book was favorably reviewed by the mainstream and gay press and was on the *New York Times* bestsellers list for six weeks. However, its author was lambasted by some lesbians and gays for his refusal to identify—to "out"—his sources in the military who were closeted homosexuals.

Researching and writing *Conduct Unbecoming,* coupled with his extensive writing for the *Chronicle* and other publications, hastened the decline in Shilts' health. He developed full-blown AIDS in 1992. On Memorial Day 1993, he participated in a commitment ceremony with his lover, Barry Barbieri, a film student.

Randy Shilts died from AIDS on 17 February 1994, at his ten-acre ranch along the Russian River in Guerneville, California. His life and work were commemorated in numerous articles in both the mainstream and gay press. His papers are held by the James C. Hormel Gay and Lesbian Center at the San Francisco Public Library.

**Profile by
Joseph M. Eagan**

BARBARA SMITH

F or over three decades, African American writer and activist

1946– •

Barbara Smith has been at the forefront of advocacy for African

American, women's, and lesbian and gay rights issues. She has edited

African American •

major groundbreaking anthologies by black women, co-authored

writer and

several books, and was a founding publisher of Kitchen Table/Women

activist

of Color Press. She has written essays, poems, and short stories under-

scoring the underrepresentation of black women writers in particular;

the lack of recognition of the contributions of black lesbian educators,

writers, and activists; and the invisibility of black women in general. In

a short story called "Home," her contribution to the 1983 black feminist

anthology Home Girls, *which she also edited, Smith wrote: "Loving* doesn't terrify me. Loss does. The women I need are literally disappearing from the face of the earth. It has already happened."

Barbara Smith was born in the poor, urban central area of Cleveland, Ohio, on 16 November 1946. "There is nothing more important to me than home," she says in the introduction to *Home Girls*. When you examine the strong, hardworking female characters that were her role models in childhood, you begin to see why. Smith and her twin sister were raised by their mother, grandmother, and a great-aunt who had been the first in the family to move north from rural Georgia in the late 1920s. The sisters shared a bedroom with their grandmother; another larger room was for the aunt, though they seldom saw her because she was a live-in cook for a white family across town. Their mother slept on a daybed downstairs because she worked full-time and would be up and out of the house every morning before anyone else. When the girls were six, they moved in with another great-aunt whose husband eventually left because, according to Smith in *Girls,* "she was too wrapped up in her family." "I was surrounded by women who appeared able to do everything," Smith noted. "They cleaned, cooked, washed, ironed, sewed, made soap, canned, held jobs, took care of business downtown, sang, read, and taught us to do the same." Smith's mother died when she was just nine years old.

At the same time, though (and with no small irony), Smith says she learned as much about black feminism from these women's failings as from their strengths. As she daily witnessed the humiliation they suffered because they had been born black and female in a white man's world, she "inherited fear and shame from them as well as hope." "These conflicting feelings about being a black woman still do battle inside me," she says in *Girls*. "This conflict makes my commitment real."

Self-Image •

Problems

Smith's mother had been the only one of three children to finish college. Though she fought for certification as a teacher within Cleveland's public school system, she preferred to work as a nurse's aide and a cashier at a local supermarket rather than teach in the demoralizing ghetto schools, which were the only ones open to her. "I [remember] telling a white woman therapist about my mother being a college graduate and the kinds of jobs she had had," Smith told Patricia Bell-Scott in *Ms.* magazine in 1995, "and having this therapist tell me that my mother obviously had a self-image problem. The diagnosis was that I had a similar problem—no self-confidence." What this therapist and other well-meaning whites do not comprehend, Smith asserts, is that there were and still are many African Americans with college degrees forced to take jobs well below their qualifications and desires, and that low self-esteem is not the cause but the result of their situation.

Smith says she started to notice the unfairness around her at about the age of eight. She had an endless list of questions, including: Why were there no black people on television? Why were all the teachers white? Why was there anxiety in the air that she and her sister could feel whenever they ventured out of their neighborhood? Why did department store clerks ignore her? "I'm kind of a natural activist," she explained to Bell-Scott. In the early 1960s, while still in high school, Smith attended her first demonstration, a protest against the death of a white minister who had laid down in front of construction equipment ready to break ground for a new segregated elementary school. Whether the workers had rolled over him by design or by accident was never made clear. It is this devotion to activism above all else that kept Smith from pursuing an academic career, though she loves teaching, and has even robbed her of precious time to write. She told Bell-Scott, "Black feminism has always meant to me that I have a responsibility to help build and provide resources for other women of color; and a commitment to struggle requires certain sacrifices."

Smith received her bachelor's degree from Mount Holyoke College in South Hadley, Massachusetts in 1969 and her master's from the University of Pittsburgh in 1971. She began teaching at the University of Massachusetts in 1976. In 1977 she presented her groundbreaking and controversial essay "Toward a Black Feminist Criticism" at a National Conference of Afro-American Writers. It shocked many of the attendees because it publicly addressed for the first time the subject of black lesbianism as an integral part of the black literary tradition. In her essay, Smith explores lesbian relationships in classic black novels. She implies that the silence surrounding writings by black women—and black lesbians in particular—had made impossible any recognition of their roles in literary scholarship. And finally, she underscores the importance of applying feminist analysis to writings by black lesbians overall. As writer Ann Louise Keating observes in *The Gay and Lesbian Literary Heritage,* Smith "maintains that because issues concerning lesbianism and lesbian oppression emerged during the late 1960s and early 1970s from within the developing women's movement, writers' views of lesbianism are directly related to feminist issues."

Over the next decade, Smith expanded her examination to include discussions of the racial, sexual, and/or religious stereotyping and prejudice all women of color experience. In 1979, she edited with Lorraine Bell a black women's issue of *Conditions: Five,* which added issues of reproductive rights, sterilization, and violence against women to the mix. In 1981, she contributed to *This Bridge Called My Back: Writings by Radical Women of Color,* and was a founder along with writers Audre Lorde and Cherrie Moraga of Kitchen Table/Women of

Color Press, established to publish this work and others on women's issues that mainstream publishers found too radical. *Bridge* set precedent in that it examined prejudice within the women's movement itself. The book went on to win the American Book Award from the Before Columbus Foundation and still enjoys widespread popularity among both women of color and in women's studies courses across the country.

Eventually, as she told *Ms.*, Smith "came to identify as a black feminist, a lesbian, and a socialist." She was a co-founder of the Combahee River Collective (1974–1981), which sponsored a series of retreats that brought together black women writers who believed in the interconnectedness of strategies for social change. "We understood that dealing with sexual politics didn't mean that you weren't a race woman," she told *Ms.*, "and that speaking out about homophobia didn't mean that you didn't want to end poverty."

In 1982, Smith also co-edited an innovative compilation of black women's studies brilliantly titled *All the Women Are White, All the Blacks Are Men, but Some of Us Are Brave*. There Smith, along with sister editors Gloria T. Hull and Patricia Bell-Scott, presented groundbreaking essays by writers such as Alice Walker and Michele Russell that dispel myths about black women, confront racism, and represent a search for solidarity among all feminists. One of the long-suppressed issues that Smith raises is that of women's liberation being the sole purview of white female intellectuals. "White women (should not) work on racism to do a favor for someone else. . . . Racism distorts and lessens (everyone's) lives," she says in her essay on "Racism and Women's Studies." She carries this essential connection further by stressing how the political theory of feminism needs to be, by definition, a struggle by all women to free all women, lesbians included.

In 1982 Smith received the Outstanding Woman of Color Award for her writing, education, and activism, and in 1983 she added to this the Women Educators Curriculum Award. It was also in 1983 that Smith saw the publication of her celebratory collection of writings by thirty-four black lesbians living in the United States and the Caribbean, *Home Girls: A Black Feminist Anthology*. In that book, Smith called for a "return to the fold" for these women, a recognition of their contributions not only by people of their own race, but by the white-dominated, "heterosexually enforced" world of feminism. *Home Girls* is still immensely popular, both as a women's studies text and as an educational sourcebook for the wider culture. Smith's destruction of myths about black women and the substitution of clear knowledge are at the core of her ideology here. Black women are not already liberated, Smith contends, just because

Home Girls and •

Home Truths

"we have had to take on responsibilities that our oppression gives us no choice but to handle."

Smith continues to be a very visible presence in the fight for what Keating calls "a positive, self-affirming history and tradition (of the roles) black lesbian artists have played in shaping African-American literature and criticism." The proliferation of writings by and about African American lesbians is in part a response to Smith's call for their recognition and respect. Today, African American lesbian writers are imbuing their work—"at the juncture of several divergent literary traditions," according to Keating—with even more celebratory self-expression and home-girl metaphors in an effort to overcome their historic grievances with self-love and respect. And yet, in the gay and lesbian community, Smith admits to still feeling like the "invisible sister." "At the twenty-fifth anniversary of Stonewall," she told Bell-Scott, "the underrepresentation of people of color was demoralizing. . . . Very few lesbians and gay men of color, including myself, are ever invited to the leadership summits called by white gay leaders. Being omitted from a meeting or invitation list might at first seem like a small thing, but the larger issue is about the disenfranchisement of women and men of color within the movement."

It's all part of the push to mainstream, and thus disempower, the gay and lesbian movement in the United States, according to Smith. This mentality is troubling for Smith because, as she says in *Ms.,* "I want a nonhierarchical, nonexploitive society in which profit is not the sole motivation for every single decision made by the government or individuals. . . . What am I, as a black woman, going to be doing at this table—carry a tray?. . . A place at the table? Not likely. It really doesn't work for me."

The fight for inclusion and against homophobia would be most righteously and effectively led by black women, according to Smith. And yet, too may black women's organizations fear the inevitability of being labeled and dismissed as lesbians. Or perhaps they are still subscribing to the pernicious myth that "people of color need to deal with the 'larger struggle'," as outlined by Smith in *Home Girls.*

Roadblocks like these, a well as encounters with black lesbian feminists who support her work but refuse to come out publicly, remind Smith of Audre Lorde's book *Sister Outsider,* as she told *Ms.* in 1995. "It's an oxymoron because a sister is obviously someone inside the family, close, a home girl. But the sister with the lesbian feminist politics . . . is also an outsider."

Now self-described as midway in life and career, she confesses to longtime friend Bell-Scott that she has a growing appreciation for simple acts of "self-care—like a daytime nap, eating on time, and sitting quietly after a bout of running around." Nevertheless, Barbara Smith is still leading the fight for empowerment—the battle to give us back something of ourselves. Currently, and true to form, she is completing another revolutionary, first-of-its-kind endeavor, a book about the history of African American lesbians and gays.

"Almost all of my writing has been about empowerment and about trying to say to people of color, to women, to lesbians and gay men that you are really worth something, you are important, you have a history to be proud of. There is no reason to be ashamed." And there is every reason to be proud of Barbara Smith as she continues to advocate for us all.

**Profile by
Jerome Szymczak**

STEPHEN SONDHEIM

A rare individual who can brilliantly write both words and music,

Stephen Sondheim has become a giant of American musical theater,

celebrated for his creativity, artistic daring, and integrity. His complex,

unconventional musicals are not always popular with critics or audi-

ences, but are often revived with greater success. While he has never

married, the intensely private Sondheim does little to advertise his sexual

preferences.

1930– •

American •

composer

Stephen Joshua Sondheim was born on 22 March 1930, the son of dress manufacturer Herbert Sondheim and former dress designer Helen Fox Sondheim. When he was ten, his parents divorced, and he was soon escaping from his difficult mother by spending time at the home of his friend Jimmy Hammerstein. There, he formed a bond with Jimmy's father, famed lyricist Oscar Hammerstein II, who tutored Sondheim in the art of writing musicals.

After graduating from Williams College in 1950, Sondheim received a fellowship that allowed him to study music. In 1953, he moved to Hollywood when hired by Jess Oppenheimer to write scripts for the television series *Topper*. Despite this and other television work and later collaboration with Anthony Perkins on the screenplay of *The Last of Sheila* (1973), Sondheim never writes librettos for his musicals, citing dissatisfaction with his prose.

Returning to New York, he wrote songs for a projected Broadway musical, *Saturday Night*, that was never produced, then wrote lyrics for Leonard Bernstein's *West Side Story* (1957) and Jule Styne's *Gypsy* (1959), two classic musicals whose enduring success gave him lifelong financial security.

However, wishing to write both lyrics and music, Sondheim developed a musical based on the plays of Plautus, *A Funny Thing Happened on the Way to the Forum* (1962), still his most accessible work. After the ill-conceived *Anyone Can Whistle* (1964), Sondheim unwisely agreed to write lyrics for Richard Rodgers's *Do I Hear a Waltz?* (1965). Their partnership proved tempestuous, perhaps because Rodgers "hate[d] homosexuality," as Oppenheimer reports (quoted in Craig Zadan's *Sondheim & Co.*). After an eccentric television musical, *Evening Primrose* (1967), Sondheim hit his stride with three musicals directed by Harold Prince, which each earned Sondheim Tony Awards. In *Company* (1970), married couples ponder their friend Bobby, an attractive, thirty-five-year-old man who refuses to marry; some believe Bobby is, or must be read as, homosexual, though the play is not explicit. Guy Livingston archly commented in *Variety* that the musical was "for ladies' matinees, homos and misogynists." *Follies* (1971), surrealistically depicting the reunion of two former show girls and their husbands, was triumphantly revived as an album and television special in 1985. *A Little Night Music* (1973), based on Ingmar Bergman's film *Smiles of a Summer Night,* was lighter in tone and featured Sondheim's first hit song, "Send in the Clowns," which won a Grammy Award as song of the year.

Still working with Prince, though growing more adventurous, Sondheim next offered *Pacific Overtures* (1976), a Kabuki-style recounting of Japan's westernization, while a revue created without his participation, *Side by Side by Sondheim* (1976), garnered new respect for his music. *Sweeney Todd, the Demon Barber of Fleet Street* (1979) outrageously chronicled the exploits of a murderer and the woman who bakes the corpses into meat pies. Perhaps the best Sondheim/Prince musical, it was unfortunately followed by a monumental failure, *Merrily We Roll Along* (1981), their last collaboration. Sondheim then received a Pulitzer Prize for what some call his masterpiece, *Sunday in the Park with George* (1984), which depicted George Seurat's painting of his famous work and the artistic struggles of his descendant. Next came *Into the Woods* (1987), a blend of traditional fairy tales with dark overtones, and *Assassins* (1991), which offended many because of its subject matter, people who tried to murder American presidents. Reactions to *Passion* (1994), based on the film *Passione d'Amore,* were typical: critical raves and brickbats, several Tony Awards, and lackluster ticket sales.

While the theater is Sondheim's focus, he sometimes works for films, scoring *Stravinsky* (1974) and *Reds* (1981), and writing songs for *The Seven Per Cent Solution* (1976) and *Dick Tracy* (1990); a song from the latter film, "Sooner or Later," won an Oscar for best original song. Other honors include membership in the American Academy and Institute of Arts and Letters—which he called "One of the few honors that I've been given that means anything to me . . . because it's awarded by peers"—and a 1990 position as visiting professor of drama and musical theatre at Oxford University.

An unusual public controversy occurred in 1992, amidst congressional efforts to reign in the National Endowment for the Arts because of grants to Robert Mapplethorpe and others: Sondheim angrily rejected the NEA's National Medal of Arts Award because the endowment had been, he announced, "transformed into a conduit, and a symbol, of censorship and repression rather than encouragement and support." Perhaps it was not a popular gesture, but this idiosyncratic visionary has never been interested in popularity.

Profile by
Gary Westfahl

KITTY TSUI

Kitty Tsui makes a dynamic career from her identity as a Chinese

American lesbian. Her life and work thus far provide an essential

corrective to minority politics, both by defining ethnic difference within

the lesbian community and by modeling sexual difference within the

Asian American community. Kitty Tsui is an award-winning chroni-

cler of the rich complexities of balancing more than one identity.

1952– •

Asian American •

writer

Tsui was born in Hong Kong in 1952, and spent her childhood in California, receiving a B.A. in creative writing from San Francisco State University. She currently lives in the Midwest with her beloved Hungarian Vizsla dog, Meggie Too.

Tsui's poetry and prose have been published in over thirty-five anthologies, including *Asian American Sexualities: Dimensions of the Gay and Lesbian Experience* (1995), *Lesbian Erotics* (1995), *Chloe Plus Olivia* (1994), and *Making Waves: Asian Women United of California* (1989). She is the recipient of the CLAGS 1995 Ken Dawson Award for research in gay and lesbian history and was listed in the 1990 Lambda Book Report as one of the fifty most influential people in gay and lesbian literature. She has been featured in three films, *Women of Gold* (1990), *Framing Lesbian Fashion* (1992), and *Cut Sleeve* (1992).

Although known primarily for her writing and activism within the Asian Pacific Lesbian Movement, Tsui is also a competitive body-builder, winning a bronze medal at the Gay Games in San Francisco in 1986 and a gold medal in Vancouver in 1990.

Tsui is the author of three books to date: *The Words of a Woman Who Breathes Fire* (1983), a book of poems, prose, and dramatic pieces; *Breathless* (1995), erotica for lesbians; and a historical novel, *Bak Sze, White Snake* (not yet published). These books point to her versatility in terms of genre, while she remains committed to a politics of inclusion and tolerance in the lesbian community.

The Words of a Woman Who Breathes Fire, written in the 1980s tradition of identity politics, focuses on ethnic and class differences among urban lesbians. Tsui struggles for self-definition in these poems, as a Chinese American woman who loves women and as a writer who refuses to be encumbered by literary stylistic traditions. In the first poem, "It's in the Name," the speaker condemns the dominant culture's confusion of Asian women with each other—"it happens all the time./ orientals so hard to tell apart." The book's conclusion, however, is more upbeat, with "A Celebration of Who I Am," and an inter-generational dramatic monologue of two women's voices, "Poa Poa Is Living Breathing Light."

Because her female and Chinese heritage is so central to Tsui, she includes several poems honoring her grandmother, whose struggles as an immigrant actress and Cantonese opera singer mirror the poet's own creative efforts. *The Words of a Woman* is dedicated to Tsui's grandmother, Kwan Ying Lin, her "first and closest connection." The poem "Chinatown Talking Story" describes her grandmother's American career: "the gold mountain men said/ when kwan ying lin/ went on stage/ even the electric fans stopped." Kwan, too, loved women and left her husband to live with another actress.

Other poems describe her family's ignorance concerning her love for women; for example, in "A Chinese Banquet," Tsui is unable to invite her lover home for a traditional meal because the category "same-sex lover" does not exist for her parents. However, Tsui insists that Chinese women come with strength: "born into the/ skin of yellow women/ we are born/ into the armor of warriors."

A large part of Tsui's fight is for lesbian autonomy. Her second book, *Breathless,* continues the theme of inclusivity. This collection of erotica covers many varieties of lesbian sexual desire, from charged glances to sex toys to sado-masochism to cutting. While some stories involve violence and are not for the faint-hearted reader, many are also simply funny as well as sexy. One story in particular, "the foodie club," contains sensual descriptions of exotic (and erotic) edibles, leaving the reader to imagine whatever sexual activities go with them. Another story, "rain," describes two old women, long-time partners, who rediscover their sexual selves. *Breathless* combines questions of love, commitment, loyalty, and loneliness with raw bodies doing amazing and, depending on your perspective, horrifying or titillating things.

As Tsui writes in an early poem, "este poema is for the crazywoman/ who lets me wear her favorite blue shirt/ and takes my tongue into her mouth/ and massages it." For Kitty Tsui, we are all potential crazy women, if we can learn to celebrate each other and ourselves as she does.

**Profile by
Catherine A. Wiley**

URVASHI VAID

*U*rvashi Vaid is well known in the United States as a veteran activist

in gay, lesbian, and feminist movements. Her long commitment to civil

rights began in her college days, where in her early twenties she was

already vocal in conferences and protests, as well as being involved in

volunteer work and organizing for feminist and civil rights issues. More

recently, from 1986–92, she was the public information director and

executive director of the National Gay and Lesbian Task Force (NGLTF).

In 1994, Time *magazine listed her in "The Fifty"—their directory of*

America's most promising leaders, age forty and under, who had the

ambition, vision, and community spirit to lead America into the new

millennium.

1958– •

Asian American •

activist

Although Urvashi Vaid was born in India in 1958, she immigrated to the United States in 1966 along with her family. Vaid was part of the second wave of Indian migration to the United States and was raised with a middle-class ethos in Potsdam, New York. Her parents were literary writers and teachers—her mother was a teacher and poet, and her father a novelist who taught literature and writing at the State University at Potsdam. In high school, although Vaid had not heard about gay liberation, she considered herself "pro-civil rights, anti-war, and a women's libber," she writes in her book *Virtual Equality.* Her first passion was for rock and roll music, but simultaneously, she began to acquire the tools for activism. Vaid's involvement in activism grew substantially throughout the coming years. In college, at Vassar, she was involved with anti-apartheid groups, was part of protests against financial cutbacks to education, and also participated in women's music concert groups. In 1979, at the age of twenty-one, Vaid had joined the women's movement in Boston. At the same time, the First National March on Washington for Gay and Lesbian Rights took place. Moreover, she became an active participant in the civil disobedience protests at the Seabrook nuclear plant in New Hampshire as part of the LUNA Group (Lesbians United in Non-Nuclear Action).

In 1980, while attending Law school at North Eastern University, Vaid proclaimed her homosexuality to her parents through her sister. These years were a crucially formative period for her political awareness of gay and lesbian visibility while she volunteered for the non-profit newspaper *Gay Community News*. In 1983, during the Reaganite era, Vaid worked as an attorney for the National Prison project of the American Civil Liberties Union (ACLU) and continued the work she began in 1977 with Roadwork. Her involvement with the ACLU heightened the awareness of the treatment of prisoners with HIV and AIDS. It was during this time that Vaid met Jeff Levi of the National Gay Task Force, who would influence her to consider gay rights activism as something she could focus on full time. By 1987, when the Second National March for Gay Rights took place in Washington, she left the ACLU and became active in media organizing, strategizing, and policy making, and was employed as the public information director of NGLTF. In a movement largely dominated by gay white men, Vaid became the first woman of color to direct the NGLTF. At the helm of the NGLTF, Vaid hoped to broaden the movement's base by asking for self-reflections that could include class, gender, and race issues. She left the NGLTF both for personal and political reasons after working there for six and a half years. In 1995, after Vaid's sabbatical time to "think and feel" in her home in Provincetown, her book *Virtual Equality: The Mainstreaming of Gay & Lesbian Liberation* was published. The book has had mostly positive reviews, and Vaid has spoken of enthusiastic crowds gathered in gay, lesbian, and independent bookstores during her six-week book tour in early 1996. In her book, she explains her decision to leave NGLTF as grounded in a need to spend more quality time with her lover and soulmate, Kate Clinton, as well as to re-look at and re-think where her visions for the gay and lesbian movement would best be realized.

Virtual Equality thus emerges as a consideration of the gay and lesbian movement as it approaches its sixth decade of political activism. Vaid finds that the community's goals of "cultural visibility, political representation and civil rights" have yet to be fully realized. She examines the disappointment gays and lesbians feel when "unprecedented cultural possibility" is followed by the "persistence of prejudice and stigmatization" that they have challenged for decades. To her this is much like a state of "virtual equality," since although there is a perception that gays and lesbians have achieved parity, this parity rests on a simulated reality. The appearance of acceptance by straight America is ironic in that it possesses the promised trappings of equality and progress and actually belies what it cannot move beyond—its virtual foundations. Vaid explores this prevailing state of the gay/lesbian movement by looking candidly at its strengths and problems, its involvement in electoral politics, and its responses to mainstreaming. She asks probing questions of the movement's guiding principles and looks at possibilities and crisis areas for future leadership.

As a lesbian and leader of color, Vaid herself experienced a large share of criticism and attack from within the gay and lesbian movement for some of her views and actions; for example, her decision to protest the American involvement in the Gulf War, and her support for direct action strategies in Washington. One of the chapters in her book focuses on leadership conundrums, detailing ambivalences and divisions regarding what is expected of leaders in the movement. All the chapters of this book show Vaid's presence, experience, hopes, and disappointments as an activist, organizer, policy maker, and strategist for gay and lesbian socio-cultural visibility. She acknowledges some of her own limitations, while also critiquing some of the working ideologies inside the movement. Vaid's tone is action-oriented: there is a pragmatic immediacy conveyed through lists, outlines, overviews, names of people and organizations, definitions, explanations, things done, and those needing to be done. She urges those working in the movement to blend out, instead of mostly blending in, and to reach out on the micro and macro levels, mobilizing families and friends as much as national campaigns. Her suggestions include creating discussion groups, focusing commitments, mentoring, pooling resources, reading, exploring and discovering groups in local areas, and being politically aware of multiple levels of differences and commonalities. Vaid's vision of the movement is one that would be multi-issue oriented—allowing for allies and coalitions by including race, class, and gender issues alongside issues of sexual orientation. Echoes of her vision resonate through her speech for the March on Washington in 1993, and in her "After Identity" speech (May 1993) where she called for the end of bigotry, racism, domestic violence, sexism, and hate, along with the call to end homophobia. However, her book is sometimes contradictory or unclear about the issues of commonalities and differences, and how to resolve the problems of sorting through multilevel issues when identity politics get fissured along these lines.

Vaid's current project includes starting a much-needed think tank named the Center for Progressive Renewal (CPR), whose goal is to plan strategies and offer a voice for gay and lesbian rights.

Profile by
Marian Gracias

GORE VIDAL

F *or fifty years, Gore Vidal has been one of America's most prolific*

and provocative writers. Best known as a novelist, he is also a distin-

guished essayist and has written numerous plays, screenplays, television

scripts, stories, and poems. An acknowledged "homosexualist"—the

term he coined and prefers—Vidal has sometimes created gay charac-

ters and addressed gay issues, but sexual orientation is only one of his

many concerns.

1925– •

American writer •

Eugene Luther Gore Vidal was born on 3 October 1925, at West Point, New York, the son of Eugene Vidal, West Point professor and later director of the Bureau of Air Commerce, and Nina Gore Vidal. During an unsettled childhood, he grew close to his grandfather, Oklahoma Senator Thomas Gore, who first inspired his lifelong interest in politics. When Vidal was nine his parents divorced, and Nina married Hugh Auchincloss; when they also divorced, Auchincloss married Jacqueline Kennedy's mother, making the Kennedys one of the many aristocratic families that Vidal was related to or acquainted with. Despite his

background, Vidal has regularly rallied against the American elite class and its pernicious control over American society.

At one prep school, Vidal had an intimate relationship with Jimmy Trimble. Trimble was later killed in World War II, and subsequently eulogized in Vidal's memoir *Palimpsest* (1995) as the major love of his life. After graduating from Exeter, Vidal served in the United States Army during World War II in the Aleutian Islands, an experience that provided material for his first novel, *Williwaw* (1946), published when he was nineteen. Impressively self-educated, Vidal never bothered to attend college and, after briefly working in New York as an editor for E. P. Dutton in 1946, devoted himself to writing novels. Although *In a Yellow Wood* (1947) briefly touched upon homosexuality, it wasn't until his remarkable third novel, *The City and the Pillar* (1948), that the topic came to the forefront. Vidal broke new ground in making his protagonist, a young gay man, a thoroughly "normal" person despite his sexual orientation; its lurid conclusion, the hero's murder of a former male lover who had spurned him, was changed in a 1965 revision to a forcible rape.

After publishing *The City and the Pillar,* Vidal believes he was blacklisted by the critical establishment and, for whatever reason, his next novels—*The Season of Comfort* (1949), *A Search for the King: A Twelfth-Century Legend* (1950), *Dark Green, Bright Red* (1950), *The Judgment of Paris* (1952), and *Messiah* (1954)—were not greatly successful. Vidal lived in Guatemala from 1947 to 1949, then went to Europe, where he associated with Tennessee Williams and other celebrities. Since 1950, he has lived with Howard Austen, but Vidal says the relationship is not sexual, as Vidal preferred sex with anonymous young strangers.

Having purchased a home in New York, and needing more money, Vidal wrote three detective novels as Edgar Box—*Death in the Fifth Position* (1952), *Death before Bedtime* (1953), and *Death Likes It Hot* (1954)—and began writing for television, moving to Hollywood in 1955. In addition to scripts for anthology series such as *Studio One, Suspense,* and *Omnibus,* Vidal also wrote screenplays—*The Catered Affair* (1956), *I Accuse!* (1958), and *Suddenly, Last Summer* (1959)—and while uncredited, worked extensively on *Ben-Hur* (1959), suggesting a gay subtext to director William Wyler. In 1957, he adapted his television script, the science-fiction satire *Visit to a Small Planet* (1955), as a successful Broadway play (but had nothing to do with the 1960 film), and wrote a few other plays, notably *The Best Man* (1960), which he adapted as a 1964 film.

While in Hollywood Vidal became a celebrity of sorts, serving as on-screen narrator of his 1960 teleplay, *The Indestructible Mr. Gore,* about his grandfather, then making guest appearances on numerous television programs and hosting a syndicated panel discussion show, *The Hot Seat,* in 1964. He was noted for heated televised exchanges with William F. Buckley when they were commentators during the 1968 political conventions, and Norman Mailer on *The Dick Cavett Show.* Beginning in 1962, Vidal spent most of his time in Rome, becoming a permanent resident of Italy in 1971 while maintaining a home in California, so he was less visible on the Hollywood scene; still, he appeared on the soap-opera spoof *Mary Hartman, Mary Hartman* in 1976 and, more recently, in the films *Bob Roberts* (1992) and *With Honors* (1994). He also worked on a television documentary about Venice that generated his book *Vidal in Venice* (1985).

Vidal's other moments in the public eye have been as a politician. He first ran an unsuccessful campaign as the Democratic candidate for a New York seat in the United States House of Representatives in 1960. From 1961 to 1963 he served, at President John F. Kennedy's request, on the President's Advisory Committee on the Arts, though he did no work for it; in the early 1970s he was involved with two left-wing political parties, the New Party and the People's Party; and in 1982 he competed in the Democratic primary for a California seat in the United States Senate.

Despite continuing work for the theater—*Weekend* (1968), *An Evening with Richard Nixon* (1972)—and films—*The Last of the Mobile Hot-Shots* (1971), *Caligula* (1980), *Dress Gray* (1986), *The Palermo Connection* (1991)—and despite his flirtations with politics, Vidal has worked primarily on novels since 1964. These include *Two Sisters: A Memoir in the Form of a Novel* (1970), his most autobiographical fiction, and two massive reconsiderations of classical Greece and Rome, *Julian* (1964) and *Creation* (1981). *Washington, D.C.* (1967) launched a series of interrelated novels chronicling American political history: they are, in order of internal chronology, *Burr* (1973), *Lincoln* (1984), *1876* (1976), *Empire* (1987), *Hollywood* (1990), and *Washington, D.C.* These meticulously researched, charming, and cynical novels have proven to be Vidal's most popular and critically acclaimed works. Finally, there are what Vidal calls his "inventions"—wildly imaginative and satirical novels. The first, and most notorious, was *Myra Breckinridge* (1968), a novel that some condemned as pornography, telling the adventures of a gay man who became a woman. Its sequel, *Myron* (1974), transported the protagonist, now male again, to Hollywood in the 1940s. *Kalki* (1978) described the end of the world brought on by a messiah figure, while *Live from Golgotha: The Gospel According to Gore Vidal* (1992) depicted time-traveling television crews and reporters descending upon Jesus Christ's crucifixion. *Duluth* (1982), Vidal's favorite novel and perhaps his best "invention," assails modern American culture as encapsulated in a surrealistic Duluth, which simultaneously borders on Canada and Mexico.

No discussion of Vidal can neglect his innumerable, often brilliant essays, collected in *Rocking the Boat* (1962), *Sex, Death and Money* (1968), *Reflections upon a Sinking Ship* (1969), *Homage to Daniel Shays: Collected Essays, 1952–1972* (1972), *Matters of Fact and Fiction* (1977), *The Second American Revolution and Other Essays* (1982, winner of the National Book Critics Circle Award for criticism), *Armageddon? Essays, 1983–1987* (1987), *At Home: Essays 1982–1988* (1989), *A View from the Diner's Club: Essays, 1987–1991* (1991), *Screening History* (1992), *The Decline and Fall of the American Empire* (1992), and *United States: Essays 1952–1992* (1992, winner of the National Book Award for nonfiction).

In "Writing Plays for Television," published in *Homage to Daniel Shays,* Vidal writes, "I am at heart a propagandist, a tremendous hater, a tiresome nag, complacently positive that there is no human problem which could not be solved if people would simply do as I advise." The statement is sometimes taken as Vidal's credo. But a subsequent reference to "this sort of intensity, no matter how idiotic" also reveals his ironic, sometimes self-deprecating, wit. Vidal complains that he lives in an era that ignores its writers, but his enormous energy, passion, and creativity have made him a difficult writer to ignore.

**Profile by
Gary Westfahl**

JOHN WATERS

John Waters has been dubbed the King of Puke, the Pope of Trash,

the Vizier of Vulgarity, the Titan of Terrible Taste, and the Lord High

Poohbah of Repulsion, according to Rolling Stone *magazine. His films,*

which in fact exhibit varying degrees of bad taste and have recently

become more mainstream, have earned him a huge cult following as

well as a measure of sometimes grudging critical respect. With imagina-

tion and wit, Waters subverts traditional societal norms, and yet, as he

himself notes, his films are basically moral stories in which "the bitter

people are punished and those who are happy with themselves win."

1946– •

American •

filmmaker

Born and raised in Baltimore, Waters attended Catholic schools, and it was there that he met his muse, Divine, at a time when the future 300-pound transvestite was just Glenn Milstead, another misfit hanging out. Waters produced his first film in 1963 at the age of seventeen. It was entitled *Hag in a Black Leather Jacket* and cost $30. After being thrown out of the New York University film school for smoking pot, Waters returned to Baltimore to form Dreamland Productions, which produced *Roman Candles* (1966), *Eat Your Makeup* (Divine as Jackie Kennedy, 1968), *Mondo Trasho* (Divine has a divine revelation and is committed, 1969), and *Multiple Maniacs* (Divine as a murdering carnival owner, 1970). Early Waters films were done in laundromats ("because the lighting was good") and in alleys ("so we could run away"). During the filming of *Mondo Trasho,* Waters and four of his actors were arrested for conspiracy to commit indecent exposure.

In 1972, Waters produced his most notorious film, and the one that made him an underground hero, *Pink Flamingos* (Divine competing for title of "Filthiest Person Alive"). Originally screened at the University of Baltimore, the film later played in a Boston pornography theater and at midnight showings in small theaters in New York City. With its bizarre cast of characters and shocking final scene, in which Divine eats dog droppings, *Pink Flamingos* became one of the most popular and profitable underground films of the 1970s, although a Florida Grand Jury declared that it was too depraved to be shown in their state. It was later selected as part of the Museum of Modern Art's bicentennial program "American Film Comedy."

Next on the film roster came *Female Trouble* (Divine is executed by electric chair, 1975) and *Desperate Living* (a lesbian melodrama, the only early Waters film without Divine). *Polyester* (Divine and Tab Hunter as psychopathic lovers, 1981) started Waters' cautious foray into mainstream America, garnering a good review from the *New York Times* and other mainstream media.

After the publication of his autobiography, *Shock Value* (1981), Waters went on the lecture circuit, talking to audiences all over the world about his peculiar take on reality. A series of his magazine articles was published in book form in 1986, entitled *Crackpot: The Obsessions of John Waters*. During the early 1980s, Waters also taught a class in filmmaking at a maximum security prison in Baltimore. He later reported that he felt a great rapport with the inmates, being as much at odds with the system as they were but having been fortunate enough to find a healthier way of expressing his opposition.

All of Waters' film have been made with small budgets, and even the commercial releases *Hairspray* (Divine convincing as a 1960s mother and Ricki Lake as her rock-and-roll crazed daughter, 1988) and *Crybaby* (Johnny Depp as another mooning rocker, 1990), which was backed by Imagine Films, were modestly budgeted by Hollywood standards. It was *Hairspray* that finally won him a measure of mainstream approval, and when *Crybaby* was made die-hard Waters fans were sure he had sold out because the film was acceptable to those not in his cult. He became so famous his home city declared a John Waters Day (February 16, for the world premiere of *Hairspray*) and commentators began to claim that he had invented a new film genre—horror/comedy. Another measure of his acceptance is that his next film, *Serial Mom* (1994), about a murderous suburban housewife who maintains a flawless Donna Reed existence while practicing her unusual hobby, starred Kathleen Turner.

Filmmakers have a high failure rate, and many projects that seem promising never make it past the development stage. Yet Waters has had great success in getting his ideas to the public in finished form, particularly since, for most of his career, his offerings have been pretty far out on the edge. A sequel to *Pink Flamingos* died after Waters tried to raise funding for two years with no success and one of the leading actresses in the original died of cancer. But the script was published as part of a book entitled *Trash Trio* (Random House, 1988). A proposed film called *Glamourpuss* was turned down by seventeen studios before Waters gave up on it, but he may yet come back to it.

Waters lives alone in a large old house in his native Baltimore (where all his films have been set) with his extensive collections of strange memorabilia, and occasionally in his little Greenwich Village apartment.

Profile by
Debora Hill

EDMUND WHITE

*A*uthor Edmund White is a master stylist best known for his widely

1940– •

acclaimed novels, many of them semi-autobiographical treatments of

gay society that combine the best features of fiction and nonfiction.

American writer •

Proclaimed by Newsweek *to be "unquestionably the foremost American*

gay novelist," White belongs to that group of writers whose literary

reputation transcends such simplistic labels. As William Goldstein

explains in Publishers Weekly: *"To call Edmund White merely a gay*

writer is to oversimplify his work and his intentions. Although that two-

word label . . . aptly sums up White's status, the first word no doubt helps

obscure the fact that the second applies just as fittingly."

Still, White is best known for the themes of gay life in America as portrayed in novels such as *A Boy's Own Story* and *The Beautiful Room Is Empty*. And he told *Publishers Weekly* that he is "happy to be considered a gay writer. . . . Since gay people have very little political representation, we have no gay spokespeople. What happens is that there is an enormous pressure placed on gay novelists because they are virtually the *only* spokespeople."

Edmund White was born in Cincinnati on 13 January 1940, the son of a chemical engineer and a psychologist. His parents divorced when he was seven years old, and he and his sister spent many years alternating living with both parents—his father in Ohio and his mother in Chicago. He recalls being aware of his homosexuality early in life but told Leonard Schulman of *Time* magazine: "I didn't want to be gay. I wanted to be normal, to have a wife and kids." At the age of fourteen, he informed his father of his sexual orientation and asked him to pay for therapy. White spent several unhappy years in therapy before finding a gay psychologist, who helped him come to terms with his sexuality.

White excelled in his studies in Chinese at the University of Michigan, from which he graduated in 1962, having earned the prestigious Hopwood Award in 1961 and 1962 for fiction and drama. After graduation, he moved to New York's Greenwich Village and began working as an editor in the book division of Time, Inc., a position he held until 1970. But by the age of fifteen, he had already written his first novel (not surprisingly, about a boy coming to terms with his homosexuality), and it was to writing that White aspired. His play *The Blue Boy in Black* was produced Off-Broadway in 1963, and throughout the 1960s he concentrated on writing novels.

White's first published novel, *Forgetting Elena* (1973), relates the tale of an amnesia victim struggling to determine his own identity and the identities of those around him. It was applauded by critics for its satiric and insightful look at social interaction, as well as for its elegant prose. This impressive debut brought White acceptance in literary circles that included Susan Sontag and Richard Howard and gained him many notable admirers, including master novelists Vladimir Nabokov and Gore Vidal.

His next novel, *Nocturnes for the King of Naples* (1978), also won acclaim for its discerning treatment of human values and relationships. As John Yohalem wrote in the *New York Times Book Review,* "*Nocturnes* is a series of apostrophes to a nameless, evidently famous dead lover, a man who awakened the much younger, also nameless narrator . . . to the possibility of sexual friendship." J. D. McClatchy, in a *Shenandoah* review, calls White "a superior stylist of both erotic theology and plangent contrition. And his special gift is his ability to empty out our stale expectations from genres . . . and types . . . and to reimagine them in a wholly intriguing and convincing manner."

Caracole, White's 1985 novel, goes back to an earlier century and revives a more elaborate fictional form in its tale of two country lovers forcibly separated who turn to sexual escapades in a large city. The resulting story is a "a puzzling melange of comic opera and sleek sensuality," according to Christopher Lehmann-Haupt of the *New York Times.* And in the *New York Times Book Review,* David R. Slavitt describes the work as "a grand fantasy. . . . Shrewdness and self-awareness ooze from every intricate sentence, every linguistic arabesque and hothouse epigram."

Even though all of the novels received high praise from critics and good response from the public, it is the semi-autobiographical *A Boy's Own Story* that is often cited as White's best work. This first-person narrative of a gay boy's adolescence during the 1950s was described by a *Harper's* reviewer as "a poignant combination of [fiction and nonfiction] written with the flourish of a master stylist." Lehmann-Haupt of the *New York Times* found that "this is not exclusively a homosexual boy's story. It is any boy's story, to the marvelous degree that it evokes the inchoate longing of late childhood and adolescence." More than one reviewer has called *A Boy's Own Story* a "classic" work. Comparing White to James Baldwin, Herman Wouk, and Mary McCarthy, *Washington Post* writer Thomas M. Disch called the work "the strongest bid to date by a gay writer to do for his minority experience what the writers above did for theirs—offer it as a representative, all-American instance."

White followed this success with a sequel, *The Beautiful Room Is Empty,* which, although generally well received, did not quite reach the level of acclaim that was awarded *A Boy's Own Story.* One explanation for this might be the somewhat less sympathetic narrator than that of the earlier novel. Here, the narrator alternately revels in his homosexuality and rejects himself for it. Psychoanalysis and increasing surrender to sensual activity escalates the young man's battle for self acceptance. Though his sexuality troubles him, the excitement and audacity of his experiences with gay men in public restrooms seems a needed respite from the blandness of his suburban life. Sometimes the adolescent makes bold moves, as when he shouts, "Gay is good!" in a Greenwich Village demonstration. At other times, he acts out his self-loathing, as when he seduces his music teacher and then betrays him to the authorities. In an interview in Larry McCaffery's *Alive and Writing,* White commented: "To have my boy turn out so creepy seemed to be a way of alienating some gay commissars. . . . You can't show somebody in a deforming period, like the 1950s in America, and then show him as happy, healthy, the perfect role model."

White discussed those earlier, more repressive times of the 1950s and 1960s in a *Paris Review* interview. "I was writing gay books well before gay liberation and before there was a recognized gay reading public. One actually existed, although no publisher was aware of it. There was also a tremendous amount of self-repression among gay editors. A gay editor would turn down a gay book because if he admitted to liking it he would have to defend it at an editorial meeting, and that might lead other people to suspect *he* was gay." As attitudes about homosexuality began to change, the publishing world became more receptive to books by gay writers. Now, White admits to being thrilled by the recognition he has received. "I know I'll always be doing this," he told the *Publishers Weekly* interviewer, "and I know that I'll never make a living from my writing; but that's fine. It's enough to be published."

Concurrent with his career as an author, White has taught creative writing at several East Coast universities, including Johns Hopkins, Columbia, Yale, and Brown. His reviews and profiles appear frequently in *Vogue* and other magazines. He also writes travel articles and reports on contemporary trends in art and politics. Continuing his role as a social historian on the homosexual experience in America, White has written several intensely personal articles on the impact of AIDS on gay life and gay writers. In the early 1980s, he became one of the founders of the Gay Men's Health Crisis and says that he has lost some forty friends to AIDS. In 1985 White himself tested positive for HIV.

In "Residence on Earth: Living with AIDS in the '80s," an article he wrote for *Life* magazine, White observed: "Ten years ago gay men were perceived as playboys who put their selfish pleasures above family or community duties and responsibilities. Now they're seen as victims who have responded to a tragedy with dignity and courage. Above all, the lesbian and gay community is recognized as a *community,* one that is often angry and militant, generally well disciplined, always concerned."

TENNESSEE WILLIAMS

A lthough his writing career spanned more than four decades, it was

between the mid-1940s and the mid-1960s that American playwright

Tennessee Williams did the bulk of his writing. His dozens of plays, most

famous among them The Glass Menagerie, A Streetcar Named Desire,

Cat on a Hot Tin Roof, *and* The Night of the Iguana, *enjoyed lengthy*

runs in New York and earned Williams a number of prestigious awards.

His plays and subsequent movie versions starred some of the greatest

stage and screen stars of all time, including Elizabeth Taylor and

Marlon Brando. In addition, he wrote dozens of other plays, short

stories, works of short fiction, essays—including a tribute to D. H.

Lawrence—and his memoirs.

1911–1983 •

American •

playwright

383 •

On 26 March 1911, Thomas Lanier Williams was born in Columbus, Mississippi to Cornelius Coffin and Edwina Dakin Williams. He was later nicknamed "Tennessee"—a name that stuck and become the moniker by which the famous Williams was internationally known and immortalized. He was the second of three children.

Williams' older sister Rose suffered from a number of emotional disorders as a young woman, including incurable schizophrenia. She was eventually institutionalized. During her hospitalization, she was one of the first patients to undergo a prefrontal lobotomy in the United States. Williams was very fond of his sister and was greatly concerned for her welfare. Although her emotional decline was difficult for him to observe, he later wrote about her mental illness. Williams believed himself to be physically frail as a result of a near fatal bout with diphtheria when he was a child. He also believed that he had suffered irreparable heart damage.

Williams kept his own company as a young boy. He was often ridiculed by other children as well as his own father, who tormented the younger Williams with the nickname "Miss Nancy," for being less than masculine. Instead of making friends, Williams remained isolated.

The third Williams child, a boy named Dakin, was born after the family moved from Columbus to St. Louis, Missouri, when Thomas was eight. It wasn't long before the general malaise and unhappiness in young Thomas Lanier's life would lead him to writing as an escape. He entered his writing in contests and often won prizes. These early writings also gleaned him formerly lacking recognition among his peers, his parents, and his teachers.

At sixteen, Williams published his first work in the magazine *Smart Set*. The story, "Can a Good Wife Be a Good Sport," won third place in the *Smart Set* contest.

A Commitment •

In college at the University of Missouri, Williams discovered alcohol—another way to cure life's ills, or at least help him to escape from them. This early attempt at college was thought to be a failure, and Williams returned home where his father found him work in a shoe factory. The emptiness of his life and the tedium of his work led to a nervous breakdown in 1935.

to Writing

It was while the twenty-four-year-old Williams was recuperating from this breakdown in Memphis with his grandparents that he discovered drama. It was also in Memphis where his first produced play, *Cairo, Shanghai, Bombay,* was performed and Williams experienced the thrill of seeing an audience respond to his work. Determined that writing would be his career, Williams returned to college—Washington University, this time—where he began writing more seriously, and became involved with a small, local theatrical group. Unable to watch his sister Rose's deterioration, he decided to leave St. Louis. He entered the University of Iowa where he studied, wrote, and eventually earned a bachelor's degree in 1938. After graduation Williams took a year off, during which time he wandered around the country, experiencing life and gathering material for his writing. In 1939, "The Field of Blue Children," a short story published in the magazine *Story,* was the first work to appear under the name Tennessee Williams.

It wasn't long before Williams caught the eye of literary agent Audrey Wood and one of the most valuable friendships in Williams' life began. Wood was quite impressed with Williams' talent. She took him on as a client and secured several grants and scholarships that made it possible for him to write and see several works produced.

• *The Struggling*

Playwright Has

a Hit

Williams' first hopeful production, *Battle of Angels,* turned out to be a disaster. The play never completed its run in Boston, closing after just two weeks, and never made it to New York. Williams returned to the South discouraged. He spent a brief time in New Orleans but soon returned to New York, where he worked at relatively menial jobs—usher, elevator operator, waiter-entertainer.

Financial woes were especially severe for Williams during this period, and it was around this time that Wood secured him a scriptwriting contract with MGM. This, too, was a relative disaster when Williams was kept on and paid $250 a week, but advised not to return to the office. He used this time to rework *The Gentleman Caller,* the script MGM had rejected, renaming it *The Glass Menagerie.*

In 1945, *The Glass Menagerie* turned out to be Williams' first major success. The play's Broadway run lasted for almost two years, and it was chosen for the New York Drama Critics Circle Award.

Williams chronicled the low period of depression and isolation following the success of *The Glass Menagerie* in "On a Streetcar Named Desire"—an essay that later served as the introduction to the 1947 play of the same name. *Streetcar,* the play, earned Williams another New York Drama Critics Circle Award, a Donaldson Award, and a Pulitzer Prize—the first of two.

In 1946, Williams spent the summer on Nantucket with novelist Carson McCullers. This summer relationship with McCullers was the second critical relationship in Williams' life. The two admired and supported one another and spent long mornings sharing the same table as they wrote together. Williams believed that McCullers was the best American novelist of the twentieth century. Her admiration of him was equally great.

Just two years later, in 1948, *American Blues: Five Short Plays,* the collection for which Williams was given a special Group Theater Award, was published. In 1950, his first attempt at longer fiction, the short novel *The Roman Spring of Mrs. Stone,* was published. In 1961, *Roman Spring* was made into a motion picture starring Vivien Leigh and Warren Beatty.

During this time the third vital relationship in Williams' adult life began. It was also his major intimate relationship. Not until the publication of his memoirs in 1975 would he actually acknowledge the homosexuality that had characterized his life for more than a decade. Prior to 1948, a number of short-term relationships served to stave off Williams' insatiable appetites.

Williams had met Frank Merlo a number of summers earlier, but in 1948 the two men were reunited. Merlo, of Italian descent, brought Italy to Williams and, eventually, brought Williams to Italy. Williams' time in Italy provided him with rich details for later work, especially *The Rose Tattoo.*

Although their relationship was not exclusive, Williams and Merlo lived and traveled together from 1948 until Merlo's death from lung cancer in 1963. The two had only been together a short time when Williams dedicated *The Rose Tattoo,* which opened in 1951, "To Frank in return for Sicily." Also of note in 1951 was the publication of Williams' "I Rise in Flame, Cried the Phoenix"—a dramatized tribute to D. H. Lawrence.

Cat On a Hot Tin Roof opened in March of 1955. It was something of a comeback for the playwright whose last remarkable work was *A Streetcar Named Desire* more than seven years earlier. *Cat on a Hot Tin Roof* brought Williams another New York Drama Critics Circle Award and his second Pulitzer Prize.

Depression and despondency led Williams to psychoanalysis in 1957. He suffered from hypochondria, claustrophobia, fears of suffocation, and a growing dependency on alcohol. His father had died in 1957, and his grandfather two years earlier in 1955. Dealing with these losses, combined with the increasing tensions of daily life, were beginning to overwhelm him.

Freudian analysis and much reading about it filled Williams' time. *Suddenly Last Summer* emerged from this period in his life. Not

Relationships •

with Carson

McCullers and

Frank Merlo

Making a •

Comeback

surprisingly, it was judged by many to be Williams' most shocking play. Nonetheless, it was still a box-office success, and while it earned no awards, it did enjoy a lengthy run of more than 200 performances.

Williams enjoyed his last major recognition as a playwright in 1961. *The Night of the Iguana,* which opened in late December, earned him a fourth and final Drama Critics Circle Award. Despite the lack of success after *Night of the Iguana,* Williams continued to write and his plays were still being produced. But in 1963 Merlo succumbed to cancer, and Williams slipped into another severe depression, increased drug use, and greater alcohol dependency.

Memoirs was published in 1975. According to Sally Boyd, Williams was more concerned with "truth than fact" and penned a predictably "unchronological, often stream of consciousness recollection of the playwright's childhood, friendships, professional associations, periods of mental distress, successes and failures, heavily laced with detailed accounts of his sexual experiences."

Something Cloudy, Something Clear was Williams' last New York play. It is a frankly autobiographical account of Williams' relationship with Merlo and his understanding of himself. It was written in 1982, just a year before Williams' death. Viewed negatively by many, there are some among his critics who believe it to be the best work of Williams' last two decades.

In addition to the four New York Drama Critics Circle Awards and two Pulitzer Prizes, Williams also received a Group Theater Award for *American Blues: Five Short Plays* (1939); an Academy of Arts and Letters Award in 1944; the Sidney Howard Memorial Award and Sign Magazine Annual Award for *The Glass Menagerie;* and the Kennedy Honors Award in 1979. In 1952 he was elected to the National Institute of Arts and Letters, and in 1979 to the Theater Hall of Fame. Among the medals he was awarded are the Brandeis University Creative Arts Medal (1964–64), The National Institute of Arts and Letters Gold Medal (1969), and the first centennial medal of the Cathedral of St. John the Divine (1973).

Williams' career is clearly marked by extraordinary successes and monumental failures. Regardless, it cannot be denied that he enriched the world in which he lived. Certainly, his body of work earned him recognition as a major figure in mid–twentieth century drama.

**Profile by
Andrea L. T. Peterson**

MERLE WOO

M erle Woo's poetry and essays have been widely published in gay/

lesbian, feminist, Asian, and socialist periodicals and anthologies. She

is a leader in Radical Women and the Freedom Socialist Party, two

socialist feminist organizations, and has gained national attention in

her battles against employment discrimination at the University of

California at Berkeley. Since 1990, as a breast cancer survivor, she has

written and organized against this epidemic, in addition to her previous

multi-issue radical politics.

1941– •

Asian American •

writer, activist,

and educator

Born in San Francisco, California on 24 October 1941 to Helene and Richard Woo, Merle Woo learned early about racism against Asian Americans. In "Letter to Ma," published in *This Bridge Called My Back: Writings by Radical Women of Color,* Woo writes to her mother about her father: "When those two white cops said, 'Hey, fat boy, where's our meat?' he left me standing there on Grant Avenue, while he hurried over to his store to get it; they kept complaining, never satisfied. . . . I didn't know that he spent a year and a half on Angel Island; that we could never have our right names; that he lived in constant fear of being deported; that, like you, he worked two full-time jobs most of his life; that he was mocked and ridiculed because he speaks 'broken English.' And Ma, I was so ashamed after that experience when I was only six years old that I never held his hand again."

While Richard Woo came from southern China, Helene Chang was born in Los Angeles. Her father was a ginseng salesman and traveling Methodist minister. The Chang family emigrated back to Shanghai while Helene was still a child, then at age ten, because she was a girl, her parents sent Helene back to the United States by herself to be raised in an orphanage. Richard Woo is her second husband. Though neither Richard nor Helene Woo were Catholic, Helene sent Merle to Catholic schools, which she hoped would be of higher quality than the public schools.

Woo was married and the mother of two small children (Emily, born in 1963, and Paul, born in 1967) when she witnessed the Third World student strikes at San Francisco State University in 1968 and 1969. It was the beginning of many changes in her life. Woo writes in the anthology *Tilting the Tower:* "When I saw the success of the Third World student movement, that radicalized me faster than dropping Catholicism, faster than becoming a lesbian. That fast! What changed me was becoming conscious in a lightening flash that my education had been full of lies and censorship. I realized I had never read anything by people of color."

After Woo completed her master's in English at San Francisco State in 1969, she began teaching in the Educational Opportunity Program, a new program at SFSU created as a result of the student strikes. In attempting to teach English to students of color, Woo became increasingly aware that there were few teaching materials relevant to her student's lives. By 1973 Woo was teaching specific classes in Third World literature and in 1977 she proposed and taught the first Third World women's literature class in women studies.

• **Battled Alcohol**

Abuse

It was during these years that Woo realized that she was alcoholic. She writes of those years in "Letter to Ma": "You gave me, physically, what you never had, but there was a spiritual, emotional legacy you passed down which was reinforced by society: self-contempt because of our race, our sex, our sexuality. For deeply ingrained in me, Ma, there has been that strong, compulsive force to sink into self-contempt, passivity, and despair. I am sure that my fifteen years of alcohol abuse have not been forgotten by either of us, nor my suicidal depressions."

Woo sees 1975 as the turning point in her claiming control over her self-destructive compulsions. Three years later she came out as a lesbian.

After almost a decade's experience at SFSU, the University of California at Berkeley hired Woo as a lecturer in the Asian American Studies Program in the Ethnic Studies Department in 1978. The next four years saw Woo publishing in *Hanai,* a publication of the Asian American Studies Program, *Bridge,* an Asian American periodical from New York, and *This Bridge Called My Back,* the landmark anthology first released in 1981. Woo won high marks from her students during these years, but in 1982 the University declined to renew Woo's contract, citing the brand-new "four-year rule" which limited lecturers to a maximum of four year's employment.

Woo argued that her termination was the result of her outspoken politics as a lesbian feminist, unionist, student rights advocate, and leader in the Freedom Socialist Party and Radical Women, which she had joined in 1980. She told Jil Clark of *Gay Community News,* "The four-year rule was simply a pretext used to silence my criticism and outspoken politics." The American Federation of Teachers argued Woo's case before an administrative law judge who agreed and ordered the rehiring of Woo, who had been the only Berkley lecturer fired under that rule. When the University appealed the decision and stalled on the rehirings, Woo sued in federal and state courts for reinstatement. The University settled the case out of court in 1984 and rehired Woo with back pay on a two-year contract.

The situation repeated itself in 1986 when Woo's contract was again not renewed despite widespread support from students. While Woo accepted a lecturer position in women studies at San Francisco State, she also filed a union grievance charging discrimination on the basis of her race, gender, sexual orientation, and political ideology. Arbitration resulted in a decision in Woo's favor, followed by university stalling and Woo considering a lawsuit. Fate intervened in 1990 when she was diagnosed with breast cancer. Woo was already well-acquainted with the disease, especially through the illness and death in 1987 of Karen Brodine, a leader in the Merle Woo Defense Committee, Radical Women, and the Freedom Socialist Party. She dropped her case rather than spend her potentially few remaining years in litigation.

In her essay "The Politics of Breast Cancer," published in *The Very Inside: An Anthology of Writing by Asian and Pacific Islander Lesbian and Bisexual Women,* Woo reveals some of the complexity of this gendered disease:

Stricken with •

Breast Cancer

I have felt so ambivalent about my double mastectomy. I was glad to have my right breast removed six months after the mastectomy on the left side: I felt symmetrical again and relief that I didn't have to wear a prosthesis . . . [to prevent] throw[ing] out the alignment of the spine because the weight of the remaining breast pulling the spine to its side.

And although I panicked because there were large cancerous tumors and knew that I could die, I rather liked having no breasts. I go back and forth on it: On one hand I feel ugly with these two asymmetrical scars slashed across my chest, and on the other, my breasts were so large, that I felt ugly with them. The image of the petite Asian women was not ever lost on me. . . . I hated myself because I had large breasts.

Despite her own battle against cancer, Woo's passion for social justice has not wavered throughout the institutionalization of ethnic studies, women studies, and gay/lesbian studies. She sums up her political assessment of the 1990s in her essay "Forging Our Future, Building Our Roots": "The right wing is going to come down on women, and the right wing is going to come down on lesbians and gays, and we are going to be on the front line. But who is going to stand up for us on the campuses and in the community if we don't ourselves become multi-issue? If we don't ourselves address race and sex as they connect up with heterosexism and class?. . . These issues are lesbian and gay issues, and I want to see them discussed in the classroom and dealt with in the streets!"

**Profile by
Loie Hayes**

FRANCO ZEFFIRELLI

1923– •

Italian film •

director and

stage designer

As a filmmaker and stage designer, Franco Zeffirelli has scores of

worldwide productions to his credit—mostly Shakespearean or operat-

ic—that have been called either brilliant or extravagant to a fault, and

sometimes both. His personal life and politics have been equally contro-

versial, from his conservative politics to his religious fundamentalism to

his reluctantly admitted sexuality. Zeffirelli drew fire from all sides, for

instance, when he vehemently opposed Martin Scorsese's The Last

Temptation of Christ *in 1988, blaming the "Jews of Hollywood" for its*

blasphemy. He has cited, in his 1986 autobiography, the sacrifice his

mother made of her life for "her little bastard" as solidifying his stand

against abortion. In 1994, he was elected to the Italian parliament on a

strident right-wing platform. And when he came out to interviewer Edward Guthmann in the *Advocate* in June 1983, he said, in part, that he hated "to call certain human beings 'gay' [because] I see already a movement or a category. . . . I don't like that at all."

But perhaps Zeffirelli was fated to an operatic life. He was born in Florence on 12 February 1923 amid much scandal—the illegitimate son of a respected fashion designer (whose lawyer husband was in and out of sanitariums most of his later life with incurable tuberculosis) and her fabric supplier (himself married). "A name had to be invented for me," Zeffirelli says in the opening pages of his autobiography. Of the invention of such a name, he offers the following: "My mother was fond of a Mozart aria in *Cosi fan tutte* which mentions the *Zeffiretti,* the little breezes,. . . but this was misspelled in the register and came out as the previously unheard-of Zeffirelli."

After studying architecture and art at the University of Florence and Academia di Belle Arti, Zeffirelli began his career in film as an assistant to some of the greatest Italian directors of this century—Antonioni, Rosselini, De Sica—and also briefly tried his hand at acting (as the "new" Montgomery Clift) under the mentorship—and, it was assumed, more intimate tutelage—of Luchino Visconti in *Death in Venice.* In the 1940s, Zeffirelli established himself as a talented stage designer for Visconti's extravagant operas, and throughout the 1950s he staged his own lavish productions of opera (often featuring soprano Maria Callas) and theater (mostly Shakespeare).

Zeffirelli carried his stage-designing reputation for vivid eroticism amid opulent sets and costumes right into the second half of the century, when he gained notoriety as a film director. *The Taming of the Shrew* (1967), *Romeo and Juliet (1968), Brother Sun and Sister Moon* (1972), *La Traviata* (1983), *Otello* (1986), *Hamlet* (1990), and even the made-for-TV *Jesus of Nazareth* (1977) are most memorable for their lush photography, lovely lyricism, and romantic portraits well beyond the mere filming of a stage play. According to Raymond Murray in *Images in the Dark,* Zeffirelli's films have the ability to lift the viewer "out of the doldrums of everyday reality and into a world of beauty, love, and tragedy." Then again, there were also the incredible bombs to account for, including *Endless Love* (1981), *The Champ* (1979), and the never-released *Young Toscanini,* with Elizabeth Taylor. True to form, Zeffirelli blames the short-sighted avarice of the Hollywood "machine" for his failures. "How on earth had I allowed this to happen," he says in his autobiography, "I who had directed Callas, Magnani and Olivier, the operas of Puccini, Verdi, etc., who had handled tempestuous superstars like Elizabeth Taylor and Richard Burton [both in *The Taming of the Shrew*], who had made a box-office hit out of Shakespeare?"

Zeffirelli's personal life and politics have remained as non-emblematic as his career. When he came out in the *Advocate* article—albeit rather academically (and some say schizophrenically)—he clearly stated that he did not like to talk about his sexual inclinations, that people were not "special" because they liked one thing better than another in bed, and that calling certain human beings gay "ghettoized" the concept to everyone's detriment. At the same time, however, and to his credit, he alluded to a gay sensibility by telling Guthmann that "it happens that people who have to go through this particular sexual syndrome are forced to refine certain receptive instruments in the mind and soul: they become much more sensitive, more ready to talk and to deal with things of the spirit. They suffer more than the normal person. I think it is not easy to be a gay. I know this. You have to go through a very, very anguishing time."

In the spring of 1994, Zeffirelli augmented his controversial life by being elected to the Italian parliament as a member of the right-wing Freedom Alliance party, representing the Sicilian town of Catania. As he told *New Perspectives Quarterly,* the Freedom Alliance party represents the beginnings of "direct democracy" in Italy, a repossession of "personal destiny from the ruling/political classes." When asked how such politics effect a "man of the image" like himself, Zeffirelli casts an eye toward the future:

> The image is the reality of our times. . . . Now television creates prime ministers and presidents. That is progress. It will be the future of politics everywhere. And after the image, something else will come because man is restless and will continue to invent new ways of expressing himself and of disseminating information.

**Profile by
Jerome Szymczak**

A CLOSER LOOK

• ROBERTA ACHTENBERG

Address

HUD Fair Housing & Equal Opportunity, 451 7th St. SW, Room 5100, Washington, D.C. 20410.

References

Achtenberg, Roberta. Interview with Andrea L.T. Peterson, March 1996.

Achtenberg, Roberta, with others. *Sexual Orientation and the Law*. New York: Clark Boardman, 1985.

Additional biographical information provided by Roberta Achtenberg's campaign office in San Francisco.

• ALVIN AILEY

References

Ailey, Alvin. *Revelations: The Autobiography of Alvin Ailey*. Secaucus, NJ: Carol Pub. Group, 1995.

"Ailey, Alvin, Jr. (obituary)" in *Current Biography Yearbook 1990*: 63.

Ailey Dances, produced by ABC Video Enterprises. Long Branch, NJ: Kultur, 1982.

"Alvin Ailey" in *Obituary Annual, 1989*: 749–751.

"Alvin Ailey at the Met celebrating 25 years of dance" in *Ebony* (Chicago), October 1984: 164.

Barnes, Clive. "Burning Bright" in *Ballet News* (New York), November 1983: 13–15.

————. "Remembering Ailey" in *Dance Magazine* (New York), February 1990: 138.

Cook, Susan. *The Alvin Ailey American Dance Theater*. New York: Morrow, 1978.

Dixon, Brenda. "Black Dance and Dancers and the White Public: a Prolegomenon to Prob-

lems of Definition" in *Black American Literature Forum,* April 1990: 117–121.

Dunning, Jennifer. *A Life in Dance*. Reading, Massachusetts: Addison-Wesley Publishing, 1996.

Estell, Kenneth. *African America: Portrait of a People*. Detroit: Visible Ink, 1994.

Gold, Sylviane. "Thirty years with Alvin Ailey: The Ailey Generations" in *Dance Magazine* (New York), December 1988:40.

Gresham, Jewell Handy. "Dance of Life" in *Nation,* January 8, 1990: 40.

Grimm, Thomas, producer. *An Evening with the Alvin Ailey American Dance Theater*. Denmark: Danmarks Radio/ZDF/RM Arts, 1986.

Hackney, C. "Ailey, Alvin—In Memoriam" in *Black Perspective in Music*, 1990: 214.

Hering, Doris. "Alvin Ailey Dance Theater at Clark Center" in *Dance Magazine* (New York), February 1962: 60.

In Black and White. Detroit: Gale, 1985: 9–10.

Ipiotis, Celia and Jeff Bush, producers. *Alvin Ailey*. New York: ARC Videodance, 1989.

Latham, Jacqueline Quinn Moore. *A Biographical Study of the Lives and Contributions of Two Selected Contemporary Black Male Dance Artists: Arthur Mitchell and Alvin Ailey: in the idioms of ballet and modern dance, respectively*. Denton, Texas: Phd Dissertation, 1973.

Maynard, Olga. *Judith Jamison: Aspects of a Dancer*. Garden City, New York: Doubleday, 1982.

Mazo, J. H. "Ailey, Alvin (1931–1989)—In Memoriam" in *Dance Magazine* (New York), February 1990: 111.

Moore, W. "Ailey, Alvin (1931–1989)" in *Ballet Review,* Winter 1990: 12–17.

For more •

information

Pinkney, Andrea Davis. *Alvin Ailey.* New York: Hyperion Books for Children, 1993.

Weir, John. *"Revelations: The Autobiography of Alvin Ailey"* in *Advocate,* March 7, 1995: 61–62.

● EDWARD ALBEE

Address

14 Harrison St., New York, New York 10013-2842.

References

Albee, Edward. "Which Theatre Is The Absurd One?," in *New York Times Magazine,* 25 February 1962: 30–31, 64, 66.

Bronski, Michael. "Edward Albee," in *Gay & Lesbian Literature.* Detroit, Michigan: St. James Press, 1994: 3–5.

Current Biography Yearbook. New York: H. W. Wilson Co., 1963.

MacNicholas, John and Stephen M. Vallillo. "Edward Albee," in *Concise Dictionary of American Literary Biography: The New Consciousness, 1941–1968.* Detroit: Gale Research, 1987: 11–30.

New York Times Biographical Service. Ann Arbor, Michigan: University Microfilms International, vol. 24, nos. 1–12, 1993.

Rood, Karen L., ed. *Dictionary of Twentieth Century Culture: American Culture After World War II.* Detroit: Gale Research, 1994.

Taubman, Howard. "Not What It Seems: Homosexual Motif Gets Heterosexual Guise," in *New York Times,* 1961.

● PAULA GUNN ALLEN

Address

Department of English, University of California–Los Angeles, 405 Hilgard Ave., Los Angeles, California 90024.

References

Allen, Paula Gunn. "Beloved Women: Lesbians in American Indian Culture." *Conditions* 7 (spring 1981): 67–87.

———. *The Blind Lion.* Berkeley: Thorp Springs Press, 1974.

———. "'Border' Studies: The Intersection of Gender and Color." In *Introduction to Scholarship in Modern Languages and Literatures,* 2d ed., edited by Joseph Gibaldi, 303–19. New York: Modern Language Association of America, 1992.

———. *A Cannon Between My Knees.* New York: Strawberry Press, 1983.

———. *Coyote's Daylight Trip.* Albuquerque: La Confluencia, 1978.

———. *Grandmothers of the Light: A Medicine Woman's Sourcebook.* Boston: Beacon Press, 1991.

———. "The Medicine Song of Allie Hawker." In *Intricate Passions: A Collection of Erotic Short Fiction,* edited by Tee Corinne, 119–23. Austin: Banned Books, 1989.

———. *The Sacred Hoop: Recovering the Feminine in American Indian Traditions.* Boston: Beacon Press, 1986.

———. "Selections from *Raven's Road.*" In *Living the Spirit: A Gay American Indian Anthology,* edited by Will Roscoe, 134–52. New York: St. Martin's Press, 1988.

———. *Shadow Country.* Los Angeles: American Indian Studies Center, University of California, Los Angeles, 1982.

———. *Skins and Bones: Poems 1979–87.* Albuquerque: West End Press, 1988.

———. "Some Like Indians Endure." In *Living the Spirit: A Gay American Indian Anthology,* edited by Will Roscoe, 9–13. New York: St. Martin's Press, 1988.

———, ed. *Spider Woman's Granddaughters: Traditional Tales and Contemporary Writing by Native American Women.* Boston: Beacon Press, 1989.

———. *Star Child.* Marvin, South Dakota: Blue Cloud Quarterly, 1981.

———, ed. *Studies in American Indian Literature: Critical Essays and Course Designs.* New York: Modern Language Association of America, 1983.

———, ed. *Voice of the Turtle: American Indian Literature 1900–1970.* New York: Ballantine Books, 1994.

———. *The Woman Who Owned the Shadows.* San Francisco: Spinsters, Ink, 1983.

———. *Wyrds.* San Francisco: Taurean Horn Press, 1987.

● DOROTHY ALLISON

Address

P.O. Box 14474, San Francisco, California 94114.

References

Faderman, Lillian. *Odd Girls and Twilight Lovers: A History of Lesbian Life in Twentieth Century America.* New York: Columbia University Press, 1991.

Garrett, George. "No Wonder People Got Crazy as They Grew Up" in the *New York Times Book Review,* 5 July 1992: 3.

Huston, Bo. "A Storyteller out of Hell" in *Advocate,* 7 April 1992: 70–72.

Jetter, Alexis. "The Roseanne of Literature" in *New York Times Magazine,* 17 December 1995: 54–57.

Kenan, Randall. "Sorrow's Child" in the *Nation* 28 December 1992: 815–16.

Megan, Carolyn. "Moving Toward Truth: An Interview with Dorothy Allison" in *Kenyon Review 16,* 1994: 71–83.

• PEDRO ALMODOVAR

Address

El Deseo SA, Ruiz Perello 15, Madrid 28028, Spain.

References

Current Biography Yearbook, 1990. New York: H. W. Wilson Co., 1990.

International Who's Who, 57th ed., 1991–92. London: Europa Publications, 1991.

Thomson, David. *Biographical Dictionary of Film.* New York: Alfred A. Knopf, 1994.

• JAMES BALDWIN

References

Leeming, David A. *James Baldwin.* New York: Knopf, 1994.

Troupe, Quincy, editor. *James Baldwin: The Legacy.* New York: Simon and Schuster, 1989.

• ARTHUR BELL

References

"Arthur Bell, 51, a Columnist, Homosexual Rights Activist," in *New York Times,* 4 June 1984: IV, 18.

"Arthur Bell: Two or Three Things We Loved About Him," in *Village Voice* (New York), 26 June 1984: 10–11.

Bell, Arthur. *Dancing the Gay Lib Blues: A Year in the Homosexual Liberation Movement.* New York: Simon and Schuster, 1971.

————. *King's Don't Mean a Thing: The John Knight Murder Case.* New York: Morrow, 1978.

Contemporary Authors. Detroit: Gale Research, vols. 85–88, 1980.

Contemporary Authors. Detroit: Gale Research, vol. 112, 1985.

Duberman, Martin. *Stonewall.* New York: Dutton, 1993.

Ortleb, Charles. "Arthur Bell," in *Christopher Street,* February 1979: 61–3.

Schneiderman, David. "A Death in the Family," in *Village Voice* (New York), 12 June 1984: 3.

Teal, Donn. *The Gay Militants.* New York: Stein and Day, 1971.

• NANCY BEREANO

Address

c/o Firebrand Books, 141 The Commons, Ithaca, New York 14850.

References

Bereano, Nancy. Interview with R. Ellen Greenblatt, 1996.

• LEONARD BERNSTEIN

References

Burton, Humphrey. *Leonard Bernstein.* New York: Doubleday, 1994 [All the references in this text refer to Burton's biography, unless otherwise indicated].

Machlis, Joseph, *Introduction to Contemporary Music.* New York: W.W. Norton & Co., 1961.

Peyser, Joan, *Leonard Bernstein.*

Siegmeister, Elie, ed. *The New Music Lover's Handbook.* Harvey House, Inc., 1973.

• RON BUCKMIRE

Address

Department of Mathematics, Occidental College, 1600 Campus Road, Los Angeles, California 90041. Email: ron@abacus.oxy.edu.

References

All the information in this essay was found on the Internet. Much of the information can be found on Ron Buckmire's home page: http://abacus.oxy.edu/~ron/ or in the Queer Resources Directory: http://www.qrd.org/QRD/

Quotes are taken from email correspondence with Ron Buckmire and from the QRD FAQ (Frequently Asked Questions).

● CHARLES BUSCH

Address

c/o Jeffrey Melnick, Harry Gold Agency, 3500 West Olive, Suite 1400, Burbank, California 91505; c/o .Marc Glick, Glick and Weintraub, 1501 Broadway, Suite 2401, New York, New York 10036-5503.

References

Anderson, Lisa. In *Chicago Tribune,* 10 November 1993.

Brantley, Ben. In *New York Times,* October 1993.

Bruckner, D. J. R. "Stage: 'Vampire Lesbians of Sodom'," in *New York Times,* 20 June 1985.

Busch, Charles. Interview with Ira Brodsky. 11 April 1996.

Current Biography, June 1995. New York: H. W. Wilson, 1995: 11.

Pacheco, Patrick. In *New York Times,* 23 July 1989.

Witchel, Alex. "Shopping with: Charles Busch; After Divas, It's a Challenge to Play a Man," in *New York Times,* 19 October 1994: C1.

● PAUL CADMUS

Address

P.O. Box 1255, Weston, Connecticut 06883-0255.

References

Davenport, Guy. *The Drawings of Paul Cadmus.* New York: Rizzoli, 1989.

Hunter, Sam, and John Jacobus. *American Art of the 20th Century.* New York: Abrams, 1973.

Kirstein, Lincoln. *Paul Cadmus.* New York: Imago Imprint, 1984.

Sutherland, David. *Paul Cadmus: Enfant Terrible at 80.* David Sutherland Productions, 1984.

● PAT CALIFIA

Address

2215R Market St. #261, San Francisco, California 94114.

● MICHAEL CALLEN

References

Berkowitz, Richard, and Michael Callen. *How to Have Sex in an Epidemic: One Approach.* New York: News from the Front Publications, 1983.

Callen, Michael. *Purple Heart.* New York: Significant Other Records, 1988.

———. *Surviving AIDS.* New York: Harper Perennial, 1990.

———, ed. *Surviving and Thriving with AIDS: Hints for the Newly Diagnosed.* New York: People With AIDS Coalition, 1987.

———, ed. *Surviving and Thriving with AIDS: Collected Wisdom.* New York: People With AIDS Coalition, 1988.

Demme, Jonathan, dir. *Philadelphia.* TriStar Pictures, 1993.

Dunlap, David W. "Michael Callen, Singer and Expert on Coping with AIDS, Dies At 38," in *New York Times,* 29 December 1993: D19.

Flirtations. *The Flirtations.* New York: Significant Other Records, 1990.

Flirtations. *Live, Out On the Road.* N.p.: Flirt Records, 1992.

Folkart, Burt A. "Composer Callen Loses 12-Year Fight with AIDS," in *Los Angeles Times,* 29 December 1993: B1, B4.

Gottlieb, Michael et al. "Speaking of the Plague. . . ," in *U.S. News & World Report* (Washington, D.C.), 17 June 1991: 23–4.

Greyson, John, dir. *Zero Patience.* Zero Patience Productions Ltd., 1993.

Merrett, Jim. "Take My HIV, Please," in *Advocate,* 22 March 1994: 72–73.

● MARGARETHE CAMMERMEYER

Address

1715 S. 234th St., Seattle, Washington 98198-7522; American Lake VA Medical Center, Department Neuroscience, Tacoma, Washington 98493.

References

Cammermeyer, Margarethe with Chris Fisher. *Serving in Silence.* New York: Viking, 1994.

● DEBRA CHASNOFF

Address

Women's Educational Media, 2180 Bryant Street, #203, San Francisco, California 94110. E-mail: WEM DHC@aol.com.

References

Chasnoff, Debra. Interview with Susie Day. 19 April 1996.

"Dykes' Night OUT at the Oscars," in *OUT/LOOK* (San Francisco), Summer 1992: 31–4.

Herman, Ellen. "Academy Award-Winning Lesbian Speaks," in *Gay Community News* (Boston), 9–21 May 1992: 8–9.

———. "Oscar Springs Filmmaker into the Spotlight," in the *Boston Globe,* 9 April 1992: 1, 78.

Malkin, Marc S. "One Woman General Electric Won't Soon Forget," in *Bay Windows* (Boston), 9–15 April 1992: 1, 10.

Rosenfeld, Megan. "Bringing Bad Things to Light, GE Expose Gets Debra Chasnoff an Oscar . . . and Maybe Even a Second Phone," in *Washington Post,* 23 April 1992: A1, D10.

● AARON COPLAND

References

"Aaron Copland." Brochure, London: Boosey & Hawkes, 1996.

Austin, William W. "Aaron Copland" in *The New Grove Dictionary of American Music.* London: Macmillan Press Ltd., 1986: vol. 1, 496–504.

Copland, Aaron. Conversations with Michael E. O'Connor, 1983–87.

Copland, Aaron, and Vivian Perlis. *Copland: 1990 Through 1942.* New York: St. Martin's/Marek, 1984.

Copland, Aaron, and Vivian Perlis. *Copland: Since 1943.* New York: St. Martin's, 1989.

Moor, Paul. "Fanfare for an Uncommon Man" in the *Advocate* (January 15, 1991): 54–55.

● MICHAEL DENNENY

References

Denneny, Michael. E-mail interview with R. Ellen Greenblatt, 1996.

● MARTIN DUBERMAN

Address

475 W. 22nd St., New York, New York 10011.

References

Berney, K. A. *Contemporary Dramatists.* 5th ed. Detroit: St. James, 1993.

Contemporary Authors, New Revision Series. Vol. 2. Detroit: Gale Research, 1981.

Duberman, Martin. *Cures: A Gay Man's Odyssey.* New York: Dutton, 1991.

———. *Midlife Queer: Autobiography of a Decade, 1971–1981.* New York: Scribner, 1996

Malinowski, Sharon, ed. *Gay and Lesbian Literature.* Detroit: St. James, 1994.

Russell, Paul. *The Gay 100: A Ranking of the Most Influential Gay Men and Lesbians, Past and Present.* New York: Carol, 1995.

Who's Who in America, 1996. Vol. 1. New Providence, New Jersey: Marquis, 1995.

● MELISSA ETHERIDGE

References

Bream, Jon. In the *Minneapolis Star and Tribune,* 12 February 1990.

Cohen, Rich. In *Rolling Stone,* 29 December 1994/12 January 1995.

Current Biography Yearbook 1995. New York: H. W. Wilson, 1996: 154–157.

Littlejohn, Maureen. "Forever Etheridge," in *Modern Woman,* April 1996.

Lustig, Jay. "Melissa Etheridge: Impending Parenthood Leads to a Change in Attitude," in the *New Jersey Star-Ledger,* 27 August 1996.

Novak, Ralph. In *People,* 8 August 1988.

Schruers, Fred. "Melissa Etheridge," in *US,* December 1995.

Smith, Patricia. In the *Chicago Sun Times,* 5 August 1990.

Thomas, Elizabeth. "Melissa Etheridge," in *Contemporary Musicians.* Detroit, Michigan: Gale Research, vol. 4, 1991.

Warden, Steve. "Melissa Etheridge: Feeling Free," in *Access,* January/February 1996.

Wild, David. In *US,* January 1994.

● LILLIAN FADERMAN

Address

English Department, California State University, Fresno, California 93740.

References

Faderman, Lillian, ed. *Chloe Plus Olivia: An Anthology of Lesbian Literature from the Seventeenth Century to the Present*. New York and London: Penguin, 1994.

Faderman, Lillian. *Odd Girls and Twilight Lovers: A History of Lesbian Life in Twentieth-Century America*. New York: Columbia UP, 1991.

Faderman, Lillian. *Scotch Verdict*. New York: William Morrow, 1983, reissue Columbia UP, 1993.

Faderman, Lillian. *Surpassing the Love of Men: Romantic Friendship and Love Between Women Sixteenth Century to the Present*. New York: William Morrow, 1981.

Schwartz, Arie. "Surpassing the Odds" in *10 Percent*, June 1994: 67–70.

● BARNEY FRANK

Address

U.S. House of Representatives, 2210 Rayburn HOB, Washington, D.C., 20515.

References

Congressional Directory, 104th 1995/96. Washington, D.C.: United States Government Printing Office, 1995.

Congressional Quarterly's Politics in America: 1996. Washington, D.C.: CQ Press, 1995.

Current Biography Yearbook, 1995. New York: H. W. Wilson Company, 1995.

Frank, Barney. *Speaking Frankly: What's Wrong With the Democrats and How to Fix It*. New York: Times Books/Random House, 1992.

Hohler, Bob. "Brawler on the Hill," in *Boston Globe*, 21 May 1995.

Kaufman, Jonathan. "The Problem With Being Too Frank," in *Boston Globe*, 17 September 1989.

Kosova, Weston. "Frank Incensed: Outspoken Rep. Barney Frank; Interview," in *New Republic*, 6 March 1995.

Morganthau, Tom. "Barney Frank's Story," in *Newsweek*, 25 September 1989.

Romano, Lois. "Barney Frank, Out of the Closet," in *Washington Post*, 2 July 1987.

Wilkie, Curtis. "Barney Frank: Making of a Pragmatist," in *Boston Globe*, 10 June 1993.

● ALLEN GINSBERG

Address

c/o Bob Rosenthal, P.O. Box 582, Stuyvesant Station, New York, New York 10009-0582.

References

Ginsberg, Allen. *Collected Poems: 1947–1980*. New York: Harper & Row, 1985.

———. *Cosmopolitan Greetings, Poems 1986–1992*. New York: Harper Perennial, 1994.

———. *Howl and Other Poems*. Introduction by William Carlos Williams. San Francisco: City Lights Books, 1956.

———. *Kaddish and Other Poems. 1958–1960*. San Francisco: City Lights Books, 1961.

———. *Mind Breaths: Poems, 1972–1977*. San Francisco: City Lights Books, 1977.

———. *Planet News, 1961–1967*. San Francisco: City Lights Books, 1968.

Miles, Barry. *Ginsberg: A Biography*. New York: Simon and Schuster, 1989.

Schumacher, Michael. *Dharma Lion: A Biography of Allen Ginsberg*. New York: St. Martins Press, 1992.

● JEWELLE GOMEZ

Address

206 Fairmount Street, San Francisco, California 94131.

References

Crowley, Karlyn. *"The Gilda Stories,"* in *Belles Lettres: A Review of Books by Women* (North Potomac, MD), vol. 7, no. 3, Spring 1992: 60–61.

Findlen, Barbara. "Bold Types," in *Ms.* (New York, N.Y.), July/August 1991: 87.

Johnson, Judith E. "Women and Vampires: Nightmare of Utopia?," in the *Kenyon Review* (Gambier, OH), vol. 15, no. 1, Winter 1993: 72–80.

Olendorf, Donna, ed. *Contemporary Authors*. Detroit: Gale Research Inc., vol. 142, 1994: 159–160.

Sherman, Susan. In *New Directions for Women* (Englewood, NJ), November–December 1991.

● MARGA GOMEZ

Address

c/o Irene Pinn, P.O. Box 460368, San Francisco, California 94146.

References

Guthmann, Edward. "A Chip Off The Old Block" in *San Francisco Chronicle,* 5 November 1995.

Horowitz, Simi. "Marga Gomez" in *New York Native* 10 May 1993.

Pollon, Zélie. "Marga Gomez Is Definitely Going Places" in *Deneuve,* October 1994 (4:5), pp. 24–27, 54.

Reser, Phil. "Marga Gomez Lifting Spirits, A Family Tradition" in *San Francisco Hot Ticket,* September 1988.

Troy, Patricia. "Marga Gomez" in *Venice,* April 1994.

Valdes, David. "Pretty Wonderful" in *Bay Windows,* 12 May–18 May 1994.

West, Blake. "Marga Gomez Goes Public" in *Metroline,* 2–15 February 1995.

● BARBARA GRIER

Address

c/o Naiad Press, P.O. Box 10543, Tallahassee, Florida 32302-2543.

References

Boucher, Sandy. "Clinging Vine" in *Heartwomen: An Urban Feminist's Odyssey Home.* San Francisco: Harper & Row, 1982, pp. 212–230.

Grier, Barbara. "Climbing *The Ladder* to Success: Naiad Press" in *Happy Endings: Lesbian Writers Talk about their Lives and Work* by Kate Brandt. Tallahassee, Florida: Naiad Press, 1993, pp. 99–108.

———. "The Garden Variety Lesbian" in *The Coming Out Stories,* ed. Susan J. Wolfe and Julia Penelope Stanley. Watertown, Massachusetts: Persephone Press, 1980, pp. 235–240.

———. Interview with R. Ellen Greenblatt, 1996.

Lesbian Tongues: Lesbians Talk About Life, Love, and Sex. Washington, D.C.: Pop Video, 1989. 90 min.

Troxell, Jane. "Naiad Press Founders Celebrate 20 Years of Personal and Professional Triumphs" 3 (May/June 1992): 8.

● MARILYN HACKER

Address

230 West 105th Street, #10A, New York, New York 10025.

References

Finch, Annie. "An Interview on Form," in *American Poetry Review,* 25(3), May/June 1996: 23–27.

Hacker, Marilyn. *Love, Death, and the Changing of the Seasons.* New York: Norton, 1986.

———. *Selected Poems 1965-1990.* New York: Norton, 1994.

Hammond, Karla. "An Interview with Marilyn Hacker," in *Frontiers,* V(3), 1981: 22–27.

Mitchell, Felicia. "Marilyn Hacker," in *Dictionary of Literary Biography,* 120. Detroit: Gale, 1992: 102–08.

● BARBARA HAMMER

Address

E-mail: http://www.echonyc.com/~lesbians.

References

Ayscough, Suzan. "Nitrate Kisses," in *Variety* (New York), 1 February 1993: 100.

Brownworth, Victoria A. "The Final Frontier," in the *Advocate,* 7 February 1995: 61–63.

Canby, Vincent. "Postwar Western Gay Culture," in *New York Times,* 9 April 1993: C-10.

Levy, Owen. "Hammer Aims to Break out of the Ghetto," in *Moving Pictures Berlinale,* 23 February 1996.

Murray, Raymond. *Images in the Dark: An Encyclopedia of Gay and Lesbian Film and Video.* Philadelphia: TLA Publications, 1994.

Rountree, Cathleen. *Coming into Our Fullness: On Women Turning Forty.* Freedom, California: The Crossing Press, 1991.

Willis, Holly. "Uncommon History: An Interview with Barbara Hammer," in *Film Quarterly* (Berkeley, California), Summer 1994: 7–13.

● HARRY HAY

References

Burnside, John. *Who Are the Gay People? And Other Essays.* San Francisco: Vortex Media, 1989. A Radical Fairy's Seedbed no. 5.

D'Emilio, John. *Sexual Politics, Sexual Communities, The Making of a Homosexual Mi-*

nority in the United States, 1940–1970. Chicago: University of Chicago, 1983.

Harry, Hay. *Radically Gay: The Story of Gay Liberation in the Words of Its Founder*. Boston: Beacon Press, 1996. Will Roscoe, ed.

Katz, Jonathan, ed. *Gay American History: Lesbians and Gay Men in the U.S.A*. New York: Crowell, 1976.

Timmons, Stuart. *The Trouble With Harry Hay, A Biography*. Boston: Aylson, 1990.

● ESSEX HEMPHILL

References

Broder, Michael. "Essex Hemphill," in *Black Writers*. Detroit, Michigan: Gale Research, 1994: 299–301.

———. "Essex Hemphill," in *Gay & Lesbian Literature*. Detroit, Michigan: St. James Press, 1994: 180–181.

Hemphill, Essex. *Ceremonies: Prose and Poetry*. New York: New American Library, 1992.

Hemphill, Essex, ed. *Brother to Brother*. Boston: Alyson Publications, 1991.

Morse, Gary and Joan Larkin, eds. *Gay & Lesbian Poetry in Our Time: An Anthology*. New York: St. Martin's Press, 1988.

Poulson-Bryant, Scott. "New Faces," in *Village Voice* (New York), 28 June 1988: 24f.

Tarver, Chuck. *Network* (New York), December 1990.

Trinidad, David. In *Village Voice Literary Supplement* (New York), June 1992: 7–8.

● DAVID HOCKNEY

Address

7508 Santa Monica Boulevard, West Hollywood, California 90046-6407.

References

Alberge, Dalya. "Hockney's Camera Puts New Technology in Focus," in the *Times* (London), 3 June 1996: 3.

Friedman, Martin. *Hockney Paints the Stage*. London: Thames and Hudson, 1983.

Hockney, David. *David Hockney by David Hockney: My Early Years*, edited by Nikos Stangos. London: Thames and Hudson, 1976.

———. "R. B. Kitaj and David Hockney Discuss the Case for a Return to the Figurative...," in the *New Review*, vol. 3, no. 34 (February 1977): 75–77.

———. "No Joy at the Tate," interview with Miriam Gross, in *Observer*, 4 March 1979, review section: 1–2.

———. *Paper Pools*, edited by Nikos Stangos. London: Thames and Hudson, 1980.

———. *That's the Way I See It*, edited by Nikos Stangos. London: Thames and Hudson, 1993.

Livingstone, Marco. *David Hockney*. Rev. ed. London: Thames and Hudson, 1988.

Melia, Paul, and Ulrich Luckhardt. *David Hockney: Paintings*. Munich and New York: Prestel, 1994.

Melia, Paul, ed. *David Hockney*. Manchester and New York: Manchester University Press, 1995.

Webb, Peter. *Portrait of David Hockney*. London: Chatto and Windus, 1988.

● HOLLY HUGHES

References

Brown, Joe and Kara Swisher. "Holly Hughes's Main Man" in *Washington Post*, 18 March 1995, p. DO2.

Carr, C. "The Lady is a Dick: The Dyke Noir Theater of Holly Hughes" in the *Village Voice* (New York), 19 May 1987, p. 32.

Davy, Kate. "Reading Past the Heterosexual Imperative: *Dress Suits to Hire*" in the *Drama Review* 33, spring 1989, pp. 153–170.

Harris, William. "The NEA Four: Life After Symbolhood" in *New York Times*, 5 June 1994.

Hughes, Holly. *Clit Notes: A Sapphic Sampler*. New York: Grove, 1996.

Jaques, Damien. "Holly Hughes' Annual Fall Gig is Still Engrossing" in *Milwaukee Journal Sentinel*, 28 September 1995, p. 8.

Nichols, John. "The Bete Noire of the Radical Right" in *Capital Times* (Madison, WI), 10 October 1994, p. 1C.

Schneider, Rebecca. "Holly Hughes: Polymorphous Perversity and the Lesbian Scientist" in the *Drama Review* 33, spring 1989, pp. 171–183.

Stone, Laurie. "Holly Daze" in the *Village Voice* (New York), 13 February 1996, p. 11.

———. "Holly Hughes: Her Heart Belongs to Daddy" in *Ms*. September/October 1994, p. 88.

———. "Mama Mia" in the *Village Voice*, 16 February 1993.

———. "Tongue Untied" in the *Village Voice,* 22 March 1994, pp. 92, 96.

Welsh, Anne Marie. "Monologues Hold Audience Spellbound" in the *San Diego Union-Tribune,* 6 May 1995, p. E-6.

Wilmoth, Charles M. "The Archaeology of Muff Diving: An Interview with Holly Hughes" in the *Drama Review* 35, fall 1991, pp. 216–220.

● ALBERTA HUNTER

References

Alberta Hunter: My Castle's Rockin' (film). New York: View Video, 1992.

Taylor, Frank C. and Gerald Cook. *Alberta Hunter: A Celebration in Blues*. New York: McGraw-Hill, 1987.

● KARLA JAY

Address

392 Central Park West 11M, New York, New York 10025.

References

Duberman, Martin. *Stonewall*. New York: Dutton Books, 1993.

Jay, Karla. *The Amazon and the Page*. Bloomington: Indiana University Press, 1988.

Jay, Karla, ed. *Dyke Life: A Celebration of the Lesbian Experience*. New York: Basic Books, 1995.

———. *Lesbian Erotics*. New York: New York University Press, 1995.

Jay, Karla and JoAnne Glasgow, eds. *Lesbian Texts and Contexts: Radical Revisions*. New York: New York University Press, 1990.

● BILL T. JONES

Address

Bill T. Jones/Arnie Zane & Co. Image Artists, 853 Broadway, Suite 1706, New York, New York 10019.

References

Jones, Bill T. *Last Night on Earth*. New York: Pantheon Books, 1995.

Jones, Bill T. and Arnie Zane. *Body Against Body: The Dance and other Collaborations of Bill T. Jones & Arnie Zane*. New York: Station Hill Press, 1989.

Gates, Henry Louis, Jr. "The Body Politic" in *New Yorker,* 21 November 1994, pp 112–124.

Jowitt, Deborah. "Bill as Bill" in the *Village Voice* (New York), 20 October 1992.

Kaplan, Larry. "Delicate Dance" in *POZ Magazine,* June/July 1994, pp 40–44, 69.

Kaye, Elizabeth. "Bill T. Jones" in *New York Times Magazine* 6 March 1994, Section 6.

Shapiro, Laura. "Dancing in Death's House" in *Newsweek,* 7 November 1994, pp 66–68.

Stearns, David Patrick. "Dancing with Death" in *USA Today,* 31 October 1994, Cover story, Life section.

● CLEVE JONES

References

"And Sew It Goes" in *Mother Jones* 14 (January 1989), 34–35.

Haberman, Douglas. "Humanitarian award honors 'activist side, scientific side'" in the *Desert Sun* (17 February 1996), E-18.

Hawkins, Peter S. "Naming Names: The Art of Memory and the NAMES Project AIDS Quilt" in *Critical Inquiry* 19 (Summer 1993), 752–779.

Jones, Cleve. "AIDS Quilt: A Call for Research" in *San Francisco Examiner* (30 November 1995), A-16.

● FRANK KAMENY

References

Fox, Sue. "At 70, Activist Frank Kameny Is Still Fighting," in *Washington Blade,* 19 May 1995.

Katz, Jonathan Ned. *Gay American History: Lesbians & Gay Men in the U.S.A.* New York: Penguin Books, 1992.

Shilts, Randy. *Conduct Unbecoming: Gays & Lesbians in the U.S. Military*. New York: St. Martin's Press, 1993.

Tobin, Kay and Randy Wicker. *The Gay Crusaders*. New York: Arno Press, 1975.

● JONATHAN NED KATZ

Address

c/o Joan Raines, Raines & Raines, 475 Fifth Avenue, New York, New York 10017.

References

Abelove, Henry, Michèle Aina Barale, and David M. Halperin, eds. *The Lesbian and Gay Studies Reader*. New York: Routledge, 1993.

Chauncey, George. *Gay New York: Gender, Urban Culture, and the Making of the Gay*

Male World, 1890-1940. New York: Basic Books, 1994.

D'Emilio, John. *Making Trouble.* New York: Routledge, 1992.

Duberman, Martin, Martha Vicinus, and George Chauncey, Jr., eds. *Hidden from History: Reclaiming the Gay and Lesbian Past.* New York: Meridian, 1989.

Greenberg, David F. *The Construction of Homosexuality.* Chicago: University of Chicago Press, 1988.

Katz, Jonathan Ned. *Coming Out! A Documentary Play about Gay Life and Liberation in the U.S.A.* New York: Arno Press, 1975.

————. *Gay American History: Lesbians and Gay Men in the U.S.A.* New York: Crowell, 1976.

————. *Gay/Lesbian Almanac: A New Documentary.* New York: Harper and Row, 1983.

————. *The Invention of Heterosexuality.* New York: Plume, 1995.

Morton, Donald, ed. *The Material Queer: A LesBiGay Cultural Studies Reader.* Boulder, Colorado: Westview Press, 1996.

● LARRY KRAMER

References

Drane, Janice E. "Kramer, Larry" in *Contemporary Authors,* Volume 126. Detroit: Gale, 1989, pp. 239–241.

Kramer, Larry. *The Destiny of Me.* New York: Penguin Books, 1993.

————. Interview with Joseph E. DeMatio, 8 May 1996.

————. "A Man's Life, and the Path to Acceptance" in *New York Times,* 4 October 1992.

————. *The Normal Heart.* New York: New American Library, 1985.

————. *Reports from the Holocaust: the Making of an AIDS Activist.* New York: St. Martin's Press, 1989.

————. "When a Roaring Lion Learns to Purr" in *New York Times,* 12 January 1995.

Shnayerson, Michael. "Kramer vs. Kramer" in *Vanity Fair,* October 1992, pp. 228–231, 293–297.

Winokur, L.A. "Larry Kramer" in the *Progressive,* June 1994, pp. 32–35.

● k. d. lang

Address

c/o Sire Records, 75 Rockefeller Plaza, New York, New York 10019.

References

k. d. lang Background Info, in *Obvious Gossipy.* World Wide Web, 1996.

Stolder, Steven. "Q and A with k. d. lang," in *San Francisco Chronicle,* Datebook, 15–24 February 1996.

The New Rolling Stone Encyclopedia of Rock and Roll, edited by Patricia Romanowski and Holly George-Warren. New York: Rolling Stone Press, 1995.

Johnson, Brian D. "A Lighter Side of Lang," in *Maclean's,* 6 November 1995.

Starr, Victoria. *k.d. lang: all you get is me.* New York: St. Martin's Press, 1994.

Ali, Lorraine. "k. d. lang," in the *Rolling Stone,* 30 November 1994.

Leland, John. "Escape from Nashville," in *Newsweek,* 27 April 1992.

Leblanc, Larry, and Richard Flohil. "Best of the 80's," in the *Canadian Composer,* Winter 1991.

Gillmor, Don. "Torch and Twang: Country Music's k.d. lang," in *Reader's Digest* (Canadian), October 1990.

Gore, Lesley, "Lesley Gore on k. d. lang . . . and vice versa," in *Ms.,* July–August 1990.

Scott, Jay. "Yippee-i-o k. d.," in *Chatelaine,* January 1988.

● AUDRE LORDE

References

"An Interview: Audre Lorde and Adrienne Rich." *Signs* 6, Summer 1981. Reprinted in Audre Lorde, *Sister Outsider.* Trumansburg, N.Y.: The Crossing Press, 1984.

Christian, Barbara. "Dynamics of Difference" in the *Women's Review of Books* I, August 1984. Excerpted in *Contemporary Literary Criticism,* 71. Detroit: Gale, 1992.

Cook, Blanche Wiesen. "Audre Lorde: Friend of Friends" in *Transcending Silences: The Life and Poetic Legacy of Audre Lorde.* Eds. Gayle Louison and Mora J. Byrd. New York: The Franklin H. Williams Caribbean Cultural Center African Diaspora Institute, 1994. First printed in the Program of Audre Lorde Memorial

Service. Cathedral of St. John the Divine, 18 January 1993.

Dictionary of Literary Biography, Vol. 41: *Afro-American Poets Since 1955.* Detroit: Gale Research, 1985.

Griffin, Ada Gay, creator, and Michelle Parkerson, director. *A Litany for Survival: The Life and Work of Audre Lorde.* Third World Newsreel, 1995. Referred to as *Litany* in essay.

Hull, Gloria T. "Living on The Line: Audre Lorde and 'Our Dead Behind Us'" in *Changing Our Own Words: Essays on Criticism, Theory and Writing by Black Women.* Ed. Cheryl A. Wall. New Brunswick, N.J.: Rutgers, 1989. Excerpted in *Contemporary Literary Criticism,* 71. Detroit: Gale, 1992.

Lorde, Audre. *A Burst of Light.* Ithaca, N.Y.: Firebrand Books, 1988.

———. *The Marvelous Arithmetics of Distance: Poems 1987–1992.* New York: Norton, 1993.

———. *Sister Outsider.* Trumansburg, New York: The Crossing Press, 1984.

———. *Uses of the Erotic: The Erotic as Power.* Out and Out Books, 1978 (available through The Crossing Press). Reprinted in *Sister Outsider.*

———. *Zami: A New Spelling of My Name: A Biomythography.* Trumansburg, New York: The Crossing Press, 1982.

Ridinger, Robert. "Audre Lorde" in *The Gay and Lesbian Literary Companion.* Eds. Sharon Malinowski and Christa Brelin. Detroit: Visible Ink Press, 1995.

Russell, Paul. *The Gay 100.* New York: Citadel Press, 1995.

Upton, Elaine. "Audre Lorde" in *Contemporary Lesbian Writers of the United States: A Biobibliographical Critical Sourcebook.* Eds. Sandra Pollack and Denise D. Knight. Westport, Conn: Greenwood Press, 1993.

● GREG LOUGANIS

Address

P.O. Box 4130, Malibu, California 90265-1430.

References

Biographical Dictionary of American Sports: Basketball and Other Indoor Sports. New York: Greenwood Press, 1989.

Cray, Dan. "Heart of the Diver," in *Time,* 6 March 1995.

Galvin, Peter. "Below the Surface," in *Advocate,* 4 April 1995.

Goff, Michael. "Depth of a Diver," in *Out,* April 1995.

Hickok, Ralph. *Who's Who of Sports Champions: Their Stories and Records.* Boston: Houghton Mifflin Company, 1995.

Louganis, Greg. *Breaking the Surface.* New York: Random House, 1995.

Mallon, Bill. *Quest for Gold: The Encyclopedia of American Olympians.* New York, 1984.

Polly, John. "Greg Louganis' Wild Ride," in *Genre,* December–January 1996.

Quintanilla, Michael. "The Truth Shall Set You Free," in *Los Angeles Times,* 28 February 1995.

● PHYLLIS LYON & DEL MARTIN

Address

651 Duncan St., San Francisco, California 94131; telephone: (415) 824-2790.

References

D'Emilio, John. *Sexual Politics, Sexual Communities.* University of Chicago Press, 1983.

Lyon, Phyllis and Del Martin. Interview with Marvin S. Shaw, 17 October 1996.

———. *Lesbian/Woman* (Twentieth Anniversary Edition). Volcano Press, 1991.

Sue, Eleanor and Pam Walton. *Forty Years of Women's Herstory* (video). Sue Walton Productions, 1996.

● IAN McKELLEN

Address

c/o James Sharkey, 21 Golden Square, London W1R 3PA, England.

References

Gibson, Melissa. "Ian McKellen," in *International Directory of Theatre, volume 3: Actors, Directors and Designers,* edited by David Pickering. Detroit: St. James Press, 1996: 503–506.

Katz, Ephraim. *The Film Encyclopedia.* New York: HarperCollins, 1994: 872.

● CHERRIE MORAGA

Address

c/o Chicano Studies Department, University of California, 3404 Dwinelle Hall, Berkeley, California 94720.

References

Anzaldua, Gloria and Moraga, Cherrie, eds. *This Bridge Called My Back: Writings by Radical Women of Color.* Watertown, MA: Persephone Press, 1981.

Castillo, Ana. Review in *Third Woman,* 1986, p. 135.

Moraga, Cherrie. *Loving in the War Years.* Boston: South End Press, 1983.

Pollack, Sandra and Knight, Denise D., eds. *Contemporary Lesbian Writers of the United States.* Westport, CT: Greenwood Press, 1993.

● MARTINA NAVRATILOVA

Address

c/o International Management Group, 1 Erieview Plaza, Cleveland, Ohio 44114.

References

Faulkner, Sandra (with Judy Nelson). *Love Match—Nelson vs. Navratilova.* Birch Lane Press.

Frayne, Trent. *Famous Women Tennis Players.* New York: Dodd, Mead & Company.

International Herald Tribune, 18 July 1996.

Miller, Neil. *Out of the Past—Gay and Lesbian History from 1869 to the Present.* New York: Vintage Books, 1995.

Navratilova, Martina (with George Vecsey). *Martina.* New York: Alfred A. Knopf, 1985.

● JOAN NESTLE

Address

215 West 92nd Street, New York, New York 10025.

References

Brownworth, Victoria A. "Joan Nestle: The Politics of *The Persistent Desire,*" in *Advocate* (New York), 2 June 1992: 39.

Metz, Holly. In the *Progressive* (Madison, Wisconsin), August 1989: 16–17.

Nestle, Joan. *A Restricted Country.* Ithaca, New York: Firebrand Books, 1987.

Nestle, Joan and John Preston, eds. *Sister & Brother: Lesbians and Gay Men Write About Their Lives Together.* San Francisco: Harper, 1994.

Nestle, Joan and Naomi Holoch, eds. *Women on Women 3: A New Anthology of American Lesbian Short Fiction.* New York: Plume, 1996.

Rochman, Susan. In *Contemporary Lesbian Writers of the United States,* edited by Sandra Pollack and Denise D. Knight. Westport, Connecticut: Greenwood Press, 1994.

Stanely, Deborah A. In *Gay & Lesbian Literature.* Detroit, Michigan: St. James Press, 1994: 279–280.

Summers, Claude J., ed. *The Gay and Lesbian Literary Heritage.* New York: Henry Holt, 1995.

● SIMON NKOLI

References

Gevisser, Mark and Edwin Cameron. *Defiant Desire: Gay and Lesbian Lives in South Africa.* New York: Routledge, 1995.

Krouse, Matthew and Kim Berman. *The Invisible Ghetto: Lesbian and Gay Writing from South Africa.* London: The Gay Men's Press, 1995.

Patron, Eugene J. "Out in Africa" in the *Advocate,* 17 November 1992, pp. 45–47.

Shenitz, Bruce. "Coming Out in South Africa" in the *Progressive,* March 1990, p. 14.

● RUDOLF NUREYEV

References

Andersen, Christopher. *Jagger Unauthorized.* New York: Dell, 1993.

Barnes, Clive. *Nureyev.* New York: Helen Obolensky, 1982.

Buckle, Richard. *Nijinsky.* New York: Simon & Schuster, 1971.

Fonteyn, Margot. *Autobiography.* London: W.H. Allen, 1975.

Martins, Peter. *Far From Denmark.* Boston: Little, Brown, 1982.

Stuart, Otis. *Perpetual Motion. The Public and Private Lives of Rudolf Nureyev.* New York: Simon & Schuster, 1995.

● PRATIBHA PARMAR

References

Amos, Valerie, and Pratibha Parmar. "Challenging Imperial Feminism," in *Feminist Review* (London), July 1984: 3–19.

"Becoming Visible: Black Lesbian Discussions," in *Feminist Review* (London), July 1984: 53–72.

Blackman, Inge, Mary McIntosh, Sue O'Sullivan, Pratibha Parmar, and Alison Read. "Perverse Politics," in *Feminist Review* (London), Spring 1990: 1–3.

Chamberlain, Joy, Isaac Julien, Stuart Marshall, and Pratibha Parmar. "Filling the Lack in Everybody Is Quite Hard Work, Really. . . ," in *Queer Looks: Perspectives on Lesbian and Gay Film and Video*. Toronto: Between The Lines, 1993: 41–60.

Gever, Martha, John Greyson, and Pratibha Parmar. "On a Queer Day You Can See Forever," in *Queer Looks: Perspectives on Lesbian and Gay Film and Video*. Toronto: Between The Lines, 1993: xiii-xv.

Kuhn, Annette, ed., with Susannah Radstone. *The Women's Companion to International Film*. London: Virago Press Ltd., 1990.

Murray, Raymond. *Images in the Dark: An Encyclopedia of Gay and Lesbian Film and Video*. Philadelphia: TLA Publications, 1994.

Parmar, Pratibha. "Other Kinds of Dreams," in *Feminist Review* (London), Spring 1989: 55–65.

———. "That Moment of Emergence," in *Queer Looks: Perspectives on Lesbian and Gay Film and Video*. Toronto: Between The Lines, 1993: 3–11.

Parmar, Pratibha, et al. "Queer Questions," in *Sight and Sound* (London), September 1992.

●TROY PERRY

Address

c/o Universal Fellowship Metropolitan Community Churches, 5300 Santa Monica Blvd., #304, Los Angeles, California 90029-1196.

References

Contemporary Authors. Vol. 109. Detroit: Gale Research, 1983.

Dynes, Wayne R., ed. *The Encyclopedia of Homosexuality*. 2 vols. New York: Garland, 1990.

Enroth, Ronald M., and Gerald E. Jamison. *The Gay Church*. Grand Rapids, MI: Eerdmans, 1974.

Melton, J. Gordon, ed., *The Encyclopedia of American Religions*. Third ed. Detroit: Gale Research, 1989.

"NCC Rejects Ties With Gay Church" in *Christian Century*. 109, 2 December 1992, p. 1097.

Perry, Troy D., with Thomas L.P. Swicegood. *Don't Be Afraid Anymore: The Story of Reverend Troy Perry and the Metropolitan Community Churches*. New York: St. Martin's, 1990.

———., as told to Charles L. Lucas. *The Lord Is My Shepherd and He Knows I'm Gay: The Autobiography of The Reverend Troy D. Perry*. Los Angeles: Nash, 1972.

Who's Who in America, 1996. Vol. 2. New Providence, NJ: Marquis, 1995.

●DEB PRICE

Address

c/o *Detroit News,* 1148 National Press Building, Washington, D.C., 20045; phone: (301) 270-1594.

References

Price, Deb. E-mail interview with R. Ellen Greenblatt, 1996.

Price, Deb and Joyce Murdoch. *And Say Hi to Joyce: America's First Gay Column Comes Out*. New York: Doubleday, 1995.

●ADRIENNE RICH

Address

c/o W. W. Norton Co., 500 Fifth Avenue, New York, New York 10110-0002.

References

Blain, Virginia, and others, editors. *The Feminist Guide to Literature in English*. London: Batsford, 1990.

Farwell, Marilyn R. "Toward a Definition of the Lesbian Literary Imagination," in *Sexual Practice, Textual Theory: Lesbian Cultural Criticism*. Cambridge: Blackwell, 1993.

Gelpi, Barbara Charlesworth, and Albert Gelpi, editors. *Adrienne Rich's Poetry and Prose*. New York: Norton, 1993.

Rich, Adrienne. "Compulsory Heterosexuality and Lesbian Existence," in *Adrienne Rich's Poetry and Prose*. New York: Norton, 1993.

———. "An Interview with David Montenegro," in *American Poetry Review,* January–February, 1991.

———. "It Is the Lesbian in Us. . . ," in *On Lies, Secrets and Silence: Selected Prose 1966–1978*. London: Virago, 1980.

———. "Notes Toward a Politics of Location," in *Women, Feminist Identity and Society in the 1980s*. Amsterdam: John Benjamins, 1985.

———. *Of Woman Born: Motherhood as Experience and Institution*. New York: Norton, 1986.

———. "Split at the Root: An Essay on Jewish Identity," in *Adrienne Rich's Poetry and Prose*. New York: Norton, 1993.

———. "When We Dead Awaken: Writing as Re-Vision," in *On Lies, Secrets and Silence: Selected Prose 1966–1978*. London: Virago, 1980.

West-Burnham, J., "Adrienne Rich," in *The A–Z Guide to Modern Literary and Cultural Theorists*. London: Prentice Hall/Harvester Wheatsheaf, 1995.

● MARLON RIGGS

References

Avena, Thomas. *Life Sentences: Writers, Artists, and Aids*. Mercury House: San Francisco, 1994.

Guthmann, Edward. "Marlon Riggs—A Voice Stilled," in the *San Francisco Chronicle,* 27 April 1994: E-1.

Hafferty, Bill. "Film Maker Reacts to Buchanan Commercial," in the *San Francisco Chronicle,* 28 February 1992: C-4.

Julien, Isaac. "Long Live the Queen," in the *Village Voice,* 26 April 1994: 60.

Murray, Raymond. *Images in the Dark: An Encyclopedia of Gay and Lesbian Film and Video*. Philadelphia: TLA Publications, 1994.

Vaucher, Andrea R. *Muses from Chaos and Ash: Aids, Artists, and Art*. New York: Grove Press, 1993.

Walters, Barry. "Filmmaker's Social Views Untied," in the *San Francisco Examiner,* 14 June 1993: E-5.

● RuPAUL

Address

c/o World of Wonder, 1157 North Highland Ave., 1st Floor, Los Angeles, California 90038.

References

De Jonge, Peter. "My Dinner With Kirsty," in *Harper's Bazaar* (New York), February, 1996.

"Forecasts," in *Publisher's Weekly* (New York), 24 April 1995.

Review of *Blue in the Face*. In *Rolling Stone* (New York), 5 October 1995.

Review of *Lettin' It All Hang Out*. In *Booklist* (Chicago, Illinois), 15 May 1995.

Review of *Lettin' It All Hang Out*. In *Library Journal* (New York), 15 May 1995.

Review of *Wigstock*. In *People Weekly* (New York), 12 June 1995.

RuPaul. *Lettin' It All Hang Out*. Westport, Connecticut: Hyperion Books, 1995.

Tresniowski, Alex. "Talking With RuPaul," in *People Weekly* (New York), 10 July 1995.

● BAYARD RUSTIN

References

The Alyson Almanac. Boston: Alyson Publications, 1994–95, 185–186.

Contemporary Black Biography vol. 4. Detroit: Gale Research, 1993: 210–213.

Rustin, Bayard. *Down the Line—The Collected Writings of Bayard Rustin*. Chicago: Quadrangle Books, 1971.

Rustin, Bayard. *Strategies for Freedom—The Changing Patterns of Black Protest*. New York: Columbia University Press, 1976.

Williams, Julian. *Eyes on the Prize—America's Civil Rights Years, 1954–1965*. New York: Viking Penguin Books, 1987.

● ASSOTO SAINT

References

Saint, Assotto. "Haiti: A Memory Journey," in *New Men, New Minds,* edited by Franklin Abbott. New York: Crossing Press, 1987.

Conversations with Michelle Karlsberg, Franklin Abbott, and Walter Holfrey.

● CAROL SEAJAY

Address

c/o *Feminist Bookstore News,* P.O. Box 882554, San Francisco, California 94188.

References

Brandt, Kate. "Carol Seajay Spreading the Word: Keeping Connected with *Feminist Bookstore News,"* in *Happy Endings: Lesbian Writers Talk about Their Lives and Work*. Tallahassee, Florida: Naiad Press, 1993: 141–150.

Findlen, Barbara. "Bold Types," in *Ms.* January/February 1991: 65.

Seajay, Carol. "As Important as a Lamp," in *Dykescapes,* edited by Tina Portillo. Boston: Alyson Publications, 1991.

———. "Books: 20 Years of Feminist Bookstores," in *Ms*. July/August 1992: 60–63.

———. "Feminist Bookstores Fight Back," in *Ms*. May/June 1995: 68–71.

•RANDY SHILTS

References

Contemporary Authors. Vol. 127. Detroit: Gale Research, 1989.

Current Biography Yearbook, 1993. New York: H. W. Wilson, 1993.

Dutka, Elaine. "The Shilts Legacy Lives On" in *Los Angeles Times,* 22 February 1994, pp. F1, 8.

Grimes, William. "Randy Shilts, Author, Dies at 42; One of the First to Write About AIDS" in *New York Times,* 18 February 1994, p. D17.

Malinowski, Sharon, ed. *Gay and Lesbian Literature.* Detroit: Gale Research, 1994.

Newsmakers. 1993 Cumulation. Detroit: Gale Research, 1993.

Steitmatter, Rodger. *Unspeakable: The Rise of the Gay and Lesbian Press in America.* Boston: Faber and Faber, 1995.

•BARBARA SMITH

Address

Director, Kitchen Table/Women of Color, P.O. Box 908, Latham, New York 12110.

References

Bell-Scott, Patricia. "Reflections of Home Girl." *Ms.,* 2 January 1995, pp. 59–63.

Hull, Gloria T., Bell-Scott, Patricia, and Smith, Barbara, eds. *All the Women Are White, All the Blacks Are Men, but Some of Us Are Brave.* Old Westbury, NY: The Feminist Press, 1982.

Smith, Barbara, ed. *Home Girls: A Black Feminist Anthology.* New York: Kitchen Table/ Women of Color Press, 1983.

Summers, Claude J. *The Gay and Lesbian Literary Heritage.* New York: Henry Holt, 1995.

•STEPHEN SONDHEIM

Address

c/o Flora Roberts Inc., 157 W. 57th St., New York, New York 10019.

References

Banfield, Stephen. *Sondheim's Broadway Musicals.* Ann Arbor: University of Michigan Press, 1993.

Freedman, Samuel G. "The Creative Mind: The Words and Music of Stephen Sondheim" in *New York Times Magazine,* 1 April 1984, pp. 22–23, 60.

Gordon, Joanne Lesley. *Art Isn't Easy: The Achievement of Stephen Sondheim.* Carbondale: Southern Illinois University Press, 1990.

Gottfried, Martin. *Sondheim.* New York: Harry N. Abrams, 1993.

Hirsch, Foster. *Harold Prince and the American Musical Theatre.* Cambridge: Cambridge University Press, 1989.

Ilson, Carol. *Harold Prince: From "Pajama Game" to "Phantom of the Opera".* Ann Arbor: UMI Research Press, 1989.

McLaughlin, Robert L. "'No One Is Alone': Society and Love in the Musicals of Stephen Sondheim" in *Journal of American Drama and Theatre,* 1991, pp. 27–41.

Morley, Sheridan. "Side by Side with the Sondheim Art" in *Sunday Times Magazine* (London), 4 March 1990, pp. 66–70.

Prince, Hal. *Contradictions: Notes on Twenty-Six Years in the Theatre.* New York: Dodd, Mead, & Company, 1974.

Sondheim, Stephen. "Theater Lyrics" in *Playwrights, Lyricists, Composers on Theatre,* edited by Otis L. Guernsey, Jr. New York: Dodd, Mead, & Co., 1974, pp. 61–97.

Sondheim, Stephen, and Harold Prince. "On Collaboration between Authors and Directors" moderated by Gretchen Cryer in *Dramatists Guild Quarterly* 16, summer, 1979, pp. 14–35.

Zadan, Craig. *Sondheim & Co.* Second Edition, Updated. New York: Harper & Row, 1989.

•KITTY TSUI

Address

4100 North Marine Drive, #15C, Chicago, Illinois 60613-2324.

References

Tsui, Kitty. *Breathless.* Ithaca: Firebrand Books, 1996.

———. *The Words of a Woman Who Breathes Fire.* Duluth: Spinsters, Ink. 1983.

•URVASHI VAID

Address

c/o Doubleday, Inc., 1540 Broadway, New York, New York 10036-4094.

References

"The Fifty: *Time's* Roster for the Twenty-First Century," in *Time* (New York), 5 December 1994: 48–65.

Rizzo, Cynthia. Interview with Urvashi Vaid, in *Sojourner: The Women's Forum,* January 1996: 26–27.

———. Review of *Virtual Equality,* in *Sojourner: The Women's Forum,* January 1996: 25–26.

Vaid, Urvashi. 1993 March on Washington Speech, in *Out in All Directions: The Almanac of Gay and Lesbian America,* edited by Lynn Witt, Sherry Thomas, and Eric Marcus. New York: Warner, 1995: 456–459.

———. "After Identity," in the *New Republic* (New York), 10 May 1993: 28.

———. *Virtual Equality: The Mainstreaming of Gay and Lesbian Liberation.* New York: Anchor, 1995.

● GORE VIDAL

Address

c/o Random House, 201 E. 50th St., New York, New York 10022.

References

Abbott, Steven and Thom Willenbecher. "Gore Vidal: The *Gay Sunshine* Interview," in *Gay Sunshine* (N.p.), Winter 1975/76: 20–25.

Austen, Roger. "Gore Vidal and His All-Male Eden," in *Playing the Game: The Homosexual Novel in America.* Indianapolis and New York: Bobbs-Merrill, 1977: 118–125.

Dick, Bernard F. *The Apostate Angel: A Critical Study of Gore Vidal.* New York: Random House, 1974.

Kieman, Robert F. *Gore Vidal.* New York: Frederick Ungar, 1982.

Mitzel, John, and Steven Abbot. *Myra & Gore: A New View of Myra Breckinridge and a Candid Interview with Gore Vidal: A Book for Vidalophiles.* Dorchester, Massachusetts: Manifest Destiny Books, 1974.

Parini, Jay, editor. *Gore Vidal: Writer against the Grain.* New York: Columbia University Press, 1992.

Ross, Mitchell S. "Gore Vidal," in *The Literary Politicians.* Garden City, New York: Doubleday & Company, 1978: 247–300.

Stanton, Robert J. *Gore Vidal: A Primary and Secondary Bibliography.* Boston: G. K. Hall, 1978.

Summers, Claude J. "'The Cabin and the River,' Gore Vidal's *The City and the Pillar,*" in *Gay Fictions: Wilde to Stonewall: Studies in a Male Homosexual Literary Tradition.* New York: Continuum, 1990: 112–129.

Vidal, Gore. *Palimpsest: A Memoir.* New York: Random House, 1995.

———. *Vidal in Venice,* edited by George Armstrong, photographs by Tore Gill. New York: Summit Books, 1985.

White, Ray Lewis. *Gore Vidal.* Boston: Twayne, 1968.

● JOHN WATERS

Address

c/o Bill Block, ICM, 8942 Wilshire Blvd., Beverly Hills, California 90211.

References

"Camping Out in Hollywood," in *Interview* (New York), April 1994.

"Cool Waters," in *Premiere* (London), April 1994.

"The Domestication of John Waters," in *American Film* (New York), April 1990.

Dowd, Maureen. "John Waters: Misfits' Messiah," in *Rolling Stone* (New York), 17 May 1990.

"High Water Marks," in *Entertainment Weekly* (New York), 29 April 1994.

Interview (New York), February 1990.

"John Waters: The Sick Man of Cinema," in *People Weekly* (New York), 14 March 1989.

"Kink-Meister," in *New York Times Magazine,* 7 April 1991.

New York, 28 January 1991.

People Weekly (New York), 28 January 1991.

"Prowling for Books with John Waters," in *People Weekly* (New York), 18 April 1994.

"Trumpism Is Out, but Dork-Knobs Will be In," in *Fortune* (New York), 26 March 1990.

Waters, John. *Crackpot: The Obsessions of John Waters.* New York: MacMillan, 1986.

"The Weird World of John Waters," in *Theatre Crafts* (New York), May 1990.

"What Hath John Waters Wrought?," in *People Weekly* (New York), 1 September 1989.

● EDMUND WHITE

Address

Department of English, Brown University, Providence, Rhode Island 02912.

References

Authors and Artists for Young Adults, Volume 7. Detroit: Gale Research, 1991.

Baylis, Jamie. Review of *A Boy's Own Story* in *Harper's,* October 1982: 75–76.

Clemons, Walter. "Gay Rites: A Tour Coast to Coast" in *Newsweek,* 11 February 1980: 92–93.

Disch, Thomas M. "Memories of a Homosexual Boyhood" in *Washington Post Book World,* 17 October 1982: 1.

Elgrably, Jordan. "The Art of Fiction CV: Edmund White" in *Paris Review,* fall, 1988: 46–80.

Goldstein, William. "Publishers Weekly Interviews: Edmund White" in *Publishers Weekly,* 24 September 1982: 6–8.

Lehmann-Haupt, Christopher. Review of *A Boy's Own Story* in *New York Times,* 17 December 1982: 26.

————Review of *Caracole* in *New York Times,* 9 September 1985: 19.

McCaffery, Larry. *Alive and Writing: Interviews.* University of Illinois Press, 1987.

McClatchy, J.D. "Baroque Inventions" in *Shenandoah,* fall, 1978: 97–98.

Schulman, Leonard. "Profile: Imagining Other Lives" in *Time,* 30 July 1990: 58–60.

Slavitt, David R. Review of *Caracole* in *New York Times Book Review,* 15 September 1985: 15.

White, Edmund. "Residence on Earth: Living with AIDS in the '80s" in *Life,* Fall 1989: 135.

Yohalem, John. "Apostrophes to a Dead Lover" in *New York Times Book Review,* 10 December 1978: 12.

● TENNESSEE WILLIAMS

References

Boyd, Sally. "Tennessee Williams," in *Concise Dictionary of American Literary Biography: The New Consciousness, 1941–1968.* Detroit: Gale Research Inc., 1987: 533.

Falk, Signi Lenea. *Tennessee Williams.* New York: Twayne, 1978.

Williams, Dakin and Shepherd Mead. *Tennessee Williams: An Intimate Biography.* New York: Arbor House, 1983.

● MERLE WOO

References

Clark, Jil. "Woo Sues University for Reinstatement, Pay," in *Gay Community News,* 16 April 1983.

Woo, Merle. "Forging the Future, Remembering Our Roots: Building Multicultural, Feminist Lesbian and Gay Studies," in Garber, Linda, ed. *Tilting the Tower: Lesbians Teaching Queer Subjects.* New York: Routledge, 1994.

Woo, Merle. "Letter to Ma," in Moraga, Cherríe, and Gloria Anzaldúa, eds. *This Bridge Called My Back: Writings by Radical Women of Color.* Albany: Kitchen Table/Women of Color Press, 1981.

Woo, Merle. "The Politics of Breast Cancer," in Lim-Hing, Sharon, ed. *The Very Inside: An Anthology of Writing by Asian and Pacific Islander Lesbian and Bisexual Women.* Toronto: Sister Vision: Black and Women of Color Press, 1994.

● FRANCO ZEFFIRELLI

Address

Via Lucio Volumni 37, 00178 Rome, Italy.

References

Guthmann, Edward. In the *Advocate,* June 1983.

Murray, Raymond. *Images in the Dark: An Encyclopedia of Gay & Lesbian Film and Video.* Philadelphia: TLA Publications, 1995.

New Perspectives Quarterly (Los Angeles, California), Summer 1994: 11, 51–53.

Rutledge, Leigh. *The Gay Book of Lists.* Boston: Alyson Publications, 1987.

————. *The Gay Decades.* Boston: Alyson Publications, 1992.

Vernoff, Edward and Rina Shore. *International Directory of 20th-Century Biography.* New York: New American Library, 1987.

Zeffirelli, Franco. *An Autobiography.* New York: Weidenfeld & Nicolson, 1986.

SUBJECT INDEX

415 •

BUSINESS REPLY MAIL

FIRST CLASS MAIL   PERMIT NO. 17022   DETROIT, MI 48226

POSTAGE WILL BE PAID BY ADDRESSEE

MARKETING DEPARTMENT
VISIBLE INK PRESS
PO BOX 33477
DETROIT MI 48232-9852